Philosophy of Religion

Keith Yandell's *Philosophy of Religion: A Contemporary Introduction* was one of the first textbooks to explore the philosophy of religion with reference to religions other than Christianity. This new, revised edition explores the logical validity and truth-claims of several world religions—Christianity, Judaism, Islam, Hinduism, Buddhism, and Jainism—with updated, streamlined discussions on important topics in philosophy of religion such as:

- religious pluralism
- freedom and responsibility
- evidentialist moral theism
- reformed epistemology
- doxastic practice epistemology
- the problem of evil
- ontological and cosmological arguments.

Other new features include updated Questions for Reflection and new annotated bibliographies for each chapter, as well as an updated Glossary. This exciting new edition, much like its classic predecessor, is sure to be a classroom staple for undergraduate students studying philosophy of religion, as well as a comprehensive introductory read for anyone interested in the subject.

Keith E. Yandell taught at the University of Wisconsin-Madison until his retirement in 2011. He is author of *Christianity and Philosophy*, *Basic Issues in the Philosophy of Religion*, *Hume's "Inexplicable Mystery"*, *The Epistemology of Religious Experience*, and (with Harold Netland) *Christianity and Buddhism*.

Routledge Contemporary Introductions to Philosophy
Series editor: Paul K. Moser, Loyola University of
Chicago

This innovative, well-structured series is for students who have already done an introductory course in philosophy. Each book introduces a core general subject in contemporary philosophy and offers students an accessible but substantial transition from introductory to higher-level college work in that subject. The series is accessible to non-specialists, and each book clearly motivates and expounds the problems and positions introduced. An orientating chapter briefly introduces its topic and reminds readers of any crucial material they need to have retained from a typical introductory course. Considerable attention is given to explaining the central philosophical problems of a subject and the main competing solutions and arguments for those solutions. The primary aim is to educate students in the main problems, positions, and arguments of contemporary philosophy rather than to convince students of a single position.

Ancient Philosophy
2nd Edition
Christopher Shields

Classical Modern Philosophy
Jeffrey Tlumak

Continental Philosophy
Andrew Cutrofello

Epistemology
3rd Edition
Robert Audi

Ethics
2nd Edition
Harry J. Gensler

Metaethics
Mark van Roojen

Metaphysics
3rd Edition
Michael J. Loux

Moral Psychology
Valerie Tiberius

Philosophy of Art
Noël Carroll

Philosophy of Biology
Alex Rosenberg and Daniel W. McShea

Philosophy of Economics
Julian Reiss

Philosophy of Language
2nd Edition
William G. Lycan

Philosophy of Mathematics
2nd Edition
James Robert Brown

Philosophy of Mind
3rd Edition
John Heil

Philosophy of Perception
William Fish

Philosophy of Psychology
José Luis Bermudez

Philosophy of Religion
2nd Edition
Keith E. Yandell

Philosophy of Science
3rd Edition
Alex Rosenberg

Philosophy of Social Science
Mark Risjord

Social and Political Philosophy
John Christman

Forthcoming:

Bioethics
Jason Scott Robert

Feminist Philosophy
Heidi Grasswick

Free Will
*Michael McKenna
and Derk Pereboom*

Metaphysics
4th Edition
*Michael J. Loux
and Thomas M. Crisp*

Phenomenology
Walter Hopp

Philosophy of Action
Sarah Paul

Philosophy of Film
Aaron Smuts

Philosophy of Literature
John Gibson

Social and Political Philosophy
2nd Edition
John Christman

Virtue Ethics
Liezl van Zyl

Philosophy of Religion

A Contemporary Introduction

Second Edition

Keith E. Yandell

Routledge
Taylor & Francis Group

NEW YORK AND LONDON

First published 2016
by Routledge
711 Third Avenue, New York, NY 10017

and by Routledge
2 Park Square, Milton Park, Abingdon, Oxon, OX14 4RN

*Routledge is an imprint of the Taylor & Francis Group, an informa
business*

© 2016 Taylor & Francis

First edition published 1999 by Routledge

Library of Congress Cataloguing-in-Publication Data
Names: Yandell, Keith E., 1938– author.
Title: Philosophy of religion : a contemporary introduction /
    Keith E. Yandell.
Description: 2 [edition]. | New York : Routledge, 2016. |
    Series: Routledge contemporary introductions to
    philosophy | Includes bibliographical
    references and index.
Identifiers: LCCN 2015041756 | ISBN 9780415963701 (alk. paper)
Subjects: LCSH: Religion—Philosophy. | Religions.
Classification: LCC BL51.Y275 2016 | DDC 210—dc23
LC record available at http://lccn.loc.gov/2015041756

ISBN: 978-0-415-96369-5 (hbk)
ISBN: 978-0-415-96370-1 (pbk)
ISBN: 978-1-315-67623-4 (ebk)

Typeset in Times New Roman and Gill Sans
by Apex CoVantage, LLC

Printed and bound in the United States of America by Publishers Graphics,
LLC on sustainably sourced paper.

For Sharon

Contents

Annotated Table of Contents

Chapter 1: Introduction
Four different basic types of religious traditions are described: monotheism, absolute monism, atheistic substance dualism, and atheistic non-dualism. The former two are in effect views of monotheism as ultimate versus apparent, and the latter views concern the nature of human persons.

Chapter 2: What Is Philosophy? What Is Religion? What Is Philosophy of Religion?
Philosophy is the construction and assessment of conceptual systems; religions are views of the cosmos that diagnose and propose a cure for a universal human spiritual illness; and philosophy of religion analyses and assesses the core concepts and arguments relative to these diagnoses and cures.

Chapter 3: What Sorts of Religion Are There?
Criteria are offered for discerning types of religion in terms of their doctrinal stances.

Chapter 4: What Sorts of Religious Experience Are There?
By comparison between religious and non-religious experience, and their structure and content, criteria are developed relative to reflection on the evidential potential of religious experience.

Chapter 5: The Importance of Doctrine and the Distinctness of Religious Traditions
It is argued that doctrinal difference is to be expected among diverse religious traditions and that no diagnosis or cure is offered without doctrine. This is so even for religions that may claim to lack doctrines altogether.

Chapter 6: Religious Pluralism
Assuming moral agreement among at least the major religious traditions, religious pluralists set aside the diagnoses and cures central to those traditions. Even granting the controversial assumption, the enterprise seems deeply flawed.

Chapter 7: Monotheistic Conceptions of Ultimate Reality
Comparisons and contrasts are drawn among a stylized Greek, Christian, and Hindu monotheism. These are relevant to future discussions.

Chapter 8: Nonmonotheistic Conceptions of Ultimate Reality
The basic views as to what there is according to Advaita Vedanta Hinduism, Jainism, and Theravada Buddhism are presented in philosophically accessible terms and their philosophical commitments laid out.

Chapter 9: Arguments against Monotheism
Arguments that belief in God and evil is logically inconsistent, consistent but against the evidence, and inconsistent to hold God blameless for allowing things we hold humans wrong to allow are assessed.

Chapter 10: Arguments for Monotheism
The arguments that it is impossible that God not exist and that if there are things that exist dependently then God exists are analyzed in detail.

Chapter 11: Monotheism and Religious Experience
Appeal to religious experiences that are apparently experiences of God is considered in the context of a principle of experiential evidence developed by considering counter-examples.

Chapter 12: Arguments concerning Nonmonotheistic Conceptions
The difference between arguments appealing to enlightenment experience and those appealing to other matters is noted, and arguments of the latter sort related to Advaita, Jainism, and Theravada are discussed.

Chapter 13: Enlightenment-Based Arguments and Nonmonotheistic Conceptions of Ultimate Reality
Since appeal to esoteric enlightenment experience is absolutely central to each tradition, the phenomenological description of such experiences—the way they seem to their subjects—and their use in supporting the traditions in which they occur are assessed.

Chapter 14: Religion, Morality, and Responsibility
The difference between freedom with determinism and freedom against determinism, and their connection to moral responsibility, is analyzed. Metaphysical value and moral value are distinguished and related.

Chapter 15: Faith and Reason
Faith that and faith in are distinguished. The deepest critique of faith, if it succeeds, is the claim that there are no religious claims to believe or not since they are neither true nor false. A variety of such views are discussed. Then the strategy of arguing to the best explanation, or at least as good as its competition, is discussed as a means of giving content to faith.

Chapter 16: Some Further Vistas

Paul Moser's appeal to moral experience as evidence for God's existence, Alvin Plantinga's reformed epistemology for which it is reasonable to believe in God without evidence, and William Alston's view that religious experience and belief should be seen in the context of a belief-forming practice, are sketched as further ways of giving content to faith.

Preface to Second Edition

The *Second Edition* continues the structure of the *First*: it explores central issues in philosophy of religion in comparative terms cross-culturally by considering ideas and practices from Christianity, Hinduism, Jainism, and Buddhism.

A new first chapter structures the book as a whole, providing a large-scale conceptual map for what is to come. The second chapter, after explaining the nature of philosophy, religion, and philosophy of religion, fills in that larger-scale map with the most pertinent details. It contains more precisely defined criteria than were offered in the previous edition.

Other major topical improvements to the *Second Edition* include:

- Updates to Chapter 6, "Religious Pluralism," building on the earlier focus on the work of John Hick now to discuss Paul Knitter and other newer ways of approaching religious pluralism.
- A revised and updated discussion of the problem of evil in Chapter 9, "Arguments against Monotheism."
- A new sort of disguised compatibilism, discussed in Chapter 14, "Religion, Morality, and Responsibility."
- A new concluding Chapter 16, "Some Further Vistas," which discusses the philosophy of religion in relation to three perspectives in epistemology not under review in the *First Edition*—moral evidentialism, reformed epistemology, and doxastic practice epistemology. Although presented by Christian monotheists, they have potential application to other traditions as well.

Pedagogically, the main significant new feature is a new annotated Table of Contents, with every chapter description including reference to key concepts and claims discussed therein.

Updated bibliographies are included at the end of each chapter and updated notes and a general glossary along with a general index are included at the end of the volume.

Preface to First Edition

Contemporary academia is secular. The idea that religious views of any traditional sort should guide the research or inform the worldview of any discipline is rejected out of court. Things were not always so. Professor John Bascom, former President of my own university, used to give a capstone undergraduate course in how to prove the existence and nature of God; his practice was more typical than surprising. Times have changed.

A student of mine once published a paper he wrote for a seminar he took with me. It argued that there is reason to reject a particular set of religious beliefs. In effect, the responses of his former professors ranged from *we all know that stuff is false* through *considering whether religious claims are true or false isn't part of the academic game* to *saying someone's religious beliefs are false is impolite and politically unwise*. None of these responses is atypical.

Nonetheless, both traditionally and currently, the philosophy of religion has made rational assessment of religious claims central to its purposes. Endeavoring to determine the meaning, and the truth value—the *sense* and the *truth-or-falsity*—of religious claims is part and parcel of this discipline. Some philosophers have denied that there are any religious claims, proposing that what seem to be such really are meaningless. Other philosophers have held that religious traditions can only be understood in their own terms, each describing a conceptual world inaccessible to any other so that there is no "neutral place" from which assessment can be offered. (As we will see, this misleading metaphor disguises a perspective whose incoherence has, alas, not mitigated its influence.) Taking either the *all supposed religious claims are nonsense* or the *every religion its own conceptual world unrelated to all others* line is itself opting for some philosophical views as opposed to others. Those outside of philosophy who assume one line or the other assume what desperately needs proof. In so doing, they draw intellectual drafts on empty accounts. These days, the *nonsense* line1 is seldom heard but the *own conceptual world* line is everywhere. The best way to show that the *nonsense* and the *own conceptual world* lines are utterly mistaken is to offer the sorts of assessments that these lines suppose to be impossible. That is the basic task before us. This task has three components: presentation of data, assessment of arguments, and reflection on experiences.

Presentation of Data

We begin by saying what religion is and what philosophy is. There are no non-controversial answers to these questions. Nonetheless, clarity about how religion and philosophy are construed in this text should be helpful for understanding the rest of what is said. Then we consider what kinds of religions there are, what religious experience is, and what kinds of religious experience there are. Some religious experiences, for example, are seen as experiences of God; others are not. Some religions are monotheistic; they hold that God exists and has very strong powers. Others hold that ultimate reality is not God, but something else. Both sorts of religious traditions not surprisingly offer accounts of what persons are, and one tradition typically offers a different view of this matter than another. Such differences are philosophically as well as religiously significant, and they require our attention. There is more than one concept of God, and so more than one kind of monotheism. Similarly, nonmonotheistic religions differ in terms of how they conceive of what exists and has religious importance. So we need to look at different notions of ultimate reality, conceived as divine or not.

Since the variety of religions is great, no one book could responsibly deal with philosophy of religion in connection with all of them. Our scope will include representative views from Judaism, Christianity, Islam, Hinduism, Buddhism, and Jainism. Each of these traditions is itself complex, and while we can hope to be fair, we cannot pretend to be exhaustive. One great divide among religious traditions comes between those that are monotheistic and those that are not. Our discussion will be divided along these lines with no suggestion that "nonmonotheism" is more than a label of convenience; each variety of nonmonotheism we discuss, like each variety of monotheism, will be positively characterized in terms of its own indigenous perspective.

Without any suggestion that this is their only or primary importance, religions provide the raw material for philosophical reflection. At this point, we will have our raw data for philosophical reflection. Once we have reflected briefly on how arguments can be constructed and assessed, and on how appeal to experience as evidence may be crafted and evaluated, we can turn to asking what reason, if any, there is to think that the religious perspectives already described might be true.

Escaping Incoherence

There are academic circles in which talk of truth, let alone religious perspectives being true, is about as popular as a teetotal sermon at a local pub. For this to be the line to take, it must be true (in the sense of "true" that was supposedly dismissed) that talk of truth is somehow so problematic as to require its abandonment. This line thus appears to be incoherent; it appears so because it is.

The devotees of a religious tradition typically take what their sacred texts say to be true. Nor is it beyond their ability to think what this "being true" might amount to. Monotheists will take *God exists* to be true—they will suppose that an omnicompetent being exists on whom the world depends. Some religious non-monotheists will think this claim false, and will think that such claims as *Persons are indestructible* or *Persons are nothing more than momentary states* are true. As Aristotle once said, a proposition is true if things are as it says they are, and not otherwise. Aristotle, and most devotees of most traditions, have no difficulty in understanding what this means. It is possible to educate oneself out of all possibility of learning anything. Aristotle and ordinary religious people have not suffered this injury.

Using the Data (I)

Arguments have been offered for, and others against, religious beliefs. This is so regarding both monotheistic traditions and nonmonotheistic traditions. Far from such arguments going deeply against the grain of the religious traditions, sincere and admired devotees of such traditions have offered arguments for their own perspective and against other perspectives. If it is true that some religious believers have rejected any such idea as needless if not inappropriate, others have entered enthusiastically into the enterprise. The idea that offering such arguments is somehow inherently against all religious thought and practice is not substantiated by the history of these traditions. Many of these arguments are provocative and powerful; they deserve our attention. Some of these arguments concern the existence and nature of God; others concern the nature of persons. In each case, such disputes tie in tightly with different views of salvation and enlightenment, of what one may expect and hope. The arguments interact significantly with the traditions in ways often ignored.

Related to the possibility of such arguments are competing notions of faith, of reason, and of their connections. Also related are competing views of the capacities and limits of religious language. If all claims about God, for example, are non-literal, how does this affect what sorts of arguments can be offered on behalf of these claims? Does this place them simply beyond argument altogether? *Are* all claims about God non-literal? Hence, along with considering arguments, we must discuss issues concerning the nature and scope of religious language.

Using the Data (II)

People claim to have religious experiences. We thus ask what evidence, if any, such experience provides for religious belief. Appeal to at least apparent experience of God, for example, can but need not be another version of an argument for God's existence. One could argue: *people seem to have experience of God; the best explanation of this fact is that God causes those experiences; hence there is reason to think that God exists.* Similarly, one could argue: *there seems to be a computer in front of me; the best explanation of things so appearing is that there is a computer in front of me; so there is reason to think a computer is there.* But I seem simply to see the computer; my belief that it is there is a matter of at least xx Preface to First Edition

seeming to see it and having no reason to think that things are not as they seem. I neither see something else from which I infer to my computer nor offer claims about best explanations. Similarly, many have claimed to experience God, not to have some experience of something from which they can then properly infer that God exists. We will consider religious experience, viewed as evidence for God's existence by virtue of its being a matter of "seeing God" rather than simply as a matter of its being the source of a premise in a proof of God's existence.

Differing views of persons are also supported by appeals to experience, particularly to introspective and enlightenment experiences. How such experiences should be described, and what significance they bear, is a matter of central dispute, particularly between such nonmonotheistic traditions as Jainism and Buddhism. Further, competing accounts of what persons are connect closely with diverse accounts of morality and of value generally. These close connections are no insignificant part of what gives the disputes their importance to the traditions involved. Discerning these traditions widens one's understanding of the views involved, and enriches the sorts of possible assessments of competing appeals to experience. Closely connected with these topics are competing notions of human survival of death and whether any of them have any basis or support.

Summary

The core of philosophy of religion, as of philosophy generally, is metaphysics and epistemology, systematic attempts to give defensible answers to the questions *What is there?* and *How can we know what there is?* At the core of any religious tradition is its own answer to these questions, construed as and embedded in an answer to the basic problem to which the tradition addresses itself as the rationale for its existence—thus our own concentration on accounts of religious reality and religious knowledge. How is ultimate reality conceived, and how are human persons viewed in relation to ultimate reality? With what consequences for salvation or enlightenment, morality, and any afterlife there may be? What arguments are offered for, and what against, these views? What appeals to experience are made for one view and against another? What assessment should be offered of these arguments and appeals?

In sum, our intent is to describe the basic perspectives concerning ultimate reality and our relations to it as seen by several of the major religious traditions, and to ask what, if anything, there is by way of reason or evidence to think any of the claims that define these perspectives are true, or are false. The underlying conviction is that an academia in which such questions are not somewhere raised, and competing answers debated, illegitimately ignores issues of great importance, and does so without decent excuse.

Besides being important, philosophy of religion is fun. One gets to learn what people in quite different cultural contexts believe about God, the nature of persons, good and evil, salvation, and enlightenment; to see what they take to follow from these beliefs; and to think as clearly and well about them as one can. Perhaps this is not everyone's cup of tea, but for those at all inclined to it, it should be a thoroughly enjoyable project. I hope that this volume is as much serious fun to read as it was to write.

Suggested Readings

Alston, William (1967) "Problems of Philosophy of Religion," *Encyclopedia of Philosophy*, Volume 6 (New York: Macmillan), p. 286–288. A brief issue-oriented summary of the field.

Bascom, John (1980) *Natural Theology* (New York: G. P. Putnam's Sons). A presentation of arguments for the existence of God by an early President of the University of Wisconsin.

Collins, James (1967) *The Emergence of the Philosophy of Religion* (New Haven: Yale University Press). A history of the field that finds its recent roots in nineteenth-century philosophy.

Lewis, H. D. (1967) "History of the Philosophy of Religion," *Encyclopedia of Philosophy*, Volume 6 (New York: Macmillan), p. 276–285. A brief, historically oriented summary of the field.

1 Introduction

There are a great many religions being practiced as you read this sentence. Each has its ways of interpreting and responding to the world. Expressed in rites and rituals, institutions and practices, each has a view of what there is—of the cosmos as a whole and of the role and status of persons in it. Taken seriously, these views have implications for most if not all of life. Some practice withdrawing from the world, looking internally into oneself for answers to questions as to what one is and how one may flourish. Others look to a community for such answers. Many if not all treat verbal traditions or oral texts, or both, as being at least helpful and more likely authoritative in terms of discerning a proper path in life. Among these religions, we will consider four examples. Each includes a view of what there is (metaphysics), of how it may be known (epistemology), and of what has deep value (value theory, including ethics). Our choices are cross-cultural and intended to be representative of two diverse sorts of religious tradition. No disrespect is intended to any religious tradition in this selection. The field is too vast to cover in one volume, and one cannot help being selective. The idea is to provide very diverse samples. One type is monotheistic, centering on God. The other is non-monotheistic, centering on the individual. The former considers how one may be rightly related to a personal God, the other how we may become rightly related to an impersonal ultimate reality. Within these broad categories, there are further differences. Within monotheism (among other alternatives) there are philosophical sources in Plato and Aristotle; the Semitic religions Judaism, Christianity, and Islam; and two Hindu varieties developed by Ramanuja and Madhva. Among these we will largely consider Christianity in the sense of what seems the most generally agreed-upon central doctrines without entering into denominational disputes. A similar practice will be followed with respect to our other examples. Hindu thought also contains a religious tradition Advaita Vedanta, with 'Vedanta' referring to the teaching of the Vedas, ancient Hindu sacred texts. 'Advaita' means non-dual. It is Advaita's view that persons, physical objects, and God are appearances, and what is real is an impersonal, qualityless Brahman. Developed classically by Shankara, this view is probably best presented in comparison and contrast to the relentless monotheism of the later Ramanuja, though the emphasis will be on the perspective of Advaita Vedanta as an example of a type of religious tradition distinct from our other three. A quite different approach is taken by Jainism, another Indian religious tradition. It holds that there are two fundamentally distinct sorts of existents, immaterial souls or minds and material particles of which physical objects are composed. Neither are viewed as created, both are held to be beginningless and endless, and the view is atheistic. Jainism is basically doctrinally homogenous in contrast to the varieties of Vedantic religion. Indian thought also offers our fourth example of a distinct religious tradition, namely Theravada Buddhism. Known as "The Tradition of the Elders" (the early followers of the Buddha) this tradition contrasts sharply to Jainism. For Jainism, the ultimate constituents of the world are things or substances, things that endure over time and throughout change. Crucially, on this view, minds are indestructible. Theravada view the cosmos (nirvana aside) to be entirely composed of conscious states and physical states, each of which is momentary, lasting barely long enough to exist at all. A mind on this view is a causally linked bundle of conscious states at a time and another entirely new bundle at the next time, the new bundle being caused by the old. The series is nothing more than the individual bundles. A physical object is analogously structured, with non-conscious states as its constituents. Later Buddhist traditions often drop out the reference to non-conscious states.

The goal of our religions is salvation in the case of monotheism and enlightenment in the case of our nonmonotheistic traditions. The former involves sinners, persons who have acted in ways that are against God's will, repenting of those sins and asking God's forgiveness. Assuming the repentance is genuine, God will forgive and grant the repentant sinner everlasting life with God and other believers. This is, of course, a very brief account of the matter, but perhaps it will serve to make clear how different the monotheistic view is in this regard from the nonmonotheistic views. The typical term for the goal of our other religions, as noted, is 'enlightenment.' The conceptual background to this idea contains reference to reincarnation and karma. The basic idea of reincarnation is that each person beginninglessly and, without becoming enlightened, endlessly is in a cycle of birth and rebirth into one new life after another. The law of karma can be thought of as a mindless rule book that states the penalties to be exacted for wrong actions and rewards for good actions. Then it is the nature of the universe that these penalties be exacted to their full limit, no merciful exceptions allowed. Only if a person has an enlightenment experience in which the truth of the Jain (in one case) or the Buddhist (in another case) is existentially seen can one become enlightened. This can occur only in a lifetime in which all remaining karmic credits and debits can be paid out. Only by coming to existentially believe a true doctrine can enlightenment be achieved, so getting the doctrine right matters. This gives us a taste of some of the views discussed in what follows.

Suggested Readings

Christianity

Davis, Stephen T. (2006) *Christian Philosophical Theology* (Oxford: Oxford University Press). A good example of work at the crossroads of philosophy and theology.

Gilson, Etienne (1955) *History of Christian Philosophy in the Middle Ages* (New York: Random House). Survey of a highly significant period of Christianity by a renowned historian of philosophy.

McGrath, Alister (2010) *Christian Theology: An Introduction* (West Sussex, UK: Wiley-Blackwell). Nicely covers Christian thought from the church fathers to modern times.

—— (2012) *The Christian Theology Reader* (West Sussex, UK: Wiley-Blackwell). Fine companion to the above.

Osborn, Eric (2009) *The Beginning of Christian Philosophy* (Cambridge: Cambridge University Press). A good historical introduction to earliest Christian philosophy.

Hindu Vedanta

Dasgupta, Surendranath (2000) *A History of Indian Philosophy* (Delhi: Motilal Banarsidass). In five volumes, detailed and balanced; arguably the successor to Radhakrishnan.

Deutsch, Eliot and Dalvi, Rohit (2004) *The Essential Vedanta: A New Sourcebook of Advaita Vedanta* (Ilford, Essex, UK: Wisdom Books). Good collection of Advaita texts.

Ganeri, Martin (2015) *Indian Thought and Western Theism: The Vedanta of Ramanuja* (New York: Routledge). Compares "qualified non-dualistic" Vedanta with Western scholastic theism.

Radhakrishnan, Sarvepalli (2009) *History of Indian Philosophy* (Oxford: Oxford University Press). From Rig Veda to Ramanuja, in two volumes, views Advaita as the consummation of Indian philosophy; has become a classic.

Sarma, Deepak (2003) *An Introduction to Madhva Vedanta* (Farnham, Sussex, UK: Ashgate). Good general introduction to dualistic Vedanta.

Jainism

Dundas, Paul (2002) *The Jains* (New York: Routledge). Brief account of historical Jainism including scripture and tradition.

Jacobi, Hermann (2005) *Jaina Sutras* (London: Forgotten Books). Jain sacred scriptures.

Jaini, Padmanabh (1998) *The Jaina Path of Purification* (Delhi: Motilal Banarsidass). The Jain route to enlightenment.

Paniker, Agustin (2012) *Jainism: History, Society, Philosophy, and Practice* (Delhi: Motilal Banarsidass). A rounded view of the roles of the tradition.

Sharma, Arvind (2001) *A Jaina Perspective on the Philosophy of Religion* (Delhi: Motilal Banarsidass). Book by an accomplished interpreter of Indian philosophy.

Buddhism

Bodhi, Bhikkhu and His Holiness the Dalai Lama (2005) *In the Buddha's Words: An Anthology of Discourses from the Pali Canon* (Ilford, Essex, UK: Wisdom Books). A good introduction to Theravada scripture.

Emmanuel, Steven (2013) *A Companion to Buddhist Philosophy* (Oxford: Wiley-Blackwell). Covers a broad range of topics, including conceptual foundations, metaphysics, epistemology, and ethics.

King, Richard (1999) *Indian Philosophy: An Introduction to Hindu and Buddhist Thought* (Washington, DC: Georgetown). Brief and yet comprehensive.

Siderits, Mark (2007) *Buddhism as Philosophy: An Introduction* (Indianapolis, IN: Hackett). An introduction to Buddhist philosophy with relevant texts.

Warder, A. K. (2008) *Indian Buddhism* (Delhi: Motilal Banarsidass). A careful scholarly account that focuses on social implications but also gives an account of how Buddhist traditions developed.

Williams, Paul, Tribe, Anthony and Wynne, Alexander (2013) *Buddhist Thought: A Complete Introduction to the Indian Tradition* (New York: Routledge). As excellent as it is ambitious.

Part I
Philosophy and Religion

2 What Is Philosophy? What Is Religion? What Is Philosophy of Religion?

Philosophy

What Is Philosophy?

No non-controversial answer is possible, and this is not a book about what philosophy is. So I will just say what I take philosophy to be, and go on to do philosophy.[1] Philosophy is the enterprise of constructing and assessing categorial systems. The tasks necessary to this enterprise are philosophical tasks, and the requisite skills are philosophical skills. The tasks in question, and the skills, need not be restricted to only philosophical ones. The obvious example of cases in which not only philosophical tasks and questions are necessary is in the "philosophy of" disciplines—philosophy of the arts, mathematics, logic, physics, biology, history, or religion, for example.[2] A categorial system is, not surprisingly, a system of categories. A category is a basic concept, primitive in the sense that it is not analyzable in terms of other concepts. The categories of a full-blown philosophical system will be concepts of things or entities (in the broadest sense of 'thing' or 'entity'), thoughts, or values.[3] Philosophy is the enterprise of constructing and assessing categorial systems. Much of Ancient, Medieval, and Modern philosophy was deliberately pursued systematically. Plato, Aristotle, Aquinas, Descartes, Leibniz, Spinoza, Locke, Berkeley, Hume, and Kant all constructed complex systems of philosophy. Their intent was, as a later philosopher put it, "to see things, and see them whole"—to develop an integrated account of (say) things, knowledge, and values. Much of contemporary philosophy has been suspicious of any such large-scale endeavors and has tended to stick to particular problems. Nonetheless, in dealing with particular problems, these philosophers too accepted general claims that placed constraints on what they could consistently accept elsewhere; even philosophy concerned only with particular problems is implicitly general.

I take religious claims to be neither more nor less open to rational assessment than any other sorts of claims. Any difference there is concerns difficulty, not possibility. Nor do I see any reason to think that offering rational assessment of religious claims is in principle harder than, say, assessing attempts to offer a unified theory for all of physics, or to solve the problems of the foundations of modal logic. Contrary to the preferences of some philosophers, some Religious Studies professors, and even some religious thinkers themselves, religious traditions do partly consist of literal propositions, belief in which constitutes being a member of the tradition, the falsehood of which is inconsistent with the tradition being a means to salvation or enlightenment. These traditions are anything remotely like what they claim to be only if what they say is true. I shall offer respect to the diversity of religious traditions by taking those claims seriously enough to try to see what can be said for and against them.

One can easily ask *How can you tell whether a religious belief is true or not?*, try to think of some general way in which this could be done, and give up. That question is a paralysis question. There is no single answer to it; religious claims are made about quite a diversity of things, and some must be assessed in one way and others in other ways. The only sensible way to proceed is on a claim-by-claim, case-by-case basis; given enough cases, one may then be able to general-ize. In what follows, I will try to understand, and then assess, a variety of religious beliefs. The sorts of assessments offered will typically be relevant to other, similar claims not mentioned here. There are simply too many religions to deal with all of them in one book, even if one knew enough to do that. If you like to think in terms of books having agendas, my major agenda is to show, by detailed argu-ment, that it is possible to rationally assess religious beliefs. In this respect, it runs against a belief that is very popular in our culture, namely that matters of religion are simply private affairs concerning how you feel about big things. This belief seems to me patently false.

It also runs against the tendency in some (certainly not all) Religious Studies circles, and (worse) even among some philosophers, to the effect that to think of religions as seriously containing propositions whose truth greatly matters so that accepting them involves accepting claims is to misunderstand them. It is possible to reply to such philosophers on their own terms. Since it challenges the very pos-sibility of faith, we will do so in our chapter on Faith and Reason. Another reply is given by looking carefully at what is supposedly meaningless in the sense of being neither true or false—by doing philosophy of religion to show the falsity of this view by looking at the actual authoritative texts of religious traditions, and seeing what they actually do say. It is highly unlikely that the scriptures of the world religions really say nothing that is true or false—that is, that they say noth-ing. Even if one wanted to say that all the apparent declarative sentences in these sources were really imperatives, an imperative makes sense only in the context of a set of truth-value-bearing propositions. Efforts to claim that so-called religious propositions are not meaningful because (a) they are not mere reports of what can be sensed, or (b) they cannot be falsified by appeal to sensory evidence, or (c) they cannot be confirmed by sensory observation alone, commit intellectual suicide. *They* make no claim that can be tested by appeal to any or all of (a), (b), and (c); on their own terms, they convey no sense. Thus they rule out nothing. If we can properly believe only what science tells us, then we cannot properly believe that we can properly believe only what science tells us. I grant that much can be learned by tracing the myriad mistakes made by those who suppose that there is no such thing as a religious truth or falsehood. But the success rate for those who have most vociferously asserted this has been dismal, and we may draw the veil of silence over their efforts. Others feel that trying to assess religious beliefs is not really polite, something no nice person would do. I note that those who possess these standards for politeness or nicety do not find much support in the religious traditions themselves. There we find real disagreement and argument. The religious traditions typically are not patron of such philosophical politeness—or political correctness. They do not say that those who reject the idea that seeking for religious truth, and arguing for or against religious doctrines—being impolite—are to be shunned. Those who reject serious inquiry into the truth or falsity of religious beliefs, by firmly rebuking and rejecting those who think this task worthwhile, themselves engage in what on their own terms is itself a sad lack of politeness. Such notions of politeness and nicety are cases of failure of nerve and unwillingness to think hard about some of the most important matters.

The book that follows offers a sustained argument. It does not offer a particular philosophical system, though no doubt its philosophical commitments (as would any others) considerably constrain the sort of system that one who accepts them could consistently accept. Arguably, some sorts of religious tradition come off better under rational assessment than do others. As the argument develops it will become clear as to how there can be a basis for such judgments.

Objectivity

Objectivity is rightly prized in philosophy as elsewhere. To be objective in the relevant sense is, roughly, to accept or reject a belief on the basis of what can be said in favor of, and what can be said against, its truth, no matter whether one would prefer the belief to be true or not. There are two views about objectivity that I reject. On one account, a book on the philosophy of religion can be objective only if it conforms to the pattern "Tradition A says this, Tradition B says that, Philosopher C argues against this in this way, but Philosopher D argues against the same thing like that, and now everybody decide for themselves without the author interfering." The assumption is that description can be objective, but assessment cannot be. Of course the author or authors of such a text have had to decide what was important enough to be favored by their attention, which interpretations of the traditions so favored were probably accurate, what arguments were the more interesting and forceful, what could properly be said about these arguments, and the like. It remains baffling as to why one should suppose *these* assessments can be objective whereas assessments of the religious beliefs themselves are impossible, particularly since offering the relevant descriptions involve tasks very similar to those included in making assessments. If it is granted that one can be objective about description, it is arbitrary to think that one cannot be objective about assessment. The other view is that objectivity is impossible to obtain about anything. There is obviously no reason to take this view seriously. It proclaims *Objectivity about any belief is impossible to obtain* and so if its proponents are right they are just being so kind as to share a small bit of their autobiographies, something on the level of *I don't like seafood*, which of course has no philosophical relevance whatever. If they are wrong, then again we need not worry about their claim. The truth about objectivity is that it is hard to achieve, especially about things that matter, and that one can do one's best to try. Sometimes one succeeds. For an easy example, the objective truth is that if James says *Nothing said in English is ever true*, what he says is either true or false. If it is false, then it is false. But if it is true, then it is false. So, either way, it is false.

Religion

What Is Religion?

Our world contains a perplexing diversity of religious traditions. Increasingly, representative congregations or conclaves of these traditions can be found in any major city. Our question is simply *What is religion?* Responsible answers will reflect what one finds in traditions universally agreed to be religious.[4]

A Definition of Religion

Broadly speaking, definitions of 'religion' tend to fall into one of two classes. One sort of definition is substantial or doctrinal; a given religion is defined in terms of the beliefs its adherents accept that make them adherents of that religion, and religion generally is characterized in terms of beliefs that all religions are alleged to share. Another sort of definition is functional or pragmatic; 'religion' is defined in terms of what it is alleged that all religions do or what the social function of religion is alleged to be. Some definitions, of course, are somewhat less than objective. Marx's claim that religion is the opiate of the people is not proposed as a scholarly and neutral definition of religion—or, even if it is presented as neutral, it isn't. It is a functional definition rather than a substantial definition. "Religion is the superstitious acceptance of the belief that God exists" is a non-neutral substantial definition. "Religion is the act of getting right before God" is a non-neutral definition that is partly substantial and partly functional.

As a basis for answering our question, we need a neutral definition. A neutral definition will not presuppose some particular answer to any of our substantial philosophical questions. It will not presuppose that some particular religious tradition is true (or false) or that no religious traditions are true (or false). For reasons that will become clear shortly, it will be nice if the definition can be both functional and also recognize the important point made by attempts to give a substantial definition. Consider this definition: **a religion is a conceptual system that provides an interpretation of the world and the place of human beings in it, bases an account of how life should be lived given that interpretation, and expresses this interpretation and lifestyle in a set of rituals, rites, institutions, and practices.** This is a functional definition; it views religions as providing persons with accounts of their world and their place in it—interpretations that are relevant to day-to-day living and that are given life in institutions, practices, and rituals. It recognizes the importance of religious activities. It also recognizes the importance of a doctrinal element in religious traditions. If doctrines without rituals are empty, then rituals without doctrines are blind. By 'rituals' here one should not think only of a Catholic Mass or a highly liturgical Anglican or Lutheran Service. A Plymouth Brethren celebration of the Lord's Supper or a Baptist celebration of adult baptism is a ritual in the sense of being a religious activity charged with theological meaning. The intent is that this definition be neutral in the sense recently characterized. Social science treatments of religion tend to focus on the institutions, rites, rituals, and practices, viewed either collectively as cultural artifacts or individually as sources of personal meaning. Philosophical discussions of religion tend to focus on the doctrines that religions offer and live by. These approaches are supplementary, not competitive, though academics often play down, or even deny, the importance of what they do not happen to study. Since this definition includes a conceptual component, it is inevitable that some reject it as too intellectual in spite of its containing emphasis on the embodiment of religion in institutions, rites, rituals, and practices. The tendency to downplay the centrality of doctrine to religion is as pervasive as the reluctance to consider truth or falsehood in connection with religious belief.

Another Definition

A different, but compatible, characterization of religion makes use of the notions of diagnosis and cure. A religion proposes a *diagnosis* (an account of what it takes to be the basic problem facing human beings) and a *cure* (a way of permanently and desirably solving that problem): one basic problem shared by every human person[5] and one fundamental solution that, however adapted to different cultures and cases, is essentially the same across the board. Religions differ insofar as their diagnoses and cures differ. For example, some religions are monotheistic and some are not. Hence some diagnoses are offered in terms of alienation from God and cures are presented that concern removing that alienation, while other diagnoses and cures make no reference to God. Other diagnoses will find the basic problem is the unsatisfactory nature of human life and offer a cure that altogether removes one from the human condition.

Philosophy of Religion

What Is Philosophy of Religion?

Metaphysics, epistemology, and ethics are disciplines within philosophy. Metaphysics is the enterprise of constructing and assessing accounts of what there is. Epistemology is the enterprise of constructing and assessing accounts of what knowledge is and how it can be attained. Ethics is the enterprise of constructing and assessing accounts of what makes actions right or wrong, what makes persons good or evil, what possesses intrinsic worth, what sort of life is worth living, and how these matters are related.[6] Philosophy of religion combines these enterprises in offering philosophically accessible accounts of religious traditions and assessing those traditions. Nothing very complex need inherently to be involved in offering philosophically accessible accounts of religious traditions, though there will be complex cases. The idea is to offer clear and literal[7] expressions of key doctrines. It is not unusual for a religion to contain metaphysical, epistemological, and ethical commitments. Then philosophy of religion will offer philosophically accessible accounts of these commitments and consider what can be said for and against the philosophical positions that have been taken.

A further feature of philosophy is worth highlighting. As Edmund Gettier once remarked, in philosophy you do not really understand a position unless you understand the arguments for it.[8] Such claims as:

A.   All that exists is minds and ideas.
B.   If a proposition P is necessarily true then **P is necessarily true** is also necessarily true.
C.   The existence of evil is logically compatible with the existence of God.

are such that one does not understand them unless one also grasps the reasons that can be offered on their behalf. This is why trying to teach philosophy without discussion of arguments is like trying to teach mathematics without reference to numbers. The reason, then, why we will pay attention to arguments is that this is a book in philosophy. Speculation unsupported by reasons is not science. Neither is it philosophy.

Questions for Reflection

1.   Explain what "Philosophy is the construction and assessment of categorial systems" means.
2.   Explain and assess the claims "The claim that objectivity is impossible is self-defeating" and "Objectivity is possible."
3.   Distinguish between functional and substantial definitions of religion.
4.   Give and explain a definition of 'religion.'
5.   Give and explain a definition of 'philosophy of religion.'

Notes

1.   Everett Hall (1958) *Philosophical Systems* (Chicago: University of Chicago Press) offers what I take to be the best book ever written on the nature of philosophy, though the final chapter disappoints.
2.   Cf. Alvin Plantinga's (Professor of Philosophy at the University of Notre Dame) remark to the effect that good philosophizing is just thinking really hard and well is right so far as it goes, and it is what one thinks about that makes one's thought philosophical.
3.   Cf. the comments by Everett Hall (1960) *Philosophical Systems: A Categorial Analysis* (Chicago: University of Chicago Press), p. 3–6, on what Medieval philosophers said

regarding *being, truth, and goodness.* Thoughts that something is so are either true or false, and *being true or false* is essential to their nature. So *thing, thought, and value,* like *being, truth, and goodness*, come under theory of reality, theory of knowledge, and ethics, which are the core disciplines for the philosophy of religion.

4. In terms of specifics, our focus will be on Judaism, Christianity, Islam, Hinduism, Buddhism, and Jainism—on Semitic and (South Asian) Indian religion.

5. By gods and goddesses as well, if there are any; by every person other than God.

6. Need it be said that these characterizations, accurate so far as they go, do not begin to plumb the complexities of these disciplines?

7. The view that all language, or all religious language, is non-literal is unfortunately widespread. It will be discussed further. As my comments here reveal, I take the view to be false.

8. The degree to which this is, or is not, peculiar to philosophical claims does not matter for our purposes; it is enough that it is true of philosophical claims.

Suggested Readings

Bertocci, Peter (1951) *An Introduction to the Philosophy of Religion* (Englewood Cliffs, NJ: Prentice-Hall). Covers a wide range of issues in the philosophy of religion with a detailed discussion of the teleological argument.

——— (1970) *The Person God Is* (London: George Allen and Unwin, Ltd.). Detailed presentation of theistic personalism (the view that persons are irreducible—not a complex made up of simpler things—and [in the case of God] ultimate).

Brightman, E. S. (1940) *A Philosophy of Religion* (New York: Prentice-Hall). Also covers a wide range of issues, arguing for the view that God is finite.

Burtt, E. A. (1951) *Types of Religious Philosophy* (New York: Harper and Brothers). After discussing Greek and biblical thought, considers major traditions and some issues in philosophy of religion.

Eliade, Mircea (1959) *The Sacred and the Profane: The Nature of Religion* (San Diego, CA: Harcourt, Brace, and World). Finds the core of religion in a (sometimes suppressed) sense of the sacred, in the non-rational numinous—a sense of the uncanny (in its stronger forms) that is irreducible to other feelings.

Hall, Everett (1960) *Philosophical Systems: A Categorical Analysis* (Chicago: University of Chicago Press). A brilliant analysis of the nature of philosophy.

——— (2010) *What is Value?: An Essay in Philosophical Analysis* (New York: Routledge). An application of Hall's view of philosophy to the property of having value. An account and application of the view of philosophy much like that assumed in this text.

MacIntosh, H. R. (1940) *The Problem of Religious Knowledge* (New York: Harper and Brothers). Discussion of wide range of theories of religious knowledge.

Otto, Rudolph, *The Idea of the Holy* (Oxford: Oxford University Press). A classic that finds the core of monotheistic religion in numinous experience, an experience of a holy and unique being.

Pals, Daniel (2008) *Introducing Religion: Readings from the Classical Theorists* (Oxford: Oxford University Press). Reading from Tylor through Geertz.

Patterson, Robert Leet (1970) *The Philosophy of Religion* (Durham, NC: Duke University Press). An account of the natures of philosophy and religion followed by a discussion of issues in the philosophy of religion.

Sire, James (2015) *Naming the Elephant: Worldview as a Concept* (Downer's Grove, IL: IV Academic). A very accessible account of the history of the notion and the role of worldviews in human life.

Smart, Ninian (1999) *Worldviews: Crosscultural Explorations of Human Beliefs* (New York: Pearson). Explores major religious and secular views of the world in terms of their conceptual organization, ways of assessing what has worth, and social structures.

Stausberg, Michael (2009) *Contemporary Theories of Religion: A Critical Companion* (New York: Routledge). Seventeen theories of religion presented by scholars representing philosophy and the social sciences.

Thomas, George F. (1970) *Philosophy and Religious Belief* (New York: Charles Scribner's Sons). Discussion of grounds of belief, God and the world, and freedom and grace.

—— (1973) *Religious Philosophies of the West* (New York: Charles Scribner's Sons). Discusses the positions of Western philosophers of religion from Plato through Tillich, with glance beyond.

Thompson, Samuel (1955) *A Modern Philosophy of Religion* (Chicago: Henry Regnery). Another account of the natures of philosophy and religion followed by a discussion of issues in the philosophy of religion.

Wieman, H. N. and Meland, Bernard Eugene, eds. (1936) *American Philosophers of Religion* (Chicago: Willett, Clark, and Co). Varieties of philosophies of religion held in American culture.

Yandell, Keith (1971) *Basic Issues in the Philosophy of Religion* (Boston: Allyn and Bacon). Contains criteria for assessing worldviews.

3 What Sorts of Religion Are There?

Monotheistic Religion

Some religious traditions are monotheistic. These traditions center on God, a being that is thought of as not depending on anything else for existence whereas the existence of everything else depends on God.[1] We will be concerned with three historical sorts of monotheism—Greek, Semitic, and Hindu.

Semitic monotheisms—Judaism, Christianity, and Islam—typically hold such claims as the following. God created the world in the sense that everything there is except God depends on God, and not conversely. The world that God created is real, not illusory, and that it exists is a good, not an evil, state of affairs. Human persons are created by God and in God's image with the dual consequence that every person has (in Kant's terms) dignity, not price (every individual has a unique worth derived from the fact of being created in God's image), and that the basis of ethics is realizing one's nature as made in God's image by imitating the behavior ascribed to God (insofar as this is possible to creatures). Human individuality is real, not illusory, and it is good that individual persons exist, not evil. God loves all persons in the sense of willing their ultimate good and acting for it. Central to being made in God's image is the capacity for loving oneself and others in this sense of willing their ultimate good and acting for it. Love in this sense is thus primarily volitional, not primarily emotional. God is all-knowing, all-powerful, all-good, and as made in His image people have some knowledge, power, and capacity for goodness. (This is, of course, quite different from human nature being "inherently good" in the sense that persons cannot help being good moral agents—inherent value is not the same as inherent goodness.) God is providential in the sense of governing the course of history and moving toward an end (the kingdom of God), so that time and the historical process are one-directional (not cyclical), and time and historical events and persons are real, not illusory, and it is a good, not an evil, that there are temporal and historical processes. God is holy in the dual sense that He is unique, alone worthy of being worshipped, and that He is morally pure or righteous. Thus worship is not a preliminary religious experience to be later transcended; its appropriateness is built into the nature of the Creator/creature distinction, which is not dissolvable. Since God is righteous, God judges sin (i.e., that which persons freely do to thwart others and themselves becoming mature good persons); since God loves all persons, this intolerance of sin follows from the nature of divine love. Thus human sin and guilt are real, not illusory, and it is held better that persons act freely as moral agents than that they be unable to sin. The basic religious problem is sin, not ignorance, and the basic religious need is for forgiveness, not for more information or enlightenment. Salvation, the solution of the basic religious problem is by grace (God's unmerited favor), not by human effort (or, for some traditions, not by human effort alone).[2]

Not every variety of monotheism holds that God has acted in the sense of bringing about events. Semitic monotheism holds that God has acted in history at real times and in real places to give revelation to persons and to act on their behalf.[3] In these traditions, religious doctrine *essentially* concerns certain persons and contains essential references to events. Religious knowledge is primarily gained through revelation (a process initiated by God) rather than through reflection, meditation, self-abasement, good works, yoga, and the like. Hindu monotheism views salvation as release from the beginningless and potentially endless round of birth and rebirth under the law of karma. The law of karma is administered by God and God has the power to release persons from the cycle of rebirth. There is a central theme of divine grace, God's unearned favor, which can rescue from the birth after rebirth. Sometimes this is viewed as sufficient of itself, but otherwise enlightenment is viewed as a joint product of divine grace combined with the human merit of good works. Insofar as there is such a thing as Greek monotheism, in Plato God is a Designer rather than an absolute creator, and for Aristotle is an Unmoved Mover who does not act but who is viewed as a final cause with the nature of everything else imitating the already fully realized nature of the Unmoved Mover in virtue of its inherent teleological tendency to become as perfect an example of a thing of its kind as is possible to it. The Mover does not act on the world, or even know any contingent truths (true propositions that might have been false) but does know the necessary truths (of logic, mathematics, metaphysics). Neither prayer nor worship play a role here.

Nonmonotheistic Religion

Indian nonmonotheistic religions such as Advaita Vedanta Hinduism, Theravada Buddhism, and Jainism, hold such claims as these. This world is a place of suffering and "unsatisfactoriness." There is a cycle of birth and rebirth.[4] There is a law of karma—one's misdeeds yield bad consequences to oneself and one's good deeds yield good consequences to oneself. The basic religious problem is that of escaping the round of birth and rebirth (*samsara*) and the way to do so is through enlightenment experience (roughly *moksha* for the Advaita Vedantin, *kevala* for the Jain, *nirvana* or *nibbana* for the Theravadin). The natural world (roughly, the set of objects of sensory experience) is in some sense unreal or illusory (except for Jainism). In Advaita only qualityless Brahman exists. For Theravada we misread our experience as that of an enduring subject of experience and take the external world to be made up of enduring objects, and there is neither enduring subjects nor enduring objects. The person, or self, (except for Jainism) of everyday experience—the "empirical self"—is in some sense unreal or illusory. There is no course of history toward an end or fulfillment. For Advaita temporal and historical processes are also in some sense unreal or illusory, and for Theravada we take processes to occur to something that endures. The basic religious problem is (in a rather technical sense of the word 'ignorance') ignorance, not sin (there is no God to sin against) and the basic religious need is for enlightenment, not for forgiveness (there is no God to forgive). Religious knowledge is gained through meditation, not through revelation (there is no God to offer revelation) and no religious doctrine essentially concerns certain persons or contains essential reference to places. Salvation comes through one's own efforts (there is no God to help), and involves the cessation of at least the "empirical self." Enlightenment experience is self-authenticating—in it one learns the truth and by having the experience one learns it in such a manner that no other evidence could show that what one supposedly learned was false.[5]

Reincarnation and Karma Doctrine

The doctrines of reincarnation and karma provide a general background to Indian Religion. Even those religions that do not accept it literally provide a reinterpretation of it. The basic idea is that everyone beginningless goes from one life to another without end unless enlightenment occurs. These reincarnations may occur in many places and under diverse circumstances as determined by one's actions in previous lifetimes. A good deed yields positive consequences and an evil deed earns negative consequences determined by an iron-clad natural law. The exception is in monotheistic traditions God can forgive wrong action and prevent the negative consequences.

One might find the idea of there being karmic laws governing a reincarnation cycle that may never end quite attractive—a sort of free cosmic travel program in which you go from life to life forever. If you live a sufficiently good life, your next life will be full enough of positive consequences to make it desirable. The indigenous perspective contains no such optimistic view.

Presumably, one cannot guarantee one's next lifetime will be lived in a good enough way to yield happy circumstances. But this is a minor consideration compared to the actual indigenous view, as the following passages make clear.

A Hindu text, Maitri Upanishad I, 3,4, reads as follows:

> In this ill-smelling body which is a conglomerate of bone, skin, muscle, marrow, flesh, semen, blood, mucus, tears, rheum, feces, urine, wind, bile, and phlegm . . . what is the good of the enjoyment of desires? . . . In this body, which is afflicted with desire, anger, covetousness, delusion, fear, despondency, envy, separation from the desirable, union with the undesirable, hunger, thirst, senility, disease, sorrow, and the like, what is the good of the enjoyment of desires? . . . we see this whole world is decaying . . .
>
> In this sort of cycle of existence what is the good of the enjoyment of desires when after a man has fed on them there is seen repeatedly his return to earth? . . . In this cycle of existence, I am a frog in a waterless well.

A story in its Jain version:

> A traveler . . . journeying through a dense forest . . . encountered a mad elephant which charged him. . . . As he turned to flee, a terrible demoness with a sword in her hand appeared before him and barred his way. There was a great tree near the track, and he ran up to it . . . but he could find no foothold in its smooth trunk. His only refuge was an old well . . . and into this he leapt. As he fell, he managed to catch hold of a clump of reeds which grew from the wall. . . . Looking down, he saw that the bottom . . . was surrounded by snakes which hissed at him. . . . In their midst was a mighty python, its mouth agape waiting to catch him. . . . Raising his head, he saw two mice . . . busily eating away at the roots. Meanwhile, the wild elephant ran up to the well and, enraged at losing its victim, charged at the trunk of the tree. Thus he dislodged a honeycomb which hung from a branch above the well [which] fell upon the man. . . . Angry bees swarmed round his head and tormented him. . . . But one drop of honey fell on his brow, rolled down to his face, and reached his lips. Immediately, he forgot his peril and thought of nothing else than getting another drop of honey.

A Theravada text:

> What then is the Holy Truth of Ill? Birth is ill. Decay is ill. Sickness is ill. Death is ill. To be disjoined from what one likes means suffering. Not to get what one wants, also that means suffering. In short, grasping at any of the five Skandas (the five elements of personality) involves suffering.

We have a Hindu description of someone in samsara as a frog in a waterless well, a Jain text picturing someone in samsara as helplessly clinging to a clump of reeds waiting to fall into a python's mouth, and a Buddhist text describing life in samsara as suffering. This is not the material from which a cosmic travel firm could cull advertisements. This is what provides the backdrop for much of India's religious tradition.

Doctrines Specific to Advaita Vedanta

For the Advaitin, ultimate reality (that which does not depend on anything else for its existence) is apersonal and eternal, unchanging, and permanent. The real self (*Atman*) is identical to this ultimate reality (*Brahman*) and in moksha learns this truth, thereby escaping samsara, losing all individuality, and being "absorbed" into Brahman. As an Advaita texts says:

> The man who has once comprehended Brahman to the (real) Self does not belong to this transmigratory world . . . there prevails the false notion that the Lord (i.e., Brahman) and the transmigratory world are different.[6]

Doctrines Specific to Jainism

For the Jain, there are an infinite number of real (non-illusory) things which are eternally distinct from one another. Among these distinct things are persons (souls, *jivas*) who can attain enlightenment in which (a) omniscience is attained, and (b) personal identity, or individuality, is not lost. Though the Jains believe in individual immortality, they do not believe in a Deity. Two Jain texts tell us:

> Modifications cannot exist without an abiding or eternal something—a permanent substance.[7] Liberation is the freedom from all karmic matter, owing to the non-existence of the cause of bondage and to the shedding of the *karmas*. After the soul is released, there remain perfect right-belief, perfect right-knowledge, and the state of having accomplished all.[8]

Doctrines Specific to Theravada (= Hinayanna) Buddhism

For the Theravada Buddhist tradition, an individual person is a set of elements, each momentary and transitory, and everything else is made up of momentary, transitory states. There is no enduring self (Atman) nor is there an unchanging ultimate reality (Brahman). In nirvana, one learns this truth concerning "impermanence." Depending on which of the competitive interpretations one accepts, final nirvana is the cessation of even this transitory self with consequent release from all desire. In any case, no series of bundles of momentary states is more than that in a nirvanic state. A Buddhist text asserts the following:

> Nagasena (or any other person's name) is but a way of counting, term, appellation, convenient designation, mere name for the hair of my head, hair of my body, . . . brain of the head, form, sensation, perception, the predispositions and consciousness. But in the absolute sense there is no ego.[9]

The implication is that there is no enduring subject of experience—indeed, no subject of conscious states who is distinct from those states. Persons reduce without remainder to collections of conscious states, the collections being nothing over and above the states. For Advaita, reincarnation belongs only to the level of appearance, not to the level of reality. For Jainism and Theravada it is real, and there is a difference as to what transmigrates = for the Jain, an enduring soul, for the Theravadin, a series of causally connected bundles of conscious states.

Criteria for Individuating Religions

It is natural to take one's cue for identifying distinct religious traditions from our characterization of that in virtue of which a tradition is religious, namely the presence of both diagnosis and cure. One result goes as follows:

Difference and Incompatibility

(1) Religion A differs from Religion B if the disease that A diagnoses is different from the disease that B diagnoses.

(2) Religion A differs from Religion B if the cure that A prescribes is different from the cure that B prescribes.

(3) Religion A differs from Religion B if what must exist if A's diagnosis is correct is different from what must exist if B's diagnosis is correct.

(4) Religion A differs from Religion B if what must exist if A's cure is successful in curing what it diagnoses is different from what must exist if B's cure is successful in curing what it diagnoses.

(5) Religion A differs from Religion B if, according to A, what must be known in order to achieve or receive salvation or enlightenment is different from what, according to B, must be known in order to achieve or receive enlightenment.

Incompatibility

(6) Religion A differs from Religion B if at least part of what must exist if A's diagnosis is correct cannot coexist with at least part of what must exist if B's diagnosis is correct.

(7) Religion A differs from Religion B if at least part of what must exist if A's cure is correct cannot coexist with what must exist if B's cure is correct.

(8) Religion A differs from Religion B if what one must know in order to become saved or enlightened according to A cannot be true if what one must know in order to become saved or enlightened according to B is true.

Criteria (1) and (2) appeal directly to what we have suggested is at the core of a religious tradition. Criteria (3) and (4) appeal to religion-relevant metaphysical difference as determined by the core. Criterion (5) appeals to a religion-relevant epistemological difference as determined by the core. Criterion (6) focuses on the question of the compatibility of what must exist if both of two diagnoses are true. Criterion (7) raises the same question concerning cures. Criterion (8) considers the compatibility of what two traditions require to be known for salvation or enlightenment.

Some Applications:

If we very briefly list first the diseases diagnosed, and the cures proposed, by Christianity, Advaita Vedanta, Jainism, and Theravada Buddhism, we get this result:

DIAGNOSES:

CHRISTIANITY: sin, separation from God

ADVAITA: ignorance of the identity of each Atman (person) with qualityless Brahman

JAINISM: false belief that one is dependent for existence on one's body; ignorance of one's inherent immortality as an immaterial jiva or soul

THERAVADA: false belief that one is an enduring mental substance; ignorance that one is nothing more than a causally linked collection of conscious states at a time and a causal series of collections over time, with a great many psychological attachments to fleeting things and events

CURES:

CHRISTIANITY: repentance and confession, commitment to God through Christ

ADVAITA: having an esoteric experience in which one realizes that one is identical to qualityless Brahman

JAINISM: having an esoteric experience in which one recognizes one's distinctness from one's body and lack of dependence on it, freed from the limitations of knowledge and power that embodiment imposes

THERAVADA BUDDHISM: an esoteric experience in which one sees the absence of an enduring subject of experience—indeed of any experiential subject at all—and is released from all attachments

With due apologies for the brevity and inadequacy of these summaries, they are sufficient to allow us to see that applying criteria (1) and (2) yields four religious traditions, each with its diagnosis and cure that differs from all the others. Hence we have four religious traditions on both criteria.

Criterion (3) deals with what must exist if a tradition's diagnosis is correct. Without going into details we can represent the answers in these terms:

What Must Exist if the Diagnoses Are Correct:

CHRISTIANITY: persons who have committed and are guilty of sin, a holy and loving God

ADVAITA: every person under illusion that they are distinct from qualityless Brahman and the non-personal Brahman to which each is identical

JAINISM: immortal persons embodied in inessential physical bodies who mistakenly identify themselves with their bodies

THERAVADA: collections of momentary states causally connected into bundles, which are related causally in a series containing belief in an enduring subject of experience
Criterion (4) concerns what must exist if the cure a tradition proposes is successful:

What Must Exist if the Cures Are Accurate:

CHRISTIANITY: a holy, loving God who becomes incarnate in Christ

ADVAITA: Brahman without qualities

JAINISM: kevala experience, which involves permanent escape from karma and reincarnation cycle and detachment from one's body

THERAVADA: final nirvana, which involves escape from karma and reincarnation cycle
Criterion (5) refers to what must be known in order to be saved or enlightened.

CHRISTIANITY: the news concerning the death and resurrection of Christ
(how this relates to those who have never heard the news varies within Chris-
tendom and is beyond our topic here)

ADVAITA: that the level of appearance is illusory and the level of reality alone
real

JAINISM: that one is neither identical to, nor dependent for existence on, one's
body

THERAVADA: that the self is illusory and attachment to anything prevents
enlightenment

Criteria (6) through (8) concern not merely difference but incompatibility. Of
course if two diagnoses, or cures, or recipes for salvation or enlightenment are
logically inconsistent, the difference is deeper than it would be otherwise. The
result is clear: given criteria (1) through (8), each of our traditions is a distinct
religion. The application of the criteria to other traditions will discern still more
religions.

There are other criteria. For example: Religion A differs from religion B if the
sacred verbal traditions or texts of A are different from the sacred verbal traditions
or texts of B, or A's rites and rituals are different from B's, or A's institutions are
different from B's. Further, one could replace "different from" by "incompatible
with." At this point, one will need to understand the goals and purposes involved,
which require doctrinal considerations.

Suggestions as to Common Features

We have distinguished between religions in terms of their most deeply religious
concerns specified in their cores. Of course one can use broader, vaguer terms
with different results. Religions that fall into different categories given our criteria may be classified together on other criteria. There is no more problem or
conflict about this than there is in the fact that Volkswagens and Chevrolets fall
under the same category if our category is automobiles and a different category
if it is products of German industry. Among the more popular of the general clas-
sifications intended to put as many religions in the same basket as possible are
"object of ultimate concern" (Tillich) and "source of self-transcendence" (Hick).
The former casts its nets widely, so that pursuit of wealth or sport counts as
religious, as is the case of the man who turned down an earlier occasion of heart
transplant so he could watch his alma mater play a bowl game. There are uses
for such wide categories, but they are not tied as closely to the actual contents of
religious traditions as seems important for extended philosophical reflection. The
second houses a deep ambiguity neglect of which yields considerable confusion.
To transcend the self may mean seriously following the Semitic second com-
mandment in the famous "You shall love the Lord your God with all your heart,
mind, soul and strength, and your neighbor as yourself," which is intended in
horizontal as well as vertical terms to include love and aid given for the sake of

the one loved, not for gain or recompense. This occurs in the context of a belief that men and women are created in the image of God, which grounds human dignity. There is another quite different, at least nearly opposite, sense in which to transcend oneself is to give up one's personal identity, or one's belief in or sense of personal identity. Compassion, which is also elicited by self-giving love, is prized as a means of losing attachment to everything one can lose. Behaviorally, the one sort of compassion may look just like the other, but the respective roots and goals differ deeply.

To put the point in a different way, one popular suggestion is that all religions have in common the goal of enabling its participants in achieving self-transcendence. This proposal contains a deep ambiguity. What self-transcendence means obviously depends on what transcendence amounts to. The ambiguity is easily extended—what transcendence involves is self-lessness. This leads to the question *What, exactly, is self-lessness?* At this point, it is high time to remove the ambiguity.

The goal of self-lessness, understood one way, is to seek as a metaphysical goal the obliteration of attachment to anything. The goal of self-lessness, understood another way, is ethical, roughly amounting to living a life of service to others. One sense of the term conveys the idea of transcending being a self, or transcending the idea that there is a self at all. The other, in a context in which being a self includes having great worth to be developed and not lost, promotes growth of the self into its potential as a moral agent. There is a difference between not being selfish and not wanting to be a self.

No doubt there are psychological goals (e.g., to live in a world that is not meaningless and in which one has an identifiable place) and sociological goals (e.g., to be a part of a social group in which one is accepted and with which one shares values and interests). Religious traditions can provide and support this. These, of course, are needs and goals that are also satisfied and reached in non-religious ways. Naturally, psychology, sociology, and anthropology of religion deal with the aspects of religion relevant to their interests, collecting data and proposing theories to explain that data; this is not competitive to philosophy of religion. Our characterization is offered with one eye on religious traditions and the other one on philosophical issues that the traditions raise. Whether or not there is an elusive essence of religion, and whether if there is our definition captures it, can be debated. Our contention is that our characterization is fair to at least many religious traditions and captures much if not all that is of interest to philosophers of religion insofar as they are on duty.

Conclusion

We have argued that, on the matters of most importance to the traditions themselves, our religious traditions differ in deep ways. Reading their doctrines nonliterally is an imperial reconstruction aimed at removing this incompatibility. The project amounts to sufficiently secularizing the traditions to turn them into stories that are intended to have moral influence. The traditions themselves are left behind. This hardly seems a means of respecting them.

Questions for Reflection

1. What philosophical issues do the core doctrines of monotheism raise?
2. What philosophical issues do the core doctrines of nonmonotheistic religion raise?
3. Are the criteria used for distinguishing between religions religiously neutral (not favoring one religion over another) and accurately applied?
4. Which doctrines in Advaita Vedanta and Christianity are most clearly opposed?
5. Which doctrines in Jainism and Theravada Buddhism are most clearly opposed?

Notes

1. Or of everything else that *can* have a source. A monotheist who holds that there are abstract objects, that abstract objects exist with logical necessity and so cannot not exist, and that what cannot not exist cannot be created but exists on its own, will not, if she is consistent, think that abstract objects can have a source of existence, and so will not take God to be such a source. The matter is controversial.
2. This is not to deny that new knowledge may be involved in attaining salvation—but that this is not all that is needed.
3. Examples: Judaism, the Passover Event; Christianity, the Cross and Resurrection; Islam, the Revelation to the Prophet.
4. Hindu monotheists accept this claim and the following two claims; they view God as the Agent behind reincarnation and karma and take enlightenment experience to involve repentance of one's sins followed by God's forgiveness and acceptance of one's worship.
5. The point is the *epistemic* one that enlightenment experience is said to yield incorrigible knowledge not the *psychological* one that it yields unretractable belief.
6. Radhakrishan, Sarvapelli and Charles Moore (1957) *Sourcebook in Indian Philosophy* (Princeton: Princeton University Press), p. 513.
7. RM, 269.
8. RM, 260.
9. RM, 284.

Suggested Readings

Buckareff, Andrei and Nagasawa, Yujin (2016) *Alternative Concepts of God: Essays on the Metaphysics of the Divine* (Oxford: Oxford University Press). Essays, pro and con, concerning non-orthodox concepts of divinity.

Christian, William (1972) *Oppositions of Religious Doctrines: A Study in the Logic of Dialogue Among Religions* (London: Macmillan). An account of how we can discover and understand disagreements among religions' essential teachings.

Larsen, Gerald James and Deutsch, Elliot, eds. (1988) *Interpreting across Boundaries* (Princeton, NJ: Princeton University Press). Investigates some of the challenges and rewards of considering religion in a cross-cultural context.

Schmidt, Wilhelm (1931) *The Origin and Growth of Religion* (London: Methuen and Company). A controversial but very interesting defense of the view that monotheism is the earliest religion.

Sharma, Arvind (2011) *Our Religions: The Seven World Religions Introduced by Preeminent Scholars from Each Tradition* (Taunton, MA: HarperCollins, Kindle). Each essay is written by a scholar who is a member of the tradition presented who also has eminent standing as an expert.

Smart, Ninian (1960) *A Dialogue of Religions* (London: SCM Press). Presents the views of various religions on central topics in the form of a dialogue.

—— (1964) *Doctrine and Argument in Indian Philosophy* (London: Allen and Unwin). Clear and comprehensive presentation of the basic claims of different Indian philosophical systems.

Smith, Huston (2009) *The World's Religions* (Taunton, MA: HarperCollins, Revised and Updated, Kindle). A classic that deals with the "inner" side of a large selection of religions.

Ward, Keith (1999) *Religion and Human Nature* (Oxford: Oxford University Press). Discusses views of human nature and eschatology from multiple religious perspectives.

4   What Sorts of Religious Experience Are There?

Structure and Content

The basic interest of religious experiences for the philosophy of religion lies in whatever potential they may have for providing information about what there is. Those who think that there are experience-independent material objects typically suppose that perceptual experience—seeing, hearing, tasting, smelling, and touching—are on the whole a reliable source of information about these objects. Moral experience is regarded by moral realists—roughly, those who think that there actually are obligations, duties, right and wrong ways of behaving, ways of being a good or an evil person, and the like—as having similar information potential. The discussion that follows is governed by two underlying queries: What sort of information about what there is might religious experiences provide, and how could one tell? While these underlying questions do not receive direct attention until later chapters, the presentation here looks forward to the discussion there.

The notion of a "kind" of experience, like so many others, is not one that is sharply delineated in everyday thought. It is a term we will need to define in a way that is fair to the experiences, but is useful for our purposes. That said, there are various sorts of religion; there are also various sorts of religious experience. The notion of a sort of experience is not immediately obvious. Let us begin with a criterion for experiences being of a different sort that has to do with the structure of an experience. Consider such experiences as feeling nauseous, dizzy, or disoriented; consider also generalized anxiety and generalized euphoria, where the force of "generalized" is to cancel out the idea that there is something in particular about which one is anxious or euphoric. Sensory experience is subject-consciousness-object (s-c-o) in structure, as are at least apparent experiences of God. In contrast, nausea and the like are subject-content (s-c) in structure. These experiences do not seem to their subjects to be matters of sensing something external, subject-content experience. To be anxious about a small dog wandering near traffic, euphoric at the thought of buttermilk doughnuts, or pained by a friend's harsh words, is to have a subject-consciousness-object experience. The phenomenology of an experience is "what it is like to the subject" to have the experience. To fear Frankenstein is to have an outer-directed experience. In another jargon, it is inherently intentional in the sense of apparently being "of something." Just as one's thought that Frankenstein would not be great to have as a neighbor is about

Frankenstein is not cancelled by there being no such being, fear of Frankenstein is not cancelled by Frankenstein's absence. The structure of both the thought and the feeling is subject-conscious object; this is an essential feature of its structure.

We now need some criteria.

> Criterion One: Experience A is of a different sort from experience B if A is of subject/consciousness object structure and B is of subject/content structure, or conversely.

Whether or not there are other experiential structures besides the two we have mentioned, an experience possessing one of the two identified structures is a different kind from the other.[1]

A central doctrine of Theravada Buddhism is that all there is to you now is a bundle of physical states that do not involve consciousness and mental states that do involve consciousness; there is no subject that has these states. A core doctrine in Jainism insists that there is a subject that has such states—states must be states of something. It adds that the subject of these states—every human being—is immortal and immaterial. Advaita Vedanta agrees with Jainism regarding what it calls the "level of experience," but its core doctrine insists that at what it calls the "level of reality" (the way things really are) there exists only qualityless Brahman. Each tradition claims that its core doctrine is seen to be true if one has its particular type of enlightenment experience. Were all three sorts of enlightenment experience reliable, you would be a subject of your experiences, a subjectless set of causally connected states, and identical to a being or state that has no properties whatever. Thus the traditions hold incompatible doctrines.

Our current interest concerns what they have in common, namely their appeal to enlightenment experience. What sort of structure does such an experience have?

Subject-consciousness-object experience, if it is reliable, is awareness of something ontologically distinct from the subject. Subject-content experience is awareness of one's own psychological and physical states. But the metaphysical structure—substantial subject in states that depend for their existence on the substantial subject whose states they are versus causally related states that are not states of anything—of persons is not one of one's mental or physical states; at least it is not typically listed along with joy and being seated, which normally one feels and is aware of by being aware of one's body. Nonetheless there are religious traditions and philosophical positions that maintain that our metaphysical structure is something we can know by direct (non-inferential) awareness. If this is also introspection, it is introspective awareness of something quite different than whether one has a headache. One's metaphysical structure is not mind-dependent nor is it something that exists distinct from and independent of oneself. We will discuss later some of the philosophical context of the Jain-Buddhist dispute. For now, we need a characterization of this sort of experience. Perhaps something along these lines will do.

> Criterion Two: If an experience, if reliable, is an awareness of something neither mind-dependent nor distinct from oneself, and so is not sensory perceptual or standardly introspective, then it is an introversive experience.[2]

Descartes claimed that when you are in pain, strictly speaking, you are aware of yourself-being-in-pain—aware of being a subject distinct from the state but aware of the state. This self-awareness is reliable and introversive. In sharp contrast, Hume claimed that when we introspect, we learn that all we are is a bundle of states. "I am in pain," stated with metaphysical care, is better expressed "A pain state is among the causally connected states that currently composes me." Jainism sides with Descartes and much of Buddhism with Hume, save that the Buddhist view grants that the Descartes-Jain view is the common sense view.

Monotheistic traditions include visions and dreams among divine revelations. These are subject-consciousness-object experiences with perceptual content. They are in one way at least like hallucinations (secularists of course will see the relation as identity)—most of their content is not veridical. Experience 2 (following) is an example. God is represented as a king sitting on a throne. It is not part of Jewish theology that the maker of heaven and earth literally sits on a throne. For the monotheist, the setting is not something that is to be taken literally; it is setting (in this case) for the verbal content of the vision. The setting is symbolic. The verbal content is literal. While it can be trickier to deal with visions (and dreams), which raise questions of interpretation not typically required by perceptual experiences, dreams are sometimes considered as, in effect, visions had by the sleeping.

There are many other ways of cutting up the experiential pie. There are perceptual—visual, tactual, auditory, gustatory, and olfactory—experiences, and moral and aesthetic experiences, for example. Nonetheless this division seems much less relevant to, and helpful for, our inquiries, and we can add others should they be added.

Experiences typically will have affective content. Enlightenment experiences standardly are described as peaceful, blissful, and having thorough absence of attachment. Monotheistic experiences often at least typically include a response of awe and reverence. These feelings are taken to be signs of, and evidence for, enlightenment experience and experience of God.

Descriptions

We next need some examples of religious experiences.

Monotheism: Jewish, Christian, Hindu

Experience 1

> Moses, tending the flock of his father-in-law Jethro, sees a bush that apparently is burning and not consumed by the fire. Then, the text of Exodus tells us:
> And Moses said, "I will turn aside and see this great sight, why the bush is not burnt." When the Lord saw that he turned aside to see, God called to him out of the bush, "Moses, Moses!" And he said, "Here am I." Then he [God] said, "Do not come near; put off your shoes from your feet, for the place on

which you are standing is holy ground." And he said, "I am the God of your Father, the God of Abraham, the God of Isaac, the God of Jacob." And Moses hid his face, for he was afraid to look at God.

(Exodus 3: 3–6)

Experience 2

In the year that King Uzziah died I saw the Lord, high and holy and lifted up; and his train filled the temple. Above him stood the seraphim; each had six wings: with two he covered his face, and with two he covered his feet, and with two he flew. And one called to another and said: "Holy, holy, holy is the Lord of Hosts; the whole earth is full of His glory." And the foundations of the thresholds shook at the voice of him who called, and the house was filled with smoke. And I said: "Woe is me! For I am lost; for I am a man of unclean lips and I dwell in the midst of a people of unclean lips; for my eyes have seen the king, the Lord of hosts!" Then flew one of the seraphims to me, having in his hand a burning coal which he had taken with tongs from the altar. And he touched my mouth, and said: "Behold, this has touched your lips; your guilt is taken away, and your sin forgiven." And I heard the Lord saying, "Whom shall I send, and who will go for us?" Then I said, "Here I am! Send me." And he said, "Go."

(Isaiah 6: 1–9)

Experience 3

I [John] was in the Spirit on the Lord's day, and I heard behind me a loud voice like a trumpet saying, "Write what you see in a book and send it to the seven churches. . . . Then I turned to see the voice that was speaking to me, and on turning I saw seven golden lampstands, and in the midst of the lampstands one like a son of man, clothed with a long robe and with a golden girdle round his breast; his head and his hair were white as wool, white as snow; his eyes were like a flame of fire, his feet were like burnished bronze, refined as in a furnace, and his voice was like the sound of many waters; in his right hand he held seven stars, from his mouth issued a sharp two-edged sword, and his face was like the sun shining in full strength. When I saw him, I fell at his feet as though dead. But he laid his right hand upon me, saying "Fear not, I am the first and the last, and the living one; I died, and behold I am alive forevermore, and I have the keys of Death and Hades."

(Revelation 1:10–18)

Experience 4

Father of all, Master supreme, Power supreme in all the worlds, Who is like thee? Who is beyond thee? I bow before thee. I prostrate before thee, and I beg thy grace, O glorious Lord. As a father to his son, as a friend to his friend, as a lover to his lover, be gracious unto me, O God. In a vision I have seen what no man has seen before; I rejoice in exultation, and yet my heart trembles with fear. Have mercy upon me, Lord of Gods, refuge of the whole universe: show me again thine own human form. I yearn to see thee again with thy crown and scepter and circle. Show thyself to me in thine own four-armed form, thou of arms infinite, Infinite Form.

(Bhagavagita (Song of the Blessed Lord) Chapter 11, paragraphs 43–46)

Comment

Examples 1–4 are subject-consciousness-object in structure. In saying this we are not assuming the experiences are veridical. Having a subject-consciousness-object experience does not guarantee the existence of the item toward which an outer-directed experience is targeted. There is an interesting phrase in 4—God is described as having an infinity of arms. This goes down well in Delhi as indicating omnipotence. It would not go down well in Detroit where seeing something with as many as eight legs can lead to a call to the exterminator. One must expect different descriptions to express the same or similar concepts as one moves from one culture to another. Also similar expressions may express different concepts. The experiences are obviously phenomenologically subject-concept-object and the at least apparent object elicits reverence and awe. It is sometimes said that a transcendent God cannot be of object of experience because such a God is not (a space and time) object. 'Object' here simply means "that which is experienced." To claim that an omnipotent cannot do this seems obviously false. (Whether God should be thought of as an eternal [timeless] being or an everlasting being [no temporal beginning, no temporal ending, and no gaps in the middle] is a point at dispute in contemporary philosophy of religion.)

Theravada Buddhism

Experience 5

This monk life leads to complete detachment, to freedom from desire, to peace, to superknowledge, to the highest insight, to nibbana.

(Digha Nikaya II, 251)

Experience 6

This is peace, this is the highest, namely the calming of the activities, the rejection of all attachment, the destruction of craving, the freedom from desire, nibbana.

(Anguttara Nikaya V, 110)

Experience 7

. . . freedom from pride, restraint of thirst, uprooting of attachment, cutting off of the cycle of existences, destruction of craving, freedom from desire, ceasing, nibbana.

(Ibid., I, 88)

Experience 8

But when I comprehended, as it really is, the satisfaction of the world as satisfaction, the misery as misery, and the escape as escape, then I fully understood and accepted full Buddha status, and the knowledge and the vision arose in me: sure is the release of my mind: this is my last birth.

(Ibid., I, 259)

Experience 9

It is recognized that there is nothing but what is seen of the mind itself where recognizing the nature of the Self-mind, one no longer cherishes the dualism of discrimination, where there is no more thirst or craving, where there is no more attachment to external things.

(Surangama)

Comment

Nirvana (= nibbana) is described in these passages in both positive terms (features it has) and negative terms (features that it lacks). Peace, superknowledge, highest insight, cutting off the cycle of existences, plus detachment, freedom from pride and desire and craving and illusion—the latter are viewed as conditions that bind one to the cycle of rebirth and the exceptionless law of karma, so that reaching nirvana means that one has escaped these conditions that pull one away from reaching nirvana. An account of nirvana is typically rather general. The question most likely to be asked about it is whether, in that state or condition (it is not a place), personal identity is retained. The basic problem is that personal identity, strictly speaking, is not retained in this, or any, lifetime. The Buddha is recorded as refusing to answer the question whether the self exists, does not exist, both exists and does not exist, or neither exists nor fails to exist. The questions assume that there is a self to survive or not survive. Further, pondering the questions does not help toward liberation from craving.[3] What Theravada Buddhists hold persons to be is one collection of ephemeral causally related momentary states at a moment, and a causally connected series of the same over time. Seeing that this is so is a central element in attaining Buddhist nirvana. To achieve nirvana is in part to perceive the truth of this doctrine. Nirvana is said to be ineffable, beyond space and time, peaceful, a blissful consciousness. One thing is clear: in nirvana there is no more to personal identity than there was under pre-nirvanic conditions. The idea is roughly this: when you see, as you do in enlightenment, that you are just one ephemeral bundle after another you will abandon all attachments. The metaphysical insight and the cessation of attachment go together.

Jainism

Experience 10

. . . with the knees high and the head low, in deep meditation, he [Mahavira, a founder of Jainism] reached Nirvana, the complete and full, the unobstructed, unimpeded, infinite and supreme, best knowledge and intuition, called Kev-ala . . . he was a Kevalin, omniscient and comprehending all objects, he knew all conditions of the world, of gods, men, and demons; whence they come, where they go, whether they are born as men or animals, or become gods or hell-beings; their food, drink, doings, desires, open and secret deeds, their conversation and gossip, and the thoughts of their minds; he saw and knew all conditions in the whole world of all living beings.

(Jaina Sutras I, 201, 202)

Experience 11

With supreme knowledge, with supreme intuition, with supreme conduct, . . . with supreme uprightness, with supreme mildness, with supreme dexterity, with supreme patience, with supreme freedom from passions, with supreme con-trol, with supreme contentment, with supreme understanding, on the supreme path to final liberation, which is the fruit of veracity, control, penance, and good conduct, the Venerable One meditated on himself for twelve years. During the thirteenth year the second month of summer, in the fourth fort-night . . . on its tenth day, when the shadow had turned towards the east and the first wake was over . . . [the Venerable One] in a squatting position, with joined heels, exposing himself to the heat of the sun after fasting two and a half days without drinking water, being engaged in deep meditation, reached the highest knowledge and intuition called Kevala, which is infinite, supreme, unobstructed, unimpeded, complete, and full . . . he was a Kevalin, omniscient and comprehending all objects; he knew and saw all conditions of the world, of gods, men, and demons; whence they come, whither they go, whether they are born as men or as animals or become gods or hell-beings, the ideas, the thoughts of their minds, the food, doings, desires, the open and secret deeds of all the living beings in the whole world; he the Arhat, for whom there is no secret, knew and saw all conditions of all living beings in the world, what they thought, spoke, or did at any moment. . . . [This is] final liberation.

(Ibid., I, 263, 271)

Experience 12

Mahavira quitted the world, cut asunder the ties of birth, old age, and death; become a Siddha, a Buddha, a Mukta, a maker of the end (to all misery), finally liberated, freed from all pains.

(Ibid., I, 264, 265)

Experience 13

Mahavira obtained the highest knowledge and intuition, called Kevala, which is infinite, supreme, unobstructed, unimpeded, complete, and full . . . final liberation.

(Ibid., I, 265, 266)

Experience 14

. . . he reached Nirvana, the complete and full, the unobstructed, unimpeded, infinite and supreme, best knowledge and intuition, called Kevala.

(Ibid., I, 201)

Experience 15

(The liberated) with their departing breath reach absolute perfection, wisdom, liberation, final Nirvana, the end of all misery.

(Ibid., I, 94)

Experience 16

Having annihilated his Karman (= karma) both meritorious and sinful, being steadfast (self-controlled) . . . [the enlightened one] crossed the ocean-like flood of worldly existence and obtained exemption from transmigration.

(Ibid., I, 111, 112)

Experience 17

. . . what is called Nirvana, or freedom from pain, or perfection, which is in view of all; it is the safe, happy, and quiet place which all the great sages reach. This is the eternal place, in view of all, but difficult of approach. Those sages who reach it are free from sorrow, they have put an end to the stream of existence.

(Ibid., I, 128)

Experience 18

(Kevalins) have obtained perfection, enlightenment, deliverance, final beatitude, and . . . an end to all misery.

(Ibid., II, 158)

Experience 19

(A Kevalin) obtains perfection, enlightenment, deliverance, and final beatitude and puts an end to all misery.

(Ibid., II, 173)

Comment

Here too nirvana (= kevala) is described in terms of what features it has and what features it lacks. Here, the seeker retains personal identity (he had it in all past lives). His knowledge is no longer limited by embodiment, belief that one is one's body or that being embodied is necessary for existence is replaced by a conviction that one is simply an immaterial mental substance, and one is assured of one's immortality free from suffering and misery.

Advaita Vedanta

Experience 20

When a seer sees the brilliant Maker, Lord, Person, the Brahman-source, then, being a knower, shaking off good and evil, stainless, he attains supreme identity with Him.

(Mundaka Upanishad III, i, 3)

Experience 21

Not by sight is it grasped, not even by speech, not by any other sense-organs, austerity, or work, by the peace of knowledge, one's nature purified—in that way, however, by meditating, one does behold him who is without parts.

(Ibid., III, i, 8)

Experience 22

That which is the finest essence—the whole world has that as its self. That is Reality. That is Atman. That art thou.

(Chandogya Upanishad VI, ix, 4)

Experience 23

Now, when one is sound asleep, composed, serene, and knows no dreams— that is the self (Atman) . . . that is the immortal, the fearless. That is Brahman.

(Ibid., VIII, xi, 1)

Experience 24

Then Usasta Cakkayan questioned him. "Yajnavalkya," said he, "Explain to me who is Brahman present and not beyond our ken, him who is the self in all things." [Yajnavalkya replies:] "Verily, he is the great, unborn self, who is this (person) consisting of knowledge among the senses. In the space within the heart lies the ruler, the lord of all, the king of all."

(Brhadaranyaka Upanishad III)

Comment

The doctrinal context is this: what we refer to as a person is an Atman that is plagued by illusion that there is the world there appears to be with physical objects, human beings, cows, mountains. This is the level of appearance, and Brahman (God) exists in this world. So long as the Atman continues to suffer from this illusion, it stays in the cycle of rebirth and under the law of karma. Enlightenment comes via an experience in which one recognizes the illusion as an illusion and the identity of the Atman and Brahman, conceived as qualityless Brahman in which there are no distinctions to be made.

Direct/Indirect Experience

The question as to what counts as a direct experience of something quickly gets complicated. The simplest example is introspection—pain does not need an intermediary from which we infer that we are in pain. Other sensations fit the same pattern. You do not have to infer that you are adding two and two from your writing down the thought and then inferring that you are having it. Sensory perception is often viewed similarly. If you see a computer screen, you do not need to think "There seems to be a computer screen there; if there seems to be a computer screen there, there probably is one; so probably there is a computer screen there." While it may be a cardboard model for advertising, a hologram of a screen, or the content of a hallucination, you will take it to be the case that there is a screen there, and the practice of doing that will work nicely. But there is a position held by competent thinkers, who offer arguments for their view, that what one is directly aware of in sensory perception is not the object perceived but sense data that are caused by the object, and the sense data gives you generally reliable information about physical objects in your environment (indirect realism). But then one never has direct awareness of any mind-independent objects. What, then, justifies your belief that there are such objects? One answer is: nothing, there just are the mind-dependent sense data (roughly, idealism). Another is that nothing justifies the belief on the sense data view, so our choices are skepticism and the view that we are directly aware of mind-independent physical objects (direct realism). With this light touch on the epistemology of perception, we can turn briefly to analogous questions concerning religious experiences.

We begin with subject-consciousness object experience—apparent experiences of God. Experience 2 has Isaiah having a vision in which God sits on a throne. God is not, according to Jewish theology, a material being. So God does not sit. The visual images are representative of God as ruler but are not to be taken literally. What about the verbal message? That is trickier. God is not a native Hebrew speaker, but there is no reason why an omnipotent, omniscient being could not cause sound waves that amount to "Whom shall I send for us?"

So perhaps the verbal communication is direct experience of God, thereby expressing thoughts God literally has. (Objections to the idea that anything said about God can be literal will be discussed in a later chapter. We can note for now that the claim that God is such that nothing literal can be said about God is itself something literal said about God, and further the question arises as to how one knows that nothing said about God can be literally true.)

So where do our monotheistic religious cases fit? One could view them as indirect because they may come at the end of a specified process. Perhaps Mary at least seems to experience God, after having gone through a sort of preparatory religious procedure intended to reach that success. Perhaps she offered a prescribed sacrifice, and then entered a house of worship and prayed. Perhaps if John at least seems to experience God after he has fasted, gone to a worship service, confessed his sins, and taken Communion; and then only then prays humbly for God's presence. What is not clear is why any of this should make the experience indirect. For one thing, it is not at all a central doctrine of most sorts of monotheism that if one does A, B, and C, then this will constrain God to appear. The view of God as sovereign typically prevents there being a ritual the performance of which is supposed to guarantee a divine visit. Further, nothing in either person's behavior places them behind a veil that God could not pass through.

One suggestion is that whatever in a vision or dream represents God as having a feature that an immaterial being cannot have, take that as the setting for whatever may be direct. Thus the words Isaiah hears may be direct—God actually having the thoughts the words expressed—whereas the throne is setting for the words, there to identify to Isaiah who is their source. So perhaps this is a sensible way to distinguish what is direct versus indirect. The basic idea is that while all of the experience is caused by God, the setting part of a dream or vision is not accurate to what God is, and the part that is accurate regarding God is the best candidate for being direct experience; God, as immaterial, has no vocal cords, but as omnipotent can cause words that do communicate thought that God has. The setting imagery, while perhaps caused by God, is not true of God or the sender who is not in a literal temple. So long as the information content is correct, perhaps whether we call the hearing of the voice is direct experience or not is not crucial—God has been reliably experienced if the words express God's thoughts, and that is enough. We will leave this suggestion for further reflection, which should include what to say concerning symbolic features of such experiences as 1–4, and in response to the question as to whether all of our experiences can be indirect (and if they all are, from what does the inference that makes an experience indirect begin?).

What, then, of the non-theistic cases? Theravada Buddhism, Jainism, and Advaita Vedanta (concerning the level of reality) are non-theistic. For Jainism enlightenment experience is awareness of one's being immaterial, immortal, and omniscient. It is thus an introversive experience—one is aware of one's nature. Common sense, everyday experience reveals oneself as a subject of experience rather than a series of ephemeral bundles of conscious states. Enlightenment experience adds to common sense, correcting the tendency to think of oneself as simply physical or dependent for existence on the physical. It more accurately sees the nature of the jiva or soul. For Theravada, it is again the structure of what we call persons that is exposed in enlightenment experience. Assuming such experiences occur, both in the Jain and the Buddhist case, the experience is direct and intravercive. If both are introversive, then introversive experiences can be mistaken, since at least one of the Jain and the Buddhist experiences must be incorrect as to what the structure of persons really is.

Questions for Reflection

1. What, exactly, is a phenomenological description and why is it important to have them?
2. Are the criteria for different kinds of experience clear and properly applied?

3.   Suppose we learned somehow that sensory perception was always unreliable. Would it follow that all sort of subject-consciousness-object experience was unreliable?
4.   What, if anything can be learned about the possible evidential potential of religious experience by reflecting concerning the types of non-religious experience?
5.   Suppose your friend Kim has what you both take to be a religious experience—say, one that seemed to be an experience of God. Could this be evidence for you that God exists? Why, or why not?

Notes

1.   Perception as s-c-o is generally accepted. Introspection of sensations and introspection of psychological attitudes phenomenologically differ in that, save for generalized anxiety, etc., the latter has an object—something feared or hoped, and are outer-directed.
2.   A technical term used as defined.
3.   Though the idea that there is an enduring self is sometimes viewed as dangerous precisely because it leads to what the tradition views as unfortunate attachment.

Suggested Readings

Dan, Joseph (2003) *The Heart and the Fountain: An Anthology of Jewish Mystical Experiences* (Oxford: Oxford University Press). Presents numerous selections from Jewish mysticism, with commentary.

Happold, F. Crossfield (1991) *Mysticism: A Study and an Anthology* (London: Penguin Books). Independent of a controversial view of mystical experience are some twenty-six selections from Hinduism, Plato, and Christianity plus a final example from nature mysticism.

James, William (1902) *Varieties of Religious Experience: A Study in Human Nature* (London: Random House). Gifford Lectures with lots of reports of religious experiences described by James as "extreme" examples, classified by their effects and the personality types of those who have them, presented in the context of James's pragmatism and pluralism.

Katz, Steven T. (2012) *Comparative Mysticism: An Anthology of Original Sources* (Oxford: Oxford University Press). Selections from Jewish, Christian, Islamic, Hindu, Buddhist, Confucian, Taoist, and Native American sources.

McGinn, Bernard (2006) *The Essential Writings of Christian Mysticism* (New York: Random House). Nearly one hundred selections from Christian mystics.

Otto, Rudolph (1958) *The Idea of the Holy* (Oxford: Oxford University Press). A classic. Highly influential discussion of experience of the holy, which Otto calls "the numinous"—the uncanny at its most extreme, where awareness of the numinous humbles the subject; the numinous content of religious experience is reducible to no other felt content.

Pike, Nelson (1960) *Mystic Union: An Essay in the Phenomenology of Mysticism* (Ithaca, NY: Cornell). Careful discussion of the prayers of Quiet, Union, and Rapture in several Medieval mystics, in which Pike argues that, upon careful examination, the phenomenology of these states is theistic.

Radhakrishnan, Sarvepali and Moore, Charles (1967) *A Sourcebook in Indian Philosophy* (Princeton, NJ: Princeton University Press). A standard reference work with a very useful collection of Hindu, Buddhist, and Jain texts that include descriptions.

Stace, Walter T. (1966) *Mysticism and Philosophy* (New York: Lippincott). Standard statement of view on which mystical experience is not subject-consciousness-object. Divides mystical experience into extrovertive (experience of unity of nature in which the subject is included) and introvertive (which is devoid of concepts and images).

Wiebe, Phillip H. (2004) *God and Other Spirits* (Oxford: Oxford University Press). In a sober and scholarly manner, quotes and discusses reports of experiences that their subjects regard as encounters with God and other spirits, thus including in his examples a wider than typical range of experiences.

Zaehner, R. C. (1960) *Concordant Discord* (Oxford: Oxford University Press). Deserves to be a classic. Argues that Stace leaves out an important type of introvertive mysticism, namely the love mysticism of both India and the West—a type of experience that is theistic.

5 The Importance of Doctrine and the Distinctness of Religious Traditions

Doctrine

Agreement on the Importance of Doctrine

It is fairly well known that the New Testament contains such passages as that in which Jesus says "I am the Way, the Truth, and the Life; no one comes to the Father but by me."[1] One reads that "he who believes in the Son has eternal life; he who does not obey the Son shall not see life, but the wrath of God abides on him."[2] St. Peter asserted, "There is salvation in no one else [but Jesus Christ], for there is no other name under heaven given among men by which we must be saved."[3] It is less well known that the other religious traditions we have discussed have similar emphases. The Advaita Vedantin Shankara, for example, forthrightly says that "if the soul . . . is not considered to possess fundamental unity with Brahman—an identity to be realized by knowledge—there is not any chance of its obtaining final release."[4] A text from the *Jaina Sutras* bluntly tells us, "Those who do not know all things by *kevala* (knowledge), but who being ignorant teach a law (of their own), are lost themselves, and work the ruin of others in this dreadful, boundless Circle of Births. Those who know all things by the full Kevala knowledge, and who are practicing meditation and teach the whole law, are themselves saved and save others." A Buddhist text speaks plainly to this effect: "If one does not proceed in this manner [to "proceed in this manner" is to "develop the understanding which results from the study of the (Buddhist) teachings"], inasmuch as meditation on some erroneous idea cannot even clear away doubt, recognition of reality will not arise and consequently meditation will be profitless like that of the Tirthikas (i.e., non-Buddhists, especially Jains)."[5] The theme of these passages is clear enough. To put them in one jargon: there is a heaven to gain and a hell to shun; there is one way to gain heaven and shun hell, and there are plenty of ways to shun heaven and gain hell.

This insistence on the importance of doctrine comes out in another way. It is not an accident that, as we have noted, the experiences that are religiously central to our traditions are typically called *enlightenment* experiences or they are said to yield knowledge of God;[6] they are described as *cognitive*. An Advaitin description of moksha goes like this: "When a seer sees . . . the Brahman-source, then, being a knower, shaking off good and evil, stainless, he attains supreme identity with

Him."[7] The Jaina Sutras speak of "the highest knowledge and intuition, called 'Kevala' which is . . . final liberation."[8] A Theravada text says, "The monk life leads to complete detachment, to freedom from desire, to cessation, to peace, to superknowledge, to the highest insight, to nibbana."[9] Correspondingly, the New Testament says, "We know that the Son of God has come and has given us understanding so that we may know Him who is true."[10]

This feature of religion is often regarded with sadness or disapproval, an unfortunate but accidental feature that can be removed from religious traditions with gain and without loss. Such suggestions fail to understand what a religion is. A doctor who diagnoses Mary as having migraine headaches and proposes Darvon and stress reduction as cure differs from a doctor who diagnoses Mary as feigning pain and recommends psychoanalysis. The one thinks that Mary's pain is real and requires medical attention; the other thinks that Mary has no pain and is faking it and thus offers no remedy for pain at all. The first doctor, if she is competent and confident of her diagnosis, will predict continuing anguish for Mary as long as her migraine headaches are ignored. The second doctor, if he is competent and confident of his diagnosis, will predict continuing fakery on Mary's part until she faces her childhood. This is what one would expect; it does not arise from either or both of the doctors being immoral, loving controversy, or taking pleasure in the thought of the suffering of others.

One who sincerely embraces a religious tradition accepts that tradition's diagnosis and cure of what it takes to be a deep problem in dire need of treatment. The founders, authorities, texts, doctrines, and experiences of the tradition are focused on properly diagnosing and successfully curing the believer's illness, which it takes to be an illness we all share. A sincere Christian, Advaita Vedantin, Theravada Buddhist, and Jain will differ as to the diagnoses they accept and the cures they embrace. Each will take the others' diagnoses to be in error and the others' cures to be ineffective regarding what the real problem is.

To actually believe that John is a sinner in need of God's forgiveness, or that John is unknowingly identical to qualityless Brahman, or that John at a time is but a cluster of momentary states and over time a series of such clusters and will unfortunately remain so unless he recognizes his nature and enters nirvana, or that John is actually an enduring and indestructible self-conscious being whose embodiment hides his omniscience and existential security, is also to think that anything incompatible with the diagnosis and cure that one accepts is false. If it is true (as it is) that the National Basketball franchise that has won the most championships is the Boston Celtics, it is not another thing for it to be false that the Celtics are not this franchise. If it is true that we are in need of God's gracious forgiveness, and that this is the basic religious problem that I share with all others, then if my belief is true it is not another thing for it to be false that this is not the basic religious problem that I share with all others. The same holds for the truth about any other proposed diagnosis. Any diagnosis is either true or not true. The same applies to whether any cure gets things right.

It is worth noting and emphasizing that the passages quoted above are not simply exceptions that do not deeply reflect the perspectives that we have been discussing. A religion typically offers an account of the conditions in which we exist, a conception of the religious problem that we face because of existing in those conditions, and a solution to that problem that is viewed as realistically facing and resolving that problem under those conditions. Different religions see those conditions differently. They hence describe the basic religious problem differently. They therefore offer different solutions. If you think that all religion is a crock, you will not take seriously those descriptions of the conditions in which we exist, and the problem that we thereby face; they will not describe live options for your acceptance. But you can still see that they are different and that the solutions offered are different. If you think that we are not in danger from fire or from flood, you will not think we need a fire extinguisher or an ark. But you can still see that the fire-fearers disagree with water-fearers in their analysis of our troubles and in their proposed remedies.

Relativity of Religious Problems?

It has been suggested that, just as different people have different diseases, so they may have different basic religious problems. One form this might take is to view religions as alternative therapies and propose that when therapy is needed we have experts who can direct patients to what seems the most appropriate religious milieu. This might lead to a new discipline—spiritology, perhaps—in which psychologists and psychiatrists made the analysis of a person's problem and a spiritual director who was intimately acquainted with a set of religious practices would place the patient in contact with what seemed the religious traditions most cordial to the patient's psyche (of course the exact arrangements would be worked out by those involved). This is in entire accord with secularized forms of religion, and all that would be required would be to psychologize the religious traditions. Different strokes for different folks. How successful such an enterprise might be is not clear. Getting agreement on the criteria for success might be rather difficult.

The suggestion of different strokes for different folks has a different application. That comes in the idea that different people actually have the different illnesses the non-psychologized diverse religions diagnose. This is a quite different program because it includes taking seriously the cures actually proffered by the religions themselves. As we have seen, the diagnoses and cures presuppose that the world is mind-independently structured in certain ways with certain contents. They presuppose a certain list of metaphysical claims, or at least one of a constrained set of such claims. They are not metaphysically neutral. They cannot be coherently divorced from their associated metaphysical perspectives without psychological (or some other) reduction. But the present suggestion does not intend to be reductionistic.

As we have said, religious traditions focus on what they take to be the deepest religious illness and suppose it to be shared by all human beings. This is not arbitrary on their part—the problem, however construed, is one viewed by these traditions as closely connected to human nature. On their view, the problem *is* human nature, or it is due to a universal misuse of capacities possession of which is constitutive of being human, or the like. They take it that everyone lives in the same cosmos, has the same nature, and is disjointed or warped in essentially the same way. From their perspective, to seriously propose that different persons have different religious problems at the deepest level is tantamount to suggesting that not all human beings are members of the same species. This suggestion is incompatible with at least most religious traditions, and there is little if any reason to think it true. The viewpoints expressed in the passages recently quoted, then, is exactly what one would expect from anyone who was sincerely committed to the religious tradition in question—who took that tradition's diagnosis and cure to fit their condition and meet their deepest religious needs. There is no good reason to think it wicked of religious believers to hold the views these passages both express and speak to, their deepest needs. Sincere Marxists, Socialists, Feminists, Freudians, Supplyside Economists, Animal Rights Activists, Right to Choose Advocates, Right to Life Advocates, and Secular Humanists hold similar views regarding the issues on which they have deeply held views. That is, they actually believe what they say and act on.

Consider again for a moment the what the diagnoses and cures offered by the traditions we are considering: living in appearance and experiencing reality in an enlightenment experience in which you realize you are identical to a qualityless reality; thinking oneself to be a material body that has dependent existence and having an enlightenment experience in which you discover that you are essentially immaterial and indestructible, so that your enduring existence is secure; discerning in an enlightenment experience that you are not an enduring being but are composed of one collection of simultaneous conscious states at a time and a causal series of such collections over time; and recognizing yourself as a creation by God who has sinned and needs repentance of those sins and God's forgiveness. For one person to have all these problems would require that she be altogether bereft of properties, an always enduring mental substance, one unenduring collection of conscious states after another, and an enduring person who has sinned and need divine redemption. No one person can manage to be all these things. Each diagnosis is correct only if each other diagnosis is mistaken. Each diagnosis requires that the world be one way rather than another, and the worlds in question are logically incompatible worlds. The same holds for the proposed cures. The different strokes for different folks, so far as religious diagnoses and cures go, is logically inconsistent.

Truth-Claims

Religions make what are sometimes called "truth-claims," though of course that is redundant since to make a claim in the sense of asserting something is to say that what is asserted is true. Truth-claims are just claims; there are *false* claims but there aren't any "falsity-claims." *Of course* religions make claims—if they asserted nothing, there would be no religions. Sometimes—particularly when a religious tradition is under rational scrutiny, or when a would-be believer recognizes that she thinks what she would like to be her religion is false and wants to keep it anyway—a religious tradition may be presented as claiming, and even may claim, that it makes no claim except that it makes no claims. But once the crisis is over, we are back to talking about God and sin and salvation, or Atman and Brahman and moksha and identity, or jivas and kevala and enlightenment, or momentary states and nirvana and release from the Wheel. It is in the very nature of a religion to offer an account of our situation, our problem, and its solution. Not every problem can arise in every situation; not every problem has the same solution. The account of our problem depends on the account of our situation; the account of our salvation depends on what we are and what we need to be saved from. To accept a religion is to embrace some particular and connected account of the situation and problem and solution.

Two popular contemporary perspectives often keep people from seeing religious differences. One is a popular sort of academic quasi-religion that has as one of its doctrinal claims that religions do not differ. The other is the sort of popular religious perspective that supposes all religions to be down-deep identical; this sort of religion, of course, is different from those religions (most if not all others) that do not think that religions do not differ.[11] If you accept the claim that all religions are the same as part of your secular religion, you may have as much trouble in admitting that not all religions are the same as members of the Flat Earth Society have in admitting the earth is an oblate spheroid.[12]

The thing to note here[13] is that none of these sorts of views can be made compatible with any of the religious traditions we have been describing; they are not expositions of, and they are plainly incompatible with, those perspectives. This is highly relevant, since these views are often presented as compatible with, if not as expositions of, one or more of these traditions; they are not.

The question arises as to whether, in some significant sense, all religions are really the same. As we have seen, in various senses they are not. They teach different doctrines, and if some of those doctrines are true then others are false. They appeal to experiences that differ in content and structure; if some of those experiences are reliable then the others are not. They propose different diagnoses and cures, and if one of those diagnoses is true then others are false and if one of those cures is genuine then the others are not. So, in various senses of the same— making the same claims, appealing to the same experiences, proposing the same diagnoses, offering the same cures, agreeing on the structure and content of the world—it is emphatically false that all religions are the same. What other senses of "are the same" might there be?

Identity

Two Kinds of Identity: Content Identity and Function Identity

The question as to whether all religions are the same raises another: The same regarding what? Once we see this, we can see our question splitting in two: Do all religions have the same doctrinal content? Do they all serve the same psychological and/or social function? Do all religions have content-identity, and do they all have function-identity? The answers are connected. At the basic of doctrinal difference is divergent views of what (if anything) exists independently; what (if anything) is that on which everything else depends for continued existence; how deep in the nature of things personal self-awareness, reason, and morality are; what (if anything) makes a person good; how (if any way) life should be lived; whether ultimate intrinsic worth resides in persons; and (if there is one) what the afterlife includes. These are all metaphysical issues, and differences here color one's morality in profound ways. Considering the diagnoses and cures, and the metaphysical and value differences embedded in diagnoses and cures, which are deep in the religious traditions in which they are offered, are the strong beginnings of answers to the questions just raised.

Low Standards for Identity: Vagueness, Generality, and Trivial Results

In spite of the partial descriptions we have offered of four religious traditions, it is possible to answer the question concerning content-identity affirmatively. So long as one makes the suggested criterion for identity of content vague and general, one can get the result that all of our religious traditions have identity of content. Thus one might suggest that all religious traditions (or at least those canvassed here) agree that a person's life does not consist in the abundance (or paucity) of material possessions; here is some identity of content. The same goes for identity of function. Thus one might suggest some such claim as *all religions provide meaning to life for their adherents*; to that extent, our religious traditions have identity of function.

In spite of the fact that the matters on which our traditions agree are neither obvious nor unimportant, there is a sense in which the result that one gets by using such vague and general criteria for identity of content or function is trivial. The result that all religions are the same regarding content and/or function is purchased at two prices. One price is that what each tradition regards as most important is entirely left out. The other price is that the traditions themselves hardly make an appearance before they are judged identical and dismissed; most of the relevant information about the traditions is not used, and that ignoring of central religious content does not respect the religions or really much discuss them, their content having largely been filtered out. I suggest, therefore, that we use high standards for content-identity and function-identity among religions.

High Standards for Identity: Clarity, Specificity, and an Interesting Thesis

What these standards should be is not far to seek. Two religious traditions have identity of content if and only if they teach the same doctrines. Two religious traditions have identity of function if and only if they serve the same psychological or social function.

Some Common Themes

All of the religions described earlier agree on such claims as these: human life is not limited to three-score-and-ten years on this earth; nothing that we can lose is of ultimate value (this is one moral of the Jain story); pleasure is not the ultimate good; violence is not an end in itself; there is a correct description of our actual cosmic situation, our consequent basic religious problem, and its real and accessible solution; some actual religious tradition has the truth about these matters; it is foolish to live only for power or pleasure or wealth. These are not obvious or trivial truths; plenty of people would reject, say, more than three of these claims. Suppose that someone suggests that all religions have the same content if they all agree on some such claim as *A few years of life on earth under present conditions is not all there is* or *Materialistic values are inadequate as a basis for living.* It plainly is worth noting that at least our four religious traditions—and many others as well—share these themes. Claiming, as I shall, that it is false that all religions are the same need not blind one to seeing that they agree on some things. But none of the things that they agree on are what the traditions themselves take to be the most important. I will argue that in fact the things they disagree about are the most important.

Two Sorts of Doctrines: Metaphysical and Moral

If one looks at the accounts we have given of four religious traditions, it is clear that they include claims about at least two sorts of matters: what there is, or metaphysics, and what there ought to be, or ethics. I will briefly draw out some of the metaphysical, and some of the moral, claims that are constitutive of these religious traditions.

Some Kinds of Metaphysics

Arguably *the*, and certainly *a*, central sort of religious experience within the classical monotheisms, Christianity included, is what Rudolph Otto, in *The Idea of the Holy*, called "numinous" experience (though there are problems with his second-order characterizations of it.)[14] In such an experience, the subject of the experience at least seems to experience an awesome Being who is unapproachable save on its own terms, majestic, overpowering, independent, living, possessed of great energy, unique, compelling, both attractive and dangerous. Typical responses come in terms of awe, a sense of creaturehood and dependence, worship, and guilt for one's sins. Plainly these experiences have a subject/consciousness/object structure; they at least seem to be encounters with something that exists quite distinct from and independent of the experiencing subject.

The relevance of this to our current topic is this: within the Christian tradition, experience and doctrine both emphasize the role of a Creator and Providence on whom all else depends. Between God and any human person there is a one-way dependence relationship; it is blasphemous to deny the

Creator-creature distinction. For Advaita Vedanta, what seems to be creature really is, not strictly the Creator, but at any rate underived Being. Creaturehood, sin, forgiveness, and the Divine Person as well, are illusory; all there is, is qualityless and apersonal Brahman. Jainism ascribes to each person, as he or she really is as opposed as to how he or she seems to be, the independence of everything else that Christianity ascribes to God alone. It denies that there is any Creator, but denies as well that personal individuality is illusory or should or even can be lost in a sea of qualityless being. The Theravadin accepts neither God nor the Jain substantival soul, maintaining that all there is, is transitory save for *nirvana* itself, the attaining of which involves not only the cessation of desire but apparently the cessation of individuality. In one sense, of course, setting aside the deep problems with such a notion, being identical to a qualityless and so apersonal Brahman and being absorbed into an apersonal state does not give one much to choose between, and some of his Vedantic critics accused Shankara of being a crypto-Buddhist.

However one should decide the question of the identity of the Advaita Vedanta Brahman and the Theravada *nirvana*, it is clear that at the least ultimate reality is conceived quite differently in Christianity and Jainism, on the one hand, and Advaita Vedanta and Theravada on the other. So is the nature and status of human beings. There is not identity of content here. It is false that all religions are doctrinally the same.

Some Kinds of Morality

The highest good for Advaita Vedanta is achieving moksha; the highest good for Jainism is achieving kevala; the highest good for Theravada is achieving nirvana. Our traditions recognize a distinction between experience had now that guarantees later escape from the Wheel, and post-mortem liberation itself. The highest good we can have in this life is achieving experiences that guarantee liberation at death. A key question in understanding how liberation is understood is this: Is personal identity retained in enlightenment? The Advaita answer and arguably the Theravada answer, for different reasons, is negative; the Jain answer is positive. All other values in these traditions are secondary to the end of enlightenment. In a tradition in which persons do not survive into final enlightenment, persons cannot themselves have deep intrinsic value or inherent worth. So they lack such worth in Advaita Vedanta and Theravada, and possess it in Judaism, Christianity, Vedantic Monotheism, and Jainism. Thus the metaphysics and ethics of our religious traditions differ greatly. This is a difference in content that cannot be removed, without utterly altering the religious traditions at their core.

My argument here can be stated briefly as follows. Our four traditions deeply differ in their morality in the ways noted; they embrace different, and importantly incompatible, values. Two religious traditions are functionally identical only if their basic values—what they take to have inherent or intrinsic worth—are similar, for the lifestyles that religions sanction are functions of the intrinsic values they embrace. Hence our traditions are not functionally identical.

There is an objection to my argument that goes as follows. It is possible that a tradition embraces one set of values and that its adherents follow another. Thus the fact that two traditions sanction different values does not entail that they are not functionally identical, for their adherents may follow similar or identical values.

This objection embodies a popular mistake. The values a religion embraces are those its authoritative oral traditions and written texts, as interpreted by its accepted leaders, sanction. If the adherents of a tradition do not embrace the values their own tradition sanctions, they are to that degree heretical or hypocritical, and nothing about religious functionality follows from their behavior or their value commitments. Attempts to evaluate religious traditions by looking at the behavior of its adherents is worthless as evidence regarding the tradition; what is evidentially relevant is what values the tradition's authoritative texts sanction.

Diversity

I suggest, on the basis of what we have already said, that it is a plain fact that there is doctrinal diversity between religions; it simply is false that all religions are the same regarding content.

The Agreement on the Importance of Doctrine Undercuts the Attempt to Both Represent the Traditions and Deny that Doctrine Matters

A matter on which our traditions do agree prevents anyone from successfully claiming to represent these traditions and yet going on to say that while there are doctrinal divergences these do not really matter. Those who try to do this may be contemporary secularists who do not care about religious matters or professors who think that tolerance for different opinions requires that the deep differences should be downplayed. They may be adherents of the rare religion that says that all religions are really the same even though in fact they are not. They may be adherents of one or another religious tradition who either do not know their own tradition very well or are just confused. They may be religious pluralists who reduce religions to a compatible morality and take as non-literal everything that does not fit through their conceptual and pedagogical filter. But it is clear that, in their traditional forms, religious traditions take as essential to salvation precisely matters on which there is deep disagreement among religious traditions.

Tolerance and Respect

An argument sometimes is offered that two people who really respect one another cannot knowingly disagree on ultimate religious matters, and since we respect each other as persons we cannot really disagree on ultimate religious, even though we may seem to. One of my two Ph.D. advisors, who by the way did respect each other, was an orthodox Rabbi and the other an atheist; both became my lifelong friends. I regret that I never saw anyone try to persuade my Rabbi friend that he really did not disagree with Christianity or atheism or my atheist friend that he really believed in God; it would have been interesting. The reply to this argument is that since people plainly do manage both to knowingly differ on basic religious matters and yet respect one another, tolerance is compatible with known difference on ultimate matters.

It has become popular to argue that if Kim and Kay are both religious—say, one a Vedantic monotheist and the other a Theravada Buddhist—and know each other to be about equally intelligent, well-informed, and intellectually honest, each should grant that the other is as likely right as he or she is. Whether one can be enlightened in a Theravada context, and forgiven of one's sins by God in a Vedantic context, compatibly with putting this view in practice is a question worth asking. If part of the popular view is that one should proportion one's belief to the evidence, then it seems that each would have to suspend judgment, and presumably thereby be unsure whether enlightenment or salvation has occurred. Faith in a context in which one is as unsure as one is sure—that is, in doubt—as to such matters may dilute the medication required for cure beyond the measure at which it is successful. How that goes will have to be thought through regarding each religious tradition.

There is a difficulty with this view that lies just below the surface. Call the view the Tolerance Balance Policy (TBP)—one is intolerant unless one grants that anyone who accepts a different religion than oneself is as intelligent, relevantly informed, and intellectually honest as oneself if one does not grant that the other is as likely right as one is regarding one's own. It is not obvious that the TBP should be limited to religious belief. Its serious application to philosophy would produce an epistemic modesty of colossal magnitude. Its chance of general adoption is the academy is minute. Suppose, then, one suggested that the TBP be limited to beliefs where difference in belief is not unlikely to lead to violence of some sort. Call the result of this modification the Restricted Tolerance Balance Policy (RTBP). This would not restrict the policy to religious belief. Political beliefs, beliefs about the right to dwell on a given plot of land, and legal conflicts begin a long list. There is a certain charm to the thought of a presidential debate with every statement of policy disagreement closing with "But my opponent is as likely right as I am." Both TBP and RTBP face the same difficulty, namely that equally intelligent, relevantly informed, and intellectually honest people will have different views concerning the correctness of either view of what counts as rational belief, and (if there is such a thing as epistemic ethics) whether either policy could be validly derived from the principles of epistemic ethics. So if we were to follow the policy's requirements we would not follow the policy's requirements. Perhaps it would be better to work to expand the belief that it is not permissible to kill or maim those with whom one disagrees on things that matter deeply to both self and neighbor.

The Plain Fact of Functional Diversity on High Standards

I suggest on the basis of what we have said that it simply is plain that there is not functional identity among religious traditions. They hold such divergent values that the ends they seek and the values they inculcate make it impossible for them to serve the same psychological ends or the same social functions, unless we describe these ends or functions with high generality. There may be some point to doing so sometimes, but if we ever want to look with any care at the religious phenomena we shall have to do so with far more specificity and clarity than will allow us to maintain cross-religious functional identity.

The Doctrinal and Functional Diversity of Religious Traditions

Our original question was: Are all religions really the same? This split into further questions: Have they the same content? Have they the same function? Any culture that wants survival success will frown on members of the culture having free license to kill each other, flee all interpersonal cooperation, and so on, and so is likely, if it long endures, to favor survival-promoting behavior. This need not amount to more than mores to prevent extinction based on prudence. On high standards that yield a significant conclusion rather than low standards that yield a trivial conclusion, the answers to our questions are "No" and "No."

What Does It Matter?: The Answer to This Question Depends on Whether Any of the Traditions Are True

One's answer to *What difference does it make?* will depend on what view one takes of the religious traditions. If one supposes that all religious traditions are false, then probably it will not make all that much difference though it is still important in our world to know what the religious traditions say and do. Suppose, however, one accepts one of the religious traditions. In one way, the answer is the same whichever of our traditions you accept. Consider the monotheisms, Advaita, Jainism, and Theravada Buddhism. Suppose one of the traditions has the diagnosis and the cure just right. If you embrace the right one and then read all the others as if they said the same thing, you will be wrong three times about what the other religions teach but you will have saved your soul (or whatever). If you accept a wrong one, and then read all the others as saying what that one says, then you hide from yourself the truth that you need by identifying it with the falsehood that you believe.

In another way, the answer to *What difference does it make?* will depend on what tradition one accepts. For in each case the conception of what believing and living the truth will bring is importantly different, as is the conception of what one gets when one believes and lives a falsehood.

There is a complicating factor that I mention in conclusion. I suspect that what most deeply motivates people to maintain that all religions are the same is that they cannot stand the idea that anyone be sincere and not be saved (or whatever). Sometimes this involves their thinking that no matter what anyone thinks, so long as they are sincere, they deserve heaven—even if all they sincerely believe in is pleasure seeking or hatred and torture. But sometimes it involves believing that anyone who sincerely is seeking the truth and wants to do what is right must somehow make it home, religiously speaking. They think that since right belief is taken in religious traditions to be basic to being saved (or whatever), then if everyone who seeks salvation is to make it home, religiously speaking, all religious traditions must have the same beliefs. In some religious traditions at least, it is possible to respond with some degree of sympathy to this suggestion without denying the plain facts of the matter. Reincarnation traditions tend to talk here of other lives in other times and climes. The classical monotheisms talk of people being judged by their response to the truth that is available to them, and recently even of a "baptism of desire" in which genuine desire for the truth is taken as tantamount to possession of it. Exactly how this is developed will differ from tradition to tradition, and sub-tradition to sub-tradition, and doing this in any detail is not part of my task here. I merely point out that the connection between correct belief and being saved (or whatever) is by no means always taken in a wooden graceless way, particularly not within the classical monotheisms. But that is another story. Our story in this chapter ends when we have noted that it is false that all religions are the same regarding doctrine any more than they are the same regarding diagnosis and cure, or regarding the experiences they take to be essential to salvation or enlightenment, or in what they take to be or have the deepest moral or religious value.

Questions for Reflection

1. What is the rationale that underlies the religious exclusivist texts quoted in this chapter?
2. What is the importance of the claims shared by religious traditions?
3. What is the importance of the claims particular to a religious tradition?
4. Can you construct a religion that makes no claims about what there is?
5. Distinguish between functional sameness and substantial sameness. Which will seem more important to our four religions, and—in each case—why?

Notes

1. John 14:6.
2. John 3:36.
3. Acts 4:12.7.
4. George Thibaut, tr. (1962) *The Vedanta Sutras of Badarayanna with the Commentary of Sankara* (New York: Dover Publications; originally published 1896), Vol. II, p. 399.
5. Geshe Sopa and Elving Jones, *A Light to the Svatantrika-Madhyanika*, p. 62; privately circulated.
6. The knowledge in question is not construed as merely knowledge by description, but there is no pretense of a knowledge by acquaintance that does not include some knowledge by description.
7. *Munkara Upanishad* III, i, 3.

8. Ibid., I, 271.
9. *Digha Nikaya* II, 251.
10. I John 5:20.
11. B'hai and Advaita Vedanta both hold this view; so do various secularized versions of Protestantism and Catholicism.
12. Another factor promoting the view "all religions are the same" is a popular sort of mind-set that has persuaded itself that religions make no claims at all. Sometimes this rests on some principle of meaning (that is likely not to meet its own standard). Sometimes it is based on a view of what it is to know that something is true (that is likely not to be knowable on its own standards). Sometimes it rests on some sort of relativism (that is likely in turn to make relativistic the view that no religion makes truth-claims). Sometimes it rests on a new account of truth (that will serve its intended purpose only if it is true in the a sense of truth of which it gives no account). Each of these perspectives has its own varieties, and it would take some space to describe, and more space to discuss, these views. The present author has argued against such view in *Christianity and Philosophy* (Grand Rapids, MI: Eerdmans, 1984) and *Hume's "Inexplicable Mystery": His Views on Religion* (Philadelphia: Temple University Press, 1990), as well as in "Empiricism and Theism," *Sophia*, Vol. 7, No. 3, October 1968, pp. 3–11; "A Reply to Nielsen," *Sophia*, Vol. 7, No. 3, October 1968, p. 18, 19; "Some Varieties of Relativism, *International Journal For Philosophy of Religion*, Vol. 19, 1986, pp. 61–85.
13. I have written about these views elsewhere.
14. Cf. the present author's *Basic Issues in the Philosophy of Religion*, Chapter One.

Suggested Readings

Carr, Brian and Mahalingham, Indira (1996) *Companion Encyclopedia of Asian Philosophy* (London: Routledge). Contains discussions of issues, views, and figures in Persian, Indian, Buddhist, Chinese, Japanese, and Islamic philosophy.

Chakravarti, Siddhanta and Shri Nemichandra, ed. and tr. (1927) *The Sacred Books of the Jain, Vol. V, Commatsara Jiva-Kanda (The Soul)* (Ajitashram, Lucknow (India): Central Jaina Publishing House). Jain teaching on the soul, with commentary by translator.

Frank, Daniel H. and Leaman, Oliver (1997) *History of Jewish Philosophy* (London: Routledge). A comprehensive volume on the nature and foundations of Jewish philosophy and its Medieval, modern, and contemporary representatives.

Gombrich, Richard (2009) *What the Buddha Thought* (Sheffield, UK: Equinox). Explanation of Buddhist thought by a famous senior scholar.

Kelly, J. N. D., ed. (2006) *Early Christian Doctrines* (London: Bloomsbury Academic). Account of early Christian doctrines by a recognized scholar in the history of doctrine.

Lipner, Julius (1986) *The Face of Truth: A Study of Meaning and Metaphysics in the Vedantic Theology of Ramanuja* (Albany, NY: SUNY Press). A clear, excellent study of Ramanuja.

McGrath, Alister E. (1998) *Historical Theology* (Oxford: Blackwell). An historical presentation of the major figures and doctrines of Christian thought.

Nasr, S. H. and Leaman, Oliver (1996) *History of Islamic Philosophy* (London: Routledge). A very comprehensive presentation of Islamic philosophy: its history, context, representatives, fields, and issues.

Otto, Rudolph (1958) *The Idea of the Holy* (New York: Oxford University Press).

Pandurangi, K. T. (2011) *Visnu Tattva Vinirnaya of Shri Madhvacharya* (Sankarapura Bengaluru Kantaka, India: Dvaita Vedanta Studies). Work in which Madhva lays out his basic doctrines.

Quasten, Johannes (1996) *Patrology* (Allen, TX: Christian Classics Reprint). A standard reference work for the Church Fathers dealing with Patristic literature from the Apostle's Creed to the "golden age" of their Greek and Latin writings.

Ramanuja, (tr. George Thibaut) (2012) *The Vedanta-Sutras with the Commentary by Ramanuja* (Amazon Digital). Reprint from *Sacred Books of the East*, Ramanuja's Visistadvaita reading of the Sutras.

Timalsina, Sthaneshwar (2014) *Consciousness in Indian Philosophy: The Advaita Doctrine of 'Awareness Only'* (New York: Routledge). An analysis and defense of the core doctrine of Advaita.

6 Religious Pluralism

Religious Plurality and Religious Pluralism

John Hick was the philosopher whose views dominated normative religious pluralism, both in philosophy and religious studies in the later twentieth and early twenty-first century. His major exposition was *An Interpretation of Religion* (1991), and his last book *The New Frontier of Religion and Science* (2010) occupied largely the same conceptual ground of normative pluralism.[1] Normative pluralism proposes an explanation of religious experiences worldwide and argues against reducing religious experience to physical states with naturalistic causes. Descriptive religious pluralism simply records and illustrates the plain empirical fact that if you put the teachings of all world religions in a list, that list of propositions would contain many logically incompatible doctrines. Normative religious pluralism is an answer to what we should think—how we should understand—that fact in a way in which no religion is wrong. What follows gives an account of much of the content of normative religious pluralism as Hick presents it.

Hick's Purposes

John Hick's normative pluralism has two aims: to argue that the materialist view of the mind (that it is the brain) and the epiphenomenalist view of the mind (that mental states are completely determined by physical states and have no effects) are mistaken, and that his normative religious pluralism is correct. He understands by 'materialism' the thesis that, whatever matter turns out to be, it is all there is. Epiphenomenalism is the view that while there are conscious states, they never have effects. Consciousness and causality never meet. The reason he wishes to accomplish the first goal is to protect the second. He holds that all of the major religions are incompatible with materialism and epiphenomenalism—what they teach is incompatible with materialism or epiphenomenalism being true. This claim seems safe enough regarding many doctrines central to religious traditions, but it is a bit puzzling that Hick makes it. The scope within which the claim of incompatibility is safest is the scope of religious traditions as one finds them, not as Hick construes them. By the time Hick has trimmed the doctrinal sails of the various traditions that he discusses, the metaphysical views of these traditions—their teachings as to what exists and what significance their existence has—are treated as non-literal. So Christianity is not, for Hick, to be construed as teaching that there is an omnipotent, omniscient God who created the world, loves us, and became incarnate in Christ. All of that is supposedly problematically "anthropomorphic" and thus to be rejected as a childish misunderstanding of what Christianity is all about. In the spirit of equal reductionism for all, the other religious traditions also have their views about what there is and what significance their existence has, read non-literally. One way—not necessarily successful—to respond to this would be to claim that, read non-literally, religious traditions after all are not anti-materialistic. (There is a close similarity to a couple of religions that seem not to need any non-literal reading that seem much less affected by Hick's pluralism than the others, and we will consider this in more detail.) In any case, in Hick's view, religious doctrines, understood in a non-literal fashion, will remove any truth-relevant inconsistency they might have were they read as typically understood. So none of them have to be false.

Anthropomorphism

Appeal to anthropomorphism as a critique of monotheism plays a role in rejecting literal monotheistic concepts. The assumption is that literal claims about God objectionably describe God in terms applicable to anthropoids (humans). While this view has also been held as a sign of humble reverence within some monotheistic sub-traditions, it has been held as removing any claim to saying anything true or false on the part of monotheistic traditions. Often appeal is made to uses of analogy to leave some propositional content—something still sayable about God—in monotheistic traditions. This apparent joining of some parts of monotheistic traditions with those who deny that the central claims of the variety of monotheisms have any literal content—an agreement that seems to be like an agreement between carrot-haters and carrot-lovers that the haters won't eat any carrots if the lovers agree not to plant any—will be considered in a later chapter. For now, of course monotheistic traditions agree that in many ways to be anthropomorphic is to ascribe to God features that are tied inextricably to everyday human life as lived by humans, and only by humans. Such things as preferring pink shoes, maroon capes, pepperoni pizza, or Chicago Cub baseball caps share the feature that if we ascribe such things to God, we are being objectionably anthropomorphic. That much is clear. Given certain assumptions about emotions—that they cloud the intellect, that they can be felt only by embodied beings, and that having them makes their subject inferior to others like them save for not feeling emotions—can be reasons for thinking having emotions to be a defect. But to altogether lack feelings is typically taken to be a serious defect. The view of the ultimate value of human emotions differ among religious traditions. Some religious traditions preach human detachment to be central to enlightenment. Other traditions preach a doctrine of salvation that requires gratitude and humble worship. The Hebrew Bible or Old Testament writers, on this view, were highly anthropomorphic about God. A negative view regarding emotions has been held in the history of the church, underwritten by the influence of similar (not universal) Greek thought. By the time we get to emotions, the question arises whether God having them really is anthropomorphic in any demeaning sense. Even ascribing omnipotence, omniscience, and moral perfection to God counts as objectionable anthropomorphism on Hick's view. Any such description of God, which entails that God is a self-aware agent, is rejected in favor of such terms as Ground of Being, the Ultimate, the Transcendent, the Unlimited, (in Hick's case) the Real, or the like. This replaces a more determinate concept by some less determinate one, though each involves some property being ascribed to God or whatever replaces God. To the degree that this is so, Hick's Rule that no non-formal concept be applied to his replacement for God is broken. The terms 'ground' (source? basis? that on which all else depends?), 'ultimate' (independent?), 'transcendent' (transcending space and time?), 'unlimited' (including everything?)—whether or not understood in the ways suggested as possibilities— replace determinate conceptions by way of applying other non-formal concepts, and therefore ascribing non-formal properties, to whatever (if anything) is being referred to. Applying vague concepts to a supposed something breaks Hick's Rule as much as applying clearer concepts does. This of course raises questions about the term 'Real' (which at least suggests that there is something to which the term applies (it exists and is non-illusory, neither of which are non-formal). The "Big It" would have similar problems, and not carry the emotional overtones that "the Real" carried when it was used in connection with such non-formal properties as independently existing and being of ultimate importance. Hick's version of normative religious pluralism retains the emotional associations of the Real that are tied to the non-formal properties ascribed to the Real while leaving the non-formal properties that elicit the associations (which make the associations understandable) behind.

There isn't much of an argument for Hick's view, simply the assumption that regarding God as personal is objectionable because it is anthropomorphic. At this point normative religious pluralism sides with Advaita Vedanta Hinduism and Absolutist Buddhism, and opposes the bulk of Semitic Monotheism, Theistic Hinduism, and Pure Land Buddhism.

Incompatible with Materialism?

We have noted Hick's claim, central to his program, that the reality-describing claims of the world's religious traditions should be treated non-literally (that is, in this case, as not ascribing any properties to reality). To have a term to use for treating the practice of reading the descriptions of reality in all religious traditions as non-literal, we will say that a religion so interpreted has been "Hickized." Then a basic question is: *Why think that a Hickized religion is incompatible with materialism?* If the metaphysical claims of the world religions are treated as non-literal—as not intended to tell us what there is and what their significance is—how can they be incompatible with materialism?

Truth

Hick continues to speak of religious truth, but redefines the word. For Hick, a religion is not true in virtue of being accurate concerning God, the cosmos, human beings, or anything else. To be true is understood as something like "succeeding in producing people who are making progress in becoming the sort of person that receives normative pluralism's approval." (The controversial assumption is that all religions—except the ones that are not morally acceptable—share the same ethical views.) It bears no relation to describing anything correctly. It, too, is not used literally in the usual sense. It is widely (and correctly) held that a proposition is true if the world is as it says it is, and a proposition is false if the world is not as it says it is. In this sense, for Hick there is very little religious truth available.

The Real

The idea behind talk of the Real is that there is a causal, or at least an accessible, influence that breaks through (or is broken through) the concepts, institutions, and practices of every culture to cause the religious traditions of the world. The aspects definitive of each culture shape how the influence is perceived by those who belong to it. Nonetheless, each religious tradition comes to be due to the influence, and our quite varied religious experiences have the same source. This obviously invests the Real in having causal properties, or at least properties in virtue of which it is accessible, as well as whatever properties these properties presuppose. This completely ignores the denial that any non-formal concept is true of the Real, and hence of any non-formal property being ascribed to it. This denial is used when convenient and not when it is not. When dealing with the fact that different religious traditions have incompatible beliefs, it is central as providing motivation for removing literal content from these beliefs. When formulating a thesis intended to explain the diversity of religious traditions and experiences, the denial is highly inconvenient and thus must be set aside. Sadly, in the academy, various contradictions have had wide support: *All beliefs are determined by the culture that one is in, and any belief determined by one's culture is rendered irrational (except this one). It is wrong to impose one's values on someone else, since any way of life is "equally valid" with every other (all moral values are relative except the one that says it is wrong to impose one's values on another). It is unreasonable to believe anything that is not learned from science (though science does not teach this).* Hick's pluralism has added another.

The Incompatibility Question Again

Back to our question: Is the (purely hypothesized) Real such that if it exists, then materialism is false? Well, if we play his game without breaking Hick's own rules, "being material" is not true of his Real. But then neither is "being immaterial" or "being mental." For any proposition one asserts about the supposed Real, if that proposition ascribes any substantial property (any non-formal property) to the Real, then that proposition is not true of the Real. So for any metaphysical proposition you affirm about the Real, it is false, including materialism but also all of its competitors. Why is materialism worse, on Hick's view, than any other metaphysic? The fact is that every metaphysical view is out of court, not just materialism, which is no more incompatible with Hick's view than any other. Nor are we offered any logically consistent religious position to contrast to materialism, since appeal to the Real as Hick conceives it (the "no non-formal concept" claim) leaves no room for any opposing theory that ascribes non-formal properties to something—any such theory will be read non-literally.

Religious Neutrality

Hick's position, insofar as there is such a thing, is supposed to be religiously neutral—that is, to be equal in its denial of literalness to the doctrines of all religions. In fact, it is not religiously neutral. Advaita Vedanta Hinduism and some varieties of Buddhism insist that what they regard as ultimate is literally ineffable. That is, they hold a view that can be put like this: There is an X such that, for no concept C is it the case that C is true of X. Then replace 'X' by 'qualityless Brahman' or 'nirvana' (whatever term is used to refer to what the religion thinks of as ultimate) and you have the doctrine as that religion holds it. So it turns out that Hick's position is very much like Advaita Vedanta Hinduism and some varieties of Buddhism as well as very different from any variety of monotheism. The source of religious experience is not God and how it does the causing (or what makes it accessible) is not explained. But his views are near enough to the ones just referred to that religious neutrality is left far behind. The strategy of trying to eliminate incompatibilities among religious doctrines by removing the doctrines, which is what his sort of non-literal reading of them amounts to, ends up by favoring some very esoteric versions of Hinduism and Buddhism. The neutrality claim is false. Accepting the ineffability doctrine sets up an inevitably contradictory perspective. If you cannot at all describe what is allegedly central to your religion, what do you do next? You cheat. You make claims that require that whatever the central being or beings of your religion are have properties that are in some way positive toward whatever the religion promises. (There is a strand of ineffabilism in Judaism and Christianity—of Jewish and Christian thinkers who say that God is ineffable in the sense that we have defined it here. Those who have, in some sense, accepted the doctrine blatantly contradict it in developing their theology. They could not do otherwise if they were to present any Christian theology at all. The same goes for every religion that proposes a diagnosis and cure, which covers at least a great many of the world's religions.)

Religion and Morality

Why Hick supposes the supposed Real to be related to morality in any way remains unexplained. So does what feature of the supposed Real allows it to influence the world in any way. It is, in his view, objectionably anthropomorphic to think of God as personal. He says:

> We therefore need a term for the final focus of religious concern which encompasses both the theistic and non-theistic understandings of it.[2]

We need a concept that goes beyond the personal and impersonal. But what does this mean? And why should we think whatever it means (if anything) has something to do with morality? There seems as much reason (none) to think the Real is immoral, or favors immorality rather than morality, or cannot possibly care one way or the other. (Further, the varieties of naturalism, on Hick's view, must share the epistemic tie [none better evidenced than another] that characterizes the religious traditions.) But since they have no place for the Real, if (contrary to their being tied in rational support with competitors) they have a more advantageous relation to fact and evidence than normative religious pluralism enjoys, there will be excellent grounds for rejecting pluralism. The same holds for any non-naturalist perspective.

This brings out an important point. If any non-religious tradition, or any religious tradition, is rationally better supported than normative religious pluralism, then an important assumption of pluralism is false. Trying to remove its competitor by pluralism reading it non-literally is a dangerous game for the pluralist to play. It can itself be read non-literally (with at least as much plausibility as the doctrinal claims to which the pluralist applies his non-literal reading).

There remains the fact that Hick's view of the Real, insofar as there is a view, is simply speculation. Given the restriction that only formal concepts apply to the supposed Real, whether it is viewed as an active or a passive source of religious traditions, it has no explanatory force compatible with the restriction and no stateable relation to morality. The hypothesis that there is any such thing is an appeal to something, I know not what. The determination to favor no religion in normative religious pluralism ends up favoring those religions that rely on ineffability most. With neither an explanation of religious traditions, nor genuine religious neutrality, to offer, this version of normative religious pluralism is not a success.

More Recent Normative Religious Pluralism

Paul Knitter has offered a version of religious pluralism that does not appear to be riddled with contradictions.[3] Perhaps it will do as a successful version of religious pluralism. As is typical for a normative pluralist, he seeks a comparative theology of religions that gives each religion a "valid" voice. This theology—hereafter we will use 'ideology' rather than 'theology' since the idea is to include non-theistic traditions as well as theistic—is to include nothing to which any religious tradition cannot agree. Indeed, it is to include only that which, at least in principle, all humanity can accept. Given this goal, secular perspectives as well as religious ones must be considered and included. So each of our four religious traditions will be included in an ideology of religions. Then there are

Jewish, Islamic, theistic Hindu, and other Buddhist religions that are equally valid sources.

The list of religions goes on for some time, and the prospects of including them all, even leaving aside secular views, are extremely dim. Hick's solution involved reading doctrinal statements non-literally. Knitter, following suit, proposes reading doctrinal claims as "action language"—as being ethical imperatives, exhortations, principles, behavior descriptions, and the like. Metaphysics is replaced by ethics in order to make a common religious ideology possible.

This of course does not accord with the situation found in the traditions themselves. Besides offering its diagnoses and cures, often the rationale of a tradition's ethic lies in its doctrines. This rationale colors the content and application of moral concepts. Put differently, the point is that a tradition's deepest religious values impact how moral concepts and practices are understood. The replacement program leaves this rationale behind. The program also assumes the religious traditions agree on at least a substantial part of ethics. It is by no means clear that the prospects for a comparative ethical ideology of religions are as promising as normative religious pluralism hopes.

But they seem better than the prospects for a doctrinal ideology, which Hick nor Knitter seem to share.

It seems fair to characterize their common position as assuming the following:

RP1.   The basic point and value of any religion is to make its adherents better people.
RP2.   The criteria for better people contain only virtues on which the religions agree.
RP3.   Whether or not the distinctive doctrines of a religion are true is not important to whether those who adhere to a religious tradition are thereby better people.
RP4.   The doctrinal statements of all religious traditions are to be read non-literally.

A sentence or two commentary on each of these claims may serve to bring out their problematic nature, for Knitter as well as Hick. The first proposed principle ignores the diagnosis and cure proposed by a religious tradition, and takes all religions as means to an end—as having, at best, extrinsic worth. The core of tradition after tradition is to be set aside in terms preferable to the religious pluralist. The second principle supposes that one will find substantial moral agreement across the traditions. This is a large topic, but it is by no means evident that moral differences do not arise from deep differences between traditions about what has intrinsic worth. The third principle downgrades the diagnoses and cures proffered by religious traditions as having no significance for what the purpose of religions is all about. To see this, combine principles 1–4. Principle 4 chimes in with a rationale for dismissing what religious traditions find most central. The motto applied to all is "Read it non-literally." (There is also the question as to why the non-literal reading must always be moral.)

The religious pluralist justifies such core statements of its view of religions on the grounds that everyone should have an equally valid voice at the dialogue table. The hope is that religions like Thuggee can be kept out. Thuggee was a mixture of elements taken from indigenous Indian religious sources and Moslem and Christian religions. The idea was straightforward. During the dry season when travel is possible, groups of thugs would pose as merchants traveling India's roads who would join other merchants (there was apparent safety in numbers against attacks by robbers) on a geographically shared route. After the merchants got to know the merchant thugs well enough to trust them, they would sit around a campfire resting. At a prearranged signal, the thugs would spread themselves one on one behind the merchants, take the sacred thread, and strangle the merchants. They would then bury the bodies according to ritual worship of the goddess Kali (the one who is represented with a necklace of skulls); the thugs would have concluded business in a profitable matter. It is not clear exactly on what grounds Thuggee, or religions of human sacrifice and temple prostitution, are eliminated from those whose morals count in coming to terms with the universal ethical agreement supposedly found in all religions. It is not as if religious pluralists have done enough serious moral philosophy to justify them in adjudicating moral differences. The morality is largely, if not entirely, to be simply assumed.

Knitter's project of textual interpretation is made explicit in these terms:

> Recognizing the primacy of orthopraxis over orthodoxy can be used pastorally to enable Christian believers to understand the nature of New Testament language and what it means to be faithful to that language . . . the christological language and titles of the New Testament had as their primary purpose not to offer definitive, ontological statements about the person or work of Jesus but to enable men and women to feel the power of Jesus' vision. . . . It would be more accurate and pastorally effective, I think, to call the New Testament claims about Jesus as "action language."[4]

Thus his interpretive program has a highly controversial historical assumption regarding the use of language and titles of Jesus as they appear in the New Testament.[5] This assumption joins that of ethical agreement among traditions in defining the foundations of his religious pluralism. It is no more easy to see how the beliefs whose acceptance is said to be essential to becoming enlightened in Jainism (the immateriality of the immortal soul), Theravada (the lack of an enduring self and the nature of persons being their consisting of ephemeral states), or Advaita (identity of Atman with qualityless Brahman) are properly to be read as "action language" than it is to see how belief in the deity or resurrection of Jesus is to be so read. Knitter's desire to replace Jesus by "the vision of Jesus" faces analogous difficulties in the case of each of the others of our four traditions.

The difficulties of universal neutrality are illustrated by examples besides that of Thuggee. Consider the conditions laid down for the sort of dialogue approved by Knitter: dialogue must be "genuinely pluralistic—one that will avoid preestablished absolutist or definitive positions in order to allow that all the participants have an equally valid voice."[40] Along these lines, we are told that "the absolute, that which all else must serve and clarify is not the church, or Christ, or even God, but rather the kingdom and its justice."[41] This gives us two absolutes definitive of genuine dialogue—one concerning appropriate participants and one concerning its purpose. The former leaves convinced believers out—a curious feature of an inclusivist perspective. The latter expresses a view of ethics that seems to distinguish between God and the kingdom of God in a manner perhaps necessary for a religious pluralist ethic but problematic for some religious traditions. This illustrates some of the problems faced by those who wish to construct and apply a comparative ethic that leaves no one out.

Conclusion

We have argued that Hick's religious pluralism is incoherent on its own terms. It cannot make the use of the supposed Real to explain anything about the source of religious experiences. In spite of the claim to equally respect (at least the nice) religions, both Hick and Knitter pronounce on the question as to what religions are for. Many, perhaps most, religious traditions ground their moral views in their core doctrines, which are taken to be true and to provide justification for their morality. Given RP4, this element of religious morality is gone. Despite the surface equal respect for religious traditions, what the religions themselves find most important is eliminated by applying a theory on which the language in which what the tradition values most is excised by talk of its not being intended literally. For a position supposed to deeply respect all religious traditions equally, holding them to have instrumental value and so interpreting them as to leave out what they make most central this is both surprising and problematic. The basic idea, if we extrapolate, is to replace each religion by a religious pluralist understanding of it by reading the Hebrew Bible, the New Testament, the Koran, Pali Canon, Jaina Sutras, the Upanishads, and so on, after Knitter's example—as "action language." As a massive interpretational task, it is hard to believe that anyone who has read any of these texts will think that it would somehow expose their real meaning, particularly since there are plainly sections that deal with morality and sections that deal with doctrine. While these sections are not unrelated, neither reduces in meaning or truth conditions to the other. The proposal is in fact for a massive revisional enterprise. The idea that it would be welcomed by all the world's religious leaders has precious little plausibility. The price of no one being wrong in religious matters is that then no one is right in them either.

Questions for Reflection

1. What is pluralism?
2. How does Knitter's religious pluralism differ from Hick's?
3. Is religious pluralism itself a religion?

4. Is one who accepts Hick's pluralism entitled to make the claims that he does concerning the Real, given the other claims included in the position?
5. How important is it for the religious pluralist that at least all the "major" religions agree on basic morality?

Notes

1. John Hick (2005) *An Interpretation of Religion: Human Responses to the Transcendent* (New Haven, CT: Yale University Press) (second ed.) and John Hick (2010) *The New Frontier of Science and Religion: Religious Experience, Neuroscience, and the Transcendent* (Basingstoke, UK: Palgrave Macmillan).
2. Hick, *An Interpretation of Religion*, p. 36.
3. Paul Knitter (2002) *Introducing Theologies of Religions* (Maryknoll, NY: Orbis); *The Myth of Religious Superiority* (Marknoll, NY: Orbis, 2005).
4. John Hick and Paul Knitter (2005) *The Myth of Christian Uniqueness: Toward a Pluralistic Theology of Religions* (Eugene, OR: Wipf & Stock), p. 196.
5. For a very different view, see Larry Hurtado (2005) *Lord Jesus Christ: Devotion to Jesus in Earliest Christianity* (Grand Rapids, MI: Eerdmans).
6. John Hick and Paul Knitter (2005) *The Myth of Christian Uniqueness: Toward A Pluralistic Theology of Religions* (Eugene, OR: Wipf and Stock), p. 181.
7. Ibid., p. 190.

Suggested Readings

D'Costa, Gavin (1980) *Theology and Religious Pluralism* (Oxford: Basil Blackwell).
Hewitt, Harold (1991) *Problems in the Philosophy of Religion* (New York: St Martin's Press).
Hick, John (1980) *God Has Many Names* (London: Macmillan).
Knitter, Paul, ed. (2004) *The Myth of Religious Superiority* (Maryknoll, NY: Orbis). Leading exponents of the idea of religious parity seek dialogue to develop a world theology.
Knitter, Paul and D'Costa, Gavin (2011) *Only One Way? Three Christian Responses to the Uniqueness of Christ in a Religiously Pluralistic World* (Norwich, UK: SCM). Conservative and liberal Catholic and evangelical Protestant views on the uniqueness of Christ, with a proponent presenting his own view and interacting with the others.
McKim, Robert (2012) *Religious Diversity* (Oxford: Oxford University Press). An analysis and challenge to the current classificatory concepts in use in describing and analyzing religious diversity with an account of how this opens the way to exploration of commonalities between different traditions.
Netland, Harold A. (2015) *Christianity and Religious Diversity: Clarifying Christian Commitment in a Globalizing Age* (Grand Rapids, MI: Baker Academic). Defends Christian commitment to uniqueness in a changing and challenging world.
Sharma, Arvind (1993) *God, Truth, and Reality* (New York: St Martin's Press).
Smith, Wilfred Cantwell (1979) *Faith and Belief* (Princeton, NJ: Princeton University Press).
——— (1981) *Towards a World Theology* (Philadelphia: Westminster Press).

Stewart, Robert B., ed. (2013) *Can Only One Religion Be True? Paul Knitter and Harold Netland in Dialogue* (Minneapolis, MN: Fortress). Religious pluralism meets Evangelical orthodoxy.

Wainwright, William J. (1984) "Wilfred Cantwell Smith on faith and belief," *Religious Studies*, Vol. 20, pp. 353–366.

Yandell, Keith E. (1993) Some varieties of religious pluralism, in Kellenberger, James, ed. *Inter-religious Models and Criteria* (New York: St Martin's Press) pp. 187–211.

Part II

Religious Conceptions of Ultimate Reality

7   Monotheistic Conceptions of Ultimate Reality

Generic Philosophical Monotheism

For monotheism, God is ultimate reality.[1] We can call what is common between various types of monotheism *generic philosophical monotheism*, characterized as follows. The claim *X is God* is to be understood as entailing each of the following claims:

1. *X is necessarily ontologically independent* [i.e., X exists, and it is logically impossible that X depend for existence on anything].
2. *X is God* entails *X is self-conscious* [i.e., is conscious and aware of himself or herself as such; thus X is a person].[2]
3. *X is God* entails *X is transcendent* [i.e., X is not identical to the world and God does not depend on the world for existence or powers].
4. *X is God* entails *X is the highest being* [i.e., the most valuable, greatest, or best].

Greek, Semitic, and Hindu Monotheism

One significant religious difference between diverse sorts of monotheism concerns whether, and to what extent, God acts in human history. We can say that God exercises *strong providence* if and only if God acts in such a way as to bring about particular public historical events, and does so not only by causing private revelations or events; God brings about both public events and private events, and does not do the former only by doing the latter. By contrast, God exercises *weak providence* if and only if, save for creation of the world, God acts in such a way as to bring about particular public historical events, but only by causing private revelations or events; God brings about both public events and private events, and does the former only by doing the latter. Alternatively, one might be monotheistic and not think of God as providentially active at all.

Greek Monotheism

Greek,[3] understood as including generic, monotheism can be defined as follows:

1. The world has always existed.
2. God exercises neither strong nor weak providence.

3.   The world does not exist because God wants it to.
4.   Whatever is *everlastingly* true is *necessarily* true.
5.   That God exists is necessarily true.
6.   That the world exists is necessarily true.

Nonetheless, the world depends on God in two ways. First, God is viewed as immutable, unchanging, and perfect; the world is mutable, changing, and imperfect. *There being mutable things* is a state of affairs dependent on *there being an immutable thing*. There is one-way dependence but no creation, not merely in the sense that the world did not begin to exist but also in that *there being a world* is not something that God chose to be the case or could have prevented. Second, God is perfect, having no potential the realization of which would bring about divine improvement or self-realization. By contrast, the world is imperfect; it has unrealized potential the proper realization of which would improve the world. The things in the world are also imperfect, and they have unrealized potential the proper realization of which would improve them. Anything that exists has a nature or essence, a set of properties that make it the kind of thing that it is. The essence of a thing in turn determines the sorts of other properties a thing can have and hence the sorts of events in which it may participate. What something can be an effect of, or a cause of, is a function of what properties it has. Mutable things have essences. An essence defines a natural kind, and members of a natural kind can be better or worse exemplars of that kind. Some bananas and some beavers are better—better *as bananas* and *as beavers*—than others. Some bananas are bruised, fragile, overripe; some are not. Some beavers are crippled, ill, or brain-damaged; others are not. Any thing has potentialities, accessible ways of changing realization of which will further or frustrate the degree to which it is a good example of its kind. Each mutable thing strives by nature to be the best something of its kind that it can be—to magnificently exemplify what something of its sort can be. In this respect, it is as if each thing tries to be as like God (viewed as the perfect member of the kind *unmoved mover* or *immovable cause of motion*) as it can be, given the sort of thing that it is.

This view has a curious result. On it, the world can depend for its existence on God, and seek its fullest realization as a thing of its sort, without God even knowing that there is a mutable world let alone knowing about any individual thing in the world. No providence occurs, no historical persons or events bear ultimate religious significance, and no worship or prayer has any point. This sort of monotheism is abstract; it will seem cold if not dead to any Semitic or Hindu monotheist. Yet many of the arguments offered within Judaism, Christianity, and Islam, come historically from Greek monotheism. Hindu monotheism, perhaps untouched historically by Greek natural theology, nonetheless contains similar arguments.

There can be evil if Greek monotheism is true. There can be defective things, things that are poorly realized members of their kind that are incapable of becoming better realized members. There can be wrong human choices, instances in which persons voluntarily go against their knowledge of what is right. But these evils cannot be evidence against the existence of God, as God is construed in Greek monotheism. This sort of deity, as we have noted, does not even know that particular persons exist. No truths that might have been false are objects of divine knowledge, and all historical claims, biological accounts, all descriptions of physical or psychological reality, have in common the feature that even if they are true, they might have been false. A Greek deity is not culpable for lacking such knowledge; it is logically impossible that the deity of Greek monotheism have any knowledge of what might have been true. Nor can the God of Greek monotheism bring about occurrences in space or time; no divine action is possible. So while there can be natural evils ("monsters" or strongly defective members of species) and moral evils (wrong human actions), these evils cannot be evidence that Greek monotheism is false. This points to an interesting feature of monotheisms. A monotheism without any doctrine of creation or providence can offer neither God's help in salvation nor God's answer to prayer, God's forgiveness or God's aid, and neither is it possible for such a monotheism that the existence of evil be offered as any evidence against its truth. A monotheism with a doctrine of creation or providence can offer God's help in salvation or God's answer to prayer, God's forgiveness or God's aid, and it is possible that for such a monotheism the existence of evil be offered as evidence against its truth. Whether evil really is evidence against monotheism is another matter; the point is that only for certain sorts of monotheism does the question even arise.

There being things that might not have existed is something to be explained. There might not have been any human beings, any lions, any trees, any rocks, any atoms. There are all of these things. There being these things has an explanation. A common strategy, fine so far as it goes, explains the existence of larger things by reference to the existence of smaller things of which the larger things are made. But perhaps sooner or later one gets to things so small that they are not in turn made of still smaller things; call these things *simple units*. There might not have been any simple units, so their existence too has an explanation. But simple units cannot be explained by reference to the things they are composed of; they are simple, not composite. So their existence has to be explained in a different way. Alternatively, suppose that, so to speak, things are composite all the way down—everything is made up of some things that are also made up of some things, and so on forever. Then the question arises as to why there is this dizzying series of composites of composites.[4] Either way, the idea is, we must appeal to something whose non-existence is not an option, something that *exists necessarily*. So if there is anything at all, something exists necessarily. It is obvious that things do exist; so something exists necessarily. This thought plays an important role in monotheism, with Greek monotheism offering one sort of explanation and Semitic and Hindu offering an explanation of a different sort.

What, then, is it for something to exist necessarily? It is at least this: something exists necessarily only if is not possible that it depend for existence on anything else. Further, on a Greek monotheistic notion of necessity, it will be impossible that it change; only immutable things can exist necessarily. The items in our immediate environment change; they gain some qualities and lose others.

They also come to be and pass away. The class of things that change and come and cease belong to *the realm of generation and corruption*. What exists in this realm depends for its existence on something that exists necessarily, but nothing that exists necessarily can be part of this realm.

Besides existing necessarily, the deity of Greek monotheism is self-conscious. He, she, or it is also omniscient relative to logically necessary truths. But he, she, or it has no feelings and no knowledge of logically contingent truths. Whatever might have been false lies beyond its range of thought. Indeed, the only thing of which it is aware is itself and the contents of its own mind. Thus the Greek Deity does not create the world, or even know that there is a world. The Greek Deity does not know that you exist or that you have needs; it is not an appropriate target for prayer of any sort. There is no prayer that it could hear. Nor does the Greek Deity bring about any events in history; there is no notion of providence in Greek monotheism.

Being a being that exists necessarily, is immutable, self-conscious, and knows all necessary truths is regarded as the best sort of thing to be. The Greek Deity is thought of as being as magnificent, valuable, and glorious as it is possible to be. Other things have positive worth insofar as they resemble this Deity and defective insofar as they lack such resemblance. God is the perfect paradigm, the standard of worth; in this sense, morality rests on God—God provides the criterion for positive worth. There can be evil in the world as Greek monotheism conceives it. That this is a religion, of course, is highly questionable. It is not easy to see what ceremonies, rituals, practices, or the like are appropriate to its core claims. Nonetheless, it is of interest here for two reasons. Understanding it provides a nice comparison and contrast to varieties of monotheism that plainly are religions; and much of Semitic monotheism has tried to introduce much of Greek monotheism into its own perspective.

Semitic Monotheism

Semitic monotheism—Judaism, and Christianity and Islam which build on Jewish foundations—also includes generic monotheism and in addition embraces the following claims.

1.   The world has not always existed [it was created *in* time, or time was created *with* it].[5]
2.   God exercises strong providence.
3.   The world exists because God wants it to.
4.   That the world exists is not necessarily true [i.e., it is false that it is impossible that the world not exist].

Here, God could have chosen that there be no world. The world is not everlasting. Either God created time in the same act as that by which God created a world, or God created the world after a time when there was no world. God sustains the world in existence and at times brings it about that particular individuals are born or are chosen for specific religious roles and that specific events occur. A religious tradition with no Abraham, Sarah, Moses, David, Ruth, Isaiah, Micah, or any of the prophets, no exile in Egypt, no Passover, no era of judges or of prophecy, no Hebrew people chosen by God, is not Judaism. If there have been none of these people and events, Judaism is false. If Jesus did not live, or died a peaceful death in his own bed, or remained in the grave, then Christianity is false. If Mohammed never existed, or was always an atheist, or was a wealthy merchant entirely uninterested in religion and never claimed to receive any revelation, then Islam is false. With room for debate about exactly the scope of the claims, the Semitic monotheisms have in common that their core doctrines refer to particular persons and particular events.

The deity of Greek monotheism cannot act, unless everlasting contemplation of necessary truths is acting. The deity of Semitic monotheism can act. The God of Semitic monotheism acts in history; it is unthinkable for Greek monotheism that the deity be able to so behave, and unthinkable for Semitic monotheism that the deity not be able so to behave. The deity of Greek monotheism is not the God of history; that would be beyond her power and beneath her dignity. The deity of Semitic monotheism is the God of history, not by necessity but by choice; this is not beyond his power or beneath his dignity.

Within Semitic monotheism, Jewish and Moslem monotheisms assert that God creates and providentially rules the world; God acts in history, ordains prophets, and gives revelations. Christian monotheism agrees, but also claims that God has become incarnate in the person of Jesus Christ. That God become incarnate, according to Jewish and Islamic monotheism, is beyond God's power and beneath God's dignity—that God be incarnate in a human being who is crucified is, if possible, even more impossible and even more against the divine status. Christian monotheism asserts that *becoming incarnate* is within the power of an omnicompetent God, and provides the supreme instance of God's wisdom and love.

Hindu Monotheism

Hindu monotheism, in addition to accepting generic monotheism, accepts these claims.

1. The world has always existed.
2. God exercises weak providence.
3. The world exists because God wants it to.
4. It is not the case that whatever is *everlastingly* true is *necessarily* true.
5. That the world exists is not necessarily true.

Hindu monotheism embraces both a beginningless world and a doctrine of creation. Here the idea that God (Brahman with qualities) creates the world teaches that while the world is everlasting toward the past, having no first moment of existence, it depends at each moment of its existence on the sustaining activity of God. God could cease sustaining the world in existence, at which point God would continue to exist but the world would not. There is an asymmetrical dependence relation between God and the world: the world depends for its existence on God's activity, but God's existence does not depend on there being a world.

The relationship between God and history, as seen by Hindu monotheism, is complex. Hindu monotheism is a religion of reincarnation and karma with karma being viewed as under God's control. In response to a person's repentance and faith, God can remit punishment, cancelling negative karma. Escape from the reincarnation cycle comes by God's grace. There are incarnations of a sort—God causes theophanies or appearances. For example, Krishna is said to appear to a devotee and to instruct him or her to build a temple on the site on which the appearance occurred. Temple traditions include stories that trace the temple's history back to such appearances. But Hindu monotheism does not include any claim to the effect that God is uniquely incarnate in any human being or provides a means for redemption in such a manner. God is capable of controlling the mind of a particular person in as extended a way and period as God wishes, and God is capable of causing whatever visions, auditory or visual, God wishes to bring about. Further, gods or goddesses, who exist dependent on God and under God's control, may take upon themselves human form. But nowhere is there unique and definitive incarnation in which God is incarnate in order to redeem the world. If nothing else, this is precluded by the fact that Hindu monotheism is not trinitarian.

There are other possibilities. Neo-Platonism, for example, is a form of monotheism distinct in various ways from those sketched here. I make no pretense to being exhaustive. My claim is only that the considerations that apply to the sorts of monotheism we shall discuss apply as well to those we do not.

Monotheisms and Atheisms

Two Different Kinds of Monotheism

Monotheisms can be distinguished on different criteria from those discussed previously. Coming to clearly grasp this requires learning some distinctions that will be useful, even crucial, to later discussions. Consider the difference between (NG) *It is a logically necessary truth that God exists* and *(CG) It is a logically contingent truth that God exists*. What (NG) says is (i) *God does not exist* is self-contradictory, (ii) there is *no* possible world in which God does not exist, (iii) there is *no* way things might have been such that God did not exist. What (CG) says is: (i*) *God does not exist* is *not* self-contradictory, (ii*) there *is* a possible world in which God does not exist, (iii*) there *is* a way things might have been such that God did not exist.

It may appear that a monotheist should much favor (NG) over (CG), and indeed some monotheists think this is so. But other monotheists do not think this; after all, what (ii) and (iii) do is just say what (i) says, putting it in different terms. They are not *further* differences between the two sorts of monotheist beyond their difference regarding (i) versus (i*).[6] A monotheist who accepts (CG) typically will also accept *(CG*) It is logically impossible that God depend for existence on anything else*. Since she thinks that *God exists* is true, she will think both that

God exists and that God exists with perfect independence. The difference between types of monotheism—between a monotheism to which (NG) is essential and a monotheism to which (CG) is essential—is not unimportant. Here is why.

Suppose that Tim thinks that there are frogs and Tom thinks that there are not. Tom is wrong, and Tim is right. Suppose that Tex agrees that there are frogs, but also thinks that *Necessarily, there are frogs* is true. This is a remarkable belief on Tex's part. It entails that under any logically possible condition, there are frogs; frog extermination is logically impossible. Not even God could get rid of frogs. Tim thinks that there are frogs all right, but he denies that there would be frogs no matter what, that it is logically impossible that frogs be exterminated; he supposes that God could create a frogless world—all of which Tex denies.

Just as one or the other of Tim (who thinks there are frogs) and Tom (who thinks there are not) is right, so one or the other of Tim (who thinks there might not have been frogs) and Tex (who thinks it is logically impossible that there not have been frogs) is right. Again, of course, Tim wins. But notice the difference between the Tim/Tom and the Tex/Tim disagreements. We can represent them as follows:

TIM/TOM:
TIM: There are frogs. [F]
TOM: There are no frogs. [not-F]
TEX/TIM:
TEX: It is a logically necessary truth that there are frogs. [Necessarily, F]
TIM: It is not a logically necessary truth that there are frogs. [Not-(Necessarily, F)]

Tim and Tom hold contradictory beliefs. So do Tex and Tim. What Tex believes to be logically necessary, Tim believes not to be logically necessary. We can also put the dispute between Tex and Tim this way:

TEX/TIM*:
TEX: It is self-contradictory that there be no frogs. [Necessarily, not(not-F)]
TIM: It is not self-contradictory that there be no frogs. [Not-(Necessarily, not(not-F))]

Tex thinks something logically impossible that Tim thinks logically possible.

Logical necessity and *logical possibility* are *modalities*. We can put the difference between the disagreements in yet another way: the Tim/Tom disagreement is about the *truth* of *There are frogs*; the Tex/Tim dispute is about the *modality* of *There are frogs*. Disputes about whether there are frogs has, of course, no religious content. But the pretend disputes about frogs are paralleled by disputes about God.

The NN Principle

A final point will place us in position to complete our discussion. A *modal* proposition is a second-order proposition[7] that says about some first-order proposition that it is necessarily true, necessarily false, or logically contingent. Here is a bit of the logic of modal propositions.[8] Where P is any proposition:

1.   Necessarily, P [= It is not possible that P be false]
2.   Necessarily, not-P [= It is not possible that P be true]
3.   Contingent, P [= It is not impossible that P be true and it is not impossible that P be false]

express the possible modalities regarding P. They entail, respectively,

4.   Possibly, P
5.   Not-(Possibly, P)
6.   Possibly, P

where "possibly" means, not "maybe" but "it is logically possible that" or "P is not self-contradictory."

A proposition of the form expressed in 1 through 6 is a second-order proposition; it says of a first-order proposition that it is necessary, contingent, or possible.

What the NN thesis tells us is this:

> NN: Every true modal proposition is necessarily true, and every false modal proposition is necessarily false; it is logically impossible that there be a contingently true or a contingently false modal proposition.

This applies to any order of modal propositions—Np, N[Np], N[N(Np)], and so on, as well as Cp, N[Cp], Possibly p, N[Possibly p], and so on.

Regarding Kinds of Monotheism and Atheism

A little reflection suggests that, since a monotheist thinks that *God exists* is true, she can either take it to be a logically necessary truth or take it to be a logically contingent truth. She cannot remain a monotheist and think it false. Similarly, since an atheist thinks that *God exists* is false, she can take it to be a logically necessary falsehood or a logically contingent falsehood.

Thus there are exactly four alternatives here:

1.   (NG): it is a logically necessary truth that God exists.
2.   (CG): it is a logically contingent truth that God exists.
3.   N(not-G): it is a necessary truth that God does not exist.
4.   C(not-G): it is a logically contingent falsehood that God exists.

What (NG) amounts to is this: *Necessarily, it is true that God exists.* What (CG) amounts to is: *It is true that God exists, and it is false that Necessarily, it is true that God exists.* Hence one sort of monotheism—that which accepts (NG) or that which accepts (CG)—is false. Further, given the NN thesis, whichever sort is false is *necessarily* false. Similarly, either N(not-G) or C(not-G) is false, so one sort or the other of atheism is false. Further, whichever sort of atheism is false is *necessarily* false.

Ultimate reality, then, according to monotheism, consists in the existence of an omnipotent, omniscient, morally perfect self-conscious Being that cannot depend for its existence on anything else. This being either is such that *Necessarily, God exists* is true or else such that *God exists is true, and it is logically necessary that God does not depend for existence on anything.* The difference between kinds of monotheism will come up again when we consider argument, pro and con, regarding monotheism.[9,10]

There are, then, different varieties of monotheism, some of which we have described. There are different monotheistic notions regarding what has ultimate reality in the sense of depending for its existence on nothing else.

A Few Comments Regarding Monotheism and Non-Ultimate Reality

Typically, monotheists have commonsensically held that there are persons and there are physical objects. Monotheism typically holds that *If there are persons then God created persons* and *If there are physical objects then God created physical objects.* The term 'physical objects' here should be so understood as to include not only artifacts (cars, chairs, pens) but also natural objects (carrots, zebras, and galaxies). God created the latter and the things from which the former are made. Monotheism typically adds that among the things created, those most like God are persons—self-conscious agents capable of acting rightly and wrongly, loving and hating, worshipping God and rebelling against God. There are different views within monotheism about even the broad details of how exactly to understand the relations between God and the world, some of which will come up later—in particular, those regarding determinism, freedom, and agency.

There are different views of what laws of nature are, and different accounts of how laws of nature are related to God. Roughly, a physical theory is a systematized attempt to explain observed physical phenomena. Such a theory will assume that certain sorts of things—say, *A-type-things*—exist and behave[11] in certain ways, and that certain general statements (laws) are true, and that one can then explain the existence and behavior of other types of things given that there are A-type-things and that the laws are true. Suppose simply for convenience that all the other natural sciences reduce to physics, and that somehow we have discovered the entirely correct physics. Then what the entirely correct physics included as basic laws would constitute the actual laws of nature. How should those laws be thought of?

On one account, they are abstract objects—propositions of some such form as (L1) *If A-type-things exist and condition C obtains, then B-type things will exist* or (L2) *If A-type things behave in way W1, and condition C* holds, then B-type things will behave in way W2.* On this view, true statements of forms (L1) and

(L2) will be necessary truths. God's role in creation will not be deciding what laws are true, but rather of deciding whether A-type and B-type things shall exist, and whether conditions C and C* will obtain. Thus if it is a law that *Water freezes at 32 degrees*[12] (if I may oversimplify) then, on the present account, *If there is water then it freezes at 32 degrees* is a necessary truth, and what is up to God is whether *There is water* and *It is 32 degrees where water exists* are ever true.

On another account, laws of nature are truths about the dispositions of natural objects. If water is what this glass contains, then—the idea is—it is an essential feature of the stuff in this glass that it freezes at 32 degrees.[13] Natural laws reflect the essential properties of natural objects and what happens to things with such properties in various environments. But on this account too *If there is water then it freezes at 32 degrees* is a necessary truth. If God creates water, God creates something that freezes at 32 degrees.

On either account, there might be considerable choice of what universe, if any, is created. The laws in question are expressed as *conditionals* or statements of the form *If A then C*. What holds that *A* place is the *antecedent* and what occupies the *C* place is the *consequent*. On the first view described, there might be various ways of putting individual laws together into logically consistent groupings such that a universe could be created containing the things referred to in the antecedents of these particular laws. There would be as many choices between orderly worlds as there were such sets of laws. On the second way of putting things, a similar result arises. The *essence* of some object is the set of properties necessary and sufficient for its existence: the set of properties it cannot exist without and the existence of which in an object suffices to make that thing.[12] Let an *essence description* be a description of a universe in which one or more logically compatible kinds of things coexisted. Every essence description would pick out a different world that God might create.

There are other conceptions of laws, or perhaps of conceptions on which there really aren't any laws. On another view, for example, what we call laws are only generalizations that we may discover to be strictly false though still fairly accurate, and that there is no more to a law than that—a typically accurate generalization which may well be false, and in any case is as explanatorily deep as things get. On this view, explaining why some generalizations are accurate and others are not is not going to be possible—not at any rate for the class of generalizations that have the widest scope.

There seems to be good reason to think that there are basic laws that are probabilistic—laws of the form (L1*) *If A-type-things exist, and condition C obtains, then the probability of a B-type-thing existing is .987* or (L2*) *If A-type things behave in way W1, and condition C* holds, then the probability of B-type things behaving in way W2 is between .997 and .999.*

The philosophical interest of such matters, insofar as they relate to monotheism, has to do with how different notions of the relations between God and the world, and of God and laws of nature. They relate to questions about creation, determinism, freedom, and responsibility—matters for later reflection.

Questions for Reflection

1. What are the tenets of our stylized Greek monotheism? Is it a religion?
2. What are the tenets of Hindu monotheism? Is the claim that the universe has always existed incompatible with a doctrine of creation?
3. What are the tenets of Semitic monotheism?
4. What is a modal proposition?
5. Why are there, modally speaking, just two types of monotheism and two types of atheism?

Notes

1. It is logically consistent with monotheism that there exist abstract objects that possess logically necessary existence. Abstract objects have no causal powers, are not self-conscious or even conscious, and exercise no creation or providence. They are of little if any *religious* interest. It is a necessary truth that *If X has logically necessary existence then there is nothing Y such that Y is distinct from X and X depends on Y for X's existence.* So if *There are abstract objects that have logically necessary existence* is true, it is also true that *There exists something whose existence does not depend on God.*

   God's status as creator, and any coherent notion of divine sovereignty, does not require that something that cannot depend for its existence on anything else depend for its existence on God or deny that the existence of such things is logically possible. But the only candidates for being something of this sort would seem to be things that exist with logical necessity.

2. Trinitarian monotheists speak in this fashion, though typically holding that God is three persons in one substance; other monotheists speak of God as personal while adding that it is proper to speak in this way because God is more like a person than God is like anything else. The latter claim rests in part on views concerning the alleged limits of descriptions of God. For a monotheistic tradition to make even the comparatively weak religious claims central to Greek monotheism, God must be self-conscious. For a monotheistic tradition to make the more robust religious claims characteristic of Judaism, Christianity, Islam, or Hindu monotheism, God must be a self-conscious agent—one who knowingly and purposively acts. A self-conscious agent is a person.

3. Roughly Aristotelian in content.

4. If the point isn't clear, consider a parallel case. If I want to know why the explanation of the existence of this very duck that walks the shore in front of me, the answer is that it had parents. But if I want to know the explanation of there being any ducks at all, I cannot properly be told about there being duck parents; there being duck parents is (part of) what I want explained.

5. Arguably, this claim is *typical of but not essential to* Semitic monotheism.

6. The Exodus, Chapter Two passage in which God, in standard translations, makes self-reference by using the terms "I am" seems not to require a stronger philosophical reading than that expressed by something like *God exists, and it is logically impossible that God depend on anything else for existence.*

7. Of course N[Np]—Necessarily, Necessarily, p—is a third-order modal proposition, and one can on up the ladder. We will go to third-order in a moment.

8. Here is a little more: (1) P *entails* proposition Q if and only if it is logically impossible that P be true and Q be false (i.e., if *P, but not Q* is a contradiction); (2) No necessary truth entails a necessary falsehood; (3) No logically contingent proposition entails a necessary falsehood; (4) No necessary truth entails any logically contingent proposition; (5) Every necessary falsehood entails any proposition whatever [this assumes the rules *If P then (P or Q)* and *If (P or Q) and not-P, then Q* or their equivalent]; (6) Every logically contingent proposition entails every necessary truth; (7) Every logically contingent proposition entails some, but not all, other logically contingent propositions.

9. The logical relations between these views go as follows. Where NT=necessarily true; NF=necessarily false; CT=contingently true; CF=contingently false, the relationships are:

   1. If **NG** is the case, then **CG, N(NOT-G)**, and **C(NOT-G)** are NF.
   2. If **N(NOT-G)** is the case, then **NG, CG**, and **C(NOT-G)** are NF.
   3. If **CG** is the case, then **NG** and **N(NOT-G)** are NF and **C(NOT-G)** is CF.
   4. If **C(NOT-G)** is the case, then **NG** and **N(NOT-G)** are NF and **CG** is CF.

10. These matters are relevant to arguments to be considered later. It is the case that (A) A proof of a necessary truth can contain only necessary truths as premises, and (B) A proof of a logically contingent proposition must contain at least one logically contingent proposition among its premises. It is also, of course, true that (C) No false proposition can be proved, and (D) No argument that contains a false premise is a proof, even if its conclusion is true.

11. "Behave" here is an anthropomorphism that unfortunately is seldom recognized as such.

12. *That this is approximate, and not a basic law, does not matter. Anyone who wants more sophisticated examples is free to supply them.*

13. Or a feature that follows from its essential features.

14. Strictly, essences typically are thought of as defining *kinds* of things; the view that there are, in addition to essences of kinds of things, also essences of individuals is much more controversial.

Suggested Readings

Bartley, C. J. (2002) *The Theology of Ramanuja: Realism and Religion* (New York: Routledge). Places the thought of the great monotheistic Hindu theologian in the context not only of his own tradition but by identifying his opponents in the larger context of Hindu thought.

Cohn-Sherbok, Daniel (1996) *Medieval Jewish Philosophy* (Surrey: Curzon). Brief, good discussion of perhaps the most flourishing period of Jewish philosophy.

Davidson, Herbert (1987) *Proofs for Eternity, Creation, and the Existence of God in Medieval Islamic and Jewish Philosophy* (Oxford: Oxford University Press). Detailed discussion of Jewish and Islamic Medieval philosophers on arguments concerning the dependence and duration of the created world and arguments for God's existence, with some reference to Christian philosophers.

——— (1992) *Alfarabi, Avicenna, and Averroes on Intellect* (Oxford: Oxford University Press). Fine discussion of theories of the mind held by three leading Islamic philosophers.

Drozdek, Adam (2007) *Greek Philosophers as Theologians* (Farnham, Sussex, UK: Ashgate). Argues that Greek philosophers, despite lack of theological language, discussed the attributes of God in terms different from popular conceptions.

Erickson, Millard (2013) *Christian Theology* (Grand Rapids, MI: Baker Academic). A comprehensive treatment of the central topics of Christian belief.

Frank, Dan and Leaman, Oliver, eds. (2000) *The Jewish Philosophy Reader* (New York: Routledge). A comprehensive anthology covering the central topics of Jewish beliefs.

Kellner, Menachem (1986) *Dogma in Medieval Jewish Thought* (Oxford: Oxford University Press). Good discussion of the systems of Jewish thought that are more doctrinally oriented than others.

Kroner, Richard (1956) *Speculation in Pre-Christian Philosophy* (Philadelphia: Westminster Press). This book, and the next two, discuss the development of Christian thought in interaction with ancient, Medieval, and modern philosophy.

——— (1959) *Speculation and Revelation in the Age of Christian Philosophy* (Philadelphia: Westminster Press). See previous reference.

——— (1961) *Speculation and Revelation in Modern Philosophy* (Philadelphia: Westminster Press). See Kroner (1956) comment.

Leaman, Oliver (1985) *An Introduction to Medieval Islamic Philosophy* (Cambridge: Cambridge University Press). Fairly brief, good discussion of perhaps the most flourishing period of Islamic philosophy.

Lipner, Julius (1986) *The Face of Truth* (Albany: SUNY Press). Fine explanation of the thought of the Hindu theologian–philosopher Ramanuja.

Lott, Eric (1976) *God and the Universe in the Vedantic Theology of Ramanuja* (Madras: Ramanuja Research Society). Another fine discussion of Ramanuja.

——— (1980) *Vedantic Approaches to God* (London: Macmillan). Excellent discussion of the three major figures of Hindu Vedantic thought: Shankara, Ramanuja, Madhva.

McGrath, Alister (1994) *Christian Theology* (Oxford: Blackwell). Good historical discussion of the types and themes of Christian thought.

Sharma, B. N. K. (2014) *Philosophy of Sri Madhvacarya* (Delhi: Motilal Barnsidass). Deals with Madhva's epistemology and metaphysics and the views based on them, and finds parallels with Aquinas.

Watt, W. Montgomery (1973) *The Formative Period of Islamic Thought* (Edinburgh: Edinburgh University Press). Good discussion of early Islamic philosophy.

8 Nonmonotheistic Conceptions of Ultimate Reality

Jainism has basically one account of ultimate reality; there are (and always have been) persons and there are (and always have been) the physical elements of which observable physical things are composed. There is no Deity on which either depends for existence or arrangement. The Jain tradition is doctrinally homogenous, so there is no need to say that it is this rather than that type of Jainism that is being described.

The Buddhist traditions range from the Theravada view, described here, through the Absolutism that is part of Mahayana and the at least nearly monotheistic perspective of Pure Land. For the moment, let us leave nirvana out of the account. Theravada Buddhism holds that (besides nirvana) what there is encompasses only momentary, dependent things. These things are[1] momentary states, some mental and some physical (some involving consciousness, some not). Much of later Buddhism accepts only mental states. These two claims[2] are as nearly orthodoxly Buddhist as anything; those who denied them were regarded as heretics: everything is radically impermanent, transitory, fleeting; nothing exists independent of other things.

Advaita Vedanta Hinduism is itself a variety of Absolutism, which we will describe in contrast to the non-Absolutist views of two other varieties of Vedantic Hinduism. Advaita Absolutism holds that all that exists is qualityless Brahman. There is one thing, not many, and this one thing of course stands in no relation to any other thing. Nor does this one thing have any qualities whatever.

The task before us in this chapter, then, is to come to understand these three quite different, but all nonmonotheistic, accounts of what there is. Since Advaita Vedanta is perhaps best understood by contrast with the other varieties of Vedanta, which are monotheistic, beginning with it provides the easiest transition from the discussion of the previous chapter.

Advaita Vedanta Hinduism

Three major philosophers of Vedantic persuasion, with generally suggested dates, are Shankara (788–820 a.d.), Ramanuja (1017–1137 a.d.), and Madhva (1197–1276 a.d.). Shankara holds to Advaita Vedanta or unqualified non-dualism; Ramanuja holds to Visistadvaita or qualified non-dualism; Madhva holds to Dvaita or unqualified dualism.

It may be helpful to understand Shankara's views in contrast with those of Ramanuja and Madhva. Let *the world* be all bodies and all minds other than God. Ramanuja holds that God and the world are in a relationship of asymmetric dependence—the world depends on God but not God on the world. He then takes the world to be God's body in a somewhat technical sense of *body*. The world is God's body in the sense that God can affect any part of the world without having to do so by affecting some other part of it. One might think of one's own body as the part of the physical world that one can move without having to move anything else in order to move it; in order to otherwise affect the physical world, one has to move one's body. All dependent minds and bodies are related in this way to God; for any mind or any body, God can affect it without having to make use of some other mind or body in order to do so. Madhva rejects the notion that the world is God's body, thinking that this makes it sound as if God were dependent for existence and/or action on the world, whereas he holds that God exists independently and is capable of thought without needing any world for his self-conscious activities. Strictly, the disagreement between Ramanuja and Madhva here seems to lie in how one is to understand the notion of God's body; understood as Madhva takes it, Ramanuja too would reject the idea.

What Ramanuja and Madhva have in common—the notion that there exists an independent God and a dependent world—Shankara rejects. What exists for Shankara is nirguna or qualityless Brahman, though what *appears* to exist is a multiplicity of physical objects and persons and a personal God. Shankara sometimes explains his view by using analogies with sensory perception. For example, suppose it is the case that:

(i) There is no man in the shadows.
(ii) Bimal (a typical perceiver) sincerely reports, based on his sensory experience, "I see a man in the shadows."
(iii) What really is in the shadows is only a coat hanging on a hook.

Then:

(iv) There is something that Bimal sees.
(v) What Bimal sees does not have the nature and properties that Bimal sees it as having.

The standard Indian examples are seeing a conch shell and mistaking it for silver and seeing a rope and mistaking it for a snake; each of these follows the (i) through (v) pattern. Analogously, then, the Advaita Vedantin claims, when one reports, based on her sensory experience that there is an experience-independent physical thing, it is nonetheless true that there exists nothing sensory. As there was no man that Bimal saw, but only a coat hanging on a hook, so there is no tree or table (or any other object) that anyone senses, but only qualityless Brahman. Strictly, the analogy does not work; *taking one thing for another* is very different from *sheer hallucination*. But the negative idea is clear—it is denied that there is a mind-independent physical world. This by itself would yield only idealism—the view that there are minds and experiences with sensory content, but no mind-independent objects of sensory experiences. Shankara's view is much more radical. He claims that there are neither minds nor experiences; there is only Brahman without qualities. All experience of physical objects or of self is illusory. It is not an illusion caused by Brahman; that would require that there be effects that were not identical to Brahman. Of course Brahman itself cannot be subject to illusion (that would be a limitation).

One should not suppose that Shankara is unaware of the very considerable difficulties of his view. Consider these passages by Shankara:

(1) To refute the self is impossible, for he who tries to refute it is the self.[3]
(2) Only a deluded man could entertain the idea that he does not exist.[4]

The idea is that while it may be possible without self-refutation to deny that there are physical objects distinct from one's sensory experience, it is not possible without self-refutation to deny that one exists oneself.[5] Shankara then turns to the task of developing a perspective that he regards as fully consistent with certain central *Upanishadic* texts, particularly one that says simply "Thou art that" (the individual person is identical to Brahman). Taking this and other texts literally, Shankara opts for the view that *only* Brahman-without-qualities exists. He holds that if I exist, then—contrary to all sorts of powerful considerations—I am Brahman. The *Vedas* and *Upanishads*, along with traditional commentaries on these documents, are the sacred texts of Hinduism. *Vedanta* means "end of the Vedas"—the late part that is taken to provide the interpretation of what precedes it. *Advaita* means "non-dual" and contrasts with *Dvaita* ("dual") and Visistadvaita ("qualifiedly non-dual"), these being terms that refer to three distinct Hindu traditions, each sharing texts in common which each interprets differently and incompatibly.

The core religious dispute among these three versions of Vedanta concerns the proper interpretation of the relevant authoritative texts concerning the nature of Brahman—that being whose existence does not depend on anything else. The Advaita reading is Absolutistic (non-dualist), the Dvaita and Visistadvaita (dualist and qualifiedly dualist) readings are monotheistic.

At issue are various texts, some of which express the view that the soul or individual human person is literally identical to Brahman, others of which express the view that the human soul is more like Brahman than are other things. The core issue is which texts—the monotheistic or the Absolutistic—are to be read literally and which read non-literally.

Here is the monotheistic reading of such passages.

> Only on account of having for his essence qualities similar to those of Brahman is the soul spoken of as Brahman, as in the case of the all-wise Brahman. Since the essence, i.e. the very nature of the soul, consists only of wisdom, bliss, and other qualities similar (in some degree) to those of Brahman, there proceeds the statement that the soul is one with (like) Brahman; just as in the text, "All this is

indeed Brahman."[6] Brahman is spoken of as "identical with all (the world) on account of there being qualities in Brahman which are predicated of the whole world." The following is in the *Bhavishyat Purana*: "The souls are separate, the perfect Lord is separate, still owing to the similarity of intelligent nature they are spoken of as Brahman in the various Scriptural disquisitions."[7]

In sum: like Brahman, who is a self-conscious Person, all-wise, filled with bliss, human persons also are self-conscious, capable of possessing some wisdom and some bliss. They are similar in ways that make both persons, one an Independent Person on whom everything else depends, one a dependent person who has sinned and thus both owes her existence to, and needs gracious forgiveness from, the One on whom she depends. This, again, is monotheism. Nonmonotheistic or Absolutist Advaita Vedanta rejects this reading of such passages.

Here is the nonmonotheistic reading.

> The difference between God and the individual soul is due to these differing limiting adjuncts [namely, the mind and the senses]. When these are absolutely negated . . . then there is no God and no individual, but there remains only the eternal, absolute, and pure Brahman. . . . Scripture [*Upanishads*] says that the limiting adjuncts are accidental, and superimposed on Brahman; reasoning based on Scripture must negate them both.[8]

To thought and perception, there appear to be a multiplicity of persons and things. On an Advaita reading, the *Upanishads* deny this; so thought and perception must be "negated" in the sense that what appears to them to be so is rejected.

What exists, then, for Shankara is nirguna or qualityless Brahman, though what *appears* to exist is a multiplicity of physical objects and persons and a personal God. Until we get to the distinction between appearance and reality, he is a realist regarding objects, minds, and God; he holds that, "at the level of appearance," such things exist. Indeed, he argues strongly for their existence. But he also holds, on *Upanishadic* authority, that only qualityless Brahman exists "at the level of reality."

How are we to understand this claim? Plainly not in terms of the level of appearance being the set of things that exist dependently and Brahman being their independently existing Source. That is the position of Ramanuja and Madhva. The levels cannot be levels of reality distinguished by presence or absence of dependence. The levels presumably are in some manner levels of knowledge or belief, appearance being how things look and reality being how things are. How are we to understand this notion?

A Two-Theories Account

Taking a cue from Spinoza, a favorite among Advaita Vedantins, one might try interpreting Advaita Vedanta along the lines of saying that there are two theories related in certain ways as follows. Suppose we have two theories, each of which has its own vocabulary; then we will have two theoretical languages, replete with their conceptual perspectives or worldviews. Each, let us suppose, is exhaustive—it describes, or attempts to describe, all there is, not of course in concrete detail but in terms of general properties and kinds and the like. In each, whatever can be explained is explained. What one theory refers to is the same as what the other theory refers to, though of course each describes what it refers to very differently from of the other. No descriptive term is common between or shared by both theories.[9] Thus on the current account there are two theories or theoretical languages that have parity of description and parity of explanatory power. The entities referred to in one language are identical to those of the other, and the explanatory connections alleged in the one will be paralleled by explanatory connections alleged in the other.

According to one of these theories, individual persons, physical objects, and a personal God exists. Since the Vedantic term for person is Atman, we can all this *the Atman theory*. According to the other of these theories, all that exists is Brahman without qualities; we will call this *the Brahman theory*. We then get something along these lines:

BT. The Brahman Theory

1.   Brahman exists and has no qualities at all.
2.   Nothing but Brahman exists.
3.   Every Atman that exists is identical to Brahman.

AT. The Atman Theory

4.   There are individual Atmans (dependent persons).
5.   There is a personal Brahman and so Brahman has qualities.
6.   No Atman is Brahman.
7.   Each Atman has mental qualities.
8.   There are physical objects.
9.   Physical objects have physical qualities.

There are problems with this as an account of Advaita Vedanta. The Brahman theory has almost no descriptive content, and no explanatory content. One cannot use terms from AT to shore up BT since this mixes the theories; it would remove the alleged purity of the theoretical languages, causing each to be tainted by the another. The account requires descriptive and explanatory parity of two logically independent theories or theoretical languages. BR and AT lack such parity. Further, the account requires that the theories be equally justified. But according to Advaita Vedanta, BR and AT are not equally justified or equally accurate. Thus this seems not a successful program for stating Advaita.

A Causal Theory of Perception Account

Perhaps one can approach matters in this way. Consider the sort of causal account of perception that John Locke offered.[10] On this view, a veridical perception of a tree is analyzed like this. Suppose it is true that *Manindra sees a tree*. What makes this true is there being a tree that causes certain images in Manindra's mind. These images represent, and in limited ways resemble, the tree. Perception occurs when a perceivable object has the right sort of causal impact on a perceiver.

Then whittle the account down. Locke himself held that, for example, color qualities were the product of interaction between object and perceiver; the tree itself has no color properties. But the tree itself does have shape properties, and the shape properties of the image must resemble the shape properties of the tree if Manindra, by virtue of having the images, is seeing the tree. But suppose one thinks that there is no tree, and indeed nothing with shape properties that caused Manindra's images. Suppose Manindra's images are caused by another mind or spirit. Then all of perception is illusory in the sense that there are no objects that cause our perceptual images. Now, one might suggest, this gives us what we might call a minimally informative causal theory of perception. It may be that this theory, while it has little to commend it philosophically, is the one to use in trying to explain Shankara's theory if we wish to use sensory analogies. Even this is dubious. On this account, which goes further than Locke's, *Manindra sees a green tree* will be true only if there is no green tree that Manindra sees. In fact, all analogy with perception has vanished. Further, in order to come to Shankara's view, one must somehow keep whittling away until neither Manindra's mind nor the mind that caused the images in Manindra's mind is thought of as having any properties. One wonders if one is then offering any account of anything. Further, Brahman is not construed as the cause of anything, and so is not conceived as the cause of perception. The most sensible procedure, then, would seem to be to leave perceptual analogies alone. In effect, this is what does happen when the Advaitin appeals to levels of being or to levels of truth or to the appearance/reality distinction construed in an Advaitin way.

Reductionism and Eliminativism

Advaita accepts the claim, relative to each individual person or Atman that it is identical to

Brahman. How is this to be understood?
Consider a simple identity statement:
Ia. Cicero is identical to Tully.
What this means is simply:[11]
Ia*. 'Cicero' designates the same person as 'Tully' designates.
Shankara intends:
IIa. The Atman is identical to Brahman.[12]
to entail:
IIa*. 'Atman' designates what 'Brahman' designates.

But this tells us only a little. Idealism regarding physical objects contends that a physical object is identical to a collection of sensory images. This can be understood in either of two quite different ways as follows, using a cat named "Oscar" as our sample physical object:

> IIIa. 'Oscar' designates what 'this collection of catty images'[13] designates.
> So far, so good. Are we then to go on to IV or to V:

IV. All true statements about Oscar can be translated without remainder into (reduced to) statements about this collection of catty images.
V.   Statements about Oscar should[14] be dropped from our speech and replaced by sentences that speak only of this collection of catty images.[15]

What IV recommends is reduction; what V commends is replacement. It seems clear that the idealist, at least of Bishop Berkeley's sort, wants V. Berkeley takes statements about physical objects to be true only if there are exactly the sort of experience-independent extended objects it is the purpose of his theory to reject. Statements to the effect that there are such things, being in principle false, should be banned from our theories. The idea is that the truths cat-sentences aim at and miss, collection of catty images sentences hit.

More formally, a statement A reduces without remainder to a statement B only if it is logically impossible that A and B differ in truth value. Statements about physical objects can differ in truth value from statements about collections of catty images. So IV recommends a logical impossibility. Further, given the conditions for reduction, if the recommended reduction could be carried out, it would import talk of objects into idealistic theory. Berkeleyian idealism is a replacement theory. It is eliminativist, not reductionist.

So is Advaita Vedanta, and for analogous reasons. Consider the difference between:

IV*. All true statements about any Atman can be translated without remainder into (reduced to) statements about Brahman.
V*.   Statements about any Atman should be dropped from our speech and replaced by sentences that speak only of Brahman.[16]

Suppose that *This Atman is tired [i.e., I am tired]* is true. It has as truth conditions that I exist as the sort of being that can tire; if *Atman is Brahman* is treated as IV* requires, it will be true that *Brahman is tired*. This Shankara rejects. It is V* that his view requires. His view is eliminativist, not reductionist. It is in that context that we should understand his view that only Brahman without qualities exists.[17]

Advaita Vedanta will receive further description when we come later to ask what considerations have been offered on its behalf. In philosophy, understanding a view and understanding what can be said for and against it are not separate enterprises; they are intrinsically related, part of a single enterprise of understanding. What can be concluded thus far is that analogies to perception and theories of perception seem not helpful in coming to terms with the core of the philosophy of Advaita Vedanta.

Jainism and Buddhism

A Radical Substance View (Jainism) and a Non-substance View (Theravada Buddhism) Compared and Contrasted

Jainism and Buddhism agree that our great need is to escape the circle of rebirths and achieve enlightenment and release. But they differ in what the enlightened person finds at the end of her search, and they disagree about what the nature of the searcher is. This difference is both religious and philosophical, and will be explained in both its religious and its philosophical contexts.

The Religious Context

Jainism and Persons: Persons Are Substances[18]

For Jainism, consciousness is always someone's consciousness. There can no more be consciousness without persons than there can be triangles without angles.
   A Jain text tells us the following:

> The distinctive characteristic of a substance is being. Being is a simultaneous possession of coming into existence, going out of existence, and permanence. Permanence means the indestructibility of the essence of the substance . . . substance is possessed of attributes and modifications . . . attributes depend upon substratum and cannot be the substratum of another attribute. Modification is change of attribute.[19]

We are told that there are things (substances) that have qualities (attributes, properties) without themselves being qualities. These qualities are inherently first-order qualities (qualities of things that are not themselves qualities) and they begin and cease to be—they come into existence and go out of existence. For a quality to come into existence is for a thing that did not have it to come to have it; for a quality to go out of existence is for a thing that did have it to come to have it no longer (this is what it is for substances to undergo modifications). When things undergo modification (change of attribute) in the sense that they gain and lose qualities, they remain the same things (enjoy permanence) throughout the modifications that they undergo. Change presupposes that something is changed, and hence that something endures through the change. In sum: numerically identical things undergo change of qualities; change of one thing (quality) presupposes permanence of another thing (substance).
   The same text adds that:

> The self's essence is life. . . . The distinctive characteristic of self is attention. . . . Those with minds are knowers.[20]

Among things or substances are some whose essence is *being alive and being capable of being liberated* or *being alive and being incapable of being liberated.*[21]

Any such thing is conscious or capable of giving attention to objects of experience, and self-conscious or aware of itself as agent and as being affected by other things. These remarks serve as background to the religious point of the doctrines just noted:

> That which should be grasped by self-discrimination is "I" from the real point of view.[22]
>
> The soul has the nature of knowledge, and the realization of this nature is Nirvana; therefore one who is desirous of Nirvana must meditate on self-knowledge.[23]

According to Jainism, knowledge of the nature of the self or person is achievable through meditative self-awareness; such knowledge is constitutive of achieving enlightenment. The most desirable modification—namely, enlightenment—neither changes the nature of the self or person or jiva nor removes his capacity for awareness or her status as a knower:

> After the soul is released, there remain perfect right-belief, perfect right-knowledge, perfect perception, and the state of having accomplished all.[24]

Here, persons are enduring self-conscious substances, retaining numerical identity over time and retaining identity as individual persons in their enlightened state. Thus in the *Jaina Sutras*[25] one reads that when the Venerable Ascetic Mahavira had become enlightened, he was

> omniscient and comprehending all objects; he knew and saw all conditions of the world, of gods, men, and demons: whence they come, whither they go, whether they are born as men or animals . . . or become gods or hell-beings . . . the ideas, the thoughts of their minds, the food, doings, desires, the open and secret deeds of all living beings in the whole world; he the Arhat, for whom there is no secret, knew and saw all conditions of all living beings in the world, what they thought, spoke, or did at any moment.

Mahavira—founder of Jainism and achiever of enlightenment—is conceived as being the same person post-enlightenment as he was pre-enlightenment. Nor does post-mortem achievement of full and final enlightenment/nirvana alter this.

Buddhism and Persons: Persons as Bundles[26]

A Buddhist text tells us that:

> Whether Buddhas arise, O priests, or whether Buddhas do not arise, it remains a fact and the fixed and necessary constitution of being that all its constituents are transitory. This fact a Buddha discovers and masters, and when he has discovered and mastered it, he announces, teaches, publishes, proclaims,

discloses, minutely explains, and makes it clear, that all the constituents of being are transitory. . . . Whether Buddhas arise, O priests, or whether Buddhas do not arise, it remains a fact and the fixed and necessary constitution of being, that all its elements are lacking in an ego (substantial, permanent self-nature). This fact a Buddha discovers and masters, and when he has discovered and mastered it, he announces, teaches, publishes, proclaims, discloses, minutely explains, and makes it clear, that all the elements of being are lacking in an ego.[27]

A longer and more familiar passage reads as follows:

Just as the word "chariot" is but a mode of expression for axle, wheels, chariot-body, pole, and other constituent members, placed in a certain relation to each other, but when we come to examine the members one by one, we discover that in the absolute sense there is no chariot; and just as the word "house" is but a mode if expression for wood and other constituents of a house, surrounding space in a certain relation, but in the absolute sense there is no house; and just as the word "fist" is but a mode of expression for the fingers, the thumb, etc. in a certain relation; . . . the word "tree" for trunk, branches, foliage, etc. in a certain relation, but when we come to examine the parts one by one, we discover that in the absolute sense there is no tree; in exactly the same way words "living entity" and "ego" are but a mode of expression for the presence of the five attachment groups, but when we come to examine the elements of being one by one, we discover that in the absolute sense there is no living entity there to form a basis for such figments as "I am" or "I"; in other words, that in the absolute sense there is only name and form. The insight of him who perceives this is called knowledge of the truth.[28]

We are told here that there are constituents that are transitory. Further, there are collections of simultaneous constituents (call these simultaneous bundles) and there are collections of successive constituents (call these successions of bundles). Successions of bundles are made up of sequential simultaneous bundles and so-called physical objects are successions of bundles.[29] More importantly for our purposes, so-called persons are successions of bundles. There are no constituents that endure; each moment sees an entirely new constituent population. Successions of bundles are the only candidates for possessing numerical identity over time.

Review, Comparison, and Contrast

I.   Reincarnation and Karma

The Jain and Buddhist traditions share belief in reincarnation and karma. Reincarnation doctrine teaches that each person beginninglessly lives one life after another, and will do so endlessly unless he becomes enlightened. Karma doctrine (in its nonmonotheistic version, which is the version relevant to Jainism and

Buddhism) teaches that one inescapably receives the merit or demerit due; right or wrong actions not disinterestedly done yield weal or woe, and no one escapes their due recompense. Embedded in these doctrines is a *justice requirement*: the recipient of the recompense must be the doer of the deed for which recompense comes—she, and not another.

2.   Change

On the Buddhist perspective described above, collections of simultaneous constituents are replaced by new collections of simultaneous constituents. No changes occur; replacement occurs.

A further Jain text reads:

> There cannot be a thing which is devoid of its modifications of birth and decay. On the other hand, modifications cannot exist without an abiding or eternal something—a permanent substance, for birth, decay, and stability (continuance)—these three constitute the characteristic of a substance or entity.[30]

"Birth and decay" refers to the comings and goings of qualities, "stability or continuance" to substances. Change requires permanence.[31]

3.   Simplicity

Jain persons lack constituents. They have no elements and are incomposite. A Jain person at a time T is a self-conscious substance that exists at T. If she is embodied at T, her body is not *part* of her at T. Her thoughts at T are thoughts but not parts; her qualities at T are qualities but not parts. A person that exists at times T1 and T2 does not have a T1-part and a T2-part. One might say: *All of her exists at T1 and all of her exists at T2—she is not temporally scattered.* She has a life, and that life (in some sense, at least) can have parts—say, one part where she is a student in Delhi and another part where she is a professor in Benares. Her life can have parts or segments; she cannot. She is an incomposite substance, a self-conscious mind. While *being alive* (not to be confused with *being embodied*) is essential to a person, a person is not identical to any particular life or series of lives. A person could have lived lives other than the one he did live, and he *has* a life, and a long series of lives, without *being* any or all of those lives (whatever exactly that might amount to).

Buddhist persons have constituents. They have elements and are composite. A Buddhist person at a time T is a simultaneous bundle that exists at T.[32] Her thoughts at T are thoughts that are parts of her at T; her qualities at T are qualities that are parts of her at T. A person that exists at times T1 and T2 does have a T1-part and a T2-part, the former being a bundle of elements-simultaneously-existing-at-T1 and the latter a bundle of elements-simultaneously-existing-at-T2. One might say: *At no moment of a person's existence does all of her exist at once—she is temporally scattered.* If a person could exist at just two moments, half of her would exist at each moment. If a life is composed of one simultaneous bundle followed by another followed by another, a person *is* a life, and that life has as many parts are there are moments at which some simultaneous bundle or other occurs in the life-series. While *being alive* (not to be confused with *being embodied*) is essential to a person, a person is identical to the particular series of lives that she lives.[33]

A Basic Difference between the Jain Doctrine and the Buddhist Doctrine of Persons

The difference between the Jain and the Buddhist accounts of what it is to be a person is important but it can be difficult to grasp. Here is another way of putting it.

Consider an atom of the sort that Isaac Newton believed in. In his physics, an atom in effect was a tiny pellet—a billiard ball shrunk to miniscule proportions. An atom was as small as anything can get, and was composed of no parts whatever. Homogenous and ultimately tiny, atoms (Newton taught) are the things of which larger physical items are composed.

Suppose that at time T1 there is just one atom; call it Alice1. Suppose that at time T2 there is also just one atom; call it Alice2. Then ask: Is Alice1 identical to Alice2? The answer is "Yes" provided Alice1 has stayed in existence from T1 through T2. Otherwise, Alice2 is a new atom.

Now suppose that instead of being a material atom, Alice1 is a person, a self-conscious immaterial mind, and the same for Alice2. Then ask: Is Alice2 identical to Alice1? The answer is "Yes" provided Alice1 has stayed in existence from T1 through T2. Otherwise, Alice2 is a new person.

Suppose Alice1 exists only at T1 and Alice2 exists only at T2; then they are not identical. This is the Buddhist answer to the identity of any incomposite thing over time. If there is such a thing as an Alice, it is simply a matter of there being a series composed of Alice1 at T1 and Alice2 at T2 (and perhaps Alice3 at T3 and so on). An Alice over time is a series of momentary Alices-at-one-time.

The difference, then, is that on a Jain account a person is one incomposite thing that exists over time—that endures through a series of times—whereas on a Buddhist account a person is a series of composite things no one of which exists over time.

The Importance of the Accounts of Persons

To one trained in contemporary academic contexts, it may seem unlikely if not wildly implausible that issues in metaphysics, and disputes about such issues, be taken to be of central religious importance—to be viewed as matters centrally affecting salvation or enlightenment versus damnation or ignorance. But of course we do not get to decide how these things are viewed; the indigenous authors and interpreters of normative texts, and the participants in the relevant rites and institutions related thereto, decide them. Thus on both Jain and Buddhist accounts of the matter, getting these metaphysical matters right[34] is central to becoming, and constitutive of being, enlightened. Further, from a Jain perspective, the Buddhist account ascribes too little (essentially, nothing) to *being a person* for any enlightenment to be possible, and from a Buddhist perspective the Jain account ascribes too much to *being a person* for enlightenment to be possible. One might say: the Buddhist thinks the Jain soul is too heavy to safely ride in the Great Vehicle and the Jain thinks the Buddhist (non)soul too frail to get in the boat.

Some Consequences

1. Action

Suppose that, as we would ordinarily say, Jamie fires three shots at Josie in order to scare her into revealing where her parents have hidden their life savings—shot 1 at time T1, shot 2 at time T2, shot 3 at time T3. On the bundle account, what fired shot 1 was a simultaneous bundle that exists only at T1; similarly for shot 2 and a simultaneous bundle that exists only at T2 as well as shot 3 and a simultaneous bundle that exists only at T3. One "element" fires shot 1, another fires shot 2, another fires shot 3. No simultaneous bundle fires all three shots. A succession of bundles fires shots only insofar as its simultaneous-bundle members fire shots; it *just is* those members. On a Jain account, a self-conscious substance fires the three shots—Jamie is numerically the same at T1, T2, and T3, and at each time he fires a shot.

2. Memory

Suppose that, as we would ordinarily say, Jamie is arrested for firing shots at Josie, and sadly remembers his wickedness toward her. On the Jain account, numerically the same self-conscious being who fired the shots thinks of himself as having done so. Memory[35] of performing an action involves numerically the same self-conscious substance who performed it thinking about himself having done so. On a Buddhist account, (reliable) memory is a matter of a later simultaneous bundle containing a state that represents an earlier simultaneous bundle acting in a certain manner, where it is true of the earlier simultaneous bundle that it did so act, and where the earlier and later simultaneous bundles are elements in the same succession of bundles.

As we have noted, the doctrines of reincarnation and karma require that appropriate recompense (weal or woe) come to each person for her own previous actions—actions not atypically in some lifetime prior to the one previously being lived.[36] Not only Mahavira but also the Buddha is represented as remembering, upon becoming enlightened, all of his past reincarnational life.

The Jaina and Buddhist traditions, then, provide us with a sharply contrasting account of what a person is—a person *at* a time and a person *over* time. For the Jaina traditions, a person at a time is a self-conscious substance and over time is a self-conscious substance that exists continuously. For the Buddhist traditions, a person at a time is a bundle of momentary states and over time is a sequence of such bundles. So we have two quite different views of what a person is, and thus two quite different views of what it is for a person to be the same person at one time as at another.

Conclusion

Three nonmonotheistic views of ultimate reality have been described. For one, what exists is simply and only a qualityless being, nirguna Brahman.[37] For another, what exists are minds and physical elements. On both views, what is *ultimate* is *incomposite* (not made of parts) and *independent* (not depending for its existence on anything). For a third view, what is ultimate is physical and mental states, each momentary, transitory, and impermanent. Here *ultimate* bears the sense of *incomposite* but not of *independent*, as each state is conceived as existing dependently on other states. Nothing is thought to have existential independence.

Questions for Reflection

1. Why, in the end, do analogies to perceptual experience, whether simple or complex, fail to communicate the core of Advaita Vedanta doctrine?
2. What does Advaita Vedanta doctrine affirm? What does it deny?
3. For Advaita, what is it that suffers constant illusion and what does Advaita say can be done about it?
4. Consider and assess this brief argument: (i) John has illusions. (2) John's apparent awareness of himself is illusory (part of an illusion). (2) If John's apparent awareness of himself is illusory, then John himself is an illusory. (3) You have to be real in order to have illusions. (4) John is real.
5. Explain the Jain account of persons, and its implications for action, memory, and personal identity.
6. Explain the Buddhist account of persons, and its implications for action, memory, and personal identity.

Notes

1. Subject to a philosophical qualification noted in a later chapter.
2. Technically, impermanence and co-dependent arising.
3. *Commentary on the Brahma-Sutra*, II, 3, 7.
4. *Pancandasi*, III, 23–24.
5. Further, Shankara's writings contain a sophisticated version of the view that there are experience-independent physical objects.
6. *Chandogya Upanishad*, 3.14.1.
7. The passage is from S. Subba Rao (1904) *Vedanta Sutras* (Madras: Sri Vaisa Press),

3.3.29, p. 141; cited in J. Estlin Carpenter (1977) *Theism in Medieval India* (New Delhi: Oriental Books Reprint Corporation); first published by Williams and Norgate, London, 1921, with quotations embedded in the text as indicated.

8. K. Satchidananda Murty (1974) *Reason and Revelation in Advaita Vedanta* (Delhi: Motilal Banarsidass), pp. 3–4. First published by Ahndra University Press and Columbia University Press, 1959.

9. Strictly, no term more determinate than, say, *substance*.

10. Strictly, it is the *Essay concerning Human Understanding*, Book II (not the later Book IV) account.

11. Allowing for a particular historical context.

12. Where "the Atman" refers to each "individual person"—the view, of course, entails the remarkable consequence that there is at most only one individual person.

13. We can ignore here whether idealistic Oscar is one collection of present images or a temporally sequenced series of collections.

14. At least for serious purposes in science and metaphysics.

15. I leave "collections of catty images" vague; in fact, there is no replacement for this phrase that satisfies the idealist desiderata of (i) being phenomenologically adequate to our sensory experience and (ii) not referring to what, if it exists, if a physical object.

16. Again, for purposes of metaphysics and high religion.

17. The question remains, of course, as to what can properly replace such sentences as *I am tired*, a topic to which we will return when we come to assess Advaita Vedanta's claims.

18. Jain doctrine is classically expressed in the *Jaina Sutras*. Jain tradition is doctrinally far more homogeneous than Buddhist tradition.

19. *Tattvarthadhigama Sutra*, Chapter V, Sections 29, 30, 31, 38, 41, 42; Sarvepalli Radhakrishnan and Charles A. Moore, eds. (1952) *A Sourcebook in Indian Philosophy* (Princeton, NJ: Princeton University Press), p. 256. The *Sourcebook* is probably still the most accessible source for the passages that it contains.

20. *Loc. cit.*, Chapter II, Sections 7, 8, 29; *Sourcebook*, p. 254.

21. This is a Jain analogue of the doctrine of double predestination (some to salvation, some to damnation), albeit without a predestinator.

22 .*Samayasdra*, 325.

23. *Atmanusasna*, 174.

24. *Loc. cit.*, Chapter X, Section 4; *Sourcebook*, p. 260.

25. Herman Jacobi, tr. (1962) *Jaina Sutras* (New York: Dover Publications; originally published, 1896) Vol. I, p. 264.

26. Buddhist tradition is far less homogeneous than Jain tradition. While the doctrine that, nirvana aside, nothing is permanent, everything is momentary, and the related thesis that no momentary thing exists independently, come near to being Buddhist orthodoxy, even within Indian Buddhism there is significant doctrinal variety. My focus here is on Theravada Buddhism. The same issues arise for non-Absolutist Mahayana traditions. Absolutist Mahayana tradition is a philosophical sibling, if not twin, to Advaita Vedanta and lies outside the present discussion.

27. *Anguttara-nikaya*, iii, 134; *Sourcebook*, p. 273, 274; the text is Theravadin.

28. *Visuddhi-magga*, xviii; *Sourcebook*, pp. 284–285; the text is Theravadin.

29. Or, for Buddhist idealism, sensory contents of elements of simultaneous bundles.

30. *Sanmati Tarka*, 1.12; *Sourcebook*, p. 269.

31. Strictly, change requires **that the item that changes retain numerical identity over time**. Whether this is a matter of **permanence**, in the sense of the inherent

indestructibility that Jainism ascribes to persons, or a beginningless but nonetheless dependent numerical identity over time that persons enjoy according to Visistadvaita and Dvaita, or a non-beginningless dependent numerical identity over time that persons enjoy according to the Semitic monotheisms, is irrelevant here. I use the quoted term "permanence" for convenience; let it stand in for something like "numerical identity over time" of any of the sorts just mentioned.

32. For non-idealist Buddhism, there are bundles that contain no states of consciousness (these being the referents of typical physical object terms) and bundles that contain states of consciousness (these being the referents of typical person terms). For the idealist Buddhist, there are only the latter, and typical physical object terms refer to subsets of bundles of states of consciousness (those containing sensory content).

33. If metaphysical identity is necessary, a Buddhist person could not have lived lives other than the one she did live. This raises questions about any alleged freedom such a person could possess.

34. "Getting them right" of course involves more than being able to pass a true-false exam in metaphysics. It involves deep convictions, basic and firmly held beliefs, associated feelings and practices, and the like—"heart knowledge as well as head knowledge" as some would say. But "getting them right" does include getting them right—believing what is true.

35. I use "memory" here as a "success term" without denying that one can think one remembers when one does not (a view quite open to Jainism). If one prefers, let him for "memory" substitute "reliable memory."

36. If you want to think of various reincarnation "visits" as all comprising a single lifetime, think of the actions as having been done on earlier "visits" than those in which the recompense comes.

37. The role alleged ineffability plays in this notion will be discussed in a later chapter.

Suggested Readings

Basham, A.L. (1951) *History and Doctrine of the Ajivikas* (London: Luzac Press). Good discussion of the doctrinal content and historical development of the Jain tradition.

Carpenter, Amber (2014) *Indian Buddhist Philosophy* (New York: Routledge). Wide coverage—fifth century b.c. through eighth century a.d.—of Buddhist metaphysics, epistemology, and moral psychology.

Chatterjee, Satischandra and Datta, Dhirendramohan (1950) *An Introduction to Indian Philosophy* (Calcutta: University of Calcutta Press). A good general treatment of the various Indian philosophical systems; goes into more detail than a typical introduction.

Jaini, P. (1979) *The Jaina Path of Perfection* (Berkeley: University of California Press). A comprehensive account of Jain thought.

Jaini, Padmanabh S. (2000) *Collected Papers on Jain Studies* (Delhi: Motilal Banarsidass). Papers by an accomplished Jain scholar on reality, karma, salvation, rebirth, and omniscience.

Jayatilleke, K. N. (2013) *Early Buddhist Theory of Knowledge* (New York: Routledge). Deals with the epistemological, metaphysical, and logical-linguistic content of the Pali canon.

Mookerji, Satkari (1944) *The Jaina Philosophy of Non-Absolutism* (Calcutta: Bharati Mahavidyalaya). Good account of Jain doctrine with emphasis on one interpretation of Jain thought on which it sees claims as relative to perspectives; it is controversial as to whether this reading is correct.

Phillips, Steven (1995) *Classical Indian Metaphysics* (La Salle, IL: Open Court). Nice discussions of issues and systems.

Radhakrishnan, S. and Moore, C.A. (1952) *A Sourcebook in Indian Philosophy* (Princeton, NJ: Princeton University Press). While much of the material is philosophical only in a very loose sense, this is a useful anthology of some passages by Indian philosophers.

Rambachan, Anantanand (1991) *Accomplishing the Accomplished: The Vedas as a Source of Valid Knowledge in Sankara* (Honolulu: University of Hawaii Press). Good discussion of the view that Hindu Scripture, along with perception, inference, and so on is a source of genuine knowledge.

Ram-Prasad, Chakravarthi (2002) *Advaita Epistemology and Metaphysics: An Outline of Indian Non-Realism* (New York: Routledge). Based on basic Advaita texts, and relating views to European philosophy, argues that there is no proof of an external world.

Sharma, Arvind (2008) *The Philosophy of Religion and Advaita Vedanta: A Comparative Study in Religion and Reason* (University Park: Pennsylvania State University Press). Uses John Hick and Advaita philosophers, including Shankara, as a basis for comparison.

Warder, A.K. (1990) *A History of Indian Buddhism* (Honolulu: University of Hawaii Press). Standard history of Buddhism in the land of its origin.

Wood, Thomas (1990) *The Mandukya Upanishad and the Agama Sastra: An Investigation into the Meaning of the Vedanta* (Honolulu: University of Hawaii Press). A lucid and excellent account of Advaita.

———— (1991) *Mind-Only* (Honolulu: University of Hawaii Press). An excellent account of Theravada doctrine, lucidly argued.

Part III

Arguments concerning Monotheistic Conceptions

9   Arguments Against Monotheism

Three Questions

A theodicy is an explanation of the role that evil plays in God's overall plan. A defense regarding evil is an argument that evil does not provide evidence that God does not exist. An argument from evil is an attempt to show that the existence of evil does provide evidence that God does not exist. So there arise three questions regarding God and evil: Is there an adequate theodicy? Is there a successful defense regarding evil? Is there a successful argument from evil? While the issues that come up in the attempt to develop a theodicy are of significant philosophical and religious interest, they typically occur within the context of a fairly detailed theology, and we will not try to develop one here. With one exception, we will set the first question aside.

Reincarnation, Karma, and Evil

The doctrine of reincarnation claims that each person is embodied in a newly born body, lives a human life for however long that body lives, and when that body dies the person who has been embodied in it becomes embodied in another newly born body.[1] This process is, for each person other than Brahman or God, beginningless and ends only if the person becomes enlightened or is saved. The doctrine of karma says that the physical, social, economic, political, and so on conditions under which a person is embodied and lives a given lifetime are the conditions rendered appropriate by the person's actions in previous lifetimes. The two claims together yield a third: what evils occur to a person in a given lifetime are morally proper, being the appropriate consequences of what the person has previously done.

At least from some monotheistic standpoints, there is an attractiveness to this doctrine. All evils are just punishments. For example if an infant is stillborn or has severe birth defects, these things happen not to a person just coming to be, but to a person who has a long and intricate series of lifetimes in which he has behaved so viciously as to deserve this treatment. Bad things happen to good people because they were not always good people. This view entails, then, that:

> (EN) For any evil E that occurs to a person in lifetime N, E is the just consequence of wrong actions by that person in lifetime N or in her lifetimes prior to N.

Whether (EN) is true or not, it is logically consistent. Thus it is relevant to a use of the Consistency Strategy that we will consider shortly. Since there is little if any solid evidence in favor of the truth of the doctrines of reincarnation and karma, it would be intellectually risky to offer them as part of a theodicy of which they formed an essential part or a defense regarding evil.

To begin by offering a defense regarding evil would be premature. One would need first to have reason to suppose that evil is evidence against the existence of God. Unless there is good reason to think this, there is no need for a defense regarding evil. While it is often assumed that the religious believer should provide evidence that God exists and also provide a defense regarding evil, the idea that the religious believer should always be the one who offers arguments is without justification. The place to start in considering God and evil is by asking whether there is any successful, or at least initially plausible, argument from evil. There are quite a variety of attempts to offer a successful argument from evil. It is time to consider some of them.

The Problem of Evil

What philosophers call the problem of evil concerns whether or not the existence of evil counts against the existence of God, makes belief that God exists unreasonable, or the like. The pastoral problem of evil—how one is to deal with the evil that one faces in one's own life and the lives of those one loves—is obviously important, but it is not the (philosophical) problem of evil. A theodicy is an account of why God allows, or even causes, evil—of the role evil plays in the great scheme of things, how it relates to divine providence, how God can bring good from evil, how God's love can triumph over evil, and the like. It is understandable that someone want a theodicy. But offering a theodicy is not necessary in order to deal with the problem of evil, and it is a large topic all by itself. Here, the concern is with the problem of evil, itself quite enough to occupy one's attention.

The existence of evil is the most influential consideration against the existence of God. The fact is that there is evil in the world, and the fact is that this is at least initially puzzling if the world is created and providentially guided by a morally perfect and omnicompetent (omnipotent and omniscient) God. In this chapter, then, versions of this consideration are examined. It is often taken to be obvious that the existence of evil is at least evidence against the existence of God. Even if other, stronger considerations vote "Yes" regarding God's existence, it is claimed that evil obviously votes "No" in that election. This is questionable. The existence of evil is evidence against the existence of God only if there is some sound and valid argument in which *There is evil* is a essential premise (one without which the argument is invalid) and *God does not exist* is the conclusion. It is not obvious that there is any such argument. Anyone who claims there is such an argument may be challenged to produce it. This chapter considers various arguments that have been offered to meet this challenge.

Is the Existence of Evil Evidence against the Existence of God?

That there is evil seems to many a feature of the world that God would not have allowed. Thus they argue that since evil does exist, God does not. This inference is cogent if and only if (E) *There is evil* and (G) *God exists* are logically incompatible, or if (E) plus some set S of discernible truths is logically incompatible with (G).[2] Thus arguments from evil to the non-existence of God either claim that (E) and (G) are logically incompatible or seek some set S of discernible truths which, together with (E), is incompatible with (G)—or, if you prefer, a set S of discernible truths that, together with (E), entail the denial of (G). It is possible to consider several arguments from *(E) is true* to *(G) is false* within a brief scope, thereby gaining a good sense of how likely to succeed this enterprise is.

Failed Escapes

No typical version of monotheism can deny (E). Semitic and Hindu monotheisms hold that our basic religious problem is sin from which we need forgiveness and deliverance. But to sin is to act in a way that is evil. Typical monotheisms are religions of redemption from evil. So they cannot deny that (E) is true. Nor can monotheism consistently embrace the notion of a finite god—a Deity who, for reasons of lack of knowledge, power, or goodness, does not prevent evil. If a supposed Deity is not perfectly good, it is not the Deity of typical monotheism, so that route is closed. An omnicompetent but morally imperfect being would not be God. Suppose, then, that a being is morally perfect but limited in either knowledge or power in such a way that, for certain evils at least, it would prevent them if it could but it cannot prevent them. This being also would not be God in any typical monotheistic sense. To see this, consider a being limited in knowledge; suppose that God lacks the knowledge to prevent evil, though God has the power to do so. Suppose also that I, walking alongside my friend Jon, know that if he does not stop walking now, he will be hit by a car. Then except under really extraordinary circumstances I am wicked if I do not stop him if I know how, and except under really extraordinary circumstances I will know a variety of ways to stop him. But, by one version of the present hypothesis, God lacks that knowledge. So relative to preventing the evil of Jon's being hit by a car, I am smarter than God. But no being that I am smarter than, relative to preventing evil, is worthy of the name "God." Hence limiting divine knowledge to "solve" the problem of evil is no more successful than denying divine goodness.

Suppose instead that God's power is limited relative to preventing at least certain evils—God knows how to prevent them but lacks the ability to put that knowledge to work. But suppose Sharon's doctor knows that if she is getting a migraine, the appropriate strength pain pill plus strong sweet tea will prevent it, and typically the doctor has the power to provide both pill and tea. (There is no claim here that this treatment is successful other than hypothetically in an imaginary case.) On another version of the present hypothesis God lacks the power to so act, even though so acting would prevent evil. But no being that, relative to preventing an evil, has less power than the doctor does is worthy of the name "God." Things do not change materially if we grant God vastly more knowledge than any human has. The point to keep in mind is that for any evil God allows, on the finitist view, God may lack the knowledge to prevent it. On any account, given the evils that there are, this amounts to a very considerable degree of ignorance. Nor is it clear where to begin to claim that evils exist due to divine ignorance rather than God having some sufficient reason for allowing them. Similar remarks apply to limitations in divine power. A being appropriately limited in either or both ways is far different from God. Hence limiting divine power as a "solution" to the problem of evil is no more successful than is limiting divine knowledge.

More formally, we could follow a strategy of allowing that God could prevent any evils we could prevent but that God cannot prevent any evils we could not prevent, or any evil that required more knowledge than K or more power than P, where K represents some degree of knowledge way above what Einstein had but short of omniscience and P represent some degree of power way above that possessed by the world's strongest person but short of omnipotence. A condition of there being point to attempting some such distinction is that we have some reason to think that God could be justified in allowing the evils that can be prevented by someone who has knowledge up to degree K or power up to degree P but not be justified in allowing evils whose prevention would require more knowledge or power. So far as I know, no attempt has been made to do this, and there is no reason to think it a promising enterprise. Making the view more formal seems not to have any real advantage.

Summary Regarding a Finite Deity and Evil

The motivation to take refuge in the idea of a finite God—one limited in power and/or knowledge—can be motivated by this general assumption: the existence of an evil E is evidence against the existence of God unless it is the case that either (i) God lacks the power to prevent E or (ii) God lacks the knowledge to prevent E. Considering all the evil there is, the consequent limitation on divine power or divine knowledge is enormous. No being so limited in power or knowledge is God. It can also be motivated by a more nuanced assumption: the existence of an evil E is evidence against the existence of God unless it is the case that (i) God lacks the power to prevent E, (ii) God lacks the knowledge to prevent E, or (iii) God has a morally sufficient reason for allowing E. The actual evils that can be prevented by a being with power of degree P or degree of knowledge K are evils God has a morally sufficient reason for allowing; the actual evils that God has no morally sufficient reason for allowing are all evils whose prevention would require a degree of power beyond P and/or a degree of knowledge beyond K and God's power and knowledge end at P and K. The distinctions involved in this assumption are arbitrary; there is no reason to suppose that they correspond to any actual differences in evils, knowledge, and power.

Denying that there is evil, or so restricting one's notion of God so that God is morally imperfect or so limited in power or knowledge that preventing evil exceeds divine capacities, all are dead ends for monotheism. These "answers" to the claim that evil is evidence against monotheism are thinly disguised admissions to the charge. Monotheism has been right in firmly resisting these moves.

If the existence of evil is evidence against God's existence, this does not settle the issue as to whether God exists or as to whether it is reasonable to believe that God exists. There might, for example, be equally strong or stronger evidence in favor of God's existence. But the notion that the existence of evil actually is evidence against God's existence should not itself be accepted without careful examination. As we have noted, evil is evidence against there being a God only if (a) (E) *There is evil* and (G) *God exists* are logically incompatible or (b) if (E) plus some set S of discernible truths is logically incompatible with (G). But is either (a) or (b) true?

The Consistency Issue

Straightforward Inconsistency

One might claim that (E) and (G) are obviously logically incompatible. This claim is false. The Consistency Strategy tells us that if any three propositions A, B, and C are logically compatible, then any pair from that trio is also logically consistent provided none of A, B, or C itself is self-contradictory. Note that what a use of the Consistency Strategy can show is simply the logical compatibility of two propositions. A proper use of this strategy with regard to two propositions A and B will prove *Possibly, both A and B* are true. It will not, and is not intended to, prove that A is true or that B is true. With this limitation goes an advantage; one using the strategy need not prove that any of A, B, or C is true.

Consider, then, these propositions:

A1.   God exists.
B1.   If God allows an evil, then God has a morally sufficient reason for allowing it.
C1.   There is evil.

None of A1, B1, or C1 appear to be self-contradictory. Nor does the trio A1, B1, C1 appear to be an inconsistent set. But if none of A1, B1, and C1 is self-contradictory, and if [A1, B1, C1] is a consistent trio, then no pair of propositions from that trio are logically incompatible. One such pair is [A1, C1]. So A1 and C1 are not logically incompatible. But A1 is simply (G) *God exists* and C1 is simply *There is evil*. So *God exists* and (E) *There is evil* are not logically incompatible. Hence (a) is false. So if evil is evidence against God's existence, (B) must be true. Another use of the Consistency Strategy goes like this. Consider these propositions:
(G) God exists.
(EN) For any evil E that occurs to a person in lifetime N, E is the just consequence of wrong actions by that person in lifetime N or in her lifetimes prior to N.

(E)   There are evils.

What was true regarding the A1, B1, C1 trio seems also true of the G, EN, E trio, so it too seems to provide the basis for a successful use of the Consistency Strategy.

Problems with This Use of the Consistency Strategy?

There is a simple rule of logical inference that says this: If a proposition A plus some necessary truth N entails proposition B, then A by itself entails B. One who doubts the success of the use made of the Consistency Strategy in the preceding reasoning may try to find some necessary truth N that, together with (E), entails the denial of (G). Finding such a necessary truth would show that (G) and (E) are logically incompatible after all. Various candidates are available. Here are two:

N1.   Necessarily, if God creates at all, God will create the best possible world, and the best possible world will contain no evil.
N2.   Necessarily, a perfectly good being prevents evil insofar as it can, and an omnipotent and omniscient being can prevent any evil.

Will either of these do? (N1) or (N2) will do only if it is a necessary truth. Is (N1) a necessary truth? Is (N2) a necessary truth?

(N1) uses the notion of a best possible world—a world that contains as much moral worth as it is logically possible that a world contain.[3] Several questions arise regarding (N1). First, is the notion of a best possible world itself consistent, or is it like the notion of a highest possible integer? "I think the highest possible integer should be named Charlie" sounds fine until one remembers it is a necessary truth that *For any integer I, there is an integer I* such that I* is higher than I*; it is logically impossible that there be a highest integer. Anyone appealing to (N1) owes us an account of "best possible world" on which it is logically possible that there be such a thing. One that would not do, for example, is this: world W is the best possible world only if the number of good persons in that world is the same number as the highest possible integer. Second, (N1) requires that a best possible world contain no evil; according to (N1), the presence of evil in a world will rule it out as being the best possible. It isn't at all obvious that this is right. Suppose, for example, that any world possessed of great moral value will have virtuous agents in it—agents who are honest, brave, compassionate, and the like. But necessarily virtue is earned; one becomes virtuous of character by acting rightly again and again. For some virtues, at least, the relevant occasions of acting rightly require conquering one or another evil. Bravery requires that one have fear that one conquers; fortitude requires than one bear pain well, and hence that one bear pain; compassion presupposes suffering, and various saints offer the experiential report that so does moral and religious maturity. Perhaps some virtues require conquering evil, and some do not. But perhaps also one who has a full quiver of virtues has among them the ones that require that they been earned through conquered evil, and in the best possible world everyone's quiver of virtues will be filled with all virtue's varieties. So maybe the best possible world would contain evil after all. Third, suppose the best possible world will contain moral agents who act only freely and rightly, and that if an agent acts freely then that agent is not merely acting in the way God has built into her that she act. In the strictest sense, to create a world W is to fiat W—to so act that W obtains simply as a result of one's having so acted. But then the free actions of a created moral agent cannot themselves be created by God; if God fiats that Eve speaks truly, Eve does not freely speak truly. So perhaps, even should there be some notion of a best possible world that is not self-contradictory, that world is one that God cannot fiat—cannot, strictly speaking, create—because it is logically impossible that this be done. But then it is false that, strictly speaking, if God creates then God creates the best possible world. Fourth, there is an argument to the effect that there being a best possible world is not compatible with God being omnicompetent. The idea is that God is omnicompetent entails *No world God created would exhaust God's competence* or *For any world W that God created, God could create a world W* such that W* was better than W.* There is reason, then, to be dubious about the claim that (N1) *Necessarily, if God creates at all, God will create the best possible world, and the best possible world will contain no evil is a necessary truth.*

Perhaps things will go better if we appeal to:

N2.   Necessarily, a perfectly good being prevents evil insofar as it can, and an omnipotent and omniscient being can prevent any evil.

Reflection about (N2) brings us back to at least one of the considerations already raised regarding (N1). If a best possible world can contain evil, why think that a perfectly good and omnicompetent God would not permit evil?

There are other problems with (N2). Let the partial description of a possible person [a PDPP] be a description of a set of fully determinate properties such that, were God to, strictly speaking, create—i.e., fiat—something having those properties, God would have fiated a person. To each PDPP X, one might say, there will correspond a person if God chooses to follow the recipe that X contains. Suppose that for each PDPP X there is a truth about how the corresponding person would act if she was created. Whatever the truth is, if there is one, about whether there is any PDPP whose corresponding person would always freely act rightly, that truth is not a necessary truth. Suppose, finally, that the logically contingent fact of the matter is that there is no PDPP whose corresponding person, were she created, would always freely act rightly. A world possessing the highest possible moral worth, or any reasonable facsimile, will contain moral agents; if the truth is as assumed, then in creating moral agents to populate the best possible world, God is creating agents whose choices will introduce evil into that world. Since it is logically possible that the truth be as we have assumed, and logically necessary that the best possible world contain moral agents, it is logically possible that the best possible world contain agents who act wrongly, thereby introducing evil into that world. Hence it is not a logically necessary truth that the best possible world contains no evil. Nor is it a necessary truth that a morally perfect omnicompetent being cannot permit evil. But then neither (N1) nor (N2) is true; hence neither is the logically necessary truth that the critic sought to pair off with (E) *There is evil* for the purpose of deriving the denial of (G) *God exists*. Nor is either the basis for a successful challenge to the Consistency Strategy.[4]

The Evidential Issue

Logical Consistency with Evidential Conflict

It is not logically inconsistent of one to believe that almost no residents of Madison, Wisconsin, would vote for Prince Charles as President of the United States, that Kim is a resident of Madison, and that Kim would vote for Prince Charles as President. But if one has no particular reason to think that Kim relevantly differs from her fellow Madisonians, one believes against the evidence when one picks her as a Prince Charles supporter. *Proposition A is logically consistent with proposition B* and *The truth of proposition A is evidence that proposition B is false* are not themselves logically incompatible claims. We have found no reason to think that the existence of evil is logically incompatible with God's existence. The remaining question concerns whether nonetheless the existence of evil is evidence against the existence of God. If there being evil counts against there being a God only if either (a) (E) *There is evil* and (G) *God exists* are logically incompatible, or (b) if (E) plus some set S of discernible truths is logically incompatible with (G), and (a) is false, there remains (b). The discernible truths added to (E) need not be necessary truths; any old truths will do. Are there any?

Those who answer affirmatively take it that the existence of evil is something not to be expected if a morally perfect and omnicompetent God created the world. If Aunt Lucy is an exquisite housekeeper, and one must choose whether she is staying in guest room 21 that is neat as a pin or in guest room 22 whose floor is invisible under dirty clothing, while it is logically possible that she is staying in 22, odds are Aunt Lucy is staying in 21. If God created the world, perhaps it is logically possible that there be evils in it; but odds are there won't be. So (roughly) the assumption goes. Is the assumption right? There is at least this much to be said for the assumption. For typical monotheisms, the present state of the world is not such as to make God overly pleased; the prayer "Thy will be done, on earth as it is in heaven" has not exactly received a full answer yet. Critic and theist agree that things are not as a morally perfect and omnicompetent being would wish them to be. In Judeo-Christian terms, our world is a "fallen" world. The question remains whether the existence of evil is evidence against the existence of God.

Those who follow the strategy of seeking some set of non-necessary or logically contingent truths that, together with (E) *There is evil*, entail not-(G) *God does not exist*, tend to appeal to claims about our knowledge and what is reasonable to accept in its light. The following argument provides a simple illustration. Let an evil whose purpose, if any, is unknown to us be an apparently pointless evil.

A Simple Argument

1. There are apparently pointless evils.
2. The Apparently Pointless Evil Claim: If there are apparently pointless evils, then God does not exist.
3. God does not exist. [from 1, 2] The first premise is patently true. The conclusion follows from the premises. So the question is whether the second premise—The Apparently Pointless Evil Claim—is true. The idea behind this claim apparently is this:

  2a. The Actually Pointless Evil Claim: God would not allow actually pointless evils.
  2b. The We Would Know Claim: If an evil has a point, it will be apparent to us.

  Then it follows that:
  2c. God would not allow any evils that are apparently pointless.

And from 2c and 1 we can infer 3—the claim that God does not exist. Suppose, then, that the truth of 2a and 2b is intended as the necessary and sufficient conditions of the truth of The Apparently Pointless Evil Claim—that 2a and 2b provide both background assumptions and presuppositions of it. Then if either 2a or 2b is false, 2 will lack justification. If we have no reason to think 2a (The Actually Pointless Evil Claim) is true, or no reason to think 2b (The We Would Know Claim) true, then we will have no reason to think The Apparently Pointless Evil Claim true.

In our discussion of these matters, we will focus almost entirely on The We Would Know Claim. The question as to whether God would allow actually pointless evils is very difficult to answer, and we will not argue either for or against it. The critic obviously needs it for his argument to succeed. We will suspend judgment here regarding its truth, and discuss its meaning only to the degree that this is helpful in getting clear about The We Would Know Claim.[5]

Let us begin, then, with The We Would Know Claim. Would we know it if an evil has a point? The purposes of an omnicompetent being might well be beyond our comprehension. Hence there is no reason whatever to think that if God allows an evil E in the light of E's having a certain point P, we will know what P is. So there is no reason whatever to think The We Would Know Claim is true. Hence there is no reason whatever to suppose that The Apparently Pointless Evil Claim is true. Since we have no reason to accept The We Would Know Claim, we have no reason to think that The Apparently Pointless Evil Claim is true. Hence the Simple Argument fails. There is, however, a more sophisticated argument right next door.

A More Sophisticated Argument

It is true that, for lots of evils, we have no idea what their point, if any, actually is. What point does someone's having a migraine, a stomach ulcer, cancer, or the inability to speak have? Even if we are able to say in general what might serve as a rationale for a morally perfect omnicompetent being allowing evils, and even for allowing certain specific kinds of evils, we are not in a position to say things that would result from filling in sentences like this with the names of actual persons and actual evils in this schema: the reason why person X experienced evil Y is that the point of evil Y is Z. Doing so would presuppose a degree of knowledge we do not have. There are also evils that it is hard to say even what their point might be.

Suppose, then, we divide evils into two broad and admittedly ill-defined classes: those kinds of evils for which we can at least imagine some point, and those for which we cannot. Call these very loosely defined classes of kind of evil, respectively, imaginably pointful and unimaginably pointful. Perhaps suffering that turns a miserably selfish person into a person of compassion falls into the former class; perhaps so does even a miserably selfish person being allowed to suffer as a way of providing her an opportunity to become compassionate. Perhaps an accident that renders irrevocably comatose a loving wife and mother whose community activities alleviated much suffering falls into the class of unimaginably pointful evils.

The class of imaginably pointful evils can be further divided into those where nothing we know about a particular case renders it unavailable for being pointful in the imagined way, and cases where this is ruled out by what we know. Suppose two stingy hoarders face death by freezing and are discovered just in time to save their lives. The one becomes generous and charitable, but the other has been so completely conditioned to be mean about money that even his being rescued by Red Cross workers does not make him any more willing to be charitable. One might think of the suffering the first hoarder endured as having a point in its positive results on his character, but the latter hoarder was so set in his ways that changing was not an option, even if he nearly froze to death. Let the former sort of case be imaginably and contextually pointful and the latter sort of case be imaginably, but not contextually, pointful. A rough informal characterization of the sense of these terms is this: an imaginably and contextually pointful evil is one that, so far as we know, may occur to a person under conditions in which the evil serves some morally sufficient point—some point such that a perfectly good being who allowed the evil to occur in order that the point be served at least arguably acted rightly in so doing. An imaginably, but not contextually, pointful evil is one that might occur to a person under conditions in which the evil serves some morally sufficient point—some point such that a perfectly good being who allowed the evil to occur in order that the point be served acted rightly in so doing, but we know something about the circumstances in which the evil occurred that prevents them from being conditions of this sort. An evil is unimaginably pointful if after considerable effort we still cannot think of any condition under which the occurrence of that sort of evil might serve some morally sufficient point—some point such that a perfectly good being who allowed the evil to occur in order that the point be served acted rightly in so doing. (We leave aside the possible consideration that this hoarder is owed a chance to reform even if it is known that he will not profit by it.)

A more formal characterization of these rough distinctions can be expressed along these lines:

D1.   An evil E is imaginably and contextually pointful relative to person S if and only if (a) we can describe a condition C such that if S is in C and endures E, it is possible that her doing so will be a necessary condition of S coming to have property Q, where S's having Q is a sufficiently good state of affairs that one who allowed S to endure E for the sake of S coming to have Q would be morally justified in so doing, and (b) nothing we know about S is incompatible with S's actually being in C when S endured E.

D2.   An evil E is imaginably but not contextually pointful relative to person S if and only if (a) we can a describe condition C such that if S is in C and endures E, it is possible that her doing so will be a necessary condition of S coming to have property Q, where S's having Q is a sufficiently good state of affairs that one who allowed S to endure E for the sake of S coming to have Q would be morally justified in so doing, and (b) something we know about S is incompatible with S's actually being in C when S endured E.

By contrast:

D3.   An evil E is unimaginably pointful relative to person S if and only if we cannot describe a condition C such that if S is in C and endures E, it is possible that her doing so will be a necessary condition of S coming to have property Q, where S's having Q is a sufficiently good state of affairs that one who allowed S to endure E for the sake of S coming to have Q would be morally justified in so doing.

Imaginably and contextually pointful evils are the least plausible candidates for use in an attempt to derive not-(G) *God does not exist* from (E) *There is evil*. Thus we will consider arguments that deal with the notions of the other sorts of evils. One might begin, then, with these reflections and offer either of the following arguments.

The "Imaginably but Not Contextually Pointful" Argument

1*.   There are imaginably but not contextually pointful evils.
2*.   If there are imaginably but not contextually pointful evils then there are actually pointless evils.
3*.   There are actually pointless evils. [from 2*, 3*]
4*.   If there are actually pointless evils, then God does not exist.
5*.   God does not exist.

The key premises in this argument are (2*) and (4*); we will first consider (2*). It assumes that some restricted version of The We Would Know Claim is true—it requires only that there are some evils—at least one—such that we could tell that if it was contextually pointful, we could discern this, and we can tell that some evil lacks this feature. Even if, as we argued above, the unrestricted version is false, this restricted version might be true. Since it approves the inference from

'There are imaginably but not contextually pointful evils' to 'There are pointless evils,' what it says is tantamount to 'Evils that are not contextually pointful are actually pointless.' Is that true?

The other, similar argument is: The "Unimaginably Pointful" Argument

1**. There are unimaginably pointful evils.
2**. If there are unimaginably pointful evils then there are actually pointless evils.
3*. There are actually pointless evils. [from 1**, 2**]
4*. If there are actually pointless evils, then God does not exist.
5*. God does not exist. [from 3*, 4*]

The key premises of this argument are (2**) and (4**); we will first consider (2**). It assumes that at least for some evil—at least one—we can via imagination tell what point, if any, an evil has, and we can discern it has none. It is a differently restricted version of The We Would Know Claim. Even if, as we argued above, the unrestricted version is false, this restricted version might be true. Since it approves the inference from *There are unimaginably pointful evils* to *There are pointless evils*, what it says is tantamount to *Evils that are unimaginably pointful are actually pointless*. Is that true?

Concerning premise 2* of the Imaginably but Not Contextually Pointful Argument, *Evils that are not contextually pointful are actually pointless*, consider the following:

Suppose, for the sake of the argument, that premise 1* is true. This helps the critic only if premise 2* is also true. Granting premise 1* grants this: there are evils that may have some point, but no point we can think of that they might have is compatible with what seems true about the circumstances in which they occur. What premise 2* says is that if there are evils that may have some point, but no point we can think of that they might have is compatible with what seems true about the circumstances in which they occur, then there is no point that they do serve.

Suppose a man wears a paper bag on his head. While either the man has a mustache, or he does not, so long as the bag is over his head it is neither apparent that he does nor apparent that he does not; we just can't see. Similarly, while either an evil has a point or it does not, it is possible that we cannot tell which is the case. Competitive to premise 2*, then, is (2a*) *If there are imaginably but not contextually pointful evils then there are evils regarding which we should suspend judgment as to whether or not they actually have a point*. The relevant point is that the claim that we know, concerning at least one sort of, or even one, evil is such that no context in which it would make it pointful that actually obtains is highly implausible. The appeal here is not to mystery. Consider the claim that there are now exactly three people, neither more nor less, that are eating exactly .0031 ounces of dark chocolate before drinking exactly .33 of an ounce of Builder's tea. Whether this is so is not a mystery. But we are not going to tell if it is true. Or consider an area X in which dinosaurs once roamed and the claim that a baby Triceratops weighing exactly ninety pounds slept for six hours on point P within X on what we would date a Tuesday beginning at three a.m. Lack of data does not a mystery make. Nor do probability matters arise. For one thing, the critic's argument assumes a necessary connection between God existing and there being no pointless evils. For another, that there are so many Xs is not by itself evidence that some Xs are Ys, and the implausibility of our being able to identity lack of context pointfulness even it exists has been noted. Still further, there are hosts of counterexamples to the 'so many Xs, some are Ys' idea, even where it is logical that an X be a Y. Let N be the height of the tallest person who ever exists. Then it is possible that some person grow to N plus .01 inches, but no one will be. Where premise (2*) counsels a specific conclusion (there are pointless evils), its competitor (2a*) commends suspense of judgment regarding that conclusion. Not surprisingly, the same issue comes up again regarding the unimaginably pointful argument.

Concerning premise 2** of the Unimaginably Pointful Argument, *Evils that are unimaginably pointful are actually pointless*, consider this argument:
2**. If there are unimaginably pointful evils then there are actually pointless evils.
What this premise tells us is that if we cannot even imagine what point an evil of a certain kind might have, then it has no point. Competitive to 2** is:
2a**. If there are unimaginably pointful evils then there are evils regarding which we should suspend judgment as to whether or not they actually have a point.
Whereas (2**) counsels a specific conclusion (there are pointless evils), its competitor (2a**) commends suspense of judgment regarding that conclusion. Strictly, all that a defense requires here is that the "suspense of judgment" claim be as reasonably believed as the "actually has no point" claim, and the same goes for the preceding pair of competing claims. That there is equity of reasonability seems highly plausible. An essential element in one influential attempt to move from (E) *There is evil* to not-(G) *God does not exist* is premise (2*) (as against 2a*), and premise (2**) (as against 2a**), or some closely analogous claim. Is it (2*) or (2**), rather than (2a*) or (2a**), that are true? Perhaps the best way to decide is to consider the sort of case that makes premises like (2*) and (2**) plausible if anything does. We have argued that the scales here are not weighted in the critic's favor.

There is another argument that approaches our topic from a different angle. Its conclusion is that monotheists are inconsistent in their moral judgments. It rests on some such claim as:

(J) If one person judges another person to be acting wrongly in a given circumstance, but judges another person as not acting wrongly even though she acts in a way not morally relevantly different and in a circumstance not morally relevantly different, then she judges inconsistently.

This is a necessarily true claim. Then the idea is that monotheists do exactly this. If you can rescue a drowning child without danger to yourself, and simply stand aside and watch, you are guilty of failing to do what is right. But if you fail to do what is right, and monotheism is true, God too fails to do what is right. Yet monotheists do not judge God as having failed to do God's duty. (We assume here that God has duties to God's creatures in virtue of having created them in God's image.) So they are inconsistent in the moral judgments that they make. The reply to this objection is to make a necessary revision to (J) as follows:

> (J*) If one person judges another person to be acting wrongly in a given circumstance, but judges another person as not acting wrongly even though she acts in a way not morally relevantly different and in a circumstance not morally relevantly different, then she judges inconsistently, provided the relevant knowledge and powers of both persons fall within the range available to human agents.

The child is beyond all influence on our part once it has drowned. If monotheism is true, it is not beyond God's power. This simple case illustrates various features relevant to our discussion. The critic is very likely to accuse the believer of cheating by bringing in assumptions for which no justification has been offered. The believer will view herself as simply referring to features of her view of the world that are relevant to the charge against her, and point out that the critic, in using (J) against her, has assumed that those features of her view are false. Each argues from the place at which she begins to her conclusion. Given her belief in God's knowledge and power, the believer is not inconsistent in making the judgments she makes. Remove that—that is, ceasing to be a monotheist—the believer would become inconsistent in her judgments. But then, no longer being a monotheist, she presumably would not make any judgments concerning God and God's duties. While there are other ways of putting the objection from to theism from evil, the ones canvassed here are representative. None of them seem successful.[6]

Another argument has recently been offered that is different from those already considered in that it rests on something being absent from the world rather than there existing evils in it. We close this chapter by considering it. J. L. Schellenberg, in *The Wisdom to Doubt* writes:

> What we find, then, through careful reasoning and consideration of the heart and soul of love, in the context of more general considerations about God and creation and the need for thinking unrestricted by traditional theology, is that the existence of non-resistant belief *shows the non-existence of God*.[7]

When it comes to unjustified belief his target is Ultimism—the view that there is something ontologically basic and maximally valuable, proper relation to which constitutes our highest good. What prevents us from rationally having any Ultimist or anti-Ultimist belief is the presence in human history and contemporary life of four "modes."

Subject Mode: We are finite, prone to pride, intellectual greed, insecurity, and a host of other foibles that incline us to overrate evidence for claims we like, and to disregard alternatives. Our finitude and foibles make for evidential distortion, especially regarding propositions that are precise, detailed, profound, and attractive. This mode alone "can make short work of the claim that religious belief, or that irreligious belief, is justified" (47).

Object Mode: The proposed Ultimate would be "infinitely profound" and thus "beyond belief." (51). The depth and complexity of the ultimate, if it exists, are grounds for skepticism as to purported knowledge thereof.

Retrospective Mode: Humanity has had only a relatively short period in which to (in some sense) investigate Ultimism. Even that has been characterized by narrow loyalties, intellectual hubris, partisan violence, mistaken values, authoritarian institutions, emotional attractions that have no positive relation to evidence or truth seeking, and poor intellectual practices.

Prospective Mode: Even if our present evidence supported one sort of Ultimism, this would not justify the claim that our present evidence was representative.

Consider two principles of proper belief:

B1.   S properly believes that proposition P is true if and only if S has evidence for P, and no evidence against P—if she goes along with the evidence she has.

B2.   S properly believes that proposition P is true if and only if S has evidence for P, no evidence against P, and knows her evidence for P is representative of the overall evidence regarding P, knows that P has no alternatives that may have evidence that may have unrecognized evidence on their behalf, which evidence may be known but its relevance unnoted, accessible now but unknown, is inaccessible now but accessible in the future, or is inaccessible in the future.

Then ask the obvious question: How, given the modes, is one to justifiably hold B2 rather than B1? Even if one claims that we cannot justifiably decide between them, this leaves Schellenberg without B2, which is an essential element in his argument. While this point is worth pursuing, by itself it leaves the proposed skepticism unjustified.

Our primary concern here, however, is with his claim to have refuted theism, and Christianity in particular. He begins with a premise that a Christian is likely to grant, and continues to his atheistic conclusion:

1.   If God exists, then God will efficaciously will that every person who does not reject God has a loving personal relationship with God.
2.   Not every person who does not reject God has a loving personal relationship with God.

Therefore:

3.   God does not exist.

The argument has a simple, valid form. Thus the question concerns the truth of the premises.

It also concerns whether 2 is known to be true—whether, that is, that the following is known:

S. Schellenberg knows that not everyone who does not reject God has a personal, loving personal relationship with God—that is he has evidence for this claim, no evidence against it, knows his evidence for it is representative of the overall evidence regarding it, knows that it has no alternatives that may have evidence that may have unrecognized evidence regarding this claim, which evidence may be known but its relevance unnoted, accessible now but unknown, inaccessible now but accessible in the future, or inaccessible in the future.

Schellenberg raises an issue relevant to 2 when he argues from divine hiddenness. The idea is that were a loving God to exist, God would make the divine existence far more evident than it is. God's not being more evident is reason to think God is not there.

This objection has interested Paul K. Moser,[8] and while he is not specifically answering Schellenberg, his position is relevant.[9] Moser agrees with premise 1. He rejects premise 2 and challenges the claim that God is objectionably hidden. Moser's view requires there to be genuine good and obligations, there independent of our opinions. Schellenberg has no quarrel with this. Moser holds that the natural theology arguments for God are not of great religious interest. At best, they justify spectator belief. Suppose one or more of them does prove that God exists. One can then think *Well, that is one philosophical question settled; what is next?* without having been challenged to make any religious commitment whatever. The God of Christianity is not centrally to be found through spectator knowledge. God is primarily if not only to be found through experience that existentially challenges its subject to change—to become more loving, even to the point of loving one's enemies. The idea is that in moral experience, one can have the sense of being bound by an obligation not of one's own making, of being called to obedience to an authority with the right to command. God's revelations to us should be seen in terms of their purpose, namely to lead us into a relationship with God that changes us. This comes largely through the conscience, not through abstract reflection. Gains in knowledge come through obedience. How explicit the sense of the presence of a person need be at the outset does not greatly matter so long as, in the long run, a personal relationship is established. But failing to respond favorably to conscience prevents the relationship from developing. Moser's view is that Christianity has a built-in epistemology: God is knowable via experience that requires positive response, not merely intellectual assent. If this epistemology is ignored, then God's hiddenness in spectator terms will seem a powerful objection, but that is to approach Christianity on assumptions that already misconstrue what can rightly be expected of a Christian God.

The dispute over the hiddenness of God, then, has epistemological dimensions—is 2 true or justifiably believed? It has an ethical dimension—what is proper to expect of a loving God? It has a theological dimension—how is hiddenness related the nature of God? But given what has been said here, it seems fair to say that it is dubious that we should be confident that premise 2 in the 1–3 argument for atheism is either true or justifiably believed, either given the modes (and so as part of Schellenberg's overall argument) or as part of a more limited argument from hiddenness (given the difficulty of knowing what can legitimately be claimed concerning how someone has responded and will respond to one's moral experience). To appeal to a tiny bit of one Schellenbergian mode, we are most apt to deceive ourselves about ourselves in such matters.

Questions for Reflection

1. What makes offering a very fully filled out theodicy so difficult?
2. Are any of the attempts to show that it is logically inconsistent to believe that God exists and there is evil successful?
3. Is the notion of a best possible world coherent? What hangs on the answer to this question?
4. Is there a clear victor in the debate over evils whose point, if any, we cannot discern?
5. Is the theist inconsistent in her moral judgments regarding God and human beings?

Notes

1. Reincarnation and karma are not part of Semitic monotheism. In Hindu monotheism they operate under divine will, and karma can be broken by divine forgiveness.
2. There seems no way to guarantee that one has considered even every type of anti-theistic argument from evil, let alone every argument of every type. The best one can do is take representative examples. The same is true for arguments for God's existence.
3. For two reasons we leave aside other sorts of value, for example aesthetic. First, for simplicity. Second, it seems to the author at least that for a consistent monotheism, moral considerations considerably outweigh aesthetic.
4. It is, one hopes, obvious that the Consistency Strategy is a truth of logic quite independent of the issues to which it is applied.
5. The crux of the matter here lies in making clear what the conditions of pointlessness are. That an event occur that God did not plan for, supposing this to be possible, it only follows that God did not have a plan in mind for allowing that evil, not that God cannot give point to the evil's occurrence. Of course it would be widely denied that God could be surprised.
6. One approach to the topic of this chapter is to find it offensive to even consider. What would be offensive would be to offer the arguments of this chapter to any but the rarest of sufferers as of any real help in their suffering. That would, in almost any conceivable circumstance, be an instance of the problem we have discussed. The present author once gave a lecture on the problem of evil to an audience of college students where one coed had just lost her beloved husband, and she left the lecture in tears. Philosophy has its uses. I do not believe it is insensitive to offer the arguments of this chapter. I do believe it would be insensitive to offer them in place of compassion.
7. *The Wisdom to Doubt: A Justification of Religious Scepticism* (Ithaca, NY: Cornell, 2012), p. 206 (my italics). Strictly, Schellenberg offers two relevant claims: that religious (and naturalistic) belief are unjustified, and that theism is false. We will deal with both here.
8. See Daniel Howard Snyder and Paul K. Moser (2001) *Divine Hiddenness* (Cambridge: Cambridge University Press); J.L. Schellenberg (2006) *Divine Hiddenness and Human Reason* (Ithaca, NY: Cornell); J.L. Schellenberg (2009) *The Will to Imagine: A Justification of Skeptical Religion* (Ithaca, NY: Cornell).
9. Paul K. Moser (2012) *The Elusive God: Reorienting Religious Epistemology* (Cambridge: Cambridge University Press).

Suggested Readings

Adams, Marilyn McCord (2000) *Horrendous Evils and the Goodness of God* (Ithaca, NY: Cornell). Focuses on what God might bring out of horrific evils that would make sense of their existence in a world created and governed by a God who could prevent them.

Griffiths, Paul (1983) "Notes toward a critique of Buddhist karmic theory," *Religious Studies*, Vol. 18, No. 3, pp. 277–291. Argues that Buddhist karmic doctrine is incompatible with what we learn from contemporary physics.

Herman, Arthur (1976) *The Problem of Evil in Indian Thought* (Delhi: Motilal Barnasidas). A consideration of the idea that karmic theory allows one to solve the alleged problem of evil.

Leaman, Oliver (1995) *Evil and Suffering in Jewish Philosophy* (Cambridge: Cambridge University Press). A fine discussion of Jewish approaches to the alleged problem of evil.

Mackie, J.L. (1982) *The Miracle of Theism* (Oxford: Clarendon Press). A clear general critique of monotheism; the "miracle" is that anyone is a theist.

McBrayer, Justin and Howard-Snyder, Daniel (2003) *The Blackwell Companion to the Problem of Evil* (Hoboken, NJ: Wiley-Blackwell). Excellent selections, including a section on religion-specific theodicies—as good an anthology is you are going to find.

Ormsby, Eric (1984) *Theodicy in Islamic Thought* (Princeton: Princeton University Press). A fine discussion of Islamic approaches to the alleged problem of evil.

Pike, Nelson, ed. (1964) *God and Evil* (Englewood Cliffs, NJ: Prentice Hall). A good collection of articles that helped frame contemporary discussions.

Plantinga, Alvin (1977) *God, Freedom, and Evil* (Grand Rapids, MI: Eerdmans; reprint of 1974 edition). A detailed clear discussion of the relevance of human freedom to the alleged problem of evil.

Reichenback, Bruce (1990) *The Law of Karma* (Honolulu, HI: University of Hawaii Press). An account and critique of the doctrine of karma.

Rowe, William, ed. (2001) *God and the Problem of Evil* (Hoboken, NJ: Blackwell). A collection of excellent papers on main aspects of the problem.

Stump, Eleonore (2012) *Wandering in Darkness: Narrative and the Problem of Suffering* (Oxford). Arguing that some philosophical problems are best approached through narrative, updates the theodicy of Aquinas.

Trakakis, Nick (2006) *The God Beyond Belief: In Defense of William Rowe's Evidential Argument From Evil* (Berlin, Germany: Springer). A vigorous defense of Rowe's argument that there is no theistic solution to the problem of evil that takes into account the considerable literature on the topic.

Van Inwagen, Peter (2008) *The Problem of Evil* (Oxford: Oxford University Press). Explaining what makes a philosophical argument that inferences from suffering to the falsehood of theism are failures.

10 Arguments for Monotheism

Proof

Proof is a complex notion. In simplest terms, a proof is a valid argument with true premises. This is the standard notion of 'proof' in logic. An argument consists of premises intended to provide support for a conclusion. An argument is valid if it is logically impossible that the premises be true and the conclusion be false.[1] Any argument of the form *If A then B; A, therefore B*, for example, will be valid. An argument is sound if it has all true premises.

Given this basic notion of a proof, the contemporary philosopher George Mavrodes has noted that one of the following arguments is a proof and the other is not:[2]

Argument A

1. Either God exists or nothing exists.
2. Something exists.
So: 3. God exists.

Argument B

1*. Either God does not exist or nothing exists.
2. Something exists.
So: 3* God does not exist.[3]

Premises 1 and 1* are disjunctions—they have the forms, respectively, *Either G or N* and *Either not-G or N*. It is false that nothing exists, so the *N* disjunct is false. Necessarily, either God exists or God does not exist; either *G* is true or else *not-G* is true. A disjunction is true so long as at least one of its members is true. So either 1 is true or else 1* is true. Premise 2, which appears in both arguments, is true. Both arguments are valid. Argument A has the form: (1) Either G or N; (2) Not-N; so G. Argument B has the form: (1*) Not-G or N; (2) Not-N; so (3*) Not-G. Thus either Argument A is valid and has only true premises or Argument B is valid and has only true premises. Exactly one of these arguments is a proof in the sense of *proof* in logic—one of these arguments not only is valid but also has only true premises.

The problem is that unless we know, independently of these arguments, whether God exists, we cannot tell which argument is a proof. While the notion of a logical proof is perfectly proper for some purposes, having a proof in that, and no stronger, sense for some conclusion C is of no help in deciding whether C is true. What one needs is sufficient reason for taking argument A rather than argument B, or B rather than A, to be sound. Mavrodes notes that we need a notion of *a proof that extends our knowledge*, perhaps along these lines. *Argument A is an argument that extends our knowledge relative to its conclusion C only if:* (i) *A* is a proof in logic; (ii) we know that *A* is valid (that its premises entail its conclusion); (iii) we know that *A* is sound (that its premises are true); (iv) for each premise P of *A*, we can know whether or not P is true without having to know whether *C* is true (our knowledge of each of the argument's premises is independent of our knowing whether the argument's conclusion is true); (v) for the conjunct of all of the premises of *A* (premise one *and* premise two *and* premise three, etc.) we can know whether or not that conjunct is true without having to know whether *C* is true (our knowledge of all of the argument's premises together is independent of our knowing whether the argument's conclusion is true); (vi) for each premise P of *A*, our knowledge of P is better founded than our knowledge of *C*; (vii) for the conjunct of all of the premises of *A* (premise one *and* premise two *and* premise three, etc.), our knowledge of that conjunct is better founded than our knowledge of *C*. This, or something much like it, is the sense of "proof" in which we seek proofs that religious beliefs are true. In what follows, we will consider some of the more interesting of the many attempts to provide such proofs.

Types of Propositions

Something *has truth value* if and only if it is *either true or false*. Anything that has truth value is a *proposition*. Declarative sentences, typically used, *express* propositions; the same proposition can be expressed by various sentences in the same language or by various sentences in different languages. Thus 'The man is old and asleep, and the woman is reading' and 'The old man is asleep, and the woman is reading' are different sentences that typically express the same proposition. A proposition is either:

1. *Necessarily true* (P is a necessary truth if and only if not-P is a contradiction—e.g., *Nothing has logically incompatible properties* is a necessary truth.)
2. *Necessarily false* (P is necessarily false if and only if P is a contradiction—e.g., *Bill Russell is exactly 6'9" tall, and is not exactly 6'9" tall* is a necessary falsehood.)[4]
3. *Logically contingent* (P is logically contingent if and only if it is neither necessarily true nor necessarily false; a logically contingent proposition may be true or it may be false—e.g., *Bill Russell is exactly 6'9" tall* is a logically contingent proposition.)

Further:
4.   A proposition P is *possibly true* if and only if P is not a necessary falsehood—every necessary truth, and every logically contingent proposition, is possibly true.

Logical Necessity

Since there are different views about logical necessity, and different meanings assigned to the words 'logically necessary proposition,' a brief explanation is in order as to how logical necessity is understood here.[5]

Logical necessity is a feature of propositions, not sentences; it is not an artifact of our language or thought, and coming to see that a proposition is necessarily true is a discovery, not an invention or a discovery about our inventions. The reason for this is that necessary truths are not possibly false. Anything whose truth depends on our language or our conventions is possibly false, for our language and our conventions might never have existed at all. So neither the necessity nor the truth of necessary truths depend on our language or our conventions. Such truths are true under all conditions, and hence true in all possible worlds and across all possible cultures.

The prime example of a necessary truth in the history of philosophy is the principle of non-contradiction, which as Aristotle said is a principle both of thought and of things. It can be expressed as *Necessarily, no proposition is both true and false* or as *Necessarily, no thing can have logically incompatible properties*. These ways of putting the principle are mutually entailing; if something could have incompatible properties then propositions could be both true and false and if propositions could be both true and false then the proposition that a thing had incompatible properties could be true and so a thing could have incompatible properties.

Many contemporary philosophers, using the language of some Medieval philosophers, distinguish between *necessity de dicto* and *necessity de re*—necessity in speech and necessity in things. Suppose that Tony is a local barber and consider two sentences about him:

A.   Necessarily, Tony is a person.
B.   Tony is necessarily a person.

These sentences express different propositions. What A says is this:

A1.   Tony is a person, and it is logically impossible that Tony not be a person.

This entails:

A2.   Necessarily, Tony exists.

Of course A2 is false; however much he and his skills might be missed, Tony does not enjoy logically necessary existence. There are possible conditions in which, or possible worlds in which, Tony would not exist. No doubt for a very long time our own world was Tonyless.

What B says is this:

B1.   Tony is a person, and anything that is a person is a person so long as it exists at all; *being a person* entails *being a person necessarily* because *being a person* (unlike *being a Democrat* or *having false teeth*) is an essential property of anything that has it.

To embrace the idea that there are *necessities de re* one must think that there are essential properties or essences. B1, and hence B, is true if this idea is true; if there are essential properties or essences, *being a person* is among them.

Unfortunately (something its users do not intend) the language that contrasts *de dicto* (of speech) and *de re* necessity can easily suggest that there is one thing—say, logical necessity—and another thing—say, metaphysical necessity—and that the former is relative to language and the latter, if it exists at all, is a human-mind-independent thing. In fact, those philosophers who favor the view that there are both *necessities de dicto* and *necessities de re* view things very differently. To speak of the necessity of a dictum is to speak of the necessity not of an asserted declarative sentence but of what is asserted by that sentence—of a proposition. Necessarily true propositions, on their view, are human-mind-independently necessary and human-mind-independently true. They no more depend for their necessity or their truth on us than do *necessities de re*. There are *necessities de re* only if there are essences. One can summarily put the point like this: there are necessarily true propositions, and if there are essences, some of those necessarily true propositions will be necessarily true about essences, including some conditional necessary truths about things that have those essences to the effect that they necessarily have them if they have them at all. For example, it is true of Tony that:

B.   Tony is necessarily a person.

and that:

A*.   If Tony is necessarily a person, then the proposition *If Tony exists then Tony is a person* is a necessary truth.

Proposition B expresses a *de re* necessity. Proposition A* expresses a *de dicto* necessity.

If something X lacks logically necessary existence, then even if it has an essence E, it is not a logically necessary truth that X has E, because it is not a logically necessary truth that X exists. What is necessarily true is this: if thing X exists, and if the essence of an X is E, then X necessarily has E.

Assuming they exist at all, *necessity de dicto* is no less metaphysical than *necessity de re*—no less language-and-convention independent, no less human-mind independent, though how it is expressed is language-and-convention dependent. There being *necessities de dicto* does not require that there are essences; there are *necessities de re* only if there are essences. If they exist at all, *de re* necessities are logical necessities among things—things including but not limited to propositions. If they exist at all, *de dicto* necessities are logical necessities only of things that are propositions.

A final point on this topic. Suppose that *Water is essentially H20* is true. Then *If water exists it necessarily is H20* pairs up with *Necessarily, if water exists, it is H20*. To each *necessity de re* there corresponds a *necessity de dicto* expressible in a corresponding conditional statement. If things have essences, then insofar as our concepts of things are accurate regarding their essences, those concepts will enable us to see *de dicto* as well as *de re* necessities.

This account of necessity is controversial and a defense of it would be lengthy and complex,[6] and though I think it is also successful the purpose of presenting it is simply to explain what is meant here by logical necessity. It is an appropriate meaning for use in discussing the Ontological Argument.

Two points need to be added. One is that necessity as truth in all possible worlds is not the same as, though it includes, formally necessary truths. A formally necessary truth has a formally necessary falsehood as its contradictory. Thus *There is nothing that is round and not round at the same time and in the same respect* is symbolized roughly as *There is no x that is both R and not-R* and its denial as roughly *There is an x that is R and not-R*. The former is true, and the latter false, in all possible worlds. But *No right angle is an alligator* is a necessary truth expressible as *For all x, if Rx then not Ax* the denial of which is *For some x, Rx and Ax* which is false in all possible worlds, so its contradictory is true in all possible world, and hence necessarily true. But necessity in these cases does not lie in logical structure. If one objects that *There is an x such that x is both fully feline and fully canine* is meaningless, reflecting on the facts that *No x is both fully feline and fully canine* is true, and the denial of a truth is not meaningless, but false is the proper reply.

The return of the Ontological Argument to serious discussion in philosophy largely awaited the redevelopment of a logic that allowed one to express sentences of the form *Necessarily, P*, *Necessarily, not-P*, *Contingent, P*, and *Possibly, P*, which the Ontological Argument needs if it is to be expressed.

Purely Conceptual Proofs and the Ontological Argument

A purely conceptual proof of God's existence is an argument that is valid, has only necessary truths as premises, and has *God exists* as its conclusion. Such a proof that extends our knowledge—which of course is what is sought—will satisfy (at least something like) the other conditions noted previously.

The most famous attempts to provide such a proof constitute various varieties of the *Ontological Argument*—an argument offered by (among many others) St. Anselm in Medieval times, Descartes in the modern period, and Alvin

Plantinga in contemporary philosophy. In coming to understand this sort of argument, we begin with two definitions:

> Definition 1. *X is a logically necessary being* = *X exists* is necessarily true (*X does not exist* is self-contradictory).
> Definition 2. *X is a causally necessary being* = *X exists* is true and logically contingent, and *X is caused to exist* is self-contradictory.

A logically necessary being has, not causally, but logically necessary existence—it exists and it is not possible that it not exist.

Four Objections to the Notion of Logically Necessary Existence

There are various objections to the very idea of logically necessary existence. Here are four of the most common:

1. All necessary propositions are conditional—they have a structure properly expressed in an *If A then B* form.
2. No necessary propositions are existential—none entails that anything actually exists.
3. All necessary propositions are tautological—they have a sense property expressed in (something like) an *All A is A* or *All AB is B* form.
4. No necessary statements provide genuine information.

We can take these objections in pairs. Objection 1 tells us that all necessary statements are of the form "if A then B," which neither asserts that A exists nor that B exists. Objection 2 tells us that no necessary statement asserts that anything exists. Both 1 and 2 are false, since *There are prime numbers larger than seventeen* and *There is a successor to two* obviously are necessary truths but do assert that something exists. Objection 3 tells us that all necessary statements are true by virtue of the meanings of the words they contain, like *All uncles are uncles* and *Any aunt has a niece or nephew.* (It is allowed that there be a rule to the effect that "A" means "B or C" so that a proposition expressible in the form *All A is A* also is expressible in the form *All A is B or C.*) Objection 4 tells us that necessary truths provide no genuine information. But both *If proposition P is necessarily true, then it is necessarily true that P is necessarily true* and *If proposition P is necessarily false, then it is necessarily true that P is necessarily false* are necessary truths, and they are not tautological and they do provide genuine information. So both 3 and 4 are false.[7] None of these common objections show that the notion of logically necessary existence is incoherent.

The Ontological Argument

The Ontological Argument is an attempt to state a series of necessarily true propositions that serve as premises that entail the conclusion *God exists.* A successful argument of this sort would prove its conclusion to be necessarily true—it would show that God has logically necessary existence. Were any of the four objections just discussed to have succeeded, it would have undermined the Ontological Argument.

In constructing perhaps the most interesting version of the Ontological Argument,[8] we need some further definitions, as follows:

> Definition 3. Proposition P *entails* proposition Q if and only if *P, but not Q* is a contradiction.
> Definition 4. Proposition P is a *maximal proposition* if and only if, for any proposition Q, either P entails Q or P entails not-Q.
> Definition 5. Each maximal proposition defines an entire *possible world.*[9]
> Definition 6. A being has *maximal excellence* if and only if it is omnipotent, omniscient, and omnibenevolent in some possible world.
> Definition 7. A being has *maximal greatness* if and only if it has maximal excellence in every possible world.
> Definition 8. A proposition is *true in all possible worlds* if and only if it is necessarily true.[10]

There are various versions of the Ontological Argument. Here is one:

A. God is a perfect being.
B. A perfect being has all perfections.
C. *Having logically necessary existence* is a perfection.
D. God has *logically necessary existence.* [from A, B, C]
E. If God has *logically necessary existence* then *God exists* is necessarily true.
F. *God exists* is necessarily true. [from D, E]

While it has played a significant role in the history of philosophy it remains true that the notion of a perfection is hard to define with any precision. If the argument can be stated without appeal to this notion, so much the better. In fact, it can be so stated, and if the argument stated without the notion of a perfection fails, then so does the argument stated with that notion.

The Ontological Argument without the Notion of Perfection

Here is a formulation that makes no appeal to the notion of a perfection, though it does include certain central concepts that express what the tradition plausibly thinks are qualities that a perfect being would have.

1. *God has maximal greatness [has maximal excellence in every possible world]* is true unless it is self-contradictory.
2. *God has maximal greatness* is not self-contradictory. So:
3. *God has maximal greatness* is true. [from 1, 2]
4. If *God has maximal greatness* is true then God exists. So:
5. God exists. [from 2, 3]

The argument is plainly valid. Its form is:

1. P unless necessarily not-P.
2. Not necessarily not-P. So:
3. P.
4. If P then G. So:
5. G.

and that form is logically impeccable. If there are any problems with the argument, then, it is that one or more of its premises are false.

Premise 1 is true. *Having maximal greatness* is a matter of *having maximal excellence in every possible world*; *having maximal excellence every possible world* is tantamount to *necessarily having maximal excellence*. It is not hard to see this provided we keep in mind what the notion of maximal greatness involves, namely having *being omnicompetent in all possible worlds*. For any quality Q, to say that something has Q in all possible worlds is to say that it is logically necessary that it has Q. This claim is, as premise 1 says, true unless it is a necessary falsehood. Any proposition of the form *Necessarily, P* is necessarily true if true and necessarily false if false. *Necessarily, God has maximal greatness* is either true or false; so it is necessarily true or necessarily false. Thus, if it is not necessarily false (i.e., self-contradictory), then it is necessarily true; that is what premise 1 claims.

Premise 3 follows from premises 1 and 2; since God cannot have maximal greatness without existing, premise 4 is true; premises 3 and 4 entail premise 5. Everything depends, then, on whether premise 2 is true. Is it true? The argument for 2, and for its siblings in the arguments to follow, is essentially this: after careful reflection on 2, we can discover no reason to think it contradictory. It is not formally contradictory as expressing it in symbols shows: *For all W, there is an x such that x is omnicompetent in W*. Nor does it seem to be informally contradictory—no semantic inconsistency seems present. The problem will be that the siblings of 2 are also not formally contradictory nor do they seem to be informally or semantically inconsistent. To argue that for one of 2 and its siblings along the lines indicated—no formal inconsistency and no apparent informal consistency—must be honest about whether the same may not be true of the siblings of 2. Until all of the siblings of 2 are shown to be inconsistent and 2 alone stands triumphant over its competitors do not we have an ontological proof that extends our knowledge. So, again, is 2 true?

In considering this question, it is helpful to consider some arguments that are analogous to the current version of the Ontological Argument.

The X Argument

1x. *Necessarily, God does not exist* is true unless it is self-contradictory.
2x. *Necessarily, God does not exist* is not self-contradictory. So:
3x. *Necessarily, God does not exist* is true.
4x. If *Necessarily, God does not exist* is true then God does not exist. So:
5x. God does not exist.

This argument is also valid, and premise 1x is true for reasons exactly analogous to those noted regarding premise 1. Premise 4x is obviously true. So if premise 2x is true, then the argument is a proof. Is premise 2x true?

The Y Argument

1y. **God exists** *is logically contingent* is true unless it is self-contradictory.
2y. **God exists** *is logically contingent* is not self-contradictory. So:
3y. **God exists** *is logically contingent* is true.
4y. If **God exists** *is logically contingent* is true then *Necessarily, God exists* is false.
5y. *Necessarily, God exists* is false.

(Remember that '*Contingent, P = The modality of P* is that it is logically contingent, and a proposition that ascribes a modality to another proposition is either necessarily true or necessarily false.) This argument is also valid. Premise 1y is true for reasons exactly analogous to those that favor 1 and 1x. If it is true that **God exists** *is logically contingent* then **God exists** *is logically necessary* is false. (So then is the proposition *God has maximal greatness*, which entails **God exists** *is logically necessary*.) So if **God exists** *is logically contingent* is true, then *God has maximal greatness* is false, and that is what premise 4y says. So if premise 2y is true, then the Y Argument is sound and valid, and thus its conclusion is true. Is 2y true?

The Z Argument

1z. **God does not exist** *is logically contingent* is true unless it is self-contradictory.
2z. **God does not exist** *is logically contingent* is not self-contradictory. So:
3z. **God does not exist** *is logically contingent* is true.
4z. If **God does not exist** *is logically contingent* is true then *Necessarily, God exists* is false.
5z. *Necessarily, God exists* is false.

This argument is also valid. Premise 1z is true for reasons exactly analogous to those that favor 1, 1x, and 1y. If it is true that **God does not exist** *is logically contingent* then **God exists** *is logically necessary* is false. (So then is *God has maximal greatness*, which entails **God exists** *is logically necessary*.) So if **God does not exist** *is logically contingent* is true, then *Necessarily, God exists* is false, and that is what premise 4z says. So if premise 2z is true, the Z Argument is sound and valid, and its conclusion is true. Is 2z true?

Summary Regarding the Ontological Argument (Version 1) and the X, Y, and Z Arguments

A.   Each argument is logically valid.
B.   In each argument, the first premise is true.
C.   In each argument, the fourth premise is true.

D.   In each argument, only the first, second, and fourth premises are indepen-
     dent; the first and second entail the third, and the third and fourth entail the
     conclusion.
E.   In each argument, if the second premise is true, the argument is sound.
F.   Premise 2y is true if and only if premise 2z is true, so we need concern our-
     selves only with one of them; we will use 2y.
G.   It is logically impossible that *more* than one (or that *less* than one) of these
     three premises be true: premise 2 of the Ontological Argument, premise 2x,
     premise 2y.

What is crucial in evaluating the Ontological Argument is that this argument does
not establish which of these three premises is true. It leaves that issue completely
open. Hence the Ontological Argument fails as a proof that extends our knowledge.
Given the discussion thus far, the point can be put succinctly as follows. Consider:

> 0. Either *God exists* is (a) necessarily true, (b) necessarily false, (c) logically
> contingent and true, or (d) logically contingent and false.

The Ontological Argument requires that (a) be the right alternative. But that argument contains the thesis that (a) is the right alternative—that is what premise 2 of
the argument says. No argument is given to the effect that (a) is the right alternative. Granted, (a) does not seem self-contradictory, but neither do any of (b), (c),
or (d), each of which is incompatible with (a). So we are left without any reason
for picking (a) as the truth.

Another Look at the Ontological Argument

1.   It is logically possible that God has maximal greatness if the concept of God
     is not contradictory.
2.   The concept of God is not contradictory. So:
3.   It is logically possible that God has maximal excellence.
4.   If it is logically possible that God has maximal greatness, then God has
     maximal excellence. So:
5.   God has maximal greatness.
6.   If God has maximal greatness, then God exists in all possible worlds. So:
7.   God exists in all possible worlds.
8.   If God exists in all possible worlds, then necessarily God exists. So:
9.   Necessarily, God exists.

Exposition of Ontological Argument

From 3 on, the argument is correct. You might object to 4, but what 4 says is this:

> *Possibly, God has maximal greatness* entails *God has maximal greatness*. What
> you need to keep in mind is that *God has maximal greatness* entails *God exists*

in all possible worlds (= *Necessarily, God exists*). Thus *God has maximal great-ness* ascribes the modality necessarily true to the proposition *God has maximal greatness*. Thus, given that necessary truths are necessarily necessarily true and necessary falsehoods are necessarily necessarily false, it follows that *God has maximal excellence* is either necessarily true, or else is a necessary falsehood.

Further Discussion of Ontological Argument

There is a problem with the argument, and it starts earlier. It lies exactly in prem-ise 1 (in contrast to Version 1, where the problem arises with premise 2). Suppose what is true is *The proposition that God exists is logically contingent.* Then the following things are true: (i) *God exists* is not a contradiction; (ii) *God does not exist* is not a contradiction, and (iii) *Necessarily, God exists* is a contradiction; and (iv) *Necessarily, God does not exist* is a contradiction. If (iii) is true, then prem-ise 1 of the Ontological Argument is false. Thus if it is true that *The proposition that God exists is logically contingent is true*, premise 1 of the argument is false. Nothing in the argument shows that *The proposition that God exists is logically contingent* is not true. So the argument fails.

A Proof That Something Has Logically Necessary Existence

Consider this brief argument:

1. Necessarily, if it is possible that something have logically necessary exis-tence, then something has logically necessary existence.
2. It is possible that something have logically necessary existence.

So:

3. Something has logically necessary existence.

In other terms:

1*. Necessarily, [Possibly, something has logically necessary existence] entails [Something has logically necessary existence].
2*. [Possibly, something has logically necessary existence].

So:

3*. [Something has logically necessary existence].

The reasoning here is simple: 1 and 1* are necessary truths. Premises 2 and 2*, being modal claims, are either necessarily false or necessarily true. Neither 2 nor 2* is necessarily false. So 2 and 2* are necessarily true. The inferences *1 and 2, hence 3* and *1* and 2*, hence 3** are obviously valid. Hence conclusions 3 and 3*, being entailed by necessary truths, are themselves necessary truths. Something has logically necessary existence.

If the Ontological Argument is sound and valid, then this argument must be sound and valid; its soundness and validity is a necessary, but not a sufficient, condition of the soundness and validity of the Ontological Argument. The simple argument is powerful; perhaps it is a proof that extends our knowledge. But even if this is so, the Ontological Argument itself is not a proof that extends our knowledge.

Empirical Proofs, Argument Strategies, and Principles of Sufficient Reason[11]

In contrast to a purely conceptual proof of God's existence, an empirical proof of God's existence is an argument that is valid, has at least one logically contingent truth among its premises, has only true premises, and has *God exists* as its conclusion. Such a proof that extends our knowledge—which of course is what is sought—will satisfy the other conditions noted previously. There are various starting points for such arguments, and various strategies for going on from the beginning. For example, one might begin with the fact that there is a universe though it is logically possible that there might not have been, or that there is some particular thing (say, oneself) though it is logically possible that there not have been that particular thing, or the fact that the universe is intelligible (science is possible) though it is logically possible that there be a universe that is not intelligible. Suppose one begins with the fact that there is a universe though it is logically possible that there not have been. Then there are at least these strategies for continuing.

1. The *everlasting world* strategy: prove that the world is everlasting and dependent, then infer to a necessarily independent being on which the dependent everlasting world depends.
2. The *world-has-a-beginning* strategy: prove that the world is not everlasting past, then infer to a cause of the world beginning to exist.
3. The *inclusive* strategy: prove that *either* the world is everlasting and dependent or that the world is not everlasting past; then infer to there being either a necessarily independent being on which the dependent everlasting world depends or a necessarily independent cause of the world beginning to exist.

Which strategy a philosopher chooses may, but need not, depend on what her religious beliefs are. A Christian, like Augustine, who believes that God created time and the universe together (that God's creating a universe is both necessary and sufficient for there being time) will suppose that the universe is everlasting in one sense—there is no time at which there was no universe—but will also suppose that it is impossible that there be a time T1 at which the universe was not created and then another later time T2 at which the universe was created. We might call this *universe-time-together creation* view. In another sense, in holding this view, she will deny that the world is everlasting; on her view, there will have been a first time—time will go back so far, and no further. But a Jewish, Christian, or Moslem monotheist might perfectly well hold that time has no beginning and that God created the world at some time prior to which time flowed but no universe existed. We can call this the *creation-in-time view*. A monotheist might even hold that the universe has always existed, and the doctrine that God created the universe entails that the universe always depends on God for its existence, has always done so, and will do so as long as it exists at all. We can call this the *beginningless creation* view. On this view, *God created the universe* entails *The universe has always existed in such a way that it depends on God, God does not depend for God's existence on there being a universe, and were God to cease sustaining the universe in existence, it would not exist but God would still exist.* But there being a first time, or a first moment at which the universe began to exist, will not be entailed. A monotheist can accept any of these alternatives. Typically Jewish, Christian, and Moslem monotheists have accepted either a universe-time-together or a creation-in-time perspective. Hindu monotheism, by contrast, holds to a beginningless creation perspective. This largely has to do with their interpretations of their religious texts.

A philosopher might think that one could not decide between these alternatives by appeal to anything other than Scripture, and wish to base his arguments only on what he thought was philosophically accessible. In this case, the third strategy may well seem attractive.[12] In any case, each strategy will require its own version of the general thesis that whatever can be explained has an explanation—its own formulation of the Principle of Sufficient Reason (PSR).

Principles of Sufficient Reason

1. The Everlasting World Strategy requires something like this: (PSR1) *If it is logically possible that something depends for its existence on something else, then it does depend for its existence on something else* or *What can depend for its existence on something else does depend for its existence on something else.*
2. The World Has a Beginning Strategy requires something like this: (PSR2) *What begins to exist must have a cause of existence* or *Nothing can simply begin to exist without being caused to do so.*
3. The Inclusive Strategy requires something like this: *(PSR1) and (PSR2).*

Crucial Premises

The different strategies will also require somewhat different premises along these lines.

1. The Everlasting World Strategy requires some such premise as this: *It is logically impossible that everything that exists, exists dependently.*

2.   The World Has a Beginning Strategy requires some such premise as this: *It is logically impossible that everything that exists has had a beginning of existence.*
3.   The Inclusive Strategy requires something like this: *(a) It is logically impossible that everything that exists, exists dependently and (b) it is logically impossible that everything that exists has had a beginning of existence.*

The idea is that if the world is beginningless past, it does not exist independently [because of the truth of (a)] and if the world has a beginning it does not exist independently [because of the truth of (b)].

The inclusive strategy is safer with respect to its required premises (its core premise is weaker in what it claims)—one who uses it need not care whether the world ever began to exist or not. But it is riskier with respect to its version of the Principle of Sufficient Reason (it requires both PSR1 and PSR2).

Differences in Conclusions

The strategies, of course, will also yield somewhat different conclusions. Aristotle wants to infer from the world's existence to God's existence in a way that does not require that God have made any choices or performed any actions. Semitic and Hindu monotheists want to infer from the world's existence to God's existence in a way that does require that God have chosen to create and that God created (the choice and the act may be the same). Even if a monotheist does not think that you can successfully infer from the world's existence to God's existence, she typically will have a view about how the world is related to God. Ramanuja, for example, rejects any inference from the world's existence to God's existence, but holds that the world is everlastingly dependent for its existence on God. Among the most famous and influential of arguments for monotheism are Aquinas's Five Ways.

Arguments by Thomas Aquinas

Aquinas's arguments are of considerable historical interest. For present purposes, however, three questions matter: (i) Do any of his arguments prove their intended conclusion? (ii) If not, can one learn from them how to frame a more powerful argument for their intended conclusion or something much like it? (iii) Do his arguments suggest some other approach to the question of the truth or falsity of monotheism? Questions (i) and (ii) are considered in this chapter; the third receives attention in the later chapter on Faith and Reason.

Aquinas asks whether the existence of God can be proved and answers in the affirmative. He then offers five arguments for God's existence followed by an argument that the being referred to in the conclusion of the first argument is the same as that referred to in the conclusion of each of the other arguments. Here, too, beginning with a few definitions will enable us to state complex arguments with much greater simplicity than we could without them.

Reflexive and Irreflexive Relations

Aquinas's arguments deal with certain relationships he takes to hold between one thing in the world and another thing in the world, or between the world and God. Here are some fundamental features of relations:[13]

> Definition 1: Relation R, holding between X and Y, is *reflexive* if *X has R to Y* entails *Y has R to X*.

If Jack is the same height as Jill, then Jill is the same height as Jack; *being the same height as* is a reflexive relation.

> Definition 2: Relation R, holding between X and Y, is *irreflexive* if *X has R to Y* entails *Y does not have R to X*.

If Tim is Tom's father, then Tom is not Tim's father; *being a father, being a mother, being a parent* are irreflexive relations.

It will be useful to have two further ways of talking about relations. Let us say that if *X has R to Y* then X has R *forwardly* to Y, and that Y has R *backwardly* to X. Reflexive relations between X and Y are had both forwardly and backwardly by both X and Y. Irreflexive relations between X and Y are had only forwardly by X and only backwardly by Y.

General Structure

The general structure—the logical skeleton, as it were—of Aquinas's arguments, typically called the "Five Ways," as we will see, can be expressed either as:

1. There is an X and a Y such that X bears relation R to Y.
2. Either (a) there is an infinite series of items such that each member has R both forwardly to something and backwardly to something, or (b) there is some item that has R only forwardly.
3. Not-(a).

So:

4. (b)

or as:

1. There is an X and a Y such that X has R to Y.
2. Either (a) there is an infinite series of items such that each member has R both forwardly to something and backwardly to something, or (b) there is some item that has R only forwardly.
3. If (a) then (b).
4. If not-(a) then (b).

So:

5.   (b).

Chronological versus Concurrent Causes

If we are to understand Aquinas, it is important to distinguish between what we will call chronological versus concurrent causes.

> Definition 3: X is a *chronological* cause of Y if and only if X's doing something or having some quality at some time *before* T is necessary for Y at T.

Putting the water over the fire, causing it to boil; turning the key in the ignition, causing the car to start; throwing the ball, causing the window to break, are chronological causes.

> Definition 4: X is a *concurrent* cause of Y if and only if X doing something or having some quality *at* T is a necessary condition of Y at T.

Holding a door to keep it open; holding one's breath to keep one's lungs full; pushing the bell to keep the bell ringing, are cases of concurrent causation. It is typically cases of concurrent, not chronological, causation that Aquinas has in mind in offering his arguments. Thus criticisms based on the assumption that he has chronological causation in mind will be off target.

Themes of the Arguments

Each of Aquinas's five arguments concerns a different relationship as follows.

> Argument 1: something moving/changing something else
> Argument 2: something causing something to come to exist
> Argument 3: X can cease to exist by becoming Y
> Argument 4: things having different degrees of worth
> Argument 5: something behaving at least as if it were seeking a goal

Domains, Forwardness, and Backwardness

A finite domain is a collection having a finite number of members; a pile of forty rocks, a flock of seventy geese, a galaxy of a million stars, are finite domains. Suppose that we have a domain of three things—Al, Bob, and Carl. Suppose that an irreflexive relationship—say, *being a father*—relates Al and Bob, and Bob and Carl. Within this domain, Al stands in the relation *being a father* only forwardly, Carl stands in the relation *being a father* only backwardly, and Bob stands in the relation *being a father* forwardly toward Carl and backwardly toward Al. If this domain is all there is, Al has no father and Carl has no children. This is a domain *ordered by* an irreflexive relationship. Each member of the domain is related to every other by an instance of the same irreflexive relationship—in the case just described, by *being a father*.

Consider a different domain—a domain defined in terms of its members being ordered by a particular sort of dependence relationship. The sort of dependence in question is *nonreciprocal dependence* where *B nonreciprocally depends for existence on A if and only if B depends for its existence on A and A does not depend for its existence on B*. Suppose, then, that there exists a domain of things each of which stands in a non-reciprocal dependence relation to something, and that this domain is finite. Then it follows that some member of this domain stands in the relationship of non-reciprocal dependence only forwardly. The only alternatives are that the domain is infinite (which we have stipulated is not so) or that there is a circle of non-reciprocal dependence, which is impossible. If B non-reciprocally depends on A and C non-reciprocally depends on B and A non-reciprocally depends on C, then the relationship between A and B is *reciprocal* dependence, not non-reciprocal. A circle of non-reciprocal relationships is logically impossible. So some member of the domain must stand in the relationship of non-reciprocal dependence only forwardly[14]—i.e., must exist independently of the other members of the domain ordered by the irreflexive relationship of non-reciprocal dependence.

Aquinas takes this relationship of non-reciprocal dependence to be one involving concurrent causation—if the existence of A fully explains the existence of B, then so long as B exists it must be the case that A is causing it to exist.

It is not obvious that the world of physical things and non-divine minds is a finitely large domain of things ordered by the relationship of non-reflexive dependence. But that it is such a domain is something that at least the first three of Aquinas's arguments require.

Change, Potentiality, Actuality[15]

Aquinas defines *change* in a way reminiscent of Aristotle's philosophy.

> Definition 5. X is in actuality with respect to some property Q if and only if X has Q.
> Definition 6. X is in potentiality with respect to some property Q if and only if (i) X does not have Q, but (ii) X is the sort of thing capable of having Q.

Elk cannot be prime numbers, eggs cannot run faster than hares, and pigs cannot fly, so these things are not in potentiality with regard to these properties. Elk can be dyed pink, eggs can be swallowed whole, and pigs can be dressed in tuxedoes, so they are in potentiality with respect to these properties. Elk have legs, eggs have shells, and pigs have ears, so they are in actuality with regard to these properties.

> Definition 7. X changes with respect to property Q if and only if X moves from potentiality to actuality, or from actuality to potentiality, with respect to Q.[16]

Definition 8. Y causes X to change with respect to property Q if and only if Y causes X to move from potentiality to actuality, or from actuality to potentiality, with respect to Q.

The First Way

The First Way concerns things being caused to move, in the usual sense of going from one place to another but also in the more general sense of simply changing, in position or some other way. It is assumed that *X changing Y with respect to Q* is a relationship that is non-reciprocal—is analogous to *non-reciprocal dependence*. Thus the idea is that it cannot be the case that *X's changing Y with respect to Q* causes *Y's becoming Q* only if *Y's becoming Q* causes *Y's causing Z to become Q* and *Z's becoming Q* causes *X's causing Y to become Q*. The argument goes as follows.

1. Some things change.
2. If X changes at time T then there is something Y that changes X at T [understood as that Y is something different from X].
3. Either (a) there is an infinite series of changed and changing beings (i.e., a series each member of which is both a changed and a changing thing) or (b) there is some being that is a changing being (a cause of motion/change) but is *not* a changed being (something that changes).
4. Not-(a).

So:

5. (b).

Aquinas offers a subsidiary argument for premise 2:

2a. For all times T, and all X, X is in actuality with respect to moving at T or X is in potentiality regarding motion at T.
2b. If X is in potentiality regarding motion at T, then X is not moving at T.
2c. If X is not moving at T, then X cannot cause motion at T.
2d. Nothing can cause its own motion at T (since in order to do so it would have to both be in actuality regarding motion at T and in potentiality regarding motion at T, and that is impossible).
2e. No motion can be uncaused.

Hence:

2. If X changes at time T then there is something Y that changes X at T (so understood that Y is something different from X).

The issue of whether there can be self-moving or self-changing things was hotly disputed in the Medieval period. Scotus, for example, offered powerful arguments against Aquinas in this regard. But there is to be a replacement for premise 2 that restricts its basic idea to cases of which it is true, and we will follow this strategy.

Self-Change

The First Way, if successful, would establish the existence of a cause of change that did not change.[17] Premise 2—the denial of self-motion—is apparently problematic. There seem to be cases of self-movement—one's walking to the store, for example—and of self-caused change that does not involve movement from place to place—deliberately stopping thinking about one thing in order to reflect on another. But there are lots of changes in which something is caused to change by something else, and the best strategy for defending Aquinas here seems to be this: argue that, with respect to the sorts of qualities with which the arguments are concerned, self-change is not an option. Something depending for existence on itself—a physical object or a human mind, for example, having some feature by virtue of which it existed independently of anything else—is not a promising notion. Perhaps the simplest defense of Aquinas here is to argue as follows: we know that every physical thing, and that every human mind[18] in fact depends for its existence on the existence of other things. But *being dependent* is an essential property of everything that has it; *X is dependent for existence on something else* entails *Necessarily, X is dependent for existence on something else*. Further, *Nothing can cause its own existence* is a necessary truth; in order for something to cause its own existence, it must do so at some time T. Then, at some time T, something that causes its own existence must both not exist in order to be caused and exist in order to do the causing—a feat that is logically impossible to perform.

Even if one provides this line of reasoning on Aquinas's behalf however—even if one grants that a version of, or replacement for, premise 2 that is restricted to some such quality as *non-reciprocally causing change* will serve his purposes even if some instances of self-change are possible—his case is not made. Consider this pair of claims:

T1. For any time T1, everything that exists at T1 depends for its existence on something else that exists at T1.

T2. For any time T2, everything that exists at T2 was caused to come into existence at T2 by something that existed at T1.

The sort of dependence that T2 describes is non-reciprocal and consecutive. The sort of dependence that T1 describes is reciprocal and concurrent. The First Way requires that there be a sort of dependence that is non-reciprocal and concurrent. Suppose that T1 and T2 are true and describe the only sorts of dependence there are. Then the First Way fails. Nothing in the First Way proves that T1 and T2 are not true and descriptive of the only sorts of dependence that there are. So the First Way is not a proof that extends our knowledge. Perhaps there is the sort of non-reciprocal dependence that Aquinas requires, but we have no proof of it here.

Infinite Series[19]

It is not obvious why there cannot be an infinite series of changed and changing things, whether we have chronological or concurrent cases of causation in mind. We have seen why premise 4—the rejection of an infinite series of things changing one another regarding quality Q—is needed. Aware of this, Aquinas offers a subsidiary argument for premise 4:

4a. An infinite series has no first (earliest?) member.
4b. If a series has no first (earlier?) members, it has no later or succeeding members.
4c. If a series has neither earlier nor later members, it has no members.
4d. No series can have no members.

So:

4. Not-(a)—there is *not* an infinite series of changed and changing beings (i.e., a series each member of which is both a changed and a changing thing).

Aquinas[20] admits that there can be a temporally beginningless causal series; so presumably it is concurrent, not chronological, causality that Aquinas has in mind in this argument (and elsewhere in the Five Ways). The argument for the fourth premise is puzzling. There were sharp disputes among Medieval philosophers as to whether an infinite series was possible. Perhaps the sub-proof rests on the idea that, in constructing a series, one has to begin somewhere, and if one does not start with a first thing one will never construct even a two-member, let alone an infinitely membered, series. Then the argument is correct but irrelevant, since to firmly contend that there are series that are infinite does not contend that we have to construct them. One can reply that any actual series must be one that could in principle be constructed by someone, and an infinitely membered series could not be. But then we need another argument that any infinite series must be one that could in principle be constructed, and another to show that an infinitely membered series does not fit this description. Plainly nothing in the argument of the First Way, in either its main or its subsidiary lines of reasoning, provides anything like this. Thus the First Way seems not to be a proof of its conclusion.

Second Way

Again we begin with a couple of definitions.

> Definition 9: X is in motion *per accidens* if and only if X moves only because X is part of or is located in Y and X moves only because Y moves.

A cup of coffee set in the cup holder of a moving car moves *per accidens*; the car moves *per se*.

Definition 10. X moves *per se* if and only if X moves and X does not move *per accidens*.

The Second Way runs as follows; it takes *coming to be* or *coming to exist* as a change.

1. If X comes to be at T then X's coming to be at T is caused.
2. Nothing can cause its own coming to exist (it would have both to exist to do the causing and not exist to be caused to come to be).
3. If X comes to be at T then X is caused to come to be at T by something other than X.
4. Either (a) there is an infinite series of beings that come to be and are caused to come to be by other beings that were caused to come to be, or (b) there is a being that causes others things to come to be but is not itself caused to come to be.
5. Not-(a).

So:

6. (b)

Aquinas argues for premise 5 in this manner:

5a. An infinite series has no first member.
5b. If a series has no first member, then it has no later members.
5c. A series having neither a first nor later members has no members; a series without members cannot exist.

So:

5. There is not an infinite series of beings that come to be and are caused to come to be by other beings that were caused to come to be.

The argument for premise 5 here is identical to the argument for premise 4 of the First Way, and hence has exactly the same problems. Further, coming to exist is not a change in the thing which comes to exist; hence on the definition of change offered above, it is not a change—non-existent things have neither potentiality nor actuality. *It is possible that X, which does not exist at time T, come to exist at time T1* does not entail *X, which does not exist, has the potentiality to exist*; *X has some potentiality or other* entails *X exists*. So the Second Way is not a proof.

Third Way

Two simple definitions are helpful here.

Definition 11. X is *generable* if and only if X can be caused to come to be.
Definition 12. X is *corruptible* if and only if X can be caused to change and can be caused to cease to exist.

Aristotle and Aquinas seem to assume *X can be caused to change* entails *X can be caused to cease to exist*, and conversely, so that necessarily anything that meets one of the conditions of being generable also meets the other. It is not at all obvious that this is so. In any case, the Third Way goes like this:

1. If X is generable and corruptible then X's non-existence is possible.
2. There are corruptible and generable things.

So:

3. There are things whose non-existence is possible. [from 1, 2]
4. Assume for the sake of showing it to be false that for all X, X's non-existence is possible.[21]
5. If for all X, X's non-existence is possible then there is some time T such that nothing exists at T.
6. There is some time T such that nothing exists at T. [from 4, 5]
7. It is impossible that anything comes to exist without its being caused to do so by something that already exists.
8. If there is some time T such that nothing exists at T then for any time T* later than T, nothing exists at T*.
9. Nothing exists at T*. [from 5 through 8]
10. If there is some time T such that nothing exists at T, T has already occurred.

So:

11. T has already occurred.
12. If T has already occurred, then nothing exists now.

So:

13. Nothing exists now. [from 10 through 12]
14. If for all X, X's non-existence is possible then nothing exists now. [from 4 through 12]
15. It is false that nothing exists now.

So:

16. It is false that for all X, X's non-existence is possible.
17. If it is false that for all X, X's non-existence is possible, then something exists whose non-existence is impossible.

So:

18. Something exists whose non-existence is impossible. [from 16 and 17]

Aquinas's Third Way is read in different ways. Aquinas is read as saying either:

(a) It is impossible that all generable things exist at every single time. [Necessarily, every generable thing at some time or other does not exist.]

or:

(b) It is impossible that, at every time whatever, some generable thing exists. [Necessarily, at some time or other, no generable thing exists.]

Compare *Necessarily, every elk passes on sooner or later*; this is analogous to (a). Consider *Necessarily, at some time there are no elk at all*; this is analogous to (b). What Aquinas needs is (b); (a) will not help him. Aquinas also needs:

(c) It is impossible that everything that exists is a generable being.

This indication of what he requires is relevant to two fallacious inferences he is often charged with making in the Third Way; either would, of course, invalidate the argument.

Inference One: From A to B

Consider
A. For all X, it is possible that X corrupt.
B. It is possible that everything (simultaneously) corrupt.

A world **W** of which **A** is true might be one of which it was also true that:
C. It is not possible that W be entirely unpopulated.
But a world of which **B** was true is a world of which **C** could not be true. Hence inferring from A to B is fallacious.[22] Inferring from (a) to (b) is tantamount to inferring from **A** to **B**. If Aquinas either inferred from (a) to (b), or simply did not adequately distinguish between them, the argument fails.

Inference Two: From D to E

D. Everything at some time fails to exist.
E. Sometime, everything fails to exist.[23]

Everything is green at some time or other does not entail *At some time or other, everything is green.* Similarly, **D** does not entail **E**. Again, the inference from (a) to (b) is tantamount to inferring from **D** to **E**. If Aquinas either inferred from (a) to (b), or simply did not adequately distinguish between them, the argument fails.

   The gist of these criticisms is that even if at some time or other, each thing that exists will pass out of existence, it does not follow that they will all pass out of existence at the same time, and so long as earlier members can generate later ones, things will go on. If Aquinas is not entitled to infer from (a) to (b), then even if he is entitled to infer from (b) to (c) this will not help, since he has no legitimate way to get to (b).

Aquinas is also criticized for claiming that the alleged time at which everything would simultaneously pass away would already have occurred; why not regard the proof as (if it succeeds) proving that at some future time there will not be any generable things? His answer is that if there have been generable things for only a finite time past, then there had to be a cause of there coming to be generable things and so there is something that is not itself a generable thing, and if there have always been generable things then an infinite time has passed and in any infinite time we would have reached the time at which every thing has passed away. We can afford not to enter into this controversy.[24]

The first three of Aquinas's Five Ways begin by reference to the fact that things exist that might not have existed and that depend for their existence on something else, and that things change. They then require some such claim as *What can depend for its existence on something else does depend for its existence on something else* and *What changes is changed by something else*, as well as such claims as *If there are things that exist that depend for their existence on something else, then there is something that exists independent of anything else* and *If things are caused to change by something else, then there is something that causes change without itself ever changing.* In part for reasons given as we explained these arguments, none of them constitutes a proof that extends our knowledge. Thus the results of examining these arguments have not been very positive; none seems even close to a proof that God exists. But rearrangement and revision of the materials these arguments contain provide something stronger.

Some Further Definitions

If these materials do yield a stronger—even a successful—argument, perhaps they do so via the following argument. Once again, some definitions will make it possible to state the argument less complexly than otherwise. Further, the way the premises are stated is intended to keep them from being open to various standard objections. Note that nothing in the following argument requires that there not be various sorts of self-motion or self-change and it requires no assumptions about whether there is an infinite series of anything.

By way of reminder:

Definition 1. P is a *logically contingent proposition* = neither P nor not-P is self-contradictory.

Definition 2. P is a *logically necessary proposition* = not-P is self-contradictory.

Further:

> Definition 3. P is an *existential proposition* = P entails a proposition of the form *X exists*.
>
> Definition 4. It is *logically possible that P's truth be explained* = There is some proposition Q such that *Q's truth explains P's truth* is not self-contradictory.

To give an analysis, if it is logically possible that the existence of something X be explained, then it is logically possible that X *not* exist, and if it is logically possible that the truth of a proposition P be explained, it is logically possible that it *not* be true.

Given these definitions, we can state another version of the cosmological argument.

Cosmological Argument, Stage One

1. If it is logically possible that the truth of a logically contingent existential proposition be explained, then there actually is an explanation of its truth (whether we know what it is or not).

Premise 1 is a version of the Principle of Sufficient Reason.

2. *There exist things whose existence it is logically possible to explain* is a true logically contingent existential proposition.

There are rose bushes, there might not have been rose bushes, and there is an explanation of there being rose bushes; hence premise 2 is true.

3. There is an explanation of the truth of *There exist things whose existence it is logically possible to explain.* [from 1, 2]

Premise 3 obviously follows from premises 1 and 2, so if they are true, so is it. The success of Stage One depends on what is true regarding the first premise.

Cosmological Argument, State Two

4. The truth of *There exist things whose existence it is logically possible to explain* cannot be explained by there being things whose existence it is logically possible to explain (the existence of *those* things is just what is to be explained).

Suppose that Pat wants to know why there now are Golden Retriever puppies. She is told that there are Golden Retriever parents. She asks why there are Golden Retriever parents. She is told about Golden Retriever grandparents. Pat then wants to know why there are any Golden Retrievers at all. She cannot now be told about Golden Retriever parents, grandparents, great-grandparents, or the like; these will all be things she wants to know about—why have any Golden Retrievers at all existed? Here, one either refuses to answer, claims that there being Golden Retrievers is just a fundamental feature of the world, or explains that there were non-Golden-Retrievers that caused there to be Golden Retrievers.

If Pat asks why there have ever been any possibly explicable things at all that exist though they might not have existed, she cannot properly be told about there being possibly explicable things that exist but might not have existed; those are the things she asks about. So one can refuse to answer, claim that there being possibly explicable things that exist but might not have existed is a fundamental feature of the universe, or refer to something that is *not* such as to exist and be possibly explicable though it might not have existed. This line of thought is correct, and is what premise 4 says.

> 5. That a logically contingent existential proposition is true can only be explained by some other existential proposition being true.

If, in the relevant sense of explanation, P's truth entails Q's truth, then P entails Q. No existential proposition is entailed by a set of propositions that does not contain any existential propositions.

> 6. If an existential proposition does not concern something whose existence it is logically possible to explain, it concerns something whose existence is logically impossible to explain.

These exhaust the possibilities.

> 7. The truth of *There exist things whose existence it is logically possible to explain* can only be explained by a true existential proposition concerning something whose existence it is logically impossible to explain.
> 8. Some existential proposition concerning something whose existence it is logically impossible to explain, and whose existence can explain the existence of things whose existence it is logically possible to explain, is true.

Premise 4 is plainly true; whatever Xs are, *there being Xs* cannot explain *there being Xs*. Neither can the existence of something that might not have existed be explained other than by reference to things that exist; the existence of contingent things can only be explained by reference to something that exists, not by reference to something that doesn't exist. So premise 5 is true. Necessarily, for anything X that exists, either it is logically possible that X's existence be explained or it isn't; that is what premise 6 says. If (i) X's existence can be explained, and (ii) can be explained only by the truth of a type A proposition or by the truth of a type B proposition, and (iii) cannot be explained by the truth of a type A proposition, then it follows that (iv) X's existence can be explained by the truth of a type B proposition. Premise 7 applies this reasoning to the notions of propositions concerning the existence of things whose existence can be explained and propositions concerning the existence of things whose existence cannot be explained. Premises 4, 5, 6, and 7 entail proposition 8; if they are true (and they are) so is it. Hence Stage Two is successful.

Cosmological Argument, Stage Three

9. If some existential proposition concerning something whose existence it is logically impossible to explain, and whose existence can explain the existence of things whose existence it is logically possible to explain, is true, then something exists whose existence it is logically impossible to explain and whose existence can explain the existence of things whose existence it is logically possible to explain.

10. Something exists whose existence it is logically impossible to explain and whose existence can explain the existence of things whose existence it is logically possible to explain. [from 8, 9]

Premises 8 and 9 entail step 10, and premise 9 is, I take it, a necessary truth. So Stage Three succeeds. The conclusion thus far—*Something exists whose existence it is logically impossible to explain and whose existence can explain the existence of things whose existence it is logically possible to explain*—is interesting all by itself. Its crucial premise is its first:

If it is logically possible that the truth of a logically contingent existential proposition be explained, then there actually is an explanation of its truth (whether we know what it is or not).

Premise 1 is a version of the Principle of Sufficient Reason. Call it PSR*.

Suppose one claims the truth of every logically contingent proposition has an explanation, and that it cannot be the case that the truth of every logically contingent proposition is explicable by reference to the truth of other logically contingent propositions. Then one will be claiming that there is some logically contingent proposition whose truth is explicable by reference to some true but not logically contingent proposition—some logically necessary truth. If *P's truth explains Q's truth* entails *P entails Q*, then one is claiming that a necessary truth entails a logically contingent truth. This is necessarily false—if Q is a logically contingent proposition, it is possibly false. No necessary truth is possibly false. Were a necessary truth to entail a logically contingent proposition, then it would be possibly false. Hence no necessary truth can entail a logically contingent proposition. If there are any true logically contingent propositions—and there plainly are—then either every one of them is explicably true by reference to some other, whose truth is explicable by reference to some other, and so on, or some among them is true but its truth cannot be explained. PSR* is compatible with all this. It requires no attempt to explain contingent propositions only by reference to necessary truths, and it is compatible with there being an infinite number of contingent truths, each explained by some other contingent proposition. It is also compatible with the fact that, if there are any logically contingent propositions—and there plainly are—then some must be true: if Q is a logically contingent proposition, so is not-Q, and of [Q and not-Q] one must be true.

What it does require is that *there being logically contingent true existential statements* is possibly explicable—as it is—and hence that it has an actual explanation. If it does have an explanation, it seems that the cosmological argument has the right sort of explanation. Obviously no necessary truth will explain it, and no possibly explicable contingent proposition will explain it, and no non-existential statement will explain it. What is left, since necessary falsehoods and contingent falsehoods explain nothing, is a logically contingent existential statement whose truth is necessarily inexplicable. While it is true that of any pair composed of a logically contingent existential statement and its denial, one must be true, it might always be that it was the denial that was true. So it is not a logical necessity that there be true logically contingent existential statements. There remains, then, this question: Is it contingently inexplicable that there are true logically contingent existential statements? That there are such statements is possibly explicable, so if there is no explanation of there being such, there is a perfectly intelligible question—*Why are there any logically contingent existential propositions?*—that might perfectly well have had an answer, but that in fact has none. What PSR* denies is that this is possible—the possibly explicable is actually explicable.

Is PSR* true? There does not seem to be anything more obviously true than PSR* from which it follows. PSR* does not seem to be contradictory, and if it is true, it is necessarily true. So it is, if not contradictory, then necessarily true. But (I) *It is contingently inexplicable that there are logically contingent true existential statements* seems not contradictory, and it is, if true, then necessarily true. So if it is not contradictory, then it is necessarily true. Nothing in the cosmological argument shows that it is PSR* rather than (I) that is true. So the cosmological argument is not a proof that extends our knowledge.

There is a bit more to be said regarding PSR*. A standard objection to weaker formulations of the cosmological argument is that if one infers from the world to God, and it is logically possible that God not exist, then one might as well have stopped with the world. A cosmological argument with PSR* as an essential premise, assuming the remainder to be crafted in line with PSR*'s content, will be subject to no such objection. Further, if one rejects PSR* one is left with an ultimate mystery, an intelligible and basic question to which there might have been an answer, but is not. Reject PSR* and mystery lies on your side of the fence, not on the monotheist's side.

Cosmological Argument, Stage Four

It is at least not unreasonable to accept PSR*, and it is worth seeing how the argument that requires it continues. A few additional definitions will serve the familiar service of simplifying the statement of the argument.

D4.   Being X has necessary existential security = X exists, and *X is caused to exist or depends for its existence on something else* is self-contradictory.

D5.   Q is a basic property of X = X has Q, and X has no property Q* such that *X has Q** explains the truth of *X has Q*.

D6.   Q is a non-basic property of X = X has Q, and X has some property Q* such that *X has Q** explains the truth of *X has Q*.

D7.   X has logically necessary existence = X exists, our concept of X is accurate relative to X's existence and *X does not exist* is self-contradictory.

D8.   X has logically contingent existence = X exists, our concept of X is accurate relative to X's existence, and neither *X exists* nor *X does not exist* is self-contradictory.

Note that:

(i)   *X has necessary existential security* does not entail *X has logically necessary existence*;

(ii) *X has logically necessary existence* does entail *X has necessary existential security*;

(iii) whatever exists has either logically necessary or logically contingent existence;

(iv) while if it is logically possible that the existence of something be explained, it follows that it is logically possible that the thing *not* exist, it is not true that if it is logically possible that it *not* exist, then it is logically possible that its existence be explained;

(v)   while it is true that if it is logically possible that the truth of a proposition be explained, it is logically possible that the proposition *not* be true, it does not follow that if it is logically possible that a proposition *not* be true, then it is logically possible its truth be explained.

11. *X's existence is logically impossible to explain and its existence can explain the existence of things whose existence it is logically possible to explain* is true only if *X has necessary existential security* is true.

12. If something exists whose existence it is logically impossible to explain and whose existence can explain the existence of things whose existence it is logically possible to explain, something has necessary existential security.

13. Something has necessary existential security.

14. Both *explaining the existence of things whose existence it is logically possible to explain* and *having necessary existential security* are non-basic properties of anything that has them.

15. If *having necessary existential security* is a non-basic property of anything that has it, then the something that has necessary existential security has some other property whose possession explains its *having necessary existential security*.

16. The something that has necessary existential security has some other property whose possession explains its *having necessary existential security*.

17. The only properties that something might have that would explain its *having necessary existential security* are A: *having logically necessary existence* or B: *being omnipotent, omniscient, and morally perfect*.

18. Something has A or B.

19. The concept of something that has A but lacks B is the concept of an abstract object, and since abstract objects lack causal powers they cannot explain the existence of anything whose existence it is logically possible to explain; thus *having A* will not explain anything having the property *explaining the existence of things whose existence it is not logically impossible to explain*.

20. The concept of a being that has B but lacks A is the concept of a being that has causal powers and whose existence can explain the existence of anything whose existence it is logically possible to explain; thus *having B* will explain anything having the property *explaining the existence of things whose existence it is logically possible to explain*.

21. The concept of a being that has B and also has A is also the concept of a being that has causal powers and whose existence can explain the existence of anything whose existence it is logically possible to explain; thus *having A and B* will explain anything having the property *explaining the existence of things whose existence it is logically possible to explain*.

22. Something exists that has B.

23. The concept of something that has B is the concept of God, conceived either as having logically necessary existence or as having logically contingent existence, but in either case as possessing necessary existential security and causal powers that can explain the existence of anything whose existence it is logically possible to explain.

24. God exists.

Suppose that God exists, and is omnipotent and omniscient. Then God will lack no power, and no knowledge, failure to have which would allow some enemy to do God in. God's existence is utterly safe; it is logically impossible that this being be destroyed from without. Suppose God is also perfectly good. A perfectly good being won't commit suicide or deicide. There are no conditions under which a perfectly good being who is omnipotent and omniscient on which that being's destruction of itself would be a good thing for it to do. It is logically impossible that such a being, while remaining perfectly good, cause itself to implode.

God's moral perfection is conceived by monotheists in two different ways. On one account, what is true is *Necessarily, God is morally perfect*; on the other, what is logically contingent and true is *God is morally perfect*.[25] On the former account, it is logically impossible that God commit deicide. On the latter account, it is not logically impossible that God commit deicide, though one may properly trust God not to do so. On neither account of divine moral perfection is it logically possible that God depend on any thing for God's existence.

Two Points Relevant to the Cosmological Argument

Consider two claims:

1. *Possibly, X is contingent* entails *X is contingent* if *contingent* means *logically contingent* (= neither necessarily true nor necessarily false).
2. *Possibly, X is contingent* does not entail *X is contingent* if *contingent* means *depends for existence on something distinct from itself.*

The cosmological argument requires that both of these claims be true.

Argument for 1

A proposition has its modality necessarily; thus whatever modality a proposition lacks, it lacks necessarily. Logical contingency is a modality; hence whatever has it, has it necessarily, and whatever lacks it, lacks it necessarily. Hence if it is possible that a proposition is contingent, then it is.

Argument for 2

It is not logically impossible that X have logically contingent existence and yet it be false that X depends for existence on something else—a logically contingent and necessarily independent being would fit this description, for example.

Hence both 1 and 2 are true.

Conclusion

Besides requiring PSR*, this version of the cosmological argument is strongest if it can be shown that *Necessarily, God exists* is false. Only then (if at all) can one infer to the cause of possibly explicable logically contingent beings having the properties that a logically contingent being must have if its existence is to be necessarily inexplicable.

A Supplementary Argument

An argument distinct from the cosmological argument that nonetheless dwells in the same conceptual neighborhood is the following:

10a. It is logically possible that an omnicompetent deity exists.
10b. If it is logically possible that an omnicompetent being exists, then it is logically possible that an omnicompetent being destroy everything material.

So:

10c. It is logically possible that an omnicompetent being destroy everything material. [from 10, 10b]

10d. If it is logically possible that an omnicompetent being destroy everything material, then nothing material has necessary existential security.

So:

10e. Nothing material has necessary existential security. [from 10c, 10d]

Thus far, the argument is obviously sound and the independent (non-inferred) premises seem to be true. If this is correct, it is a useful supplement to the cosmological argument. A natural off-shoot is this argument:

10e1. If nothing material has necessary existential security, then something exists that is not material.

So:

10e2. Something exists that is not material.
10e3. If something exists that is not material, then materialism is false.

So:
10e4. Materialism is false.

The truth of 10e1 requires the conclusion of Stage Three of the cosmological argument—i.e., premise 10—and is exactly as secure as that premise is.

Aquinas's Fifth Way

The Fifth Way is one version of the Argument from Design. To say that something *seeks its own end* is to say that *it seeks its own flourishing as a member of its kind.* The following characterization of the Fifth Way reads it as asserting that each generable body seeks its own end, not that all generable bodies together seek some *universal* end or some end that characterizes the universe as a whole (e.g., universal orderliness).[26]

1. We observe generable bodies that lack awareness typically seek their own flourishing.
2. What happens typically does not happen accidentally.

So:

3. Generable bodies typically seeking their own flourishing does not happen accidentally. [from 1, 2]
4. Generable bodies typically seeking their own flourishing, if it does not happen accidentally, occurs only because they are caused to do so by an agent that intends that this occur.

So:

5. Generable bodies typically seeking their own flourishing occurs only because they are caused to do so by an agent that intends that this occur. [from 3, 4]
6. If they are caused to do so by an agent that intends that this occur, then there is an agent that intends that this occur.

So:

7. There is an agent that intends that this occur. [from 5, 6]

A different way of putting the argument invokes the distinction, but also the similarity, between artifacts and natural objects. Artifacts are made by humans; their parts are made and organized so as to produce some end or other. They are made to do something, and insofar as they are well made, they do that thing. Call the feature of having parts that were made to be organized so as to produce specific results *being operationally functional*. Then the argument goes:

1. Artifacts are operationally functional things.
2. Natural objects are operationally functional things.
3. Operational functionality in artifacts is adequately explicable only by reference to intelligence.
4. If artifacts are operationally functional things, natural objects are operationally functional things, and operational functionality in artifacts is adequately explicable only by reference to (human) intelligence, then operational functionality in natural objects is adequately explained only by reference to intelligence.

So:

5. Operational functionality in natural objects is adequately explained only by reference to intelligence. [from 1–4]
6. Operational functionality in natural objects is not caused by human intelligence.
7. What is caused by intelligence other than human is caused by non-human intelligence.
8. If operational functionality in natural objects is adequately explained only by reference to intelligence, and operational functionality in natural objects is not caused by human intelligence, and what is caused by intelligence other than human is caused by non-human intelligence, then operational functionality in natural objects is adequately explained only by reference to non-human intelligence.
9. Operational functionality in natural objects is adequately explained only by reference to non-human intelligence. [from 5–8]
10. If operational functionality in natural objects is adequately explained only by reference to non-human intelligence, then there is strong evidence that there is non-human intelligence.

11. There is strong evidence that there is non-human intelligence. [from 9, 10]

The conclusion is neither uninteresting (a newspaper editor convinced of its truth would put it in her headlines) nor as strong as *Monotheism is true*. Its religious relevance becomes obvious if one thinks what sorts of powers a being would have to have in order to cause operational functionality in natural objects.

   The Hindu monotheist Ramanuja offers the following objections to the argument from design. Reacting to Indian versions of the argument from design, Ramanuja says:

(1) There is no proof to show that the earth, oceans, etc., although things produced, were created at one time by one creator. Nor can it be pleaded in favor of such a conclusion that all those things have one uniform character of being effects, and thus are analogous to one single jar, for we observe that various effects are distinguished by difference of time of production, and difference of producers . . . for experience does not exhibit to us one agent capable of producing everything.[27]

That is, if we take our experience with artifacts as the clue to operational functionality in natural objects, often various humans cooperate in the production of an artifact, or make changes in it; the evidence cited by the argument from design suggests a committee as much as it does a single intelligence. A standard response is that one is justified in positing no more intelligences than is necessary to explain the data.

(2) Experience further teaches that earthen pots and similar things are produced by intelligent agents possessing material bodies, using implements, not endowed with the power of a Supreme Lord, limited in knowledge, and so on; the quality of being an effect therefore supplies a reason for inferring an intelligent agent of the kind described only.[28]

That is, if we take our experience with artifacts as the clue to operational functionality in nature, its intelligent causes are embodied[29] and possess limited intelligence and power.

(3) Consider the following point also. Does the Lord produce His effect with His body or apart from His body? Not the latter, for we do not observe causal agency on the part of any bodiless being; nor is the former alternative admissible, for in that case the Lord's body would be permanent or impermanent. The former would imply that something made up of parts is eternal; and if we say this was may as well admit that the world itself is eternal, and then there is no reason to infer a Lord. And the latter alternative is inadmissible because in that case there would be no cause of the body different from it (which would account for the origination of the body). Nor could the Lord Himself be assumed as the cause of the body, since a bodiless being cannot be

assumed as the cause of a body. Nor could it be maintained that the Lord can be assumed to be "embodied" by means of some other body; for this leads us into a regress in infinitum.[30]

Here, the reply is more complex. Suppose that God, like human artificers, must have a body in order for God to produce operational functionality in anything. Then God, able to produce operational functionality only through use of a body that is already is operationally functional, did not produce operational functionality in *that* body. God's own body, construed on the analogy with human artificers, has an operational functionality not produced by God. But then why not simply view all bodies as having some such intrinsic not-produced-by-God operational functionality? Ramanuja, then, concludes that "the inference of a creative Lord which claims to be in agreement with observation is refuted by reasoning which itself is in agreement with observation, and we hence conclude that Scripture is the only source of knowledge with regard to a supreme soul that is the Lord of all and constitutes a highest Brahman."[31]

David Hume, in his famous *Dialogues concerning Natural Religion*, offers criticisms similar to those of Ramanuja.[32] He views the argument from design as an inductive argument. The property relevant to the inductive inference is something like *orderliness* or *behaving in specifiable, predictable ways always or for the most part*. The things relevant to the inference are artifacts, like clocks, and natural objects, like apples or sheep. One is invited to infer from a sample class of which one has had experience (artifacts having been produced by an observable designer by an observable process) to a reference class of which one has had only partial relevant experience (one has observed natural objects though one has not observed them being caused to possess *orderliness* by a non-human intelligence). So the premises concern there being artifacts and natural objects, and both having orderliness. The conclusion is that natural objects are caused to have orderliness by a non-human intelligence.

The connecting premises point to the cause of orderliness in artifacts, namely human intelligence. The core idea is that one infer that orderliness in natural objects should be taken to have the same sort of cause—an intelligent mind—and obviously human minds do not cause orderliness in apples and goats.[33]

Hume makes these objections, among others:

(a) There are other explanations of orderliness in natural objects than that they were designed—for example, natural objects might have a sort of intrinsic order, being by nature organisms or natural machines produced by natural processes.

(b) We cannot in principle observe natural objects being caused to have orderliness by non-human intelligence nor can we in principle observe natural objects being caused to have orderliness by something else; observing an apple grow or a goat give birth are examples of orderliness, not explanations of orderliness of the sort disputers regarding the argument from design are concerned with.

(c) There is no lawlike connection that we can know of between *natural objects possessing orderliness* and *natural objects being caused to have orderliness by X*, whether "X" is filled in by reference to intelligence, natural processes, or anything else, and legitimate inductive inferences ride the rails of natural laws.

The argument from design is, in effect, an argument to the best explanation—an argument that is intended to establish that, if we follow the sorts of procedures we typically follow in making probabilistic inference, we shall come to the conclusion that there is a designer. But there obviously are other explanations of operative functionality in natural objects—for example, that material particles evolved over a long period in such a manner as to produce such items. All that is required, the proposal is, is particles of the right sorts, laws, and time. This sort of explanation of operative functionality in natural objects is intended as well to explain there being human intelligence capable of causing operative functionality in artifacts. Thus most of the philosophically interesting issues raised by arguments from design have to do with how to decide which, among a group of explanations, is best, and how exactly to understand the relevant data and formulate the theories relevant to explaining them. This sort of issue comes up again in the final chapter on Faith and Reason.

The Teleological Argument

Another argument in the same family as the argument from design, but different in what it begins with—the intelligibility of nature or the possibility of science—and its straightforwardness as an argument to the best explanation—is the teleological argument. As construed here, it is a supplement to the cosmological argument. Here is one more objection to the cosmological argument: what the conclusion of the cosmological argument does (roughly) is to say that the universe of dependent things is caused by the act of an intelligent divine agent; it says that God, who might not have created anything, acted to create dependent things. But then God's action of creating might not have occurred. So we are left, not with a being that might not have existed but whose existence it is not impossible to explain, but with an action that might not have occurred; what's the gain?—either way we stop our explanation arbitrarily. One way of construing the teleological argument, it is not an independent argument but rather is an answer to this objection to the cosmological argument.

The teleological argument is often stated as an independent argument. As stated here, it is a continuation of the cosmological argument, and offers an answer to the present objection to that argument. Again, some beginning definitions simplify the overall presentation.

D1. R is S's *sufficient reason* for doing A = S does A for reason R, there is no better reason for doing A than R, there is nothing better that S might do than A, and S's doing A is right (note that *being right* does not entail *being obligatory*; if there is more than one right way of acting in a given circum-stance, one's obligations in that circumstance are simply to act in one of those ways).

D2. R is S's *proper ultimate reason* for doing A = R is S's sufficient reason for doing A, there is no true moral proposition from which R follows in any way that justifies R, R is true, and S knows that R is true (every proposition follows from other propositions—any proposition P follows from [(Q or P) and not-Q]—but not every proposition follows from others in a way that proves it true; if we cannot have some knowledge without proving it, we cannot prove anything).

D3. S is *completely rational* in doing A = S has a proper ultimate reason for doing A.

D4. E is an *ultimate existence explanation* = E explains the truth of a logically contingent existence proposition by reference to the truth of an existence proposition whose truth it is logically impossible to explain.

Statement of the Teleological Argument

1. If an ultimate existence explanation has a teleological explanation as an essential component, then the agent referred to in that teleological explana-tion is completely rational in acting as that explanation says she acts.
2. If an agent is completely rational in acting in a certain way, then there can be no further teleological explanation of her acting in that way.
3. If there can be no further teleological explanation of an agent's acting in a certain way, then unless the existence of that agent can be explained, there is nothing relevant that is left unexplained.
4. If God created the world, God was completely rational in doing so.

According (roughly) to the conclusion of the cosmological argument:

5. God created the world.

Hence, from 4 and 5:

6. God was completely rational in doing so.

Hence, from 2 and 6:

7. There can be no further explanation of God's creating the world.

But:

8. It is not possible to explain the existence of God.

Hence, from 3, 7, and 8:

9.   There is nothing relevant that is left unexplained.

Hence the objection fails. One is not left with something explicable that is unexplained.

Conclusion

The combination of the cosmological and teleological arguments considered is one of the stronger versions of one sort at least of natural theology—the effort to present arguments that are plainly valid, have premises that are discernibly necessarily true or contingently true propositions, and infer to the existence of God. Even it, however, does not yield a proof that extends our knowledge.

Questions for Reflection

1.   What is the difference between a logically necessary and a logically contingent proposition?
2.   Consider this argument:

Possibly, something has necessary existence. (= The concept of a necessarily existing thing is not inconsistent.)
If [Possibly, something necessarily exists] then it is true that [Something necessarily exists].

So:

Something necessarily exists. (This is to be contrasted with [Necessarily, something or other exists]).
If this argument is correct, then the sort of argument that the Ontological Argument is, one that goes beyond pure thought to extra-mental existence, is possible. Is this argument correct?

3.   Does the concept of having a cause apply to, as well as within, the cosmos?
4.   What sort of argument extends our knowledge?
5.   Is a version of the cosmological argument that allows for there being a beginningless series of caused and causing beings stronger than one that does not?

Notes

1. Proposition P *entails* proposition Q if and only if *P, but not Q* is a contradiction (e.g., *There are two whales in the bay* entails *There is at least one whale in the bay*, since to assert the former and deny the latter is to contradict yourself). Another way of putting this is: P *entails* Q if and only if *P, therefore Q* is a necessary truth.

2. George Mavrodes (1970) *Belief in God: A Study in the Epistemology of Religion* (New York: Random House), Chapter Two.

3. These examples are due to George Mavrodes (1970) *Belief in God: A Study in the Epistemology of Religion* (New York: Random House).

4. For those not aware of the history of the basketball franchise the Boston Celtics, Bill Russell was the center for the Celtics' teams that won eleven of thirteen championships, and the greatest defensive center (arguably, the greatest player) ever to play the game.

5. Defending this understanding goes beyond the scope of this book. For a beginning, see Arthur Pap (1959) *Semantics and Necessary Truth* (Yale: Yale University Press), Chapter Seven, "The Linguistic Theory of the Apriori" and Alvin Plantinga (1974) *The Nature of Necessity* (Oxford: Clarendon Press).

6. For an accessible review of different relevant views, see Michael Loux (1998) *Metaphysics* (London: Routledge).

7. If you want another counter-example and are willing to have it more complicated than our other examples, here are two: *For any formal S, if S is adequate for number theory (e.g., if its axioms are strong enough to entail Peano's postulates) there will be some formula F that is both expressible in S and undecidable in S* and its corollary *For any formal system S, if S is adequate for number theory, there can be no proof within S of the claim* **S is consistent**. These are hardly uninformative or mathematically trivial.

8. Due to Alvin Plantinga; see *The Nature of Necessity* and *God, Freedom, and Evil* (New York: Random House, 1974). The former contains the fulldress, and the latter a streamlined, version of the argument.

9. Note that, on the principle *For all X, if X is actual then X is possible* that the actual world is (also) a possible world.

10. Note that to be *true in all possible worlds* and to be *included in every maximal proposition* are the same.

11. I am using 'empirical' here very broadly.

12. This strategy may also seem attractive if one wishes to hedge one's bet regarding the interpretation of Scripture on how God and the universe are related.

13. Medieval theories of relations is an interesting topic all by itself—one that would take us far afield from our current concerns. Mark Henning (1989) *Relations: Medieval Theories* (Cambridge: Cambridge University Press) provides an excellent introduction.

14. Some member of the domain must also stand in this relationship only backwardly—must depend on something else but nothing else depends on it.

15. At *De Caelo XII 258* Aquinas offers a series of claims relevant to his Five Ways. It seems worth including them here. Again, we begin with definitions:

> Definition A: X has *non-derivative necessary existence* if and only if *X does not exist* is self-contradictory.
> Definition B: X has derivative necessary existence if and only if X cannot naturally (without the action of an omnipotent being) cease to exist.

Definition C: X cannot naturally cease to exist if and only if X contains no matter or the matter that X contains cannot have any essence other than the one that it has.

Definition D: X has the power of not existing if and only if X is such that X exists only if X has the essence it has but it is possible that the stuff that X is made of come to have some other essence.

Definition E: X generates from Y at T if and only if there is a Y that exists at T − 1 and X at T contains the matter that was in Y at T.

Definition F: X corrupts at T if and only if there is a Y such that Y exists at T + 1 and the matter that was in X at T is in Y at T + 1.

Definition G: X is a natural body only if X is capable of generation and corruption.

Aquinas tells us:

1. If X always exists, then X has the power always to exist.
2. If X has the power always to exist, then X lacks the power not to always exist.
3. If X always exists then X lacks the power not to always exist. [from 1, 2]
4. If X lacks the power not to always exist then X does not generate or corrupt.
5. If X generates or corrupts then X does not lack the power not always to exist.
6. If X has the power not always to exist then X does not always exist.
7. If X generates or corrupts then X does not always exist.

Also involved seems the idea that, in some sense, *Necessarily, in any infinite time all possibilities are realized*, though it is difficult to think of any reading of this claim on which it is true.

16. More fully: For X to change or move is for X to go from potentiality to actuality or from actuality to potentiality regarding quantity, quality, or place.

17. The existence of something with causal powers—the actual capacity to bring about changes in other things—that was not itself changed in so doing—might, by itself, have slight religious relevance, but of course Aquinas has no intention of limiting himself to this one conclusion.

18. And animal mind, if such there be—we need not enter into that matter here.

19. The notion of infinity is of course complex. A nice introduction to various relevant notions is A. W. Moore (1991) *The Infinite* (London: Routledge).

20. At *Summa* I a46 2ad7.

21. The strategy here is called Conditional Proof. You assume that P, show that P plus a set of truths entails Q, and conclude *If P then Q*.

22. Let *P = possibly, P; Cx = x corrupts. Then another way of stating the criticism is this: Aquinas shifts quantifiers illegitimately, going from: $\mathbf{A} = (x)^*Cx$ to $\mathbf{B} = {}^*(x)Cx$.

23. Let Ex/t = x exists at t; (Et) = there is a t. Then the criticism is that Aquinas illegitimately goes from: $\mathbf{D} = (x)(Et)$ not-Ex/t to $\mathbf{E} = (Et)(x)$ not-Ex/t.

24. The Fourth Way is a variety of the moral argument for God's existence, and we will look at it briefly when we consider religion and morality.

25. Here, 'God' is being used as a name, not a definite description.

26. *ST* Ia 15 2 suggests the possibility of the reading that we do not give here.

Aquinas is criticized for making an inference from **A** to **B** below:

A. Every generable thing is such that an intelligent agent directs it to seek its own flourishing.

B. There is an end that all generable beings together are directed to seek.

On the present reading, no such inference is required.

27. Sacred Books Volume 48, pp. 170–171.
28. Ibid., 165—cf. p. 171 that notes that intelligent agents whom we observe to cause things also have emotions— "are connected with pleasure and the like."
29. Ramanuja thinks of the world as God's body, but a body that depends on God for its existence.
30. Ibid., p. 173.
31. Ibid., p. 173.
32. After an introductory first section, sections two through eight of the *Dialogues* deal with a dialogue concerning the argument from design. Section nine deals with an argument that is a mix of the ontological and cosmological arguments, sections ten and eleven with the problem of evil, and section twelve with natural religion. The present author has discussed all of these issues in Hume's philosophy in *Hume's "Inexplicable Mystery": His Views on Religion* (Philadelphia: Temple University Press, 1988).
33. Two points: there is also a version of the argument that has as a premise the orderliness of the physical world as a whole, rather that the orderliness of particular sorts of natural objects; the fact that we can change the sort of order we find in nature by selective breeding in no way discounts the fact that we did not bring about the order that makes such breeding possible. Both varieties of the argument are discussed further in *Hume's "Inexplicable Mystery."*

Suggested Readings

Burrell, Donald, ed. (1967) *Cosmological Arguments* (Garden City, NY: Anchor Books). An excellent collection of historical and recent discussions of the argument.

De Cruz, Helen and DeSmet, Johan (2014) *A Natural History of Natural Theology: The Cognitive Science of Theology and Philosophy of Religion* (Cambridge, MA: MIT Press). Argues that the ideas developed in theistic arguments articulate our sense of beauty, order, and design, which are universal.

Flew, Anthony (1966) *God and Philosophy* (London: Hutchinson). Philosophy of religion done on the presumption of atheism.

Haldane, J.J. and Smart, J.J.C. (1996) *Theism and Atheism* (Oxford: Blackwell). An atheist and a Catholic theist argue their cases.

Hallett, Garth (2008) *A Middle Way to God* (Oxford: Oxford University Press). Argues that a sound argument for minds other than one's own is paralleled by a sound argument for theism.

Hick, John and McGill, Arthur, eds. (1967) *The Many-faced Argument* (New York: Macmillan). An excellent collection of historical and recent discussions of the Ontological Argument.

Leftow, Brian (2015) *God and Necessity* (Oxford: Oxford University Press). Offers a new view of possibility and necessity that provides the basis for an argument for theism.

Manson, Neil, ed. (2003) *God and Design: The Teleological Argument and Modern Science* (New York: Routledge). An excellent introduction followed by strong papers on issues essential to the success of the argument.

O'Connor, Timothy (2008) *Theism and Ultimate Explanation: The Necessary Shape of Contingency* (Malden, MA: Wiley-Blackwell). Offers an account of necessity and contingency that leads to a new formulation of the cosmological argument of Leibniz.

Plantinga, Alvin, ed. (1974) *The Ontological Argument* (New York: Harper and Row). An excellent collection of traditional, and some recent, treatments of the argument.

Rowe, William (1975) *The Cosmological Argument* (Princeton, NJ: Princeton University Press). Probably the best discussion of the argument.

Swinburne, Richard (1979) *The Existence of God* (Oxford: Clarendon Press). Argues for the existence of God from a perspective in which the controversial idea of a priori simplicity is important.

11 Monotheism and Religious Experience

Our next question is whether apparent experiences of God provide evidence for God's existence. Even if the answer is affirmative, that does not settle the issue. There are various relevant considerations, among them arguments for and against, other sorts of religious experience, the status of appeals to sacred texts, and historical evidence in those cases where the truth of certain historical claims is a necessary condition of the truth of central religious doctrines. So our inquiry concerns only a part of the overall evidential question.

Phenomenologically Thick Experiences

Phenomenological Content and Description

Subject-consciousness-object experiences have phenomenological content—there is a way things seem to the subject to be, given the experience. A phenomenological description of an experience is a description that tells us how things appear to the person who has it. Consider these sentences, each of which uses the word 'seems' in a different sense:

1. Kim seems less capable than she is. (Here, 'seems' contrasts appearance to reality.)
2. It seems to Kim that she left the oven on. (Here, 'seems' reports a shaky belief on Kim's part.)
3. There seems to Kim to be a chair in front of her. (Here, 'seems' expresses how Kim is "appeared to"; whether there is a chair there or not, it remains true that if things are as they perceptually appear to Kim, a chair is in front of her.)

So there are at least three senses of 'seems'—a contrastive sense (in 1), an opinionative or belief-expressive (in 2), and an experiential and perceptual sense (in 3). Our concern is with the experiential, perceptual sense. Suppose Kim is in a room that she knows that was set up by majors in psychology and physics. There seem to be twice as many chairs in the room as there are—half of the "chairs" are in fact holograms of chairs. Not having been in the room before, but knowing that half of what seem to be chairs are not, Kim nonetheless properly says:

4.   It seems to me that there is a chair in front of me, though I have no idea
     whether I am seeing a chair or a hologram of a chair.

The 'seems' here is experiential and perceptual; it is also *phenomenological*—it
describes how things perceptually seem, whether they are that way or not. Using
phenomenological descriptions, an atheist and a theist can agree that experiences
occur in which it at least seems to the subject that she is experiencing a powerful,
holy being[1] distinct from herself. They disagree over whether there is such a being
that she perceives.

Thin Description versus Thick Description

Members of monotheistic religious traditions report what they will describe as
experience of God. Sometimes the phenomenologies of these experiences is quite
thin, for example a matter of feeling forgiven, only if one reasonably already takes
monotheism to be true does one have reason to take such experiences as reliable,
and even then only with various qualifications (e.g., is one planning to do the same
thing again tomorrow?). These seem to be experiences toward which one likely
must be disposed to interpret theistically for them to be taken as pro-theistic evidence, and they are not typically offered as pro-theistic evidence in philosophical
disputes. In contrast, subject-conscious-object experiences that have fuller theistic
phenomenologies more typically appear in such discussions. After considering a
more general issue, we will return to the topic of thicker phenomenologies.

Since sensory perception is more familiar than religious experience, we will start
with examples of sensory experience in developing a satisfactory principle of experiential evidence—a principle relevant to assessing the evidential force of experiences.
We start with this basic idea: an experience that is subject-consciousness-object in
structure, where the apparent object, if the experience is reliable, exists distinct from,
and independent of, the subject, is evidence for the existence of that object. Seeming
to see a dog on the couch is evidence that a dog is on the couch. Then the question
is whether the principle needs to be qualified, and if so how. The result should be at
least a defensible principle of experiential evidence. Then it needs to be seen whether
that principle, as it stands or with further revision, is suitable for use relative to religious experience. We will lay out the discussion by means of questions and answers,
using vision as our example, and neglecting other senses.

Experience as Direct Evidence

*Question One: Are there other approaches to religious experience as evidence
than the one pursued here?*

Yes. Here are two examples. One approach asks what the best explanation
is of the occurrence of religious experience, arguing that theism supplies this.

This requires an account of what is meant by explanation, how one decides among competitors, and why a theistic explanation is the best. Another appeals to doxastic (belief-forming) practices. They are based on particular foundational propositions that provide a framework for thinking that sets the context in which the interpretations of experiences are offered. One familiar practice concerns forming beliefs about physical objects. The practice is widespread but its foundational propositions are not necessary truths and the success of the practice depends on the degree to which those who follow it survive and flourish. Further, a practice can be evaluated in terms of the logical consistency and mutual coherence of the beliefs that arise from interpreting relevant experiences along the lines supplied by the foundations. It is also relevant to ask how well the overall view composed by the foundations and the beliefs gained from interpreting experiences as they suggest fares in terms of resolving problems and paradoxes that arise in following the practice. What is not clear is the degree to which, if at all, this interesting view escapes relativism. Practices—particularly religious ones—tend to produce incompatible views. The foundational propositions in one practice will not only be different but, in various cases, incompatible. There must then be some propositions, presumably practice-neutral, to which to appeal when one tries to assess competing practices in terms of consistency, coherence, and success in untying conceptual knots. (And, if there are such assessment-relevant propositions, in virtue of what are they epistemically more secure than the competing propositions in practice foundations? If the response is that the assessment-relevant items are procedures rather than propositions, this simply raises the question as to what propositions justify the use of these principles.) Appeal to what we have called phenomenologically thin experiences is in accord with a doxastic practice theory, depending on which propositions are included in the foundations. By contrast, here we take it that there are principles of experiential evidence to which we can appeal in deriving conclusions about the evidential force of religious experiences.

Question Two: What makes some experiences "thicker" than others?

Some experiences viewed as experiences of God are, as it were, phenomenologically thicker in that the subjects report, not of feeling forgiven, but an awareness of a being of majestic power, profound holiness, overwhelming purity, and deep love. Responses include worship, reverence, a sense of dependence, and a sense of one's sinfulness. Such experiences are reported in various formal and informal mystical traditions in Catholic, Orthodox, and Protestant contexts, in all of the Semitic monotheisms, and in Hindu monotheism. Similar reports are given by persons not associated with any mystical or religious tradition, sometimes by persons not religious by any monotheistic standard. Sometimes these experiences are sought and sometimes they simply occur. An earlier chapter lists a few descriptions of such experiences. The present question is whether the occurrence of these phenomenologically richer experiences provides any evidence that God exists. This question of experiential evidence can be answered with any care only if we ask and answer some other questions first. Here is a series of relevant questions and answers. Throughout these questions and answers, but not elsewhere, 'religious experience' will simply mean "experiences that, given their phenomenology, are, if reliable, experiences of God."

The relevant experiences are subject/consciousness/object in structure; they involve a person having an experience that, providing that the experience is reliable, involves being aware of something or someone that is not dependent for its existence on being experienced. In that respect, such experiences resemble experiences of shrubs and worms (these being typically reliable, and shrubs and worms existing independent of one's experiencing them) or of ghosts (if experiences of ghosts were reliable, then ghosts would have experience-independent existence). They have the sort of content described previously in the first part of our series of descriptions of religious experiences. They are also experiences in which the at least apparent object is not oneself, one's body, or one's mental states; they are (if reliable) experiences of something other than oneself or one's body or one's states—a being that exists distinct from and independent of oneself.

Question Three : Can any experience be evidence for just any old claim?

Distinguish between direct evidence and indirect evidence. An experience is direct evidence for a claim that something exists only if it is true that the experience in question, if reliable, just is an experience of that thing. We take it that we have exactly that sort of experience of cats and computers. An experience is indirect evidence for the existence of something only if it is, if reliable, experience of something else, where if the something else exists, then the thing in question exists. Suppose that Ralph and Mabel are hosting Mabel's sloppy brother Jim, whom they know to be the only person in the world who eats peanut butter and mustard sandwiches. Arriving home, Ralph is hopeful that his brother-in-law may have ended his visit, but is chagrined to find on the kitchen table two peanut butter and mustard sandwiches waiting to be devoured; he infers that Jim is still around, and will soon be having a snack. Seeing the sandwiches provides direct evidence of their existence, and indirect evidence of Jim's continued presence. Our concern in this chapter will be with direct evidence only, and our concern with it focuses on the conditions under which experience provides direct evidence for the existence of something. Not every experience can be direct evidence for the existence of just anything. Its at least seeming to Mary that there is tea in her cup, bread on her table, and music coming over the radio will not provide her with direct evidence that the Alps are still around, there are trolls, or that God exists. Mountains, trolls, and God are not among the things she even seems to directly experience. An experience is direct evidence only for what exists provided that experience is reliable—provided things are as that experience represents them as being. How an experience represents things as being is a function of its phenomenological content. Our concern here is with, and only with, experience as potential evidence for claims to the effect that things are as the experiences that are potential direct evidence for them represent things as being[2]—with the cases of experiences and claims where the claims match up with the phenomenological content of the experiences. Experiences will not be direct evidence for any other claims.

A Principle of Experiential Evidence

Question Four: How do we tell what an experience can be direct evidence for the existence of?

An experience can be direct evidence for the existence of something only if it is an experience in which it experientially seems to the subject to be an encounter with—a perception of—that thing. An experience in which one at least seems to perceive a coat in the closet provides one with evidence for the existence of a coat and a closet. There may not be: it is logically possible that she only seems to see a coat in the closet and there be neither or just one. The basic idea, then, is this: if Mary has an experience that, if reliable, is a matter of experiencing a coat in her closet, then she has experiential evidence in favor of things being just that way. More formally:

(P) If a person S has an experience E that, if reliable, is a matter of being aware of an experience-independently existing item X (whose phenomenological content represents there being an X), then S's having E gives S evidence that X exists.

Question Five: Can't such experiences go wrong in various ways?

Yes. If Mary is drinking a special tea that always produces coat hallucinations, it will appear to her that there is a coat, whether there is one or not. This circumstance, let us say, will cancel the evidential force of the experience relative to there being a coat in the closet. She has seemed to see a coat under circumstances where she would seem to see one whether there was one or not. So we need to revise (P) via:

(P1) If a person S has an experience E which, if reliable, is a matter of being aware of an experience-independently existing item X, and E is not canceled, then S's having E gives S good evidence that X exists.

If Mary learns that her tea has its unusual feature, she is justified in drawing no inference regarding the coat.

Suppose Mary looks in her messy desk drawer and seems to see the pen she got for her birthday. She closes the drawer, opens it again, and does not seem to see the pen. She is suddenly called away but cannot get the pen off her mind. She reflects that her original evidence has been counterbalanced, and if she goes by the evidence she suspends judgment. So we need a further revision:

(P2) If a person S has an experience E that, if reliable, is a matter of being aware of an experience-independently existing item X, and E is not canceled *or counterbalanced*, then S's having E gives S good evidence that X exists.

Suppose Mary succumbs to a rare disease the result of which is that she cannot see coats and she always seems to see a pen. Then her not seeming to see a coat is not evidence there is none, and her seeming to see a pen is not evidence that there is one. Relative to coats and pens, her experience is *compromised*. She cannot confirm or disconfirm that there is a coat in the closet or a pen in the drawer. So we need to add this revision:

(P3) If S has an experience E such that, if reliable, it is evidence that there is a mind-independent X, then unless S's experience is cancelled, counterbalanced, or compromised, S's having E is good evidence that there is an X that S experiences.

Here we need to change our strategy, since the needed qualification is more obviously applicable to religious experience than to sensory.

Suppose one discovers a discernibly powerful argument for God's non-existence, perhaps a complex but lucid demonstration that every theologically satisfactory concept of the divine attributes we have been able to form is logically inconsistent. Then the possibility of the existence of the apparent object of religious experience is seriously conceptually challenged.

Thus we need:

(P4) If a person S has an experience E that, if reliable, is a matter of being aware of an experience-independently existing item X, and E is not canceled or counterbalanced or compromised or conceptually challenged, then S's having E gives S positive evidence that X exists.

This gives at least an idea of what is meant by a principle of experiential evidence. It is hard to see how one could be sure that one had included the entire range of possible ways in which subject-consciousness-object experiences can "go wrong." All one can do is put in all the ways one can think of and be ready to add others if they are found.

We can add a principle to the effect that:

(P4*) If S (non-culpably) believes that S's experience E satisfies (P4) she is rational in taking E to be evidence that X exists.

There has been something of a shift in philosophy of religion toward asking whether religious belief is reasonable rather than pressing a claim about truth. While the truth question is more basic, the reasonability question is also important, and relative to religious belief based on subject-consciousness-object experience (P4) provides a response.

Question Six: It is hard to see how the certainty religious belief requires is going to be achieved given what you have said; isn't that a problem?

Descartes pointed out that it was logically possible, in any case of apparently successful sensory perception, that one be mistaken. While it does not follow from this being possible in *any* case, it is possible in *every* case. Descartes noted that every one of our sensory perceptions could be unreliable. So if what we mean by 'certainty' regarding a belief is that it is logically impossible we believe it and it be false, we can have no certain sensory knowledge. Similarly, it does not follow from someone's having an apparent experience of God that she cannot be wrong about its reliability. It is not a necessary truth that apparent experiences of God are reliable in the sense of genuinely being what they seem. It is also logically possible that your friends and family are fictions of your imagination. The thing to do after knowing that is to remember that it is logically possible that they are not fictions. So far as sheer logical possibilities go, things are tied. Descartes held that we can know necessary truths, that we exist, that we are in certain mental states, and how things sensorily appear to us. Even that short list has been challenged. Note that it does not include knowing any historical truths, that you have brown hair or have feet, and so on through pretty much everything in life. It is plausible that most religious believers would be content if justified religious confidence compared favorably with their belief that the objects that occupy their physical environment are actually there and much like they seem. The point is that, for any proposition the truth of which is not entailed by your believing it, you can be mistaken in believing it. (Remember every necessary truth is entailed by every proposition.) A psychological certainty often comes with salvation and enlightenment experiences. Whether this certainty is justified is a function of the degree to which the relevant traditions are true.

Question Seven: What about the claim that God is ineffable, or that religious experience is ineffable?

To say of something X that it is seriously and literally ineffable is to say that (I) *For any concept C, C does not apply to X.* Since the concept of ineffability is a concept, to make the claim that anything is seriously and literally ineffable is to assert something that is necessarily false. So neither God, nor religious experience, can be literally ineffable. It is possible to revise the thesis and say something like (Ia) *For any concept C save the concept of ineffability, C does not apply to X.* But X is ineffable entails X exists, so the concept of existence applies to X and thus (Ia) is false. One can then try (Ib) *For any concept C save the concepts of ineffability and existence, C does not apply to X.* But X exists and X has no properties is also necessarily false. One can then try (Ic) *For any concept C save the concepts of ineffability, existence, and having properties, C does not apply to X.* If the concept *having properties* applies to X, then so does the concept *having only consistent properties, not being both prime and not prime, being either good or not* and so on. By the time one has finally reached a non-contradictory thesis, serious and literal ineffability has been left far behind. It is only serious and literal ineffability that would raise a problem for our argument.

Question Eight: Isn't the sort of criticism just made merely verbal, superficial, intellectual cleverness without substance, and so worthless?

No. If one claims that nothing said in English can be true, what one says cannot be true. If one says that all sentences of more than four words are gibberish, if what one said were true one would have said nothing. If one claims that the state of Washington is a prime number, one asserts that a concrete object is identical to an abstract object, that something spatially located is identical with something that cannot be spatially located, that something that might never have existed is identical to something that (if it exists at all) has logically necessary existence. All of these claims are discernibly intellectually disreputable in the light of what they entail. The same goes for the claim that something is ineffable.

The claim that something is ineffable, while it is (like all claims) made by the use of language, is not about language—it is about God, or religious experience, or whatever is said to be ineffable. Any claim that God, religious experience, or anything else is ineffable, as it turns out, is self-defeating. If one claims instead that God cannot be described *in physical terms* or that we cannot completely describe God,[3] these claims are true. But they have nothing to do with ineffability.

Question Nine: Can't we always "explain away" any religious experience without any reference to God?

Consider some person Tom and some experience E that Tom has. To give a social science explanation of Tom's having E is to refer to some science phenomenon (SSP)—some institution, practice, community membership, phobia, desire, economic status, political role or perspective, social standing, unconscious motivations, or whatever—and to claim that Tom's having SSP is the cause of Tom's experience E. Suppose some such explanation is true. Does it disqualify E from being reliable? Suppose E is a conceptual experience—Tom's belief that social science is not simply a superstition that unscrupulous academics have developed in order to bilk money from students and government agencies. Is that conceptual experience of Tom's rendered unreliable, or at least somehow evidentially neutralized, by its being social science explicable? Suppose instead Tom's experience is that of appreciating the love of his family, respecting the environment, hoping studying hard will enable him to pass his social science course, or being shocked at the number of conspiracy theories people accept. If there are social science explanations, as there seem to be, these experiences are going to be explained by them in whatever sense social science explanations do explain anything. But their being social science explicable in no way discredits the evidential value of such experiences, if they have any in the first place. After all, the development of the social sciences themselves, their procedures of inquiry and standards of research and methods of theory testing, are all themselves social science explicable. If being social science explicable renders unreliable what is explained, social science itself is a crock.

Two things are necessary for what might be called social science debunking. The first is that the thing—the experience, belief, practice, or whatever—has been shown to be unreliable, false, unsuccessful, or otherwise defective. Then some social science explanation is appealed to in order to explain how anybody could accept an unreliable experience, a false belief, an unsuccessful practice. But all of the critical intellectual work involved in the debunking has already been done by the time social science is appealed to. Of course what typically happens is that opponents of a view simply offer the social science explanation without bothering to offer actual arguments and evidence against what they oppose, and then claim to have debunked the view they dislike, hoping that no one will notice that their own view is also social science explicable and that they haven't actually refuted anything. The assumption is that the strategy can be successful without entering in dispute as to whether the belief in question has evidential support in that whatever can be explained by appeal to natural phenomena alone is not in any respect supernatural.

The tighter argument against religious experience being evidence is this: if one can specify some set of conditions C under which religious experience R occurs—say an apparent experience of God—and explain C's obtaining in purely naturalistic terms, then—by transitivity of explanation—one has explained R in naturalistic terms. If one can reproduce R when one wants, or at least often, by bringing about a condition like C, then one is even better off regarding showing R to be part of the nexus of naturalistic cause and effect. Of course the causes of R may be subtle, and the attempt to produce it only sometimes successful, but this matters little since one has already shown that R can be caused in a fashion that makes no reference to God. Hallucinations are subject-consciousness-object in structure but are not evidence for the existence of the reality of what just seems to be there. If one can explain a subject-consciousness-object experience without reference to its apparent object, one has removed any reason to think that the experience gives reason to believe that object exists.

This is obviously a forceful argument. It deserves careful examination. The fact that it is possible to produce subject-consciousness-object experiences that seem to be awareness of some item does not discredit cases in which items of that sort are actually experienced. Further, for any experience of any human being, there presumably is some physical state such that having that experience is, or is correlated with, that state. There is some physical condition that is, or is sufficient condition for, the experience. One common monotheistic belief is that everything that exists that can be caused is held in existence by God. This is not an observable feature of things. Neither particle nor partridge carries with it an observable created-by-God feature. This does not refute the monotheistic claim, which is not empirically confirmable or disconfirmable. Its reasons lie in philosophy and theology. But the appeal to religious experience as evidence for God's existence obviously is a different matter as it makes an explicit claim of experiential confirmation. Mention of the monotheistic doctrine of creation and conservation nonetheless makes a relevant point. The fact that religious experiences at least involve the occurrence of physical states that are social (and natural) science explicable is not logically inconsistent with there being a religious explanation.

The next question is why anyone should think there is one. It will be useful to discuss this in connection with a look at some of the differences between sensory evidence and evidence, if any, from religious experience.

Question Ten: Aren't there crucial differences between sensory experience and religious experience?

There certainly are differences. They are crucial for some matters, and not crucial for others. Let such experiences as *seeing that identity is transitive, recognizing that no contradiction can be true, discerning that arguments of the form [P or Q, and not-Q; therefore P] are valid but arguments of the form [P or Q, and Q; therefore P] are invalid conceptual experiences.* There are crucial differences between sensory experiences and conceptual experiences; that fact casts no aspersions on either sort of experience and gives no reason for supposing that either is evidentially suspect. Suppose that Tara and Todd sit beside one another at morning worship. Tara and Todd both at least appear to see a stained glass window and Tara has a religious experience whereas Todd does not. If Tara were to seem to see a window and Todd were not, given that both are sighted and looking in the same place, either Tara is window-hallucinating or Todd is window-blind. But Todd's not having a religious experience does not call into question Tara's having one, nor does it raise doubts about the religious experience that Tara has. This difference sometimes is put by saying that sensory experience is public in a way that religious experience is not. Further, if one wants to see the window, simple procedures will allow this, whereas experiences of God are not producible by following a procedure. Sensory experiences typically are *controllable* where religious experiences are not. Further still, if one sees the window, one can predict that if one reaches out, one will touch it; if one raps it gently, one will hear a sound; if one tastes it, one will get a cold, smooth sensation; were one to strike it sharply with a hammer, it would break; and so on. Sensory experiences typically ground predictions and are testable by comparison with experiences from other sensory modalities. Typically, religious experiences do not ground predictions nor do there seem to be multiple religious modalities.[4]

These differences are crucial only if they underlie this difference: it is possible to cross-check sensory experiences but it is not possible to cross-check religious experiences. Since this is not so, these differences are not crucial relative to the question of whether religious experience provides evidence that God exists.

Question Eleven: How can one check religious experiences?

In exactly the ways one might expect. First, any experience that satisfies (P4) is evidence by virtue of that fact. There isn't any point in checking, say, one sensory experience against another unless each such experience has some presumptive evidential force. If it looks like my computer screen has turned solid gold, there is no point in checking unless my looking again has some evidential punch all on its own; but then the first look has evidential punch too. If there isn't any conflict among one's sensory experiences, as there very often is not, then comparison will have no negative results regarding their reliability. To the degree that there are religiously relevant similarities this counts in favor of their having evidential force. Second, one appeals to other things one knows or reasonably believes in sorting out what experiential conflicts one finds in sensory experience. If an experience is reliable only if something is false that we have good reason to believe, its reliability is properly questioned. The same holds for religious experiences. Third, if religious experiences occur, as they do, in various cultures, at various times, to people in various sorts of social, economic, political, and psychological situations, that is all to the good—it broadens the base of possible comparison of experience with experience, removes concern that religious experience is somehow tied to one culture or another, and the like.

Being Evidence versus Providing Evidence

If (P4) is true, any experience not disqualified by it *is* evidence. It does not follow that any such experience *provides* evidence to anyone who did not have it. Being evidence is a necessary but not sufficient condition for *providing evidence*. What else is required? One obvious thing is this: in order for an experience to provide evidence to one, one must believe it to be evidence, as well as its being evidence. But what else?

If one considers the logical possibilities regarding sensory experience as evidence, they turn out to include:

L1. No sensory perception is reliable.
L2. All sensory perceptions are reliable.
L3. Some sensory perceptions are reliable and some are not.

Descartes considered the possibility that there is an evil deceiver who has and uses the power to make sure that there never is what we seem to perceive. Given this, and the thesis that if it is possible that my current perception is unreliable (what I seem to see is not there), it follows that I can never be justifiably certain that I correctly perceive. But it is also possible that there is a good perceiver who has and uses the power to guarantee that every sensory perception is reliable, and from this and the thesis that my sensory perception is evidence as to the way things are (plus there being no reason to think my perception is unreliable), it is reasonable for me to think my sensory perceptions are reliable. What makes it unreasonable to think that they always are is that if one proposes that all perceptions are reliable, one will encounter cases of perceptual conflict (the stick out of the water is straight, partially submerged is bent, so that one who requires all perception to be reliable should hold the view that the stick changes shape when partially submerged).

Another, and opposite, perspective says that Mary only need (non-culpably) to have no reason to think that the experience is unreliable. If a matter is of enough importance, and there are considerations relative to whether an experience is reliable, these considerations are accessible without great effort, then it is at least arguable that one basing a belief on the evidence that his experience seems to provide should see if it does so in the light of those considerations. If he does not do so, under some circumstances, his belief is arguably unreasonable; he has not checked out what he should. The various notions involved here—matter of enough importance, relevant considerations, accessibility—are hardly lucid. For our purposes, only two things need be noted: (i) since our concern is centrally with whether religious experiences *are* evidence, and so *can provide evidence*, for religious belief, we need not enter deeply into a discussion as to exactly when a particular person is reasonable in accepting them as evidence, and (ii) if an experience does not run afoul of any of the factors mentioned in our principle of experiential evidence, or there isn't any good reason to think that they do, that greatly reduces the plausibility of claiming that one who takes them to provide evidence is unreasonable in virtue of doing so.

Question Twelve: Can you falsify—even in principle—the claim that an apparent experience of God is reliable? And if you can't, does that show that such experiences are not evidence?

You seem to have in mind the idea that if an experience can count as evidence for a proposition, then not having such an experience, in the same or similar circumstances, is evidence against that proposition. This is often true. If your seeing a car parked by a fire hydrant, your experience is not evidence for it being there unless, were it not there, you would still (seem to) see it. Otherwise, you are car-hallucinating. It is typical to test a hypothesis by finding some circumstance in which, if the hypothesis is true, a certain event will occur. If it does not, the hypothesis has been falsified. But in the theistic case, there is no such case—no circumstance in which failing to have an experience of God is evidence that God does not exist. The typical belief is that God cannot be made to offer experience of God, and that if there is none God has a good reason for not having caused one. So it looks as if the answer to your first question is that there is no case in which the failure to experience God is evidence that God does not exist, at least none consistent with standard theistic belief.

This, however, assumes that if experience E is evidence for proposition P, then E failing to occur is evidence for not-P. The assumption is false. Consider this claim: someone alive today will be alive tomorrow. Tomorrow, you can have confirming direct experiential evidence for it, but not disconfirming. So the *If an experience can vote for a proposition, it can vote against it* premise is false.

If you prefer a different example, suppose there is a hypothetical particle that behaves completely randomly and thus unpredictably. It is viewed suspiciously by the scientific community. Nonetheless, there is knowledge of what one would have to observe if one were to experimentally run across it.

If there are any of these particles, there is just one. One day scientists in various countries are running the same new experiment and get exactly the results they would get were the single special particle to interfere with the experiment. After carefully sifting the data, the scientists at every location where the experiments were run come to the same conclusion: the only available explanation of their results is that there actually is the hypothesized particle. For years scientists run the same experiment, and never again do they get results different from the typical ones. Assuming the instruments used in the new experiment are carefully checked and their readings verified, one sensible conclusion to draw is that the hypothesized particle is real. Yet its not being discerned in no matter how many experiments are run in which it makes no appearance, this produces no evidence that there is no such particle. (Here, it may help to remember the gambler's fallacy—the gambler reasons that if he bets ten times on horses on which the odds are ten-to-one that it will lose, and has lost nine times, that he is sure to win when he does the same thing a tenth time.) The point is that whether the claim that if there can be positive evidence from X occurring in circumstance C, X's not occurring in C is evidence against that proposition is true depends on the details of the context in which the claim is made. The claim is not a necessary truth, and seems false concerning experiential evidence for theism.

The Evidential Argument from Religious Experience

Another point is worth notice. One might argue in this manner: concerning religious experiences that are at least apparently experiences of God, the best explanation of the occurrence of these experiences is that God causes them, so it is more reasonable than not to believe that God causes them; if God causes them, then God exists; thus it is more reasonable than not to believe that God exists. This is an *inferential* argument from religious experience. It is compatible with the argument offered here that this inferential argument succeeds. But the argument here is not an inferential argument from religious experience.

An *evidential* argument from religious experience has a different shape. It goes like this:

> Experiences occur that at least seem to be experiences of God; if these satisfy a correct principle of experiential evidence, they are reasonably taken to be reliable; they do satisfy a correct principle of experiential evidence, they are hence reasonably taken to be reliable; if they are reasonably taken to be reliable, then they provide evidence that God exists; hence they provide evidence that God exists. The argument presented here is an *evidential* argument from religious experience, not an *inferential* argument from religious experience.[5]

Here is a basic version of the evidential argument from religious experience:

1. Experiences occur that are a matter of their subjects at least seeming to experience God.

2.   If the subjects of experiences of this sort (non-culpably) have no reason to think that these experiences are canceled or counterbalanced or compromised or conceptually challenged, then their occurrence provides them with evidence that God exists.
3.   The subjects of experiences of this sort typically have no reason to think that these experiences are canceled or counterbalanced or compromised or conceptually challenged.

Hence:

4.   These experiences provide evidence that God exists. [from 1–3]

The Principle of Experiential Evidence Applied

The first premise is an empirical truth. The argument of course also requires that premise 2 is true. Here is an argument for that premise. Premise 2 says that religious experience is not disqualified by any of the considerations included in:

(P4) If a person S has an experience E that, if reliable, is a matter of being aware of an experience-independently existing item X, and S (non-culpably) has no reason to think that E is canceled or counterbalanced or compromised or conceptually challenged, then S's having E provides S evidence that X exists. Promise 3 is an empirical truth.

Suppose, then, that Mary has what is an at least apparent experience of God. The first two relevant terms in (P4) are defined, relative to an experience providing evidence, as follows:

1.   Mary's experience is *cancelled* as evidence if she has reason to think that she would seem to experience God whether or not God exists (or at least whether God caused the experience).

(Strictly, so far as evidence goes, it presumably would not matter whether God "built it into" the world at creation or was the immediate cause of the experience.)

2.   Mary's experience is *counterbalanced* as evidence if she has reason to believe that it is just as likely that she seems to experience God if God exists as it is if God does not exist.

Suppose, then, that Mary has a religious experience in which she at least appears to encounter a majestic, holy, powerful, loving being—an experience similar to those described earlier as central to monotheistic traditions. It is very likely that Mary will have no reason to think that she would seem to experience this being even if it did not exist. This is made more likely if she has not been taking drugs that might cause such an experience. If (as was argued earlier) social (and natural) science explanations do not typically "explain away" religious experience, Mary's experiential evidence is not cancelled. She is also unlikely to have any reason to think that it is just as likely that she have the experience if the being in question does not exist as it is that she will have it if that being does exist. In the light of the truth of the basic idea of our principle of experiential evidence—that one's at least seeming to experience X is evidence that X exists unless we have some good reason to think otherwise— one claiming that Mary's experience is counterbalanced owes us some particular reason for thinking so. An argument that God does not exist, even if it had some force, would provide evidence one way; this would not entail that Mary's experience did not provide evidence the other way. If Mary knows of an apparently successful proof that any monotheistically satisfactory concept of God is self-contradictory, then her experience is conceptually contradicted, but that there is any such argument is far from obvious, and a point much disputed. If Mary's experience is counterbalanced, say by some version of the problem of evil, then it is still evidence for theism, even if, given a broader perspective, that evidence faces counter-evidence.

It seems fair to claim that the 1–4 argument makes at least a plausible case for its conclusion. Any such conclusion, for or against monotheism, is part of a long, complex dispute—one that we are partly describing.

Question Thirteen: Can you give me an example or two of experiential evidence such that, if it occurred, it would be evidence against God's existence?

Here are two. One concerns a post-mortem experience.

One: If everyone, upon dying, were to go to a place where everyone was exquisitely happy, civilized, and glad to be alive, or to a place where everyone was devastatingly unhappy, crude and violent, and devoutly wishing for their annihilation; those in the happy habitat are without exception those who have opposed the idea of God, been atheists or at least agnostics, been hostile to monotheism of any kind, and enjoyed nothing so much as committing blasphemy; those in the miserable habitat are without exception those who have, as they thought, worshipped and served God, been sincere monotheists, prayed, sang hymns, and tried to live lives in accord with monotheistic morality; societies for psychical research communicate with both habitats and receive convincing evidence that this is indeed how things are in the afterlife; scientists working in the happy habitat discover that there are fundamental laws of nature that will keep those in the happy habitat there, and those in the miserable habitat there, forever.

The other is pre-mortem.

Two: If most apparent experiences of a non-human intelligence was of a powerful being who enjoys wickedness, encourages rape and murder and torture, excruciating suffering accompanies all such experiences and those who have them become exceedingly violent and dangerous, and the only remaining religious experiences are those in which the subjects are first given experiences with phenomenologies like those of monotheistic experiences and then followed by phenomenologies in which it is explained that monotheistic experiences were given to religious fools to deceive them.

Were experiences of the first sort to occur, we would have experiential evidence against the existence of God, perhaps of the same kind as are Mary's own experience and possibly not. (Given the looseness of the notion of a *kind* of experience, one could dispute the claim that they would be of the same kind. It does not seem to matter. If the sort one experiences are not of the same kind as Mary's at least apparent experience of God, it may also be the case that the requirement that they be of the same kind is too unclear to give any force to the idea that relevant possibly confirming and possibly disconfirming experience be of the same kind.) Were experiences of sort two to occur, we would have experiences more clearly of the same kind as Mary's—experiences at least apparently of a powerful, overwhelming non-human being who was not holy and loving but wicked and hateful; these experiences would be experiential evidence against *God exists*. It is logically possible that such experiences occur. So it is not logically impossible that there be experiential evidence against God's existence.

Evidence Only for the Experiential Subjects?

Suppose one learns that explorers in northern Minnesota have discovered black squirrels, hitherto thought to inhabit only the East with their center on the Princeton University campus, though the Minnesota variety thrive on pine cones and fish as well as nuts and weigh as much as forty pounds. The explorers' squirrel-spotting and squirrel-weighing experiences satisfy (P4), and so are evidence for there being the squirrel giants. They also satisfy (P4*) and so provide the explorers with evidence for their conclusions. There is nothing to prevent one from learning from all this that northern Minnesota is blessed with giant black squirrels without oneself making a trip there. Similarly, if religious experiences occur that satisfy (P4), and so are evidence, and satisfy (P**) relative to their subjects who accept the experiences as evidence, they provide evidence for the claim that God exists. There is no reason why one cannot learn of the occurrence of such experiences, consider (P4) and (P4*) relative to one's own situation, and conclude that these experience, had by others, provide one with evidence that God exists. Indeed, there would be nothing unreasonable in taking them to be such evidence, even if their subjects did not, provided one had no reason to think that those subjects were anything other than mistaken in whatever reasons they might have for not accepting their own experiences as evidence that God exists.[6] It is an extreme skepticism regarding testimony and historical evidence to simply set aside the widespread evidence of people having at least apparent experiences of God, and a point rightly granted by most critics of theism.

Questions for Reflection

1. What, if anything, can be learned by comparing religious with non-religious experience?
2. What is a principle of experiential evidence?
3. How does one evaluate such principles?
4. How effective are social science explanations in debunking apparent experiences of God as evidence?
5. How important is the fact that religious experiences have occurred over time and cross-culturally?

Notes

1. Using "a holy, powerful being" as a brief description of the content of monotheistic religious experiences.
2. And, of course, claims logically entailed by those claims.
3. To completely describe something is to state every truth about that thing. There is nothing whatever such that any human person can completely describe it. Other than the unsurprising fact that we are not omniscient, it is hard to say that anything of particular philosophical interest follows from this.
4. For what it is worth, conceptual, moral, and aesthetic experiences are more like religious experiences in these respects than like sensory experiences.
5. Here is an extension of an evidential argument from religious experience:

   1. Experiences occur that are a matter of their subjects at least seeming to experience God.
   2. If experiences of this sort are not canceled or counterbalanced or compromised or conceptually challenged, then their occurrence is evidence that God exists.
   3. Experiences of this sort are not canceled or counterbalanced or compromised or contradicted or confuted or logically consumed or empirically consumed.

   Hence:

   4. These experiences are evidence that God exists. [from 1–3]

   It continues:

   5. If these experiences occur in various cultures, and at various times, to people of various backgrounds and socio-economic status, their evidential force is increased.
   6. These experiences occur in various cultures, and at various times, to people of various backgrounds and socio-economic status.

   Hence:

   7. Their evidential force is increased.

   While the claims that appear in the premises of this argument are interesting, controversial, and—in the present author's view—entirely defensible, discussing them in detail would take far afield—into discussions, for example, of the similarity or otherwise of at least apparent experiences of God as these occur in different times and places and religious traditions.

A final issue should be mentioned. If one sees a cup on the table and not unreasonably comes to believe that *There is a cup on the table,* in all strictness one believes more than one's current experience tells. The cup one believes is on the table, if it exists at all, is an enduring thing; one's current experience is momentary. It is not a matter of pure report of sensory experiences if one looks again and has an experience with the same sensory phenomenology that one says that the same cup is still there; it is logically possible that the old cup has passed away and been replaced by a new one. Cups have other sides, and one sees only this side; perhaps one sees only a cup facade. The point is not to provide a basis for skepticism about cups, but simply to note that even a very modest claim about an ordinary object strictly goes beyond the experiential information one currently possesses.

Underdetermination looms larger in scientific theory where there will always be more that one possible way of explaining what is observed, so that claims that various sorts of theoretical entities exist are underdetermined by the data on the basis of which such claims are made. Even religious experiences of a phenomenologically think sort—Isaiah in the temple in the presence of an awesome holy being in whose presence he senses his own sinfulness and need for forgiveness, for example—underdetermine the claims, for example, that God is omnipotent and omniscient. In religion and theology, as in everyday sensory experience and scientific theory, conceptual experiences join with sensory or religious experiences in more fully determining the concepts used to describe the objects of experience. How this goes in any given case is likely to be complex and fascinating. The next step would be to ask what reasons monotheism can supply for claiming that God is omnipotent and omniscient. But that is another story.

Suggested Readings

Alston, William (1991) *Perceiving God* (Ithaca, NY: Cornell University Press). Argues that the practice of belief formation within which Christians claim to experience God is reliable; considers a host of epistemological views.

Broad, C. D. (1953) *Religion, Philosophy, and Psychical Research* (London: Routledge and Kegan Paul). Contains a standard, rather favorable discussion of religious experience by an agnostic.

Davis, Carolyn Franks (1989) *The Evidential Force of Religious Experience* (Oxford: Clarendon Press). Argues that religious experience provides evidence for God's existence. Its strength is its detailed discussion of social science theories; supposes that there is only one kind of religious experience.

Fales, Evan (2010) *Divine Intervention: Metaphysical and Epistemological Puzzles* (New York: Routledge). Considers the question of religious experience from the perspective of laws of nature, causality, and time.

Gellman, Jerome (2002) *Mystical Experience of God: A Philosophical Enquiry* (Aldershot: Ashgate). Presentation of religious experience as evidence for God's existence and defends it against traditional and feminist objections.

Hardy, Alister (1979) *The Spiritual Nature of Man: A Study of Contemporary Religious Experience* (Oxford: Clarendon Press). Presents reports of religious experiences by "ordinary people."

Martin, C. B. (1989) *Religious Experience* (Ithaca, NY: Cornell University Press). Argues that religious experience does not provide evidence that God exists.

McNamara, Patrick (2014) *The Neuroscience of Religious Experience* (Cambridge: Cambridge University Press). An excellent way into the literature on brain correlates to religious experience.

Rowe, W.L. (1982) "Religious experience and the principle of credulity," *International Journal for the Philosophy of Religion*, Vol. 13, pp. 85–92. Argues that religious experience does not provide evidence for religious belief.

Wainwright, William J. (2006) *Reason and the Heart: A Prolegomenon to a Critique of Passional Reason* (Ithaca, NY: Cornell). Seeks a middle ground between detached reason and subjectivity via emotion-guided reason and discusses Newman, James, and especially Edwards.

——— (2015) *Reason, Revelation, and Devotion: Inference and Argument in Religion* (Cambridge: Cambridge University Press). Makes a cross-cultural case that sheer logical skill and ability needs to be supplemented by proper "habits of the heart" in order for our judgments to be sound.

Yandell, Keith E. (1993) *The Epistemology of Religious Experience* (Cambridge: Cambridge University Press). Full-dress presentation of the argument of this chapter.

Part IV

Arguments concerning Nonmonotheistic Conceptions

12 Arguments concerning Nonmonotheistic Conceptions

Appeals to Argument and Appeals to Experience

Three views are relevant here: Advaita Vedanta's claim that (i) only Brahman without qualities exists, Jainism's contention that (ii) persons are independently immortal existing beings, and the typical Buddhist view that (iii) persons are composite entities, made up of other things that are not persons and that comprise the basic constituents of the universe. These are obviously logically incompatible claims; all could be false, but not more than one could be true. If only quality-less Brahman exists, persons and non-person constituents of persons, which have qualities if they exist, do not exist—if (i) is true, (ii) and (iii) are false. If persons are not composed of non-person constituents, and of course have properties, they are not identical to Brahman; thus if (ii) is true then (i) and (iii) are false. If persons are made up of non-person constituents, then these constituents have properties and persons are composite—if (iii) is true, then (i) and (ii) are false.

These claims are defended and attacked by appeal to argument and appeal to experience. By 'appeal to argument' is meant use of arguments whose premises do not contain reports of non-conceptual experiences people have or are alleged to have had; by 'appeal to experience' is meant use of arguments that do contain reports of non-conceptual experiences people have, or are alleged to have had, or simple appeal to those reports. A conceptual experience is one in which, without appeal to sensory or introspective experience, one comes to see the meaning, and perhaps the truth value, of some proposition; seeing that nothing can have incompatible properties, noticing that it cannot be known that no one knows anything, seeing that if there are tables then there are physical objects, are examples of conceptual experiences. Highly undervalued, and often ignored, such experiences are experiences without whose possession ordinary life, let alone philosophy, would be impossible. The present chapter will be concerned with appeal to argument using contents of conceptual experiences; the next chapter will deal with appeal to non-conceptual experiences.

Advaita Vedanta

It looks as though Advaita wants to hold logically inconsistent theses. In particular, it begins with the claim that something exists but altogether lacks properties, and that something that altogether lacks properties can be identical to a variety of things that have properties and are distinct from one another. To exist and to have properties are not alternatives. Each entails the other—anything that has properties exists and anything that exists has properties. We have the concept of Santa Claus, not because Santa exists or has properties, but because—given that we have a concept of Santa—we know (to some degree) what properties Santa would have were he to exist. So we do not have a counter-example here of the to-exist-is-to-have-properties-and-to-have-properties-is-to-exist necessary connection. The idea of something that has no properties is the idea of nothing.

The identity claim is dealt with by distinguishing between the level of appearance from the level of reality—how things appear and how things are. But appear to whom? Appearances cannot appear to appearances. But the appearance/reality distinction requires that there be some reality to which things appear. Brahman is qualityless and so cannot experience appearances, and the reception of appearances is a state of ignorance that cannot with any propriety be ascribed to Brahman, which has no defects. So there is nothing left to which appearances can appear.

The Advaita claim that Nirguna Brahman is ineffable has its own enormous problems. The idea that Brahman is identical to each individual soul, which is central to Advaita, is incompatible with Brahman being ineffable. If everything at the level of appearance is identical to Brahman, then Brahman is identical to everything at the level of appearance, from which it follows that everything at the level of appearance is identical to Brahman. This inference will of course be rejected on the grounds that an appearance need not have the properties possessed by that of which it is the appearance. The problem is that if everything at the level of appearance is an appearance of Brahman, then this is true of Brahman, which is hence not ineffable. Further, if Brahman is ineffable, then we are left with the claim that *Brahman is . . .* with no sanctioned way of filling out the sentence. Even claiming that Brahman is ineffable applies a concept to Brahman, which breaks the rule that it asserts. To put the point differently, halfway toward symbolic logic, we have *There is an X such that, for any property Q, it is not the case that X has Q.* But it is also supposed to be the case that any Atman (soul) A is identical to Brahman, so Brahman has the property *being identical to A.* Then it follows that however many individual souls there may be, there are that many cases of Brahman having the property of being identical to each. (I leave aside the idea of Brahman being identical to anything else.) If one replies that Brahman is identical to A in the sense that Brahman appears to be, or as, A, then Brahman has the property *appearing as A.* Further, moksha—enlightenment experience—is supposed to confirm Brahmanic doctrine via one having a pure consciousness experience. But even supposing that there can be a subjectless and contentless experience, why should this be taken to be—and how could it be—evidence for anything? How could one tell by experience that one thing was identical to everything? Insofar as Advaita doctrine rests on experience, it seems to find no possible support that does not come from experience had by some subject who is herself only appearance. The suggestion that the bridge between the Atman (soul) of Chandra and Brahman without qualities comes by way of philosophical or theological theory. But since Brahman without qualities is said to be ineffable, this leaves the theoretical bridge attached only at one end (the Atman) with nothing at the other end to which it can be attached,

Other Vedantins have pressed these sorts of problems with Advaitan. For one example, Ramanujan,[1] a Visistadvaitan, for example, held that it was contradictory to hold that *There is an X such that for every property P, X lacks P.* (Or, if existence itself is a property, *There is an X such that for any property P other than existence, X lacks P.*) One way of putting a Ramanuja-like point is to note that to claim that Brahman, or anything else, is qualityless is to claim that it exists and deny an entailment of that very claim. Hence Advaita Vedanta metaphysics is not even possibly true. Ramanuja's critique seems decisive, and there is no point in lingering over logical impossibilities.

Jainism and Buddhism on Persons

Three Exclusive but Non-exhaustive Alternatives[2]

Three alternatives regarding the nature of mind and body are idealism, materialism, and dualism. Idealism holds that having a mental property is kind-defining relative to the only kind of substances there are; materialism gives that status to having a physical property; dualism holds that having a mental property and having a physical property are kind-defining relative to two distinct kinds of substances.[3] Thus each of these views is substantival and essentialist: each holds that there are substances that belong to a kind and hence have essences. Among mind-body dualists, some suppose minds or souls to exist without depending on anything else whatever, and so are inherently immortal; others take souls to exist dependent upon God and as immortal by grace since God could cease to support them in existence at any time. For example, the Jain view is that it is impossible that a soul cease to exist; Christianity, insofar as it accepts dualism, holds to the less radical version.

Property Dualism versus Substance Dualism

Jain dualism is one version of mind-body dualism. Insofar as religious traditions are dualistic concerning mind and body, they hold to a dualism of substances, not merely a dualism of properties. Property dualism concerning mental and physical properties holds that being a mental property defines one kind of property and being a physical property defines another kind of property, and it is logically impossible these properties belong to the same thing. A property Q is a mental property if and only if X has Q entails X is conscious, or, on a higher standard, self-aware. Not every non-mental property is a physical property; "being prime" is not a physical property, nor is "having only consistent properties." Without pretense of precision, let us refer to such properties as "abstract properties" and then suggest that property Q^* is a physical property if and only if Q^* is neither mental nor abstract. There are more concrete definitions of being a physical property;

for example, one can say that Q* is a physical property if and only if *X has Q* entails *X is spatially located* or *X is a property referred to or expressed by some predicative term used in some contemporary theory in natural science or some similar successor*. But the more concrete examples raise problems; it is not clear that there is any univocal sense in which both chairs and elementary particles are "spatially located" and "similar" in "similar successor" means "physicalistic" (or something less clear).[4]

Philosophical dislike or disdain of substance dualism will, in the current academic climate, suggest to even the most convinced property dualist, of which there are many, that they should not go further and embrace substance dualism. A substance dualist concerning mind and body holds that not only are 'being mental' and 'being physical' definitive of different kinds of properties, but each is a kind-defining property relative to a sort of substance—'being mental' constitutes one kind or essence and 'being physical' constitutes another kind or essence, it being logically impossible that any one substance belong to both kinds. Something is a substance if it has properties, is not itself merely a bundle of properties, has an essence, and (if it is temporal) can remain the same over time and through change of nonessential properties. For a substance dualist, persons are mental substances. Typically for a dualist, human beings are persons embodied in genetically homo sapiens bodies. Substance dualism, and its associated view of persons, has a highly distinguished history. For example, Plato, Augustine, Anselm, Descartes, Samuel Clarke, and Thomas Reid all held it. It also has some distinguished contemporary advocates.[5] Its popularity currently is at low tide, this arguably (if a pun be allowed) being more a matter of fashion than of substance.

Identity

Symmetry and Transitivity of Identity

The proposition *A is identical to B* entails the proposition *B is identical to A*. The propositions *A is identical to B* and *B is identical to C* entail the proposition *A is identical to C*. These two simple facts about identity are expressed by logicians by saying that identity is reflexive and transitive. Whether A, B, and C are wombats, kumquats, tuxedos, numbers, angels, or galaxies, identity among them is reflexive and transitory. To deny this is to deny that there is any such thing as identity as applied to them, which is the same as denying that there are any such things.

Numerical versus Qualitative Identity

In considering competing views of persons, and of personal identity, it is crucial to keep firmly in mind the distinction between numerical identity and the quite different matter of qualitative (so-called) identity or close resemblance. Suppose Tim has a penny in each hand, each minted in Philadelphia in 1998, both bright and unscratched. He names the one in his left hand "Cop" and the one in his right hand "Per." Cupping his hands together, he shakes the pennies and then again grasps one in one hand and one in the other. Neither he nor we were able to keep track of either penny during the shaking. In these simple circumstances, we know that Cop is still in Tim's left hand or else Cop is now in Tim's right hand, and that either Per is still in Tim's right hand or else Per is now in Tim's left hand. But we do not know which.

This simple example illustrates various important concepts. Both Cop and Per retain numerical identity over time. Cop's (and Per's) having numerical identity over time is a fact about it independent of our knowledge of it. Cop and Per are (nearly) qualitatively identical; that is why we cannot, at the end of the shaking, tell which penny is which. But each retains numerical identity over time and each remains numerically distinct from the other, independent of our knowing which is which.

Any substance is self-identical, identical to itself at each moment of its existence; identity in this sense is numerical identity. If substance X exists at time T1 and continues to exist at the next moment T2, then the X that exists at T2 is identical to the X that existed at T1; here, too, identity is numerical identity.

Numerical identity, strictly speaking, is identity; qualitative identity is a matter not of identity but of resemblance. For a dualist, personal identity is numerical identity of a person—a self-conscious substance—identity to itself at a time, and to its continuingly existing self over each of various times.[6] Temporal endurance of a simple substance is sufficient for its continuing numerical identity. For a simple substance X to endure from T through T* is for it to be the case that exists at each time from T through T*, and for any property Q such that Q is essential to X, X has Q. Especially when it comes to persons, the endurance of a single substance through time versus a series of things of momentary duration that runs from T through T*, is highly significant.

Personal Identity

General Criteria for Theories of Personal Identity

A theory of personal identity should consist of elements none of which is itself self-contradictory that are also logically consistent with one another, each of which coheres with the others in such a way as to yield a plausible account of what it is to be a person, where the account is compatible with, and explanatory of, the things we know about persons.

An Exclusive Disjunction

These are two basic sorts of views held regarding persons: persons are simple or complex. If they are simple, they are substances.[7] If they are complex, they are composed of substances or qualities or states or whatever. If they are substances, they are either mental or physical. If they are not substances, they are complex and composed of mental and/or physical qualities or states or whatever. It is logically impossible that both views be true. There are various substantival views about persons other than the Jain view (for example, that persons are material substances, that persons are created, that persons are not inherently immortal). There are other non-substantival views about persons other than the Theravada view (for example, that rather than states, it is qualities, events, processes, or the like that make up persons).[8] But the claims *Persons are simple substances*, essential to Jainism, and *Persons are not simple substances*, essential to Buddhism, are obviously exclusive. What does each entail?

Bundle Theory

A Non-substantival View of Persons

The sort of complexity account of persons that concerns us here holds that (i) persons are not substances; (ii) a person is composed of elements that are not themselves persons; (iii) these elements, whatever they are, exist only momentarily; and (iv) what makes a bundle of elements that compose a person at one time (part of) the same person as another bundle at a later time is some relation R that holds between the bundles. There is a constraint on what relation R can be. It cannot be numerical identity over time, since R is supposed to explain—to state the sufficient conditions for—numerical identity of persons over time.

The idea, then, is that a person at a time is a bundle B1 of momentary apersonal elements, that a person at another time is another bundle B2 of momentary elements. No element in one bundle can be identical to an element in another bundle. Over time, a person is a series of bundles. Our deepest concern here is with the structure of this type of view, not with its content. There are different accounts of what the alleged elements are that make up a person at a time; they may be viewed as physical, as mental, or as some of each. There are different notions of what relation R allegedly relates bundles over time into one person: resemblance, temporal continuity, memory, causality, a combination of these, and so on.

Earlier Buddhist bundle theories tell us that the bundles are composed of both mental and physical states, later theories include only mental states. For simplicity we will focus on the latter. Since the contents of a person's mind may vary considerably from moment to moment, it is entirely possible that bundle B at time T2 in series S2 may resemble bundle A at time T1 in series S1 more than the bundle that follows A in S1. The results of making resemblance the ground of linkage between bundles will shift personal identity from series to series in a random manner, its not being in reality required that Tom endures for T through T1 only if the states that compose Tom at two different times resemble one another to some high degree. Temporal continuity is important, but for any bundle that exists at T there will be an enormous class of other bundles that occur at T1. Memory as the key to linkage presupposes personal identity—one can remember doing only what one did or observed. Causality is a better choice, and it is the one chosen. One can put the Buddhist view this way. Persons are composite in three respects. First, they are composed of bundles. Second, the bundles are composed of momentary states. Third, the bundles compose a causal series that is all there is to a person. Talk of a series of bundles is a more economical way of speaking of bundles collectively and does not refer to some entity above and beyond the bundles themselves. All there is to a person at a given time simply is a bundle of conscious states, and all there is to a person over time is a series of bundles. Since each state is momentary, each bundle is momentary; no state belongs to as many as two bundles. No bundle outlasts, or is anything more than verbally beyond, its constituents. For some person—say, Amy—to perform some action at time T involves a bundle or series of bundles in a series named Amy to bring about effects. Amy's action typically will not all occur at one time; few actions take only a moment. The effects that Buddhist doctrine regards as karmic occur over a later time. If all the karmic effects happened right away, then, contrary to Buddhist doctrine, karmic effects would not lead to reincarnation. Karmic consequences, positive or negative, would be instantaneously paid out. After the action ends, the action-causing series is forever gone. Hence no karmic effects shall accrue to that series.

The Buddhist idea is that the justice requirement be met as follows: a series of bundles other than those included in the action-causing bundles will receive the relevant karmic effects, and the action-causing bundles must be a part of the series to which the effect-receiving bundles belong. The idea is that so long as action and karmic consequence occur in the same series then justice is done. But the series just is one bundle after another that are sequentially causally connected. The bundles that successively cause one another do not give rise to a third sort of thing—a series in addition to states and bundles. If a sequence of forty bundles occurs in a causal series, talk of a series simply saves one the trouble of making forty separate references in order to tell what happened. There aren't forty bundles plus a series. The net result then is that the karmic-consequence-receiving bundles are numerically distinct from the action-performing bundles, linked to those earlier bundles by a causal chain that may contain a great many bundles since it may be that karmic consequences occur in a different lifetime than the action for which they are recompense. The point is that all there is that receives the recompense is a series of bundles that may be temporally and causally far distant form the series of bundles that caused the action for which recompense is due.

The fact is that on the Buddhist view of persons that we have been discussing it is not the same item (an earlier series of bundles) that receives the karmic consequences of what an earlier item (a previous series of bundles long since gone) caused. The Buddhist ambition to make sure that persons are not primitive entities in the universe—with components that exist barely long enough to be there or all—yields a view in contradiction to the justice requirement that is basic to the law of karma (that which performs the action must receive the consequences that are due). On the Buddhist view of persons, the justice requirement that the agent of the deed be the recipient of the karmic consequences of the action is not met.

Perhaps contrasting Buddhist and Jain perspectives on karma—what claims each is entitled make given its metaphysical views—will aid clarity. The Buddhist doctrine can be put formally in this fashion:

(B1) If Lucy at T1 receives recompense for something A done by a person at time T, then Lucy at T1 is composite nonendurers that are members of

(an element of or a constituent in) a composite (conventional) endurer—
a series—in which the composite nonendurers that did A at T are earlier
members.[9]

In contrast, the Jain view put equally formally is this:

(J1) If Lucy at T1 receives recompense for something A done by a person at
time T, then Lucy at T1 is a noncomposite endurer who is numerically identical to the person (the noncomposite endurer) who did A at T.

Given (B1), the justice requirement is not met, and given (J1) it is. One of course
can reject the justice requirement in favor of the Buddhist doctrine of persons.
Nonetheless, the requirement is a significant element in karmic doctrine and an
important part of the treatment of the problem of evil in which it arises relative to
any tradition in which karmic doctrine plays an essential role.

An External Critique of the View That Persons Are Bundles[10]

There are external criticisms of Buddhist-type views—criticisms that appeal to
claims that are not part of a Buddhist-type account of persons or otherwise elements in a Buddhist perspective. There is nothing intrinsically philosophically
problematic in the notion of such a critique or in various of its instances. If I forward the hypothesis that Mahavira was a Buddhist, I am not thereby licensed to
dismiss appeals to the contrary historical evidence by noting that such evidence is
not part of my perspective; in fact, the evidence should be. There is no more reason to despise external philosophical criticism than to despise external historical
criticism. If I maintain that a rule of inference is valid if and only if everyone who
is asked about it accepts it, thereby proposing to turn logic into a sort of sociology, I cannot justifiably simply reply to the objection that the view assumed by the
criticism is not part of the view being criticized. The criticism, though external,
may be entirely correct, and the fact that I don't agree is irrelevant.

Suppose that Rita is a series of bundles of conscious states. The bundles are
connected by causation. Up until time T, the series that Ruth is runs along without problems. Then suppose the following occurs at T1: bundle B in the Ruth
series causes bundles B1 and B2, each of which then goes its own way. What
happens to Ruth? If Ruth is identical to anything at T2, it is the new B1 series or
the B2 series. Each series has, so to speak, equal right to claim to be the continuation of Ruth. But since the B1 series is not numerically identical to the B2 series,
it cannot be that both series continue Ruth, and if not both then neither. The B1
series and the B2 series, each without the other, would continue Ruth. So double
causation prevents Ruth from continuing whereas single causation would have
preserved her.

Suppose the series B1 and the series B2 are twin states. Then the existence
of two persons just like Ruth would have been prevents Ruth from continuing
to exist. The suggestion that Ruth has then given birth to twins ignores that B1

and B2 replace Ruth in the sequence. The suggestion that the B1 series continues Ruth and the B2 series is Ruth's child ignores the fact that each, in the absence of the other, would be a continuation of Ruth herself, not a child of Ruth. These consequences are the result of Ruth being construed as occurring in time slices or temporal stages related as members of a causal series rather than as one substance enduring over time.

An Internal Critique of the View That Persons Are Bundles

Internal critiques of the sort relevant here claim the Buddhist-type account is internally inconsistent, or an argument to the effect that a Buddhist-type account is inconsistent with other Buddhist claims. Jain and Buddhist doctrines now diverge on two further points. In order to express them precisely, let us adopt a bit of technical terminology, but in order to express them clearly, let it be only a tiny bit. The Jain view of persons, we have noted, entails that for any person Lucy, all of Lucy exists at each moment at which Lucy exists. Lucy contains no elements; she is incomposite; she enjoys numerical identity over time. She is, then, a noncomposite endurer. On the Buddhist view, there are no noncomposite endurers. Instead, there are noncomposite nonendurers. These are single momentary constituents. There are composite nonendurers. These are bundles of noncomposite nonendurers. There would be composite endurers were a series of bundles more than the bundles that compose it. These are successions of composite nonendurers. But talk of composite endurers is metaphysically loose, since the composite endurers are conventional entities, being in sober fact just their composing bundles.

If issues concerning justice arise in comparison between Jain and Buddhist traditions, so do issues arise regarding memory. Both stem from their contrasting views of persons and account of personal identity. The claims can again be put formally and in so doing note the parallel structure of the issues. First, the Jain doctrine:

> (J2) If Lucy at time T1 remembers performing action A at time T, then Lucy is a noncomposite endurer who is numerically identical at T and T1.

It is necessarily true that no Buddhist person/recompense pair ever satisfy (J1) (above) and that no Buddhist person/memory pair ever satisfy (J2).[11] The formal statement of the Buddhist view follows:

> (B2) If Lucy at time T1 remembers performing action A at time T, then Lucy at T1 is composite nonendurers that are members of (an element of or a constituent in) a composite (conventional) endurer in which the composite nonendurers that did A at T are an earlier members.

The idea is that all is well regarding justice and memory so long as the series of bundles that caused the action are earlier members of a series in which the consequence-receiving bundles and the action-remembering bundles are later members.

Reincarnation

Given what has already been said concerning memory and karmic justice, it is natural to wonder about reincarnation, which after all is closely connected to the justice requirement. Appeal to memory of past lives, sometimes offered in defense of the doctrine of past lives, is not nearly as central to Buddhist (or other rein-carnation-including) traditions as the doctrine of reincarnation itself. Something similar holds regarding the doctrinal centrality of theistic proofs in theistic tradi-tions: unless there are composite endurers who are things in addition to composite nonendurers (and who are persons), there will be no such thing as reincarnation as well as no recompense, or memories. But it seems that, on the Buddhist-type account, there cannot be any such thing as composite endurers save in the insipid sense in which 'composite endurers' refers to one composite nonendurer and then to another and then to another, which of course is not a sense of there being com-posite endurers in addition to there being composite nonendurers. Thus the very idea of reincarnation is threatened. (Not all Buddhist traditions accept the idea; Mahayana Absolute Idealism does not.)

A series of bundles linked causally at time T is constituted by bundle B. B then causes two bundles: B1 and B. Here is no feature of a bundle theory that prevents this from occurring, and adding such a feature would be ad hoc. Sup-pose, if this matters, that the content of B1 and B2 is properly related in terms of resemblance to B to be a continuing of the B-series. For simplicity I will assume that the content of B1 and B2 is nearly qualitatively identity. *As I noted earlier, the existence of a certain degree of resemblance seems irrelevant to whether one bundle belongs to the same series as another. But if one supposes that it is, the argument here anticipates even that consideration.* Suppose a sep-arate series is caused by each of B1 and B2. In the absence of the other, each of B1 and B2 would constitute a continuation of the series in which B occurs. As it is, both the series started by B1 and the series started by B2 have equal claim to continue the series in which B occurs. Since the B1-series and B2-series are not identical, the B-series cannot be identical to both. Hence the B-series is identical to neither. Thus the existence of someone just like Vasabhandu at T1 would prevent the continued existence of Vasabhandu at T1. So this constitutes a feature of the bundle theory of persons incompatible with what is true of per-sons, namely that the existence of someone just like Vasabhandu at T1 would prevent his existence at T1.

In sum: Theravada Buddhism holds a complexity view of persons. The Jain tradition holds a substantival view. The complexity view does not support the occurrence of karmic justice, memory over or even within lifetimes, and removes an essential part of the doctrine of reincarnation. If there are only the substantival view and the complexity view, then the substantival view has the advantage in terms of being part of a worldview that includes reincarnation and karma doctrine or even provides for memory within or over lifetimes.[12] It does not follow that it is true in the Jain version thereof.[13]

On There Being a Fact of the Matter

There is a reply to the criticisms just raised that goes as follows: suppose that there is a person—Sam, let's say—at time T. Then at time T1 there come to be two persons—Sam1 and Sam2—each of whom bears R (whatever relation the complexity theory takes to constitute being the same person) to Sam. Then we can say what we like—that Sam 1 is identical to Sam, that Sam2 is identical to Sam, that Sam has ceased to exist and been replaced by Sam1 and Sam2, that Sam1 is identical to Sam on even numbered days and Sam2 is identical to Sam on odd numbered days, or whatever. The claim is that there would be no fact of the matter about whether Sam continues to exist if Sam is followed by Sam1 and Sam2. What we say, if anything, in answer to *Is either Sam1 or Sam2 identical to Sam?* is conventional, arbitrary, or at most pragmatic; there is no true answer.

One can respond that there are contradictory answers to the question, and the complexity theory—as we have seen—entails them. What entails a contradiction is necessarily false. This critique is not something that can be successfully responded to by saying, "Well, I accept the complexity theory but when it comes to what it entails I just dismiss those entailments that are false." The question is not about what someone who holds the complexity theory feels comfortable about doing, but about whether the theory is true, and if it entails falsehoods, it isn't true. This line of reasoning is correct providing there is a fact about the relevant matter. But since the criticism denies precisely that, simply assuming there is a fact of the matter gives no real response to the criticism.

The criticism has as its target the criticism of the arguments against the Buddhist view. It is not a defense at all of the Buddhist view. That view requires that there be a fact of the matter as to questions of personal identity—that *Is the person who receives the karmic consequences of an action the same person as the one who performed it?*, *Is this person in lifetime B the same person as was incarnate in lifetime A (has reincarnation occurred)?*, and *Is this person who achieves enlightenment at time T* that same person as sought it at earlier time T?*. There being no fact of the matter as to how these questions should be answered—if the fact of the matter is that there is no fact of the matter—then this result is just as unacceptable to the Buddhist tradition under discussion as was the result yielded from the arguments at which the no-fact-of-the-matter criticism is targeted. The earlier arguments against the Buddhist view under review assumed that there is some fact of the matter, and the view entails that the facts are incompatible. It is not better for the complexity theory described earlier if there is no fact to be entailed. One could easily offer an argument that begins *Either there is a fact of the matter or not* and then offer first the argument that the complexity account either entails inconsistency or else there is no answer, either result being sufficient to show that the complexity account fails.

If it is a fact that the criticism of the earlier arguments is made, then it is a fact that someone made it. Offered criticisms do not stalk the world unchaperoned by someone who makes them. So if there is a fact of the matter about whether a criticism is made, and the fact is that it was made, then there is also a fact of the matter as to who made it. But the criticism, at its strongest, is that on the complexity view there is no fact of the matter, and if the view entails inconsistent answers this can be the starting point for an argument that on the complexity view there is no fact of the matter.

> But here is another way of seeing the problem. Consider Sam and the way things ordinarily go—Sam exists at time T and Sam exists at time T1 and no Sam1 and Sam2 crop up. If Sam-at-T is identical to—is the same person as—Sam-at-T1, then necessarily Sam-at-T is identical to—is the same person as—Sam-at-T1. The Principle of the Necessity of Metaphysical Identity (PNI): If [A = B], then Necessarily, [A = B].[14]
> We can offer a possible worlds argument for (PNI). Consider two possible worlds W1 and W2.

Deny (PNI). Suppose that A, B, and C all exist in possible worlds W1 and W2. Suppose also, as is possible if identity is contingent rather than necessary, that in W1, A is identical to B, and C is distinct from A and B. Suppose also, as is possible if identity is contingent rather than necessary, that in W2 A is identical to C, and B is distinct from A and C. If identity is contingent rather than necessary, W1 and W2 are possible as described. Now A-in-W1 is identical to A-in-W2, B-in-W1 is identical to B-in-W2, and C-in-W1 is identical to C-in-W2. But A-in-W1 is distinct from C-in-W1 and A-in-W2 is identical to C-in-W2; since C-in-W1 is identical to C-in-W2, it follows that A-in-W2 is identical to C-in-W1. Since A-in-W1 is identical to A-in-W2, it follows that "both" A-in-W1 and A-in-W2 are, and also are not, identical to "both" C-in-W1 and C-in-W2. So again metaphysical identity is necessary. (As Saul Kripke noted, the terms 'A,' 'B,' and 'C' must have "rigid designation"—that is, have the same referents in all possible worlds.)

Here is another way of developing the argument against the complexity view. The complexity view entails that personal identity over time is logically contingent, and that view is self-contradictory. Thus on a complexity view, there is no such thing as personal identity—were personal identity what a complexity view says it is, there would be no such thing. There would be a fact of the matter about Sam-at-T and Sam-at-T1 being the same person; he would not be, because there would be no such thing as being the same person over time.

Put differently, on the complexity view, with or without Sam1-and-Sam2-type scenarios, there aren't any persons—talk of persons is "conventional" is a sense in which talking about persons is a way of speaking to which nothing that is a person corresponds. This, of course, is not an account of what persons are. It is a denial that there are any persons.

Substance Theory

Jain Dualism

There are a variety of arguments for mind-body dualism of the sort Jainism embraces. Some of them are clear failures. Epistemological arguments for mind-body dualism infer from something about the way in which we know minds and bodies to the conclusion that the mind is distinct from the body. Let X = my mind's existing, or that my mind exists, as grammatical structure dictates; let Y = my body's existing, or that my body exists, as grammatical structure dictates.

Argument 1: I can think of X without thinking of Y; if I can think of X without thinking of Y, then not(X = Y), so: not(X = Y).

Argument 2: I cannot be mistaken with respect to X but I can be mistaken with respect to Y; if I cannot be mistaken with respect to X but I can be mistaken with respect to Y, then not(X = Y), so not(X = Y).

Argument 3: I cannot doubt X but I can doubt Y; if I cannot doubt X but I can doubt Y then not(X = Y), so not(X = Y).

Argument 4: I can be directly aware of X but I cannot be directly aware of Y; if I can be directly aware of X but I cannot be directly aware of Y then not(X = Y), so not(X = Y).

The problem with this sort of argument is that, in each case, the middle premise is false. 'Can' here means "it is logically possible that." Consider these objections:

Reply to Argument 1: I can [it is logically possible that I] think of the cat Socks without thinking of the Clintons' favorite cat, because it is logically possible that Socks is not the Clintons' favorite cat. But it does not follow from this that Socks is not the Clintons' favorite cat.

Reply to Argument 2: I cannot be mistaken if I think that two is greater than one, and I can be mistaken if I think that your favorite number is greater than one, but it does not follow that your favorite number is not two.

Reply to Argument 3: I cannot doubt that I exist but I can doubt that I am the one who is supposed to take out the garbage, but it does not follow that I am not the one who is supposed to take out the garbage.

Reply to Argument 4: I can be directly aware of my being in pain and I cannot be directly aware of my feeling worse than ever before, but it does not follow that my being in pain is not my feeling worse than ever before.

Epistemological arguments such as these fail to prove their conclusions. The question remains as to whether other sorts of arguments are better.

Arguments for Jain Dualism

Philosophers James W. Cornman and Keith Lehrer remark that:

Mind-body dualism seems to be essential to most religions. The body will disintegrate after death, but according to the doctrines of many religions, the soul, the immaterial part of us which is quite distinct and different from the body, will live on eternally. . . . The primary philosophical problem is to find out whether dualistic interactionism or some other position is the most plausible view about the nature of a person.[15]

This remark fits at least Jainism.

Aristotle took the Law of Non-contradiction to be a law of thought and of things. The law can be expressed in two sentences.

L1.   No thing can both exist and not exist at the same time, or have and lack the same property at the same time.
L2.   No true proposition can assert and deny the same thing.

The idea is that these are mind-independent claims—not true because of the way we use language, or the way we think, or anything else that might be otherwise. The idea, then is also that L1 and L2 are metaphysical principles, true in (and constraint on) all possible worlds—all the ways a world might be. Connected to these claims is an epistemological perspective to the effect that while mistakes are certainly possible, often one can see the truth of propositions whose denials are contradictory and recognize them as stating how things must be. One example may help. There is a simple rule of logic called conversion:

Conversion: If [if P then Q] then [not-Q then not-P]

For example, if '*There are three chairs in the room* entails *There are at least two chairs in the room* the *There are not at least two chairs in the room* entails *There are not three chairs in the room.*

Consider this less-than-thrilling exercise. Discern whether there are two people or just one person in the room: everyone in the room is 36, works in a factory, is left-handed, and a theology student. So far, you cannot tell. Further, while no one in the room will ever be in Chicago, the person or persons in the room could both be and not be in Chicago at the same time. This allows one to tell that there are two people in the room. The reasoning relies on the principle *A possible difference entails an actual difference.* That is:

1.   If there is a possible difference between A and B, then A is not identical to B.

By conversion:

2.   If A is identical to B, then there is no possible difference between A and B.

This gives us another argument for the Principle of the Necessity of Metaphysical Identity (PNI). That principle is used in an argument that many dualists accept. It can be stated as follows. Consider some person Manindra. Then:

1.   It is logically possible that Manindra is self-aware and Manindra is in no bodily states (of any sort). Premise
2.   If it is logically possible that Manindra is self-aware and Manindra has no bodily states then Manindra's being self-conscious is not identical to Manindra's being in any bodily states (of any sort). Necessary Truth

So:

3.   Manindra's being self-aware is not identical to Manindra's being in bodily states (of any sort). [From 1, 2]

So:

4.   Necessarily, Manindra's being self-aware is not identical to Manindra's having bodily states (of any sort). [From 3 plus PNI]

The argument is plainly valid. The crucial premise is premise 1. What should be said about it? It rests on our seeing that it is possible to have a world with minds and no physical states—our conceiving a world, say, with unembodied minds. The proposition *Manindra is self-aware and in no bodily states* involves no structural contradiction. It also seems to involve no semantic contradiction. But the same, in both cases, is true of the contradictory proposition to premise 1. Not surprisingly, philosophers differ regarding premise 1. We face here a problem familiar to us from our discussion of the Ontological Argument. There seems nothing contradictory in the claim that God is that being who is omnipotent, omniscient, and morally perfect in every possible world. Neither does there seem to be anything contradictory in the denial of this claim. Yet, for reasons stated earlier, one or the other is (broadly) necessarily false. Similarly, there seems nothing contradictory about the claim that minds are numerically distinct from bodies—that a world exist in which there are minds but not bodies. But if this is so, then by the Principle of the Necessity of Metaphysical Identity, minds and bodies are necessarily non-identical. Correspondingly, there seems nothing contradictory in the view that minds are identical to brains, or perhaps more of the central nervous system. Arguments to the contrary will point to proposed properties that minds have that bodies cannot have and conversely.

The dispute concerns essences—if they have essences, what are the essences of mind and of body? Descartes took the essence of mind to be that it is a thinking thing (self-aware and capable of a range of mental states, introspective, perceptual, and abstract) and the essence of body to be location in space—strictly, to be extended. It seems that one could amend the view of Descartes so that it says that to be physical is to be located in space or a constituent of something that is. It seems beyond dispute that the meaning or sense of mental terms cannot be reduced to the meaning or sense of physical terms—for example, mental descriptions.

> *Tom has thought out a Theory of Everything* cannot be restated without remainder into any statement describing any set of physical states. The meanings will not be the same. The physicalist typically will take there to be an identity of reference between the subject terms of the mentalistic sentence and the physicalistic sentence offered as its parallel, and between the predicate terms of the sentences.

For a simpler example, consider *Tom is in pain* and *Tom's C-fibers are firing*. The physicalist will insist on identity of reference, so that "pain" and "C-fibers firing" occur, respectively, in everyday discourse and scientific discourse, and correspond to the same physical state or states. Part of the dispute is due to the fact that there is something it is like to be in pain, and it is anything but obvious that this is something physical. Property and substance dualists take "being in pain" to be a mental property and physicalists take it to be a physical property. Identity theory physicalists hold that the phenomenological property (feeling of pain) and the indisputably physical property C-fibers firing, while they do not seem to be the same, really are. The grounds for this, to keep things simple, is the discovery that when the subject reports pain, an appropriately equipped observer observes C-fibers firing.

This (plus the assumption of physicalism) yields the conclusion that this is a case of identity. The property dualist and the substance dualist takes this as showing correlation and is not surprised that pain can be created by producing its correlated physical state. The physicalist is equally unsurprised when this happens, explaining the production of pain by the pain being the same as the physical state.

There being lots of embodied minds is no objection to premise 1. It is perfectly compatible with all the minds we ever encounter being embodied. What the first premise says is that being embodied is neither a necessary nor a sufficient condition for having or being a mind—that having bodily states is not an essential feature of beings that are or have minds. The oft-made comment to the effect that all the minds one has encountered have been embodied is simply not to the point as to whether minds are necessarily embodied.

Rationalist philosophers can be characterized as rejecting two theses that empiricist philosophers embrace. First, that all our concepts are derived from sensory or introspective experience. Second, that all necessarily true propositions are trivial—they are expressible in sentences of the form *All A are A* or *All AB are A* or *If P then P* or more sophisticated logical structures. The first empiricist claim bears the slogan 'all our descriptive concepts are empirical' or 'all our concepts are abstracted from sense experience.' But one can abstract out of experience only what is already there. For the empiricist claim to have clear enough sense for it to be assessed, something more must be said about the content of sensory experience. On one account, the contents of sensory experience are secondary qualities (accessible to one sense only) and primary qualities (accessible to more than one sense). A rationalist response will point to concepts like 'theory,' 'explanation,' 'confirm,' 'necessity,' and the like as not abstractable from sensory or introspective elements of our experience. They are concepts that we get in some other way than abstraction from such experience. The second empiricist claim is that necessary truths are trivial, giving us no information as to the content of the world. Rationalist philosophers will point to such things as PNI, fundamental principles in ethics, Goedel's theorem, and the like as counter-examples to the necessary = trivial claim.

This very general description of two fundamental "camps" of philosophers, though it greatly simplifies things and is nothing like adequate to the two complex traditions involved, may be helpful in seeing a difference relevant to our discussion. Rationalists grant that we cannot discern the essence of water, oat meal, iodine, or poison ivy (if, as many philosophers hold, and many deny, there are essences) by sheer reflection. These are empirical matters to be decided by experiment. But they also typically hold that in some cases, we can discern essences of things in our world by careful reflection. (Note that the term 'non-conceptual experience' does not mean experiences to which no concepts apply, there being none of these, but rather sensory and introspective experiences.) Thus while an empiricist will almost certainly insist that we should draw our conception of mind only from science, a rationalist may well insist that we can discern the essence of mind by philosophical reflection, while taking into account whatever is relevant in data presented in science. Thus rationalists and empiricists in contemporary philosophy will generally view claims like premise 1 from very different perspectives that tend to predispose empiricists to be unimpressed by the source of premise 1 in philosophical reflection whereas this feature of that premise is not nearly so likely to look suspicious by more rationalistic thinkers. (There is no intention here to disparage reflection on the nature of the mind by empiricist philosophers or consideration of relevant scientific data by rationalist philosophers.)

Being self-aware is a property with deep ramifications. A being that has it would be radically different if it irretrievably lost it; its causal powers would be greatly diminished and its causal patiencies (what could be done to it) would be significantly altered. Being self-conscious is a very plausible property for being a kind-defining property or being an essential property of anything that has it.[16] This reflection, plus introspective experience, strongly supports the view that self-awareness is essential to personhood.

In spite of the fact that mind-body dualism, which holds that there are two kinds of substances, is not subject to the sorts of critique to which complexity accounts of persons are subject, it is widely rejected and often despised in the contemporary academy. What is favored instead is materialism, the view that there are material substances but not substances of any other kind.[17] The materialism/dualism controversy is complex and fascinating. There do not seem to be such powerful arguments for materialism that dualism should be ruled out as a viable position.

Arguments against Dualism

There are widely accepted arguments against dualism. One such argument contends that materialism is simpler, positing less kinds of substance, though why having two sorts of material substance, one capable of self-consciousness and one not, is in any significant way simpler is as unclear as why appeal to simplicity of kinds of substances should carry the day (or favor materialism, since idealism is simpler than dualism in the same sense as that in which materialism is). The most frequent criticism is that the only version of dualism that is plausible is interactionism, the position that mental events cause physical events and physical events cause mental events. But mind-body interaction, we are told, is impossible—how could such different things as an immaterial substance and a material substance interact? This is perhaps the only time in contemporary philosophy in which the causal likeness principle is invoked—the claim that in order for X to affect Y with respect to some property Q, X must have Q or something like Q. There is neither criterion for what degree of similarity is required nor reason to accept the principle. Dualists find it unclear why color experience being caused by non-colored things, colds and flu by bacteria and viruses, pain by unfeeling things, and the like somehow are unproblematic whereas mind-body interaction is problematic, save on an assumption of materialism already in place. Added to the first objection is the claim (as made by many dualists) that minds, being immaterial, are non-spatial, and if there is anything non-spatial it cannot interact with anything in space. Some dualists deny this and some hold that immaterial things can be in space. Another objection is that if something immaterial did affect something material this would introduce energy into the spatial system and this would be ruled out by the very basis principle in physics that energy is conserved. The dualist reply is that the principle says that energy is conserved in closed physical systems, not in physical systems, full stop. Dualists deny that all physical systems are closed. But perhaps the basic issue lies deeper. It seems that the basic reason for the rejection of dualism as a live option in much of the contemporary academy has to do with what might be called the mapping problem: How does one relate the description of the physical world, insofar as we can provide this, to the descriptions true of everyday choices and actions? Roughly, how does one map our descriptions of the mental world onto our descriptions of the physical world?

It is tempting to deny that there is a mapping problem by suggesting that our descriptions of the physical world, cast in natural science terms, and our descriptions of persons and their freedom of thought and action, are incommensurable in the sense that they do not bear logical relations to one another—that they do not have relations of consistency, inconsistency, entailment, and the like. The problem is that the suggestion is false; given that a description of the physical world is true, there are hosts of actions not available that would be available were the physical world otherwise. For example, if the correct description D1 of the physical place of an orange is that it is at place P at time T, then at T it is not possible to bring the orange to P—it is already there. If the correct description included the information that the orange was elsewhere than P, bringing it to P would (given other features of things) be possible. In such ways, and much more complex ones, what makes a particular description of the physical world at a given time true also constrains what can be done in that world at and after that time.[18] So the incommensurability tactic fails.

Eliminative materialism, which denies that there are any mental properties, dismisses the mapping problem by denying that there is anything that mental descriptions describe. It thereby dismisses the possibility of distinguishing between good science and bad, and between science and superstition, since on its terms such claims at *Einstein's thought changed Newtonian physics* is not an acceptable type of claim since it is a mental description. The assumption that all mental descriptions can be dismissed without loss is of course accompanied by the claim that when physics has become sufficiently mature this will provide a satisfactory discourse without reference to mentality. This claim draws a check on the future that is, to say the least, controversial. Those who claim that the distinction between the mental and the physical captures not substances or properties but ways of talking fail to both solve the mapping problem and give no account of the phenomenological and explanatory differences between the mental and the material. Property dualists grant that there are both mental and physical properties, but are no better at dealing with the mapping problem than are substance dualists. Insofar as its roots are intellectual, the current disposition to dismiss dualism seems to lie in the hope that if one embraces property dualism, one can grant the phenomenological and explanatory differences between the mental and the physical and have the best chance, some day, of solving the mapping problem. If, as argued earlier, being self-conscious has strong credentials as a kind-defining property, property dualism is a longer step toward substance dualism than most property dualists would like.

Mounting a full-scale defense of a substantivalist and dualist view of persons would require more space than is available here. What has been done is this: we have argued that while epistemological arguments for dualism fail, there are metaphysical arguments of much more power in its favor, and the objections against it have much less force than is usually assumed. What follows is that, insofar as Cornman and Lehrer are right about what many religions take to be true about persons, their perspective is far more defensible than it currently is usually thought to be.

Questions for Reflection

1. What is the difference between an appeal to argument and an appeal to experience?
2. Explain and argue for and against the complexity view of persons (i.e., that they are composed of conscious states).
3. Explain and argue for or against the simplicity view of persons (i.e., that they are enduring substances that have or are in states of which they are not composed).
4. According to Theravada, how is reincarnation possible?
5. Is the Jain account of how karma works any more, or any less, coherent than the Theravada account?

Notes

1. See, for example, the selections from Ramanuja in Sarvapalli Radhakrishnan and Charles Moore, *Sourcebook in Indian Philosophy* (Princeton: Princeton University Press) or Ramanuja, *Scared Books of the East*, ed. Max Mueller (Delhi: Motilal Barnasidass).
2. That is, no more than one of the alternatives can be true, and (as we shall see) there are other relevant views besides these three.
3. A bit more fully: I take dualism to hold that X is a person if and only if X is a self-conscious being, where X is a self-conscious being if and only if X is sometimes self-conscious and X when not self-conscious nonetheless has to capacity to become so. Further, X continues to be a person only if X is a person and X shall be self-conscious in the future. Dualism, then, holds that *being self-conscious* is not a physical property, that persons are self-conscious mental substances whose essence is (or includes) *having self-consciousness*, and that no mental substance is a physical substance or an abstract object.
4. Philosophers often talk as if the notion of a mental property is obscure and the notion of a physical property is lucid. But when one comes to actual definitions of 'physical property' the supposed clarity of the idea becomes shy and hides. Some philosophers talk as if the notion of being self-conscious were itself somehow deeply obscure. There are views (and so much the worse for them) on which it is hard to see how anything could be or become self-conscious, but *being self-conscious* is a clearer notion than is *being physical*.
5. C.J. DuCasse (1951) *Nature, Mind, and Death* (Chicago: Open Court); Alan Donagan (1999) *Reflections on Philosophy and Religion* (Nicholas Perovich, ed.) (Oxford: Oxford University Press); Alvin Plantinga, "Against Materialism," *Faith and Philosophy* (2006), pp. 3–32; Howard Robinson (2016) *From the Knowledge Argument to Mental Substance: Resurrecting the Mind* (Cambridge: Cambridge University Press); John Foster (1991) *The Immaterial Self* (New York: Routledge).
6. If the relationship between qualitative so-called identity and numerical identity are not clear, one might consider some relevant necessary truths.
   Some Necessary Truths

   It is helpful, in understanding qualitative "identity" and numerical identity to see how these concepts are related; a bit of reflection should be sufficient to see that each of the following claims is true (indeed, not possibly false, and so necessarily true).

   N1. *X is nearly fully identical to* Y does not entail X is numerically identical to Y. (Identical twins are possible.)
   N2. *X at T is numerically identical to Y at T1* does not entail *X at T is fully qualitatively identical to Y at T1*. (It is logically impossible that anything at one time can be fully qualitatively identical to anything at another time; the definition of full qualitative identity, including as it does spatial and temporal properties, rules that out.)
   N3. *X at T is numerically identical to Y at T1* does not entail *X at T is nearly fully qualitatively identical to Y at T1*. (A thing can remain the same thing and yet undergo non-essential change.)
   N4. *X at T is fully qualitatively identical to Y at T1* entails *X at T is numerically identical to Y at T1* and entails *X at T is numerically identical to Y at T1*. (The claim that things that exist at different times are fully qualitatively identical is self-contradictory; see comment after N2.)

N5. *X at T is nearly fully qualitatively identical to Y at T1* does not entail *X at T is numerically identical to Y at T1*. (Something at one time can be very, very similar to something at another time without being identical to it.)

N6. *For all X, X at T is fully qualitatively identical (and hence nearly fully qualitative identical) to X at T*. (Anything at a time T is qualitatively identical to itself at T.)

N7. *For all X, if X at T is numerically identical to Y at T then X at T is fully qualitatively identical to (and hence nearly fully qualitatively identical to Y at T)*. (See comment after N6.)

7. Other possibilities are sometimes proposed—e.g., Bertrand Russell's neutral monism on which mental and physical properties are somehow reducible to other properties that are neither mental nor physical. I doubt that this particular view is defensible. Nonetheless, the discussion deals with the views most relevant to Jainism and Theravada Buddhism, and does not pretend to be a comprehensive discussion of all logically possible accounts of minds and bodies.

8. Indeed, one can intelligently argue about which of these alternative *is* the Theravada view. Our arguments will be concerned with the *structure* of the view, and not depend on which of these alternative accounts of what makes up that structure is the right reading of the Theravada account.

9. I assume for convenience that the act was itself momentary, otherwise there will also be a problem about the identity of the original agent of the action.

10. 'Critique,' of course, need not mean "refutation, or attempt to refute;" it does mean that here.

11. Save, perhaps, for the unorthodox, extremely minority-status Buddhist Personalists.

12. I think that there are only two logically possible accounts of the metaphysical structure (so to say) of persons. This is argued briefly in *A Defense of Dualism*, forthcoming in *Faith and Philosophy*, in an issue that includes all of the main papers read at the 1994 Notre Dame Conference on the Philosophy of Mind.

13. For example, the Jain view, fleshed out, includes the implausible claims that *Every person is inherently omniscient, though exercise of this capacity is frustrated by our being embodied* and *It is impossible that anything cause a person to cease to exist, though a person can be caused not to be embodied in the body she presently occupies (or in any body at all)*. That our existence involves latent omniscience and necessary ontological independence are claims quite independent of anything discussed here, and I should not like to have to defend them.

14. That is, if Sam at T is identical to Sam at T1, then necessarily, Sam at T is identical to Sam at T1—which is to be distinguished from *Sam at T enjoys logically necessary existence, as does Sam at T1*.

15. James W. Cornman and Keith Lehrer (1974) *Philosophical Problems and Arguments: An Introduction* (New York: Macmillan), pp. 238–239.

16. Materialists who are property dualists are often willing to grant that physical things come in at least two kinds—those capable of self-consciousness and those not (or at least those capable of consciousness and those not—though if the *not capable of consciousness/capable of consciousness* distinction is kind-defining or essential, it is hard to see why the same should not be said regarding the *not capable of self-consciousness/capable of self-consciousness* distinction).

17. Some philosophers have embraced the view that there are abstract objects (immaterial substances not capable of consciousness) as well as material substances. But they have continued to reject the idea that there are any mental substances.

18. This is, of course, perfectly compatible with determinism being false.

Suggested Readings

Betty, L. Stafford (2014) *Vadiraja's Refutation of Sankara's Non-Dualism: Clearing the Way for Theism* (Delhi: Motilal Banarsidass). Insightful critique of Advaita view by a theistic Vedantist.

Chau, Bhikshu Thich Thien (1999) (tr. Sarah Boin-Webb), *Literature of the Personalists of Early Buddhism* (Delhi: Motilal Banarsidass). Personalist Buddhism, rejecting the no-self view, constituted part of the Indian Buddhist tradition for centuries and was declared heretical by a Buddhist council, a rare event.

Donagan, Alan (1987) *Choice: The Essential Element in Human Action* (London: Routledge and Kegan Paul). Argues for a view of persons as enduring free agents.

Hiriyanna, M. (2009) *Outlines of Indian Philosophy* (Delhi: Motilal Banarsidass). Reprint of an older excellent work.

————— (2015) *The Essentials of Indian Philosophy* (Delhi: Motilal Banarsidass). Again, reprint of an older excellent work.

Hoffman, Joshua and Rosenkrantz, Gary S. (1994) *Substance among Other Categories* (Cambridge: Cambridge University Press). Discusses various views of what a substance is, objections to these views, and arguments for them.

————— (1997) *Substance: Its Nature and Existence* (London: Routledge). See previous reference.

Lowe, E. J. (1989) *Kinds of Being* (Oxford: Basil Blackwell). Discusses substance theories and competing theories, arguments for and against each.

————— (1996) *Subjects of Experience* (Cambridge: Cambridge University Press). See previous reference.

Parfit, Derek (1984) *Reasons and Persons* (Oxford: Oxford University Press). Defends a Buddhist-type account of persons.

Yao, Zhihua (2009) *The Buddhist Theory of Self-Cognition* (New York: Routledge). Explores the origin and development of the Buddhist view of self-awareness in external disputes and on into internal developments using original texts in four languages.

13 Enlightenment-Based Arguments and Nonmonotheistic Conceptions of Ultimate Reality

Appeals to Enlightenment Experience

Appeals to religious experience as evidence for religious belief are not, of course, limited to consideration of experiences that are taken by their subjects to be experiences of God. Appeals are made to enlightenment experiences as well. While, as noted earlier, the psychological features (detachment, calm, bliss, and the like) of Advaita, Jain, and Buddhist enlightenment experiences are very similar, the proposed doctrinal significance of the experience is quite different. Enlightenment experiences are not viewed by religious traditions in which they are prized primarily because they are believed to cure one's psychological illness. The ills they are said to cure are not depression, but the basic illness common to us all, as each particular religious tradition perceives it. If a devotee of Advaita Vedanta appeals to Advaita enlightenment experience as evidence for religious belief, it will be Advaita beliefs that are said to be supported by the experience—and analogously, of course, for Jain or Buddhist appeals to Jain or Buddhist enlightenment experiences.

The Exact Nature of the Appeals to Experiential Evidence

An appeal to experience as evidence typically involves, as we have seen, referring to a description of the experience and explicitly or implicitly assuming some conceptual connection between the occurrence of an experience that fits that description and the proposition for whose truth that occurrence is said to provide evidence. The core idea is:

1. An experience that fits description D has occurred.
2. If an experience that fits description D has occurred, that fact is evidence that proposition P is true.

So:

3. That fact is evidence that P is true.

One who wishes to make a claim like 3 regarding some religious doctrine requires that some claims like 1 and 2 are true when one replaces *D* by a relevant description and *P* by a statement of a relevant doctrine. The role of the connecting premise may be implicit, necessary for the appeal to experience but unstated. The connecting premise typically will simply be an assumed principle of experiential evidence.

Generally, Advaita, Jain, and Buddhist enlightenment experiences are called, respectively, moksha, kevala, and nirvana experiences. We can expect, then, appeals to experience of the following sort.

Advaita Vedanta

A1.   Moksha experiences (in which one realizes one's identity with qualityless Brahman) have occurred.

A2.   If moksha experiences have occurred, that fact is evidence that *We are identical to qualityless Brahman* is true.

So:

A3.   That fact is evidence that *We are identical to qualityless Brahman* is true.

Jainism

J1.   Kevala experiences (in which one realizes one's existential independence or ontological security and one's omniscience) have occurred.

J2.   If kevala experiences have occurred, that fact is evidence that *We have existential independence or ontological security and are omniscient* is true.

So:

J3.   That fact is evidence that *We have existential independence or ontological security and are omniscient* is true.

Theravada Buddhism

T1.   Nirvana experiences (in which one realizes one's nature as composed at a time of momentary elements and over time of a series of bundles of such elements) have occurred.

T2.   If nirvana experiences have occurred, that fact is evidence that *We are composed at a time of momentary elements and over time of bundles of such elements* is true.

So:

T3.   That fact is evidence that *We are composed at a time of momentary elements and over time of bundles of such elements* is true.[1]

Further, in treating these appeals to experience in the same sort of way as we treated appeals to numinous experience, the first premise of each triad must be read phenomenologically; thus we will have:

A1*. Moksha experiences (in which one *at least appears to* realize one's identity with qualityless Brahman) have occurred.
J1*. Kevala experiences (in which one *at least appears to* realize one's existential independence or ontological security and one's omniscience) have occurred.
T1*. Nirvana experiences (in which one *at least appears to* realize one's nature as composed at a time of momentary elements and over time of a series of bundles of such elements) have occurred.

These will replace A1, J1, and T1, and the beginning (the antecedent) of A2, J2, and T2 will be modified accordingly.

Two Counterbalancing Considerations

It is sometimes suggested that those who have had religious experiences are the real experts as to what those experiences show—as to what they are evidence for. This claim is often made regarding enlightenment experiences. While perhaps, just by virtue of having them, persons who have enlightenment experiences are experts about what it is like to have the sort of religious experience they have had, this does not tell us that they are experts about whether such experiences are self-authenticating relative to religious claims based on them, or that they have expertise as to whether these experiences provide evidence for the beliefs based on them.

If some have claimed that religious experiencers—those who have had religious experiences—are thereby experts about the reliability or veridicality of those experiences (about whether or not they correctly represent the world), it should be noted that others have claimed that religious experiencers are the last people one should expect to have any such expertise. They have argued that the very having of such experiences—experiences that are often emotionally very powerful and that sometimes result in instantaneous conversions or redirections of a life—renders them in no position to objectively evaluate the cognitive significance of such experiences. Further, particularly in the traditions that center around enlightenment experience, the investment in having such experiences (walking for years in a loin cloth from one end of India to the other, begging for one's bread, or spending years learning the meanings of ancient arcane texts under the relentless guidance of demanding gurus, or a near lifetime of good works—in each case instead of devoting oneself to seeking pleasure, wealth, and power) plus the status given to those who allegedly have had them (being elevated to a semi-divine status where others bow in your presence or dare not even look you in the face) is just too great for anyone who claims to have had any such experience to be trusted to be at all rational in his reasoning or judgment regarding its cognitive significance.

Whatever weight either sort of consideration has is balanced by the other sort, and neither sort justifies concluding either that religious experiencers are the experts regarding what their experiences evidentially justify, or that if those experiences serve as evidence they can only do so for those who have them. The degree to which religious experiencers in a tradition have expertise in assessing the evidential value of their experience will come out in what they say that is relevant to the issue. The influence of a secular community can be just as bias-producing as that of a religious community.

Self-Authentication

Religious experiences are often said to be self-authenticating or self-guaranteeing, so that appeal to them gives one a uniquely secure source of experiential confirmation. If this is so, it is obviously an important fact about religious experiences. It would be particularly relevant to their status as evidence for religious beliefs. What exactly, then, is it for some experience to be self-authenticating? *Self-authentication* is a three-term relation; there is a person to whom an experience authenticates, an experience that does the authenticating, and a belief or proposition that is authenticated. Further, the idea is, the belief or proposition in question is evidenced or authenticated in a particularly strong way—in such a way, in fact, that the person cannot be mistaken in accepting that belief or in believing that proposition if they base accepting or believing on having had the experience. Formally, the idea can be put in this fashion:

> Chandra's experience E is *self-authenticating* regarding proposition P if and only if Chandra has experience E, it is logically impossible that Chandra have an experience phenomenologically of sort E and proposition P be false, and Chandra rests his acceptance of P on his having had E.[2]

If there are experiences that satisfy these conditions regarding persons and beliefs, the most obvious examples do not concern religious beliefs. Suppose that Wendy, perhaps feeling philosophical, reflects that, in contrast to Santa Claus and unicorns but like salamanders and her dog, she exists. Reflection is, after all, a kind of experience, and if Wendy reflects at time T that she exists at T (a reflection that, she notes, includes her believing that she exists), then she is fully justified if she also notes that her reflecting that she exists is impossible unless she does exist; Wendy's experience of believingly reflecting on the fact of her existence is such that it is logically impossible that she do so and her belief be false. So if she rests her belief that she exists at T on the experience of believingly reflecting that she exists at T, her experience of believingly reflecting that she exists at T can be self-authenticating regarding her belief that she exists at T. If we ask, then, what sorts of beliefs there are that can receive self-authentication from experience, it seems clear that among them are: one's belief that one now exists, that one is now conscious, that one now has at least one belief, and the like. Perhaps if one believes that one is now in pain, then it is true that one is now in pain (though one can be wrong about the pain's cause and its location). These sorts of experiences and beliefs represent the least controversial cases of self-authentication.

Consider claims central to Advaita Vedanta, Jainism, and Theravada Buddhism:

> AV. *We are identical to qualityless Brahman.*
> J. *We have existential independence or ontological security and are omniscient.*
> TB. *We are composed at a time of momentary elements and over time of bundles of such elements.*[3]

Each of these claims, if they are true at all, are—as their adherents insist—true whether we know them to be true, and true independent of anyone having any enlightenment experience.[4] Further, each tradition holds that one can believe two of these three claims, and have the experience that the tradition in which it is alleged that the experience confirms that claim, without that claim being true. It seems plain that it is logically possible that one believe any of *We are identical to qualityless Brahman, We have existential independence or ontological security and are omniscient*, or *We are composed at a time of a bundle of momentary elements and over time of a series of bundles of such elements* and believe falsely, just as it is logically possible that one believe oneself to be more courageous than one is, or free from illness while a disease silently takes its toll, or devoid of pride while enamored of one's humility. It also seems possible that one have an experience that has a phenomenology that justifies its subject in believing it to be an experience of God and believe mistakenly, just as it seems possible that one has an experience that has a phenomenology that justifies its subject in believing that it is a genuine enlightenment experience, and hence that she is identical to qualityless Brahman, or is inherently immortal, or is but a bundle of momentary states at the moment and just a series of bundles over time, and be mistaken. It is not logically impossible that one have an experience in virtue of which one accepts a religious belief and that experience is not self-authenticating. Thus it may well be that in all three cases, one can have an experience that seems to be a relevant enlightenment experience, believe the corresponding doctrine, think the experience confirms the doctrine, and be mistaken on all counts. Each tradition holds views that entail that the "enlightened" members of the other two traditions are in exactly this position. For example, my having no sense of self at time T is not evidence that I really am not a self—to whom or what would it be evidence? One's having no awareness of the passing of time or of being in time does not entail that one is not or was not in time. The same holds for lack of awareness of being spatially located and in fact not being in space.

None of this is denied by even the strongest proponents of the self-authenticating character of enlightenment experiences.[5] What is claimed is not that it is logically impossible that one believe the preferred doctrine and that doctrine nonetheless be false, but that (i) it is logically impossible that one have an enlightenment experience that self-authenticates a doctrine and the doctrine nonetheless be false, and (ii) enlightenment experiences (of the right kind) are self-authenticating regarding (the right) doctrine. While (i) is true by definition of "self-authentication," (ii) is a substantial claim that we will explore.

Descriptions

In exploring it, we begin with this question: What sort of descriptions will be true of an enlightenment experience that is self-authenticating regarding, say, a Jain religious doctrine? To put the same question in a different way, what sort of phenomenology or observable features must such an experience have? Since what it is said to self-authenticate is *We have existential independence or onto-logical security and are omniscient*, it must have a phenomenology appropriate to confirming that claim. The simplest description will be something like *at least apparently recognizing one's existential independence or ontological security and one's omniscience*. There are various problems with offering this as the descrip-tion relevant for the appeal to experience as evidence.

Suppose that you and I are looking at an ancient coin. You claim it is Roman, and I claim it is Greek. I say *I see it is Greek* and regard the case as closed. You claim *I see it is Roman* and regard the case as closed. But at least one of us is wrong, and neither of us has provided any evidence by describing the experience in a way that simply assumes that our claim is true. It is not that I express my evidence by saying *I see it is Greek*; I do not thereby recite any evidence what-ever, I merely repeat my claim. If your experience is to be evidence that the coin is Roman,[6] it must be the case that there are features that the coin at least seems to have such that, if the coin has those features, it is at least probably Roman. So to speak, the phenomenology of your coin-experience must be Romanesque. For example, it may bear the likeness of a Roman emperor rather than a Greek states-man. If I am to have evidence, the coin must at least appear to me to have some feature such that, if the coin has that feature, that fact supports its Greekness. For example, it may bear the likeness of a Greek statesman rather than a Roman emperor.

The case of enlightenment experience is analogous. To simply assert, for some religious claim C, that one has an experience in which one recognizes or realizes its truth, with no specification of what it is about the experience that confirms C, is pointless so far as evidence is concerned.

Evidence about What?

Enlightenment experience is supposed to teach one about one's nature—about what one is—insofar as one is anything. For Advaita Vedanta the goal is identity with qualityless Brahman. For Jainism the goal is recognizing that one is an inde-structible, all-knowing, self-aware substance. It is typical of Buddhist traditions to deny that anything has a "same-nature" or essence. Nonetheless, it is also typical of Buddhist traditions to hold that every item that we commonsensically regard as an enduring thing is really composed at a time of a bundle of momentary elements and over time of a series of momentary bundles of elements. Whether or not one calls this a doctrine of the nature of persons or not,[7] the idea is that this is what persons really are. For each of these traditions, the goal is the truth about (what there is of) oneself.

If, however, any of these claims is true, it is true about everyone, not just about oneself; the idea is that if anyone then everyone is identical to qualityless Brahman or is an indestructible enduring mind or is composed only of momentary elements. Further, these claims can be true only if various other things are false. For example, if monotheism is true, God is ultimate and has qualities (so there is no qualityless Brahman), persons are created and endure by divine courtesy (they are not indestructible), and God is neither transient nor composed of transient elements (it is false that everything is impermanent).

Particular Experiences, Universal Claims

The various doctrines about persons are universal in scope; the experiences occur to particular individuals. When we ask whether these particular experiences provide evidence for claims that are universal in their scope, we get different results depending on the case. Suppose that enlightenment experience provides evidence that one is identical to qualityless Brahman. Will this also provide evidence that everyone else is? The question is peculiar in a way that arises from the doctrine itself. If A is identical to B and C is identical to B, then A is identical to C. So if you are identical to qualityless Brahman and I am too, we are identical to one another; so there isn't "anyone else." If there is anyone else, the doctrine is false.

Suppose that enlightenment experience provides evidence that one is an indestructible mind or is composed of momentary elements. Will this also provide evidence that everyone else is? It will do so in the presence of a doctrine to the effect that the subject of the experience is a person and what makes her a person is the same as what makes everyone else a person, assuming that one is justified in taking these additional claims to be true. Discussing these issues in any detail would take us too far away from our basic concerns here. Thus we simply note that it is widely assumed that these sorts of additional claims are true.[8] It is unsurprisingly typical that Jain and Buddhist believers take themselves to have the same nature, or lack of nature, as all other people. They share this perspective with common sense and the monotheistic traditions. Jainism does hold that some souls are not capable of enlightenment—a sort of election to lack of salvation without an Elector.

Phenomenologies That Fit the Claims

The right sort of phenomenology seems to be of this sort: for Advaita enlightenment experience, *appearing or seeming to be identical with qualityless Brahman*; for Jainism, *appearing or seeming to be an indestructible and highly knowledgeable mind*; for Buddhism, *appearing or seeming to be only a bundle of transitory states*. One might question whether these are, strictly speaking, possible phenomenological features of an experience. They seem, like *being a Roman coin*, to be features something could have only by virtue of other features also had by that thing. In the case of a Roman coin, *bearing the image of an emperor* is one such feature. In the enlightenment cases, presumably the relevant further features are such qualities as *having no sense of possessing qualities*, *feeling indestructible*, and *being aware only of states of mind*. It is, however, logically possible that one possess qualities that one has no sense of having, feel indestructible while being dependent for existence on something else, and be aware of nothing but one's current mental states without being identical to those states even at the time at which one has them. Further, that one has no sense of having qualities is possible only if one does have qualities—to have no qualities at all is simply not to exist at all, and not existing gets very much in the way of having experiences. Having a sense of being indestructible is perfectly compatible with not being indestructible, and having a sense of being momentary is perfectly compatible with being an enduring thing.

One way of putting the problems with the notion that enlightenment experiences are self-authenticating with regard to Advaita, Jain, or Buddhist doctrinal claims is this:

(i)   The claims are, if true of one at all, true of one so long as one exists, whereas in the least controversial cases of self-authentication the claims that are authenticated have to do with one's existence right now or one's current, momentary states of awareness; the claims in cases where claims to self-authentication is plausible are about a time span that corresponds, and is limited, to the time during which the authenticating experience occurs.

(ii) The quality or state ascribed to oneself by the claim is an observable quality—like being in pain—or is entailed by any quality anything has—like existing.

By contrast, the Advaita, Jain, and Buddhist claims concern times not limited to the duration of the enlightenment experience or entailed by the content of the relevant enlightenment experience. Such states as *seeming to oneself to be qualityless*, *seeming to be indestructible*, and *seeming to be momentary* are states that can easily be mistaken—one may seem to oneself to be qualityless, indestructible, or momentary without these things being in fact true.

It is important to remember here that we are not asking what sort of phenomenological features an experience might have were one's having it to lead one to accept a particular religious doctrine, especially if one had it in a context in which it was expected that such experiences might occur—for example, within a meditative tradition the very purpose of which was the preparation for having such experiences whose interpretation was built into the institutional context within which the meditative practice occurred. We are not seeking to give a psychological explanation of enlightenment experiences, but asking whether these experiences provide self-authentication for certain religious beliefs.

What follows from our discussion is that they do not. Not only is it the case that Advaita Vedanta, Jainism, and Theravada Buddhism each can claim self-authentication for a claim that is logically incompatible with the claims for which the other traditions assert that same privilege. But then the beliefs embraced by at least two of the traditions will be mistaken, so that appeal to self-authentication is insufficient to show that a doctrine for which it is clamed is true. In addition, none of the enlightenment experiences possess a phenomenology that self-authenticates the beliefs in question. It is not logically impossible that one have an enlightenment experience—whether Advaita Vedanta, Jain, or Buddhist—that possesses the relevant phenomenological features and it also is the case that the corresponding Advaita, Jain, or Buddhist doctrine be false. So enlightenment experiences do not self-authenticate doctrines based on them. The argument showing this can be made fully explicit as follows:

1. One's enlightenment experience is *self-authenticating* regarding a proposition expressing the core Advaita, Jain, or Buddhist doctrinal claim only if one seems (respectively) to be qualityless, indestructible, or momentary, and it is logically impossible that one seem to oneself to be qualityless, indestructible, or momentary, and one not be qualityless, indestructible, or momentary, and that one rests one's acceptance of core Advaita, Jain, or Buddhist doctrine on one's having seemed to oneself to be qualityless, indestructible, or momentary.
2. It is not logically impossible that one seem to oneself to be qualityless, indestructible, or momentary and one not be so.

Hence:

3. One's enlightenment experience is not self-authenticating relative to Advaita, Jain, or Buddhist doctrine.

We have argued that enlightenment experiences are not self-authenticating regarding these claims. That they are not self-authenticating regarding the religious claims often based on them does not entail that these experiences are not evidence for those claims. Evidence need not be self-authenticating. We have argued that the same is true for monotheistic claims. So the next question is: Do enlightenment experiences provide evidence for religious beliefs?

What Principle of Experiential Evidence Is Relevant?

The previous chapter explained and defended principles of experiential evidence. They are examples of claims that can provide support for premises like the second steps of the brief three-step arguments sketched early in this chapter. These principles were:

(P*) If a person S has an experience E that, if reliable, is a matter of being aware of an experience-independently existing item X, and E is not canceled or counterbalanced or compromised or contradicted or confuted or logically consumed or empirically consumed, then S's having E is evidence that X exists.

and:

> (P**) If a person S has an experience E that, if reliable, is a matter of being aware of an experience-independently existing item X, and S (non-culpably) has no reason to think that E is canceled or counterbalanced or compromised or contradicted or confuted or logically consumed or empirically consumed, then S's having E provides S evidence that X exists.

Some experiences, we have noted, are matters of someone's at least seeming to perceive something that, *if it exists at all*, exists independent of its being experienced. These have a particular structure—subject-consciousness-object. Other experiences are matters of someone's feeling a certain way. These also have a particular structure—subject-content. Seeing an apple tree is of the former sort; so is merely seeming to see an apple tree. Feeling nauseous or dizzy and experiencing generalized anxiety or euphoria are examples of the latter sort. It is important to keep in mind the differences between experiences that are subject-consciousness-object in structure and experiences that are subject-content in structure.

Subject/Content Experience and a Principle of Experiential Evidence

Treating subject-content experience as evidence requires a principle of experiential evidence different from (P*) and (P**), which refer to evidence for the existence of experience-independent things and apply to subject-consciousness-object experiences. Enlightenment experiences are construed as awareness of states, conditions, or structure of oneself as a person, or of what is commonsensically taken to be a person. Thus Advaita Vedanta proposes an enlightenment experience that is an awareness of the existence of a qualityless, undifferentiated state—if we may so put it without disrespect, an analogue of cosmic tapioca without lumps that lacks spatial and temporal properties—with which the person having the experience is identical. (One cannot say "is a part" since it has no parts.) The Jain proposal is that one is a mental substance that has no, or no essential, physical properties and has no parts of any sort, and in enlightenment experience recognizes to be the full nature of oneself as a person. That nature has a substance-property structure in which the substance is simple or incomposite. Buddhism claims an enlightenment experience in which one sees that the structure of what we take to be persons is collections of momentary conscious states that occur in a series, with 'collections' and 'series' being conventional terms that do not refer to something over and above their momentary constituents. These proposed experiences are not subject-content in the way that one's being aware of one's pain or fatigue are. The latter sort of experiences are ones in which one's subjective states are open to awareness, and no idea as to everyone else being in those states is either explicit or implicit in the experience.

Regarding subject-content states whose content is sensations—pains, generalized anxiety, generalized euphoria, dizziness, and the like, something like this seems right if not overly cautious.

(P***) If a person S has an experience E that, if reliable, is a matter of S being aware of being in an experience-dependently existing state X of S, then S's having E is evidence that S is in state X.

But enlightenment experiences are viewed as a different sort of animal. We need a principle of experiential evidence that will fit these cases. Where we allow *being in a state* to be broadly construed (so as to cover things like *having a quality*, *being an event*, and the like), consider:

(P****) If a person S has an experience E that, if reliable, is a matter of S being aware of being in an experience-independently existing state X of S, then S's having E is evidence that S is in state X.

(Note the shift from "experience-dependently" in (P***) to "experience-independently" in (P****).)

Experiencing pain, euphoria, or anxiety is evidence that one is in a state of pain, euphoria, or anxiety.[9] (We waive questions of incorrigibility.) Religious claims do not typically concern such private, momentary psychological states, and no religion bases its core doctrines on their occurrence. Being identical to Brahman or being qualityless, being indestructible or a soul that exists independently, and being a momentary being or a being whose constituents are momentary, are not features or qualities or states that are experience-dependent. What makes one a person or what we view as a person—the metaphysical structure of what determines whether we are or not—apparently can be easily confused. Descartes, Jainism, and Advaita Vedanta regarding the level of appearance take the side of our being substances with properties. Hume and generally the Buddhist tradition take the side of bundles in a series. Happily, neither philosophers nor leaders in the traditions (who sometimes overlap and sometimes do not) have not drawn the conclusion that persons belong to two species, a sustance species and a series species. Assuming they are right in avoiding this rather desperate tactic, one can be quite mistaken in what one's person-making metaphysical structure is. This is a central the point of dispute between Jainism and Buddhism. Advaita Vedanta's place in the conversation between the three traditions is harder to state. As noted, the level of appearance, according to Advaita sides with Jainism. So, for that matter, does the Buddhist account of common sense. But the Buddhist view of common sense, speaking generally, is that it is mistaken in this crucial regard, and Buddhist enlightenment experience shows this. Shankara, the most famous representative of Advaita, was accused of being a cryto-Buddhist for adopting his view of the level of reality, which on a plausible understanding of what is meant by Buddhist nirvana is nirvana by another name. Without getting into interpretive disputes, we will simply take the Advaita account of the level of appearance as it is given without worrying about its historical source. Our question is what sort of phenomenological content should be specified as providing experiential evidence for the Jain and Buddhist, and then the Advaita, doctrines.

The answer regarding the Jain and Buddhist cases is obvious. It would have to be, in each case, a description of the structure ascribed to persons by those religious traditions. The Jain claims to be aware of herself as a mental substance not dependent on anything physical and inherently immortal. (We waive discussion of the claim to omniscience.) The Buddhist claims to be aware of himself as only a collection of conscious states. This raises the question of how this awareness is possible without a subject. Something or other must be aware in the required fashion. Perhaps the bundle possesses reflexive consciousness or contains some one-or-more-membered class of conscious states that are aware of the rest? Then we need some good reason to think that this sort of reflexive awareness is provided in some manner that does not involve their being unified by being experiences of a subject, and why whatever has the reflexive consciousness must be momentary.

Sticking to the issue of whether having an experience the phenomenology of which is Buddhist in content, we have an experience in which there is awareness whose scope is only conscious states.

In the Jain case, the phenomenological requirement is that the subject seems to himself to be indestructible and completely non-physical.

To go back a step, and be as concrete as possible, the Buddhist experience must be—in the case of pain—one of feeling pain, and the Jain experience—in the case of pain—must be one of feeling oneself being in pain. For the Jain, one is aware of the pain as one's pain, of oneself being in pain, of pain as being a state one is in. These ways of putting the point converge on the idea that one's experience is not simply pain, but rather I-am-in-pain, that pain awareness is one among a great many instances of self-awareness. As an account of everyday experience the Buddhist has no quarrel, but goes on to maintain that everyday experience misleads in this regard.

There are, of course, a great many properties that one can have to which one has no introspective access. One can introspectively seem to oneself to be qualityless, indestructible, or momentary in the sense that one has an experience in which one believes this to be so, but what would make this so is not some introspectable property. It is a state of affairs that is not itself introspectively observable. Whatever security introspection provides regarding experience-dependent states does not belong to them. We are dealing with states such that, if they exist, they are not metaphysically experience-dependent. We turn to our three cases directly.

Advaita

Appearing to be qualityless seems a non-starter. What would justify one in claiming to have such an experience? Supposing one had such an experience, what would justify one in thinking it was oneself that was qualityless? Having an experience is a property, so if one manages to have an experience, one is not without properties. Doing so not only is not evidence that one is qualityless but is sufficient evidence for possession of qualities; it is logically impossible that one have any experience at all and not exist, and logically impossible that one exist without having qualities. Indian critics of Advaita Vedanta, the most famous of whom is Ramanuja, have pressed this decisive objection with great force and clarity.[10]

Jainism and Buddhism

Appearing to oneself to be indestructible is not evidence that one is indestructible. Claims of indestructibility, of course, are not made regarding the body; Jain philosophers know as well as anyone that the human body is not indestructible. What they claim, along with Plato and Platonists, is that the mind or soul or person is indestructible. The point remains, however, that the mind or soul or person having an experience in which it seems to itself to be indestructible is not evidence that it is indestructible. Not only is it logically possible that one have an experience in which it seems to one that one is indestructible though in fact one is not; it is also that having such an experience is not any evidence that one is indestructible, any more than having an experience in which one seems to oneself to be destructible is evidence that one is destructible. Similarly, a sense of one's existence as momentary, or as composed of momentary items is one thing, and one's being a momentary existent or being composed of things that exist only for an instant is another, and having a sense of one's momentariness is not evidence that one is merely momentary or that one is composed of momentary constituents. The claim that one was composed of only momentary states would require a continuing observer who watched the states come and go. But then something capable of observing and remembering what one observed would have to endure throughout the period of observation. One could try claiming that there was an observer at each moment that caused an observer at the next moment to remember what the previous observer had observed as well as doing its own observation of a new set of momentary states, but this appeals to a theory that goes well beyond anything that can be experientially confirmed in a world of momentary states. Further, the momentary observers seem to be momentary subjects of experience, and once one admits momentary subjects of experience, one needs argument that they are momentary and an explanation of how momentary subjects can learn that there are momentary subjects.

The argument can be stated along the following lines. Consider three claims, each of which is true:

1. There are states, like being in pain, feeling happy, worrying about one's health, and the like, where one's having the sense that one is in pain, happy, or worried, justifies one's belief that one is in pain, happy, or worried—such states involve phenomenological awareness of the actual state that one ascribes to oneself and one's being aware of being in such a state is evidence that one is in it.[11]
2. There are other states, like thinking that one can wave one's arms and fly, that one has grown a lion's head, or that one's head is made of glass, where

one's having the sense that one can fly, has grown a lion's head, or one's head is made of glass, does not involve a phenomenological awareness of one's actually flying, actually having a lion's head, or actually having a head made of glass, and one's having such a sense is not evidence that one is in the state that one ascribes to oneself.

When one believes on the basis of introspection that one is in one of the sorts of states that 1 describes, one typically is right. When one believes on the basis of introspection that one is in one of the sorts of states that 2 describes, one typically is wrong. Consider:

3.   There are still other states, like thinking that one is the brightest member of one's class, the most talented actor in one's school, an immortal soul, someone who will die today, and the like, where one's having the sense that one is brightest, most talented, immortal, or will die today, does not involve a phenomenological awareness of one's actually being brightest, most talented, immortal, or dying today, and one's having such a sense is not evidence that one is in the state that one ascribes to oneself.

In these cases, in contrast to those described in 2, it is not just obvious that one is not in the state mentioned. But the cases are similar in this respect: the state in question, unlike those mentioned in 1, is not a state that is introspectively accessible or discernible. One cannot, so to speak, read off of one's introspective awareness that one is in the sort of states described in 2 and 3. Nor is there any entailment between *seeming to be in the state* and *being in the state* or any relation such that *seeming to be in the state* renders it more likely than not that one is in the state.

Consider, then, this way of putting the argument:

A.   Enlightenment experiences are senses of being in a certain state and they fall into either class 2 or class 3.
B.   Senses of being in a certain state that fall into either class 2 or class 3 are not evidence that the person who has that sense is in that state.

Thus:

C.   Enlightenment experiences are not evidence that the person who has them is in the state she thinks she is in.

Hence appeal to enlightenment experience will not confirm Advaita, Jain, or Buddhist doctrine.

A Caveat

While the arguments presented thus far have a certain force, and are eminently defensible, they do not sufficiently discuss the actual contexts in which one finds the other side presented. In discussing these matters still further, it will be useful to consider first the Advaita Vedanta appeal to experience as evidence, and then the Jain and the Buddhist appeals. The critique of the Advaita appeal that one finds readymade in Indian thought is straightforward and decisive. The latter two appeals in particular are very like positions taken outside of any religious context, and are best seen in a cross-cultural context.

Advaita Appeal to Enlightenment Experience

Shankara rightly held that we do know that we exist and that we have certain properties. Chandra can know that he now exists, and that he is conscious now—and thus he can know that *For all X, if X lacks properties, then X is not me.* Further, Chandra can know that there are things that he does not know, and if there cannot be things that Brahman does not know (and this is supposed to be a necessary truth—at least it is supposed to be a necessary truth that "not knowing something" cannot be properly ascribed to Brahman) then Chandra can know that he is not identical to Brahman. If one knows both *I exist, and have P* and *There is an item—namely, X—that (if it exists) lacks P* then one can properly infer to *I am not X.* Hence the Advaita Vedanta claim—its reading of the *Upanishadic* passage "Thou art That"—is not true. Similarly, on Shankara's own view, if Chandra sees an elephant, Chandra sees a mind-independently existing large gray or albino mammal, so there are mind-independently existing large gray or albino mammals. But Brahman is not any sort of mammal at all, and so even if Brahman exists, Brahman does not exist alone.

Shankara is of course aware of such objections, and while Ramanuja, Madhva, and other Vedantins make them because they believe that Shankara has no adequate answer, the answer that he has should be noted. The answer[12] is that enlightenment experience trumps or "sublates" all other sorts of experience, and enlightenment experience is self-authenticating. Further, each sensory or introspective experience is self-defeating, because it is either subject-consciousness-object or else subject-content in structure—it includes "the making of distinctions"—and any such experience is (it is claimed) inherently unreliable. Such later critics as Ramanuja and Vadarija turn the latter claim against its author. In moksha or enlightenment experience, one is supposed to learn that one is identical to qualityless Brahman. While this is not viewed as being like learning that seven and five are twelve, or that Alaska and Hawaii are U.S. states—it is an experience said to be life-changing, transforming, accompanied with calm and bliss and freedom from desire, and the like—still it is a matter of coming to see some alleged truth. Enlightenment experience is supposed to confirm core Advaita doctrine. Suppose it does so; then it is a matter of someone learning something—a subject-consciousness-object or else a subject-content experience. If all experiences with such structures are unreliable, so is enlightenment experience. On the other hand, if enlightenment experience is reliable, then other experiences possessing a similar structure can be reliable, and all sensory and introspective experience provides evidence against the claim that only qualityless Brahman exists. Should it be replied that enlightenment experience has no object and no content, then it cannot be the case that it confirms some doctrine rather than some other. "Contentless and objectless experience" describes no possible experience, and if it did describe any experience, such an experience would not be evidence for Advaita versus Jain, Buddhist, monotheistic, or other religious claims. Without even apparent object or content, it would favor none of the traditions.

Jain-type Appeals to Experience

Both Jain and Buddhist traditions appeal to introspective experience as evidence for, or confirmation of, their particular doctrines of what a person is. From a Jain perspective—since for Jainism there is a self to have experiences—"introspective experience" here means "self-awareness" or "awareness of one's mental states," irrespective of how those states are elicited or understood. Jain enlightenment experience is taken to have the same structure, and to reveal the same substantival being, that is encountered in ordinary everyday self-consciousness. The Buddhist tradition typically takes ordinary self-awareness to be deceptive and restricts its appeal to enlightenment experiences and experiences that occur to the type achieved by those trained in Buddhist meditative traditions. Philosophers—of whom David Hume is the most famous—claim that the most ordinary of introspective experiences confirm the same view as that which the Buddhist derives from esoteric experiences. In what follows, then, we will simply speak of introspective experiences, not limiting ourselves to those that are meditative or religious. As the dispute is cross-cultural, we may as well see it in that context, quoting both European and Indian representatives of both positions. One position is propounded by Descartes, various Jain texts, and Ramanuja, and the other asserted by David Hume and various Theravada Buddhist texts.

The dispute here concerns, then, whether or not persons are self-conscious and enduring substances. This matter, at least, Descartes, Ramanuja, Jainism, Buddhism, and Hume think can be settled by appeal to introspection. They disagree as to what the introspective evidence confirms. We begin with the position that claims that introspection and enlightenment experience clearly and incontrovertibly shows that persons are enduring mental substances, and follow with the position that introspection and/or enlightenment experience clearly and incontrovertibly shows that persons at a time are but bundles of momentary states, so that over time a person can be nothing more substantial than a series of such bundles.

Descartes

Descartes writes:

> . . . of a surety I myself did exist since I persuaded myself of something (or merely because I thought of something). But there is some deceiver or other, very powerful and very cunning, who ever employs his ingenuity in deceiving me. Then without doubt I exist also if he deceives me, and let him

deceive he as much as he will, he can never cause me to be nothing so long as I think that I am something, so that after having reflected well and carefully examined all things, we must come to the definite conclusion that this proposition: *I am, I exist*, is necessarily true each time that I pronounce it, or that I mentally conceive it.[13]

The claim is that *Necessarily, the fact that I think includes the fact of my existence* and that I can know without danger of error that I am a thinking being and that I exist. Descartes does not make the false claim that *Descartes exists* is, if true, then necessarily true. In his investigations of self-consciousness he "was merely investigating these properties of which I able to attain to sure and evident knowledge"[14]—in particular such properties as pertain to the nature of Descartes as a sample person. He claims that he, as a person, is a self-conscious substance, and that this is introspectively evident. It is logically impossible that he exist without being a self-conscious being, and hence being a self-conscious being is at least part of his essence. He adds that since this is true of him as a representative person, what it is to be a person is to be an enduring self-conscious substance.

Two sorts of claims are represented here. One sort is introspective, strictly speaking; Descartes is aware of his thinking of the nature of persons rather than reflecting about triangularity, logical necessity, the nature of matter, or the prospects of his completing a letter to Elizabeth. Discerning what one is thinking about is a matter of being aware of one's thoughts—a matter of introspection. Another sort is conceptual and metaphysical—he is considering the nature of persons rather than wondering how his mother is doing or considering what to have for dinner, and by doing such conceptual thinking he can discern the nature of persons—just as, in thinking about triangles, he can discern their essence. In this special case, he holds that he has (as anyone can have) a unique advantage—what he considers the essence of is also an object of direct awareness, and thus the concept of this essence can be compared with something that has the essence the concept expresses. Thus his claim is that these two sorts of thinking—introspective and conceptual—to some degree coalesce in the case of his deliberate use of self-awareness as a source of knowledge regarding his nature as a person. He observes in himself not only his thinking and his existence but also a necessary connection between the property *Descartes thinking now* and the property *Descartes existing now* that eliminates any need for inference from the fact that he has the one property to his having the other (though of course that inference is proper). He is able to reflect that he exists only if he is a self-conscious thing—permanent loss of self-consciousness is also cessation of his existence, and he is directly aware of himself as a self-conscious substance.

Put differently, Descartes is often aware of his being in certain introspective states. Some of these states are states of abstract thought, and among these are reflections concerning the nature of persons. When he thinks of triangles, bluebirds, or waffles, Descartes is thinking of kinds of things to which he does not himself belong. Not so when he thinks of persons. When he thinks about the nature of a triangle—what it is to be one, or of a bluebird or a waffle, he does not think about his own nature; not so when he thinks of what it is to be a person. His view is that he can learn what it is to be a person by (i) noting what sorts of properties he himself has—something introspectively accessible to him, and (ii) reflecting about what properties he could exist without having and what properties he could not exist without having—something conceptually accessible to him.

Explaining his position in reply to an objection, Descartes says:

> Everything in which there resides immediately, as in a subject, or by means of which there exists anything that we perceive, i.e. any property, quality, or attribute, of which we have a real idea, is called a Substance.[15]

Since he is aware of himself as having various qualities and being in various states, he is introspectively aware of being a substance. Since allegedly he knows that it is his essence to be self-conscious—any other features not identical to or entailed by self-consciousness, he could survive without; without self-consciousness[16] he does not exist—he concludes that it is his nature as a person (and hence the nature of persons) to be a self-conscious substance.

Jainism

A Jain text tells us the following:

> The distinctive characteristic of a substance is being. Being is a simultaneous possession of coming into existence, going out of existence, and permanence. Permanence means the indestructibility of the essence of the substance. . . . Substance is possessed of attributes and modifications. . . . Attributes depend upon substratum and cannot be the substratum of another attribute. Modification is change of attribute.[17]

A substance, we are told, has attributes—properties or qualities, if you please. No attribute can exist that is not the attribute of some substance. Things come into existence in the sense that substances come to have qualities they did not have and to lose qualities they did have; through such changes, substances continue to exist and of course retain their essential qualities.

Further:

> The self's essence is life. . . . The distinctive characteristic of self is attention. . . . Those with minds are knowers.[18]

"Selves are substances"[19] and their definitive characteristic or essence is described as "life" and "attention." Further:

> That which should be grasped by self-discrimination is I from the real point of view.[20] The soul has the nature of knowledge, and the realization of this

nature is Nirvana; therefore one who is desirous of Nirvana must meditate on self-knowledge.[21]

Jainism sometimes uses 'nirvana' rather than 'kevala' to refer to enlightenment experience. Self-realization involves self-knowledge, and it "has the nature of knowledge." This obviously comes very close at least to Descartes's view of the person, mind, or soul as being a self-conscious substance. In both introspective and enlightenment experience, one appears to oneself as a thinking thing, a substance that possesses cognitive mental qualities.

Ramanuja

In a passage that expresses the same sort of view as that of Descartes and Jainism, the Hindu monotheist Ramanuja writes:

> The judgement "I am conscious" reveals an "I" distinguished by consciousness; and to declare that it refers only to a state of consciousness—which is a mere attribute—is no better than to say of the judgement "Devadatta carries a stick" is about the stick only.[22]

He adds:

> Consciousness is the illuminating, in the present moment, to its own substrate, by its own existence alone. . . . Or else, it is the establishing of its own subject by its own existence alone. . . . A conscious act is the illumination of a particular object to its own substrate by its own existence alone. . . . The nature of consciousness is to make something into an object of experience of its own substrate through its own being alone.[23]

According to Ramanuja, a person can be directly aware of herself as the subject of her experiences, including an awareness of herself. Seeing a lamp, one can be aware of oneself as so seeing. One need not infer from *Someone is seeing a lamp* to *I am someone or I am seeing a lamp*. The same experience yields the information that both of these sentences express, and it is *Someone is seeing a lamp* that requires inference if anything does, for it abstractly expresses a consequence of one's concrete first-person experience.

Ramanuja makes his allegiance to a Cartesian doctrine of the person plain when he writes:

> Now the permanence of the producer [of conscious acts], and the origination, duration, and cessation, as for pleasure and pain, of what is known as the conscious act, which is an attribute of the producer, are directly perceived. The permanence of the producer is established by recognition from such judgments as *This is the very same thing previously known by me.*[24]

The first sentence of this passage appeals to direct perception. Only in the second sentence is there appeal to argument, and the argument infers from reliable memory to the endurance of oneself as a substance.[25]

Nor, in Ramanuja's view, is this nature as a self-conscious being lost in enlightenment.

Ramanuja waxes eloquent on the point:

> To maintain that the consciousness of the "I" does not persist in the state of final release is again altogether inappropriate. It, in fact, amounts to the doctrine—only expressed in somewhat different words—that final release is the annihilation of the self. The "I" is not a mere attribute of the self so that even after its destruction the essential nature of the self might persist—as it persists on the cessation of ignorance; but it constitutes the very nature of the self. Such judgments as :"I know," "Knowledge has arisen in me," show, on the other hand, that we are conscious of knowledge as a mere attribute of the self.—Moreover, a man who, suffering pain, mental or of other kind—whether such pain be real or due to error only—puts himself in relation to pain—"I am suffering pain"—naturally begins to reflect how he may once for all free himself from all these manifold afflictions and enjoy a state of untroubled ease; the desire of final release thus having arisen in him he at once sets to work to accomplish it. If, on the other hand, he were to realize that the effect of such activity would be the loss of personal existence, he surely would turn away as soon as somebody began to tell him about "release." . . . Nor must you maintain against this that even in the state of release there persists pure consciousness; . . . No sensible person exerts himself under the influence of the idea that after he himself has perished there will remain some entity termed "pure light"!—What constitutes the "inward" self thus is the "I," the knowing subject.[26]

A similar theme is expressed in this passage:

> "May I, freeing myself from all pain, enter on free possession of endless delight?" This is the thought which prompts the man desirous of release to apply himself to the study of the sacred texts. Were it a settled matter that release consists in the annihilation of the "I," the man would move away as soon as release were only hinted at. "When I myself have perished, there persists some consciousness different from me," to bring this about nobody truly will exert himself.[27]

The "permanence" referred to here, like that of the Jain doctrine, is inherently everlasting, unlike the Cartesian doctrine (for whom it comes from God). Unlike the Jain, Ramanuja holds the permanence to be possessed only by divine courtesy and dependent on divine grace. In addition to an insistence on the distinctness, endurance, and value of the individual person or self, Ramanuja refers us to the nature of conscious experience as a basis for the view that a person is a mental substance in yet another passage:

> Some things—e.g., staffs and bracelets—appear sometimes as having a separate, independent existence of their own; at other times they present themselves as distinguishing attributes of other things or beings (i.e., of the persons carrying staffs or wearing bracelets). Other entities—e.g., the generic character of cows—have a being only insofar as they constitute the form of substances, and thus always present themselves as distinguishing attributes of those substances. . . . The assertion, therefore, that the difference of things is refuted by immediate consciousness is based on the plain denial of a certain form of consciousness, the one namely—admitted by every one—which is expressed by the judgment "This thing is such and such."[28]

The gist of this passage is that experiences that we all have are properly reported by statements of the form *I experience an X that has Q* where *X* refers to some thing and *Q* to some quality.

Descartes, Jainism, and Ramanuja—a French Catholic, an atheistic religious tradition, and a Hindu Visistadvaita Vedanta monotheist—hold that introspective (and for Jainism and Ramanuja, enlightenment) experience confirms that persons are self-conscious substances that endure through time. In briefest scope, the idea is this: *I am what I appear to be in introspective and enlightenment experience; what I appear to be in introspective and enlightenment experience is this: a mental substance; hence I am a mental substance.*

Buddhist-type Appeals to Experience

Hume

David Hume writes concerning "all of our particular perceptions" that:

> All these are different, and distinguishable, and separable from each other, and may be separately consider'd, and may exist separately, and have no need of any thing to support their existence. After what manner, therefore, do they belong to self; and how are they connected with it? For my part, when I enter most intimately into what I call myself, I always stumble on some particular perception or other, or heat or cold, light or shade, love or hatred, pain or pleasure. I never can catch myself at any time without a perception, and never can observe any thing but the perception. When my perceptions are remov'd for any time, as by sound sleep; so long am I insensible of myself, and may truly be said not to exist. And were all my perceptions remov'd by death, and cou'd I neither think, nor feel, nor see, nor love, nor hate after the dissolution of my body, I shou'd be entirely annihilated, nor do I conceive what is farther requisite to make me a perfect non-entity. If any one upon serious and unprejudic'd reflexion, thinks he has a different notion of himself,

> I must confess I can reason no longer with him. All I can allow him is, that he may be in the right as well as I, and that we are essentially different in this particular. He may, perhaps, perceive something simple and continuous, which he calls himself; tho' I am certain there is no such principle in me.[29]

Hume's claim is that all his introspection yields is awareness of independent states—say, a state of being in pain and a state of wondering where the aspirin went. At another later time, introspection may reveal, say, a desire for fish and wine and a regret that one forgot to buy either. What there is, so far as persons go, is such states, and nothing else. In briefest scope, his line of reasoning goes: *I am what I appear to be in introspective experience; What I appear to be in introspective experience is this: individual states; hence I am individual states.*

Theravada Buddhism

It is well known that this Humean view is shared by various Buddhist perspectives. A Buddhist text tells us that:

> Whether Buddhas arise, O priests, or whether Buddhas do not arise, it remains a fact and the fixed and necessary constitution of being that all its constituent are transitory. This fact a Buddha discovers and masters, and when he has discovered and mastered it, he announces, teaches, publishes, proclaims, discloses, minutely explains, and makes it clear, that all the constituents of being are transitory. . . . Whether Buddhas arise, O priests, or whether Buddhas do not arise, it remains a fact and the fixed and necessary constitution of being, that all its elements are lacking in an ego (substantial, permanent self-nature). This fact a Buddha discovers and masters, and when he has discovered and mastered it, he announces, teaches, publishes, proclaims, discloses, minutely explains, and makes it clear, that all the elements of being are lacking in an ego.[30]

A longer and more familiar passage reads as follows:

> Just as the word 'chariot' is but a mode of expression for axle, wheels, chariot-body, pole, and other constituent members, placed in a certain relation to each other, but when we come to examine the members one by one, we discover that in the absolute sense there is not chariot; and just as the word 'house' is but a mode of expression for wood and other constituents of a house, surrounding space in a certain relation, but in the absolute sense there is no house; and just as the word 'fist' is but a mode of expression for the fingers, the thumb, etc. in a certain relation; and the word 'lute' for the body of the lute, strings, etc.; 'army' for elephants, horses, etc.; 'city' for fortifications, houses, gates, etc.; 'tree' for trunk, branches, foliage, etc.; in a certain relation, but when we come to examine the parts one by one, we discover that in the absolute sense there is no tree; in exactly the same way words 'living entity' and 'ego' are but a mode of expression for the presence of the five

attachment groups, but when we come to examine the elements of being one by one, we discover that in the absolute sense there is no living entity there to form a basis for such figments as "I am" or "I"; in other words, that in the absolute sense there is only name and form. The insight of him who perceives this is called knowledge of the truth.[31]

In briefest scope, the line of reasoning is this: *I am what I appear to be in enlightenment experience; what I appear to be in enlightenment experience is this: individual states; hence I am individual states.* Buddhism typically holds that everyday experience seems to give awareness of a self, and thus supports the enduring self view. For precisely this reason, enlightenment experience is necessary to escape the sort of view that Jainism accepts.

The Duration Problem

It is impossible that one tell by immediate awareness at time T that one is, or is not, something that does, or does not, endure beyond T. Descartes emphasizes this: he knows by immediate awareness that he exists *now*—that "*I am, I exist,* is . . . true each time that I pronounce it, or that I mentally conceive it." Appeal to memory (as in the Ramanuja passage noted earlier) is required. There are obvious problems in appealing to memory to establish one's own lack of endurance, but for present purposes we shall simply set aside reference to duration and lack of duration and consider only the idea that either the Jain sort of appeal to experience can establish that persons are mental substances or the Buddhist sort of appeal to experience can confirm that persons are individual states. (The question arises as to whether 'states' is the right word—don't states have to be *states of something*? But similar questions arise about such terms as 'qualities' (of what?), 'events' (aren't events matters of substances coming to gain and/or lose qualities?), 'processes' (don't these occur to something?), and so on.)

These Buddhist passages express the doctrine that Hume claims to derive from introspective experience and that Theravada (and other) Buddhist traditions believe to be confirmed in meditative and enlightenment experience. The gist of the passages is put more succinctly via the terse claim "Consciousness is soulless."[32] Hume takes each mental state—each perception, or impression and idea, as he says—to exist independent of every other. The Buddhist traditions hold that each mental state depends for its existence on other states. But this difference aside, they agree—persons at a time are bundles of momentary states, over time are a series of such bundles, and introspective and/or enlightenment experience teaches us this sort of view.

The Contrasting Arguments

The enduring-mental-substance view and the bundle-of-momentary-states view do agree on an important and controversial claim, namely that what we appear to be in introspective, meditative, or enlightenment experience is what we are. It is not obvious that this is so. John Locke, in Book Two of his *Essay concerning Human Understanding*, offers an interesting third view. He agrees with Hume and Buddhism that what we are aware of is momentary states. He holds that momentary states can exist only as states of enduring substances. So he accepts the description of introspective data given by the momentary-mental-state theorist and the conclusion held by the enduring-mental-substance theorist, and there is at least nothing obviously incoherent about this view. It is incoherent if one thinks that what we are is exactly what introspection (etc.) reveals, but Locke does not hold that. Further, of course the view that we are simply what appears to or in our introspective, meditative, or enlightenment experience is not something that is introspectively (etc.) confirmable, and if one denies that we are only what appears to or in our introspective (etc.) experience one does not embrace a self-contradictory doctrine. Further, we have lots of tendencies, habits, dispositions, and properties that are not introspectively (etc.) available to us—some (like our ability to make logical inferences) are not always introspectively accessible, since we are not always making inferences; some, like either our being indestructible or our not being indestructible, are not ever introspectively available. Since the view that we are what we introspectively seem to be is common to both sides of the dispute, and an important part of their appeal to experience, both are—to that important degree at any rate—mistaken. That assumption is false. One could replace it by the view that our tendencies, dispositions, habits, and so on are—at least broadly speaking—properties we have, each is introspectable, even if not all are in fact introspected. But most of these properties are not introspectable at every moment and some will not be introspectable in any given introspective experience, so that part of what properties one has will not be present introspectively in any enlightenment experience. Thus not all of what we are is present. One might revise the claim regarding introspection (etc.) to claim merely that whatever structure the (real or illusory) self seemed to introspection (etc.) to have, or whatever fundamental sort it seemed to introspection to belong, was the structure it had or the kind to which it belonged. But *belonging to a kind* is not the sort of property that is introspectively discernible; if persons are *essentially self-conscious*, and *to be self-conscious* is the nature of persons, it still does not follow that *self-consciousness being the nature of persons* is somehow introspectively accessible. Similarly, if one has a triangular image before the mind's eye, and *being closed and three-sided* is essential to a triangle, it does not follow that *being closed and three-sided is essential to a triangle* are part of one's image. Neither *self-consciousness being the nature of persons* nor *being closed and three-sided* is an introspectively (etc.) accessible quality. Neither will it be reliably introspectable whether there is or seems to be a subject of experience over and above the experience since even the enduring self theorist admits that awareness of oneself can be at most at low ebb when one's experiential content is captivating, but will not be disturbed by this since one normally has no trouble, say, identifying whose pain, hope, fear, anxiety, or euphoria one is experiencing.

It is crucial here that Descartes used both introspective report and conceptual considerations.

So did Locke; so also do Ramanuja, Hume, and the Jain and Buddhist traditions. The substantivalists—Descartes, Ramanuja, and the Jain tradition—take it to be true that it is logically impossible that there be mental states that are not the states of some person in the sense of being states of some mental substance. Here Locke, who describes his experience in Humean and Buddhist terms, agrees with Descartes, Ramanuja, and the Jains in virtue of holding to the conceptual claim that *Necessarily, every experience is someone's experience.* For Jainism, Descartes, and Ramanuja, what introspection yields is not a pain, but *one's being in pain*; not a or the thought that Abraham Lincoln was once U.S. president, but *one's thinking that Lincoln was president*; not hunger, but *one's being hungry*. It is *oneself-in-some-state* that is introspected. The Buddhist tradition typically takes this to be a correct account of ordinary introspection, and to that extent agrees with the substantivalists against Hume. Hence their appeal to meditative and enlightenment experience, which they take to be different.

Hume takes persons to be, at a time, merely bundles of states. He takes introspection to reveal this, whereas the Buddhist tradition agrees with Hume's doctrine while taking his description of introspection to be true only of meditative and enlightenment experiences—experiences that have been, on the Buddhist view, purified from mistaken notions and, from the Jain view, rendered evidentially worthless by importation of Buddhist assumptions and made unnatural and non-representative of reliable human experience.

It is tempting to offer this explanation of the differences. Each perspective offers its reports of what experience teaches on report forms constructed in their own shops, substantival forms from the Jain shop and non-substantival forms from the Buddhist shop. What makes this possible regarding introspective experience and the dispute at hand is a variety of things we have noted already—the dispute is not a dispute about introspectively accessible properties or states, and it is a dispute inherently involving contrary philosophical theses. The Buddhist tradition is unwilling to rest the case on appeal to introspective or sensory experience because it thinks that this would refute its own position. It thus appeals to experiences that occur in meditative and enlightenment contexts of the right sort—e.g., not of the Jain sort. This involves a move not unlike the Advaita appeal to moksha experience as trumping others, unless Hume is right about introspective experience after all.

The problem with both the appeal-to-experience of the substantivalists and of the non-substantivalists is this: it marks out the dispute on ground that apparently cannot offer sufficient experiential evidence regarding it. The problem is not merely that there is no neutral way of describing introspective experience to which one can appeal for evidence that is of any use—though that is true. The awareness only of mental state view can be accommodated by the substance theorist by following Locke's approach. The problem is that the sorts of properties or states experience of which would be evidence are not accessible to introspective experience. *Being a substance* and *being only a bundle of states* are not more properties or features that are more introspectively accessible than are *being indestructible* or *being destructible*; both sorts of features differ in that regard from *being fatigued or worried or elated*. Equally intelligent and careful introspectors report different results. To posit two species of human being, one of the has-a-self and one of the has-no-self type has no precedent and conflicts with the universal-problem universal-cure perspectives of the religious traditions.

One stubborn fact prevents us from having a Principle of Introversive Experience: those who appeal to it do not agree on its phenomenological; description. If appeal to introspectibly accessible features are relevant to the dispute, as of course they are, they are relevant by virtue of their connection to competing theories of the self or person. The dispute then switches to the competing theories themselves—to the internal consistency, the coherence, the explanatory power, and so on, of substantival versus non-substantival theories of persons. But that is a different matter from appeal to introspective, meditative, or enlightenment experience as evidence for religious belief. It is a matter of which theory—substantivalist or non-substantivalist—can best explain memory, responsibility, self-consciousness, unity of consciousness, and the like.[33]

Questions for Reflection

1. Why, in the end, does the perceptual analogy not work as a way of expressing Advaita Vedanta?
2. What does Advaita Vedanta affirm?
3. What does Advaita Vedanta deny?
4. Explain the Jain doctrine of persons and its implications for memory.
5. Explain the Theravada doctrine of persons and its implications for memory.

Notes

1. In fact, the terminology used to refer to the relevant experiences is not as neat as these characterizations suggest. For example, Jainism not infrequently used 'nirvana' to refer to kevala experiences.
2. One might add something along the lines of *S has seen both that he had E and that it is logically impossible that he have E and P be false.* Nothing argued here will depend on whether we add this last consideration or not, so long as it is not the case that Chandra has E but believes P, not on the basis of his having had E, but on some other basis. Even if E is self-authenticating regarding a proposition P, and person S has E, E does not self-authenticate P to S if the only reason that S accepts P is not that S had E and E fits a description such that if E occurs then this is (conclusive) evidence for P. For example, if S would otherwise not accept P unless his great-grandfather had asserted P, and would have accepted P on that basis even without having had E, then even if E is conclusive evidence for P, S does not accept P on that basis and so E is not for S self-authenticating regarding P.

   One might put self-authentication along these lines: E is self-authenticating to Shandra regarding P if and only if Chandra cannot be mistaken about a belief B that P, Chandra evidentially rests his belief that P on his experience E, P cannot be false if Chandra has E, it is logically impossible that Chandra be wrong about whether Chandra has E, and Chandra believes that he had E. Again, nothing we say here would be changed if we characterized self-authentication along these lines.

3. These are only one way of putting these views, and do not exhaust the views central to these traditions. But they are accurate and representative, fully fair for illustrative purposes here.

4. Even if some claim is knowable only by someone who has an enlightenment experience it does not follow that it is true only if someone has an enlightenment experience. In fact, the relevant notion of enlightenment experience requires that such experiences essentially involve discovering what has been true all along.

5. Not at any rate so long as they think the doctrines they favor to be logically contingent truths.

6. I assume that we both have sufficient evidence that we are seeing a coin of some sort.

7. With the addition, of course, of claims about consciousness and memory.

8. I think that they are also *reasonably* accepted, save by Advaita Vedantins who claim that all of what could be said on their behalf in "sublated" and so trumped by enlightenment experience.

9. We will not worry here about second-order conscious states—e.g., one's being aware that one at least seems to perceive a tree or is having a headache similar to the one she had yesterday.

10. See, for example, the work by L. Stafford Betty, cited at the end of this chapter.

11. Philosophers who agree with the rest of what is said here may think that putting the matter in terms of evidence is not quite correct; it won't matter for our purposes whether speaking of evidence is exactly right here. For example, those who think we cannot be wrong about such states will want to talk about something stronger than evidence, which will not affect our basic point.

12. Another answer is that claims that a multiplicity of persons and physical objects exist are somehow self-contradictory, all relational claims are self-contradictory, the notion of a substance (physical or mental) is self-contradictory, or the like. But there seem to be no very good arguments for such accusations.

13. *Of the Nature of the Human Mind*, Meditation II, Haldane and Ross, eds. (1931) (Dover Publications), p. 150.

14. *Ibid.*, p. 30.

15. *Argument Demonstrating the Existence of God and the Distinction between Soul and Body, Drawn Up in Geometrical Fashion*, Definition V; p. 53.

16. One sort of dualism will take *being self-conscious* to be the nature of a person; others opt for *being capable of self-consciousness, and sometimes being so.*

17. Tattvarthadhigama Sutra, Chapter V, Sections 29, 30, 31, 38, 41, 42; *Sourcebook*, p. 256.

18. *Ibid.*, Chapter II, Sections 7, 8, 29; *Sourcebook*, p. 254.

19. *Ibid.*, Chapter II, 10.

20. *Samayasdra*, 325.

21. *Atmanusasna*, 174.

22. *Sourcebook*, p. 547.

23. G. Thibaut, tr. (1962) *The Vedanta-Sutras with the Commentary by Ramanuja* (Delhi: Motilal Barnasidass Reprint; originally published by Oxford University Press, 1904), p. 48, 55, 56.

24. *Ibid.*, p. 56.

25. Ramanuja also takes self-awareness to occur in sensory experience—a view that Jainism and (with qualifications) Descartes share.
26. Thibaut, I, i, p. 1; *Sourcebook*, p. 547.
27. *Ibid.*, p. 58.
28. *Ibid.*, p. 43.
29. *A Treatise of Human Nature*, Book One, Part IV, Section VI, of Personal Identity, p. 252.
30. Anguttara-nikaya, iii, 134; *Sourcebook*, p. 273, 274; the text is Theravadin.
31. Visuddhi-magga xviii; *Sourcebook*, pp. 284–285; the text is Theravadin.
32. Sangutta-nikaya iii, 66; *Sourcebook*, p. 280.
33. Substantivalists nonetheless have two advantages in the dispute. Hume admits that we believe that there are enduring substances and has to offer a painfully distended account of our having that belief. There is reason to take the substantivalist report form as the natural one—the one we in fact use in describing such experience. Further, even if it were to be proved that the non-substantivalist report form should be used, this—because of Locke's point—would not establish, or even provide any evidence for, the non-substantivalist point. So if there is a way around the objections offered here to appeals to introspective (etc.) experience, the advantage lies with the substantivalists. Still, the weight falls on the results of asking which view can explain memory, responsibility, self-consciousness, and the like. Appeal to enlightenment and meditative experience is made by both sides, as we have noted.

Suggested Readings

Braddon-Mitchell, David and Jackson, Frank, eds. (1996) *Philosophy of Mind and Cognition* (Oxford: Blackwell). A good survey of contemporary philosophy of mind.

Chisholm, Roderick (1976) *Person and Object* (LaSalle, IL: Open Court). Defends a substance account of persons.

Collins, Steven (1990) *Selfless Persons: Imagery and Thought in Theravada Buddhism* (Cambridge: Cambridge University Press). An excellent account of the Buddhist no-self doctrine.

Descartes, Rene, *Meditations on First Philosophy* (multiple editions). The classic presentation of mind-body dualism.

Hume, David, *A Treatise of Human Nature* (multiple editions). The classic expression of a no-self view.

Lavazza, Andrea and Robinson, Howard, eds. (2013) *Contemporary Dualism: A Defense* (New York: Routledge). State-of-the-art defense of a currently unpopular position.

Loux, Michael (1997) *Metaphysics* (London: Routledge). Contains a good discussion of substance-theories and bundle-theories.

Lowe, E. J. (2006) *Subjects of Experience* (Cambridge: Cambridge University Press). Defends a view on which subjects having experiences is metaphysically correct.

Siderits, Mark (2015) *Personal Identity and Buddhist Philosophy: Empty Persons* (Aldershot: Ashgate). Analytic philosophy is used to express and defend Buddhist no-self theory.

Yandell, Keith E. (1990) *Hume's "Inexplicable Mystery,"* (Philadelphia: Temple University Press). Contains a detailed discussion of Hume's views.

Part V

Religion, Morality, Faith, and Reason

14 Religion, Morality, and Responsibility

One obvious factor in considering religion and morality is how morality is being conceived. It is controversial to suppose that moral rules are basic to morality. For example, some hold that what is basic is the sense or recognition of the good or the obligatory on a particular occasion. None the less I will assume that what is basic in ethics as a discipline is ethical theory, that ethical theories contain one or more basic moral principles, and differ most fundamentally in the principles from which those who hold the theories reason and endeavor to properly apply to specific cases. If there is nothing closer to ethics than mores—customs adopted by a community to govern communal and individual living and having no deeper roots than the culture-relative status this gives them—then there is no such thing as morality. Put in other terms, unless there are things good in themselves or bad in themselves, ways that are right or wrong to behave, independent of the beliefs of any person or group, there is no such thing as morality. What there is, is human convention.

One way to discuss religion and morality is to start with morality. This is to start with moral theories. In principle there are a great many ethical theories, among them the view that only spiders have intrinsic worth and the view that it is always obligatory to increase the paperclip population of your home. We will consider, in any detail, three rather more plausible, and certainly more widely held, ethical theories. One ethical theory is strict egoism. Its only ethical principle is that my own interest ought to be furthered, since it alone has intrinsic goodness or is good for its own sake. Your interests have worth only if they serve my own. If they do not serve my own purposes, they are neutral, unless they harm my interests, in which case they are bad. One problem with this theory is that you can make that claim about your interests as well as I can make it about mine. Then we face the task of justifying the idea that it is only your, or my, interests that have the proposed exalted status. Anyone can claim this favored status for her interests, and there seems no good reason for one person to be seen as doing so with unique justification. One move to make at this point is to grant intrinsic worth to the interests of everyone. But if something's interests have intrinsic worth, then the something itself has intrinsic worth, so the something itself must have intrinsic worth.

The view that persons themselves have great worth—that as contemporary environmentalists affirm that landscapes have great inherent worth, persons have great intrinsic worth—has this general sort of grounding. Persons have reason, self-awareness, are capable of abstract and concrete reasoning, flourish best in relation to others in the same community, can anticipate the future and plan for it, along with many other capacities. But what sort of worth is this?[1]

The traditional, and often the contemporary, answer is that it is metaphysical worth, a gift to its owner. One can be praised for having it, but not for getting it. One's human nature was not something earned over time by some sort of deeds that one deliberately performed. As Kant puts it, persons have dignity rather than price. If your friend loses your new copy of Plato's *Republic*, she can buy you a new one and no harm done. If she takes your son for a walk, and loses him, she cannot make it right by going to an orphanage and finding a boy that looks almost the same as he does; this will not make things right. Persons are not properly replaceable in this manner. This rests on, and illustrates, Kant's dignity-versus-price distinction.

Another part of Kant's concept of persons is that they are moral agents, capable of recognizing right versus wrong action, and deciding what to do. Choices regarding such matters over time produce moral character, good or bad. One's moral character is, at least to a significant degree, the product of one's choices, and so to one's credit or blame, in a way that one's being human is not. For monotheistic traditions, it is the fact that, of all earth's creatures, persons most resemble God that is the foundation of their metaphysical worth, and the properties in virtue of which there is this resemblance include properties on which being a moral agent rests.

Divine Command Ethics[2]

Surprisingly, there is a variety of monotheistic ethics that maintains, at least in its most radical form, that nothing has intrinsic moral worth, and hence that persons have none. We look briefly at some of its varieties in discussing a famous dilemma for those who wish to relate religion and morality. At its most radical, divine command theory is voluntarist and proposes that God arbitrarily chooses what is good and bad or right and wrong. Had God chosen that people like Hitler be good and people like Mother Teresa be bad, they would be. Had God chosen that torture was mandatory and binding wounds was forbidden, they would be. One can object along these lines: this is not worrisome, since God has not turned good and bad, and duty to do and being forbidden, upside down. Divine command theory of the most radical sort in fact does not offer this comfort. There is no serious obligation on the part of a God who arbitrarily chooses what is morally positive and morally negative to stick with decisions already made. Since any decision about such matters is arbitrary, God can decide that there are seven theories of what is thought to be good, and seven theories of what is thought to be obligatory, each with its own account of what is bad and what is forbidden. God arbitrarily decides that each theory will be the correct one for one day of the week, judges people in the way supported by that day's theory, and keeps secret what theory goes with what day. None of this is inconsistent with radical divine command theory. More simply, God could decide to command nothing and then nothing would be good or bad, right or wrong. Or in a genuinely arbitrary context, one could make commands with an explicit restriction allowing for reversal at any time.

Another problem for the theory is that theism typically holds that God is the highest being—the one possessing more inherent worth that any other possibly could. But then things with significant likeness to God should have worth in virtue of that resemblance, and do so non-arbitrarily. So a theist need not accept radical divine command theory and hence is not saddled with its problems.

One could hold that God chose to have highest metaphysical worth and that this choice was arbitrary. Then metaphysical value is also arbitrary; all it would mean for God to be good was that, without reason, God approved of God. The most radical version of divine command theory has not been widely accepted within monotheism. Radical divine command theory makes the notions of divine omnipotence and sovereignty central for morality. Milder divine command theories include other divine attributes, such as love and justice, as equally central.

Euthyphro Dilemma

According to a famous argument, religion and morality are separated by an unpassable gulf. The argument is a simple dilemma posed in one of the Platonic dialogues. Euthyphro, the character after whom the dialogue is named, states the dilemma in polytheistic terms. We will recast it so that it is relevant to monotheism. Given this recasting, Euthyphro asks whether what is good is good because God approves of it or whether God approves of it because it is good. The idea is that both alternatives are unfriendly to monotheism. On one horn of the dilemma, God determines what is good without any moral reasons for doing so—there aren't any moral reasons to which to appeal until God declares what is moral. On the other horn, God—so to speak—has to look things up in a book God did not write that tells God what the correct answer is to the question *In virtue of what is something good?* So morality is based on an arbitrary divine decision—one irrationally made by drawing answers out of a heavenly hat—or God has nothing to do with determining the foundations of morality. Not a pretty picture for the monotheist, and the basis for many declarations of the autonomy of ethics from religion.

A dilemma-based argument is intended to show that there are two or more alternatives, each of which is for some reason unacceptable. Thus such an argument must be exhaustive regarding the relevant alternatives; if it leaves one out, it is at best inconclusive.[3] This problem plagues the Euthyphro argument. Suppose goodness is, so to speak, built into God's nature—that God is good by nature, necessarily good. Then there is no need for God to invent goodness—it is already in place. God's nature is the standard of goodness, and any created thing is good insofar as it relevantly resembles God or is in accord with the will of a perfectly good God. The former is so whether or not God makes commands. So while radical divine command theory is highly problematic, one can develop an account that closely relates God and morality on which God gives no commands. Further, on this view, any commands God gave would not be arbitrary; they would be consistent with, and derive from, the necessarily good nature of God.

It needs to be made clear that the question is not whether, if God commands that something be done in certain circumstances—for example, that one should bind the wounds of an injured person—it is good or obligatory that this be done. It is whether the divine command constitutes the goodness or the obligation. One way of putting this is: Would the action be good or right had it not been commanded?[4] The question here is not epistemological—it does not concern whether we would know what the right thing to do was were it not commanded. It concerns metaphysics—is binding the wounds something that is good to do? If we could not tell that it is, and were not culpable in our ignorance, it might well not be something we were obligated to do, though it would be a good thing to do it. An individual's obligations typically are relative to knowledge that we do (or ought to) have, in a way in which what is good is not.[5] There is nothing contradictory in the view that binding the wounds is good whether or not is it commanded. This is a problem with any theory that makes the goodness of a thing or the rightness of an action always to be constituted by a divine command. But the Euthyphro dilemma fails on the ground of being incomplete—of leaving out at least one relevant alternative, namely that the divine nature is inherently good and the standard for goodness, so that nothing arbitrary enters the picture.

There is a more controversial view regarding the dilemma. Suppose there are abstract objects—items not located in space, either eternal or everlasting, changeless, lacking causal powers, non-conscious, and existing no matter what. Whether or not there are other varieties of abstract objects, suppose there are propositions—the things that are, in the basic sense, true or false. Among these will be necessary truths, such as *Nothing has incompatible properties*. Among the necessary truths are moral principles—things like *Persons ought always to be respected*. (If it is needed, we could add "unless they have so acted as to give up that right" as is arguably the case of a sniper who has already killed several students and faculty by firing from a tower on campus and can only be stopped by being shot by another marksman.) The idea is that moral principles that are true are necessarily true. It can be stated as a conditional, namely *If there are persons in a world, they ought always to be respected* so it is vacuously true in a world composed only of rocks. Another feature abstract objects are often held to have is that they cannot be created. From there the view adds that there is a feature of things that God knows but did not create that states the truth about what is good or bad, right or wrong. Since abstract objects have no causal powers, they constitute no threat to anything. But God cannot create or destroy them. The Christian doctrine of creation, if is to accommodate abstract objects, has to be put in some such terms as these: *For all X that is not God, or exists and cannot need creation in order to exist, if X exists then God created X* or *If X is not God, and X might not have existed, God created X*. Monotheists disagree as to whether this way of putting the doctrine of creation in acceptable. If it is, then one horn of Euthyphro's dilemma is not problematic after all.

Ultimate Values: Buddhism

The ultimate values of a religious tradition will ramify throughout its moral perspective. For the Buddhist tradition there are two elements that are central. First, there is the unsatisfactoriness of human life, at least under reincarnation and karma conditions. Second, there is the fact that we cling to, are attached to, the things and states available in life under those conditions. Attachments are the "causal risings" of unsatisfactoriness, which is a function of the ephemeral nature of everything in this life, its unsatisfactoriness (that which is difficult to bear) and no-self (the doctrine that experience has no enduring subject, indeed no subject period—where a subject is something that has conscious states rather than is constituted by such states). Third, we need to end this attachment, and escape from those conditions to some other condition. Fourth, we can do so by following the Noble Eightfold Path. These are the Four Noble Truths of Buddhism: the fact of unsatisfactoriness, the fact that it has causes, the fact that unsatisfactoriness can be escaped by detachments, and the fact that there is a road to nirvana. The Noble Eightfold Path is that road. It includes right view (understanding the nature of things as expressed in the four truths), right attitude (acting out of compassion), right speech (speaking truth clearly, never harmfully), right action (avoiding exploitation of others), right livelihood (one based on non-exploitation), right awareness (being motivated by non-exploitation and avoiding harming others), right mindfulness (if you hold yourself dear, watch yourself well—do not return to attachment), and right meditation (beginning with the mind focused on a single object, and then expanding its scope). This brief description covers a great many things in a very short scope, but it illustrates the focus of some central Buddhist doctrines and practices. There is a metaphysic and an ethic, with the former leading directly to the latter. The path may be seen as having three elements—ethics (truths 1–3), concentration (truths 4–6), and wisdom (truths 7, 8). However this is viewed, the core idea is to move from attachments to things you will lose to a detachment that allows an enlightenment experience in which one comes to understand the nature of the cosmos, especially to "see" the emptiness (absence) of the self, and to free you from the cycle of rebirth. The diagnosis and cure set the framework for all of this.

Nirvana, the goal of the path, is conceived in various ways. Two such ways are the cessation of the sufferer and absorption into an undifferentiated peace, consciousness, and bliss that, as undifferentiated, is not anyone's peace, consciousness, or bliss. On one plausible understanding, these two ways are complementary—the sufferer as sufferer, as an individual, ceases and what was the suffered "blends into" a state that reminds one of the level of reality of Advaita Vedanta. (This is not to say that the Buddhist tradition borrowed from a Vedantic tradition.) Nirvana is often said to be beyond space and time and ineffable, which conflicts with descriptions of it as consciousness and bliss (and being beyond space and time) if ineffability entails total inexpressibility. The crucial question as to whether morality applies to nirvana is whether there are moral agents in that state (nirvana is not a place). If there are not, it does not. It seems clear that in nirvana it does not.

What we call a person is, after all, held to be but a series of momentary bundles composed of conscious states that lack a subject to experience them, where the series is not ontologically more than the bundles and the bundles are not onto-logically more than the states. The existence of any one element—one conscious state—is ephemeral and dependent on the existence of other like states. (Adding momentary non-conscious states does not change the basic ontological structure.) Nirvana is changeless, so a series "entering into" nirvana that was not "there" before seems impossible, though perhaps in the case of unindividuated states, assuming it is possible that there be such a thing, this concern for some reason does not arise.

If it is possible for a bundle to be compassionate—for there to be subjectless compassion—this is viewed as a state valuable to achieve. At least as valuable is detachment from everything. Consider a scenario in which a loving couple are married, live at a comfortable economic level, are in excellent health, and look forward to living a long peaceful life blessed by children and grandchildren. There are a thousand and more ways in which their dreams may not be realized and their lives may be nasty, brutish, and short. Better, then, that there not be attachment to the things of which their dreams are made. Only those who achieve detachment will escape the otherwise endless round of rebirths under the iron law of karma that is part of the metaphysical structure of things. The state of having escaped has the tradition's ultimate (non-moral) value.

Ultimate Values: Jainism

To Mahavira, an early Jain who became enlightened in a fashion described in the Jaina Sutras, are ascribed five basic concepts and associated principles. One is non-violence, corresponding to the rule of never taking life or harming anything. The range of possible violence is very wide. It is always wrong to deprive living things of life, or to otherwise harm them. Even atoms can be ensouled, and hence living. The most scrupulous wear masks to filter out insects that might other-wise enter the mouth, and carry brooms by which to clear the ground on which one is about to step. This is followed by the concepts of truthfulness and never stealing, the corresponding principles being easy to provide. The next concept is non-possessiveness, corresponding to avoiding the practice of being attached to possessing and acquiring things. The fifth concept is chastity—abstinence for the unmarried and the monks, marital faithfulness for the wed. The Jain "worship" service involves reflecting on, and then following, the example of Mahavira and earlier Jains who are believed to have attained enlightenment. Karma is thought of as dirt that collects on the soul, and it prevents enlightenment, keeping one in the cycle of rebirth. Ethics is cut to the pattern of preparation for enlightenment. Escape is possible only through having an experience in which one sees that one is not identical to, or dependent for existence on, one's body, but is in fact an immaterial soul with great knowledge. Thus, as with Buddhism, there is a moral path to be followed in seeking the highest good. Since personal identity is retained in enlightenment, the moral character of the achiever is retained.

For Advaita Vedanta, given the nature (or lack thereof) ascribed to the "level of reality," ethics has no application there. It applies to the level of appearance. The goal of life is the realization of one's identity with qualityless Brahman. This contrasts with the theistic Vedanta of Ramanuja and Madva, where the goal, in effect, is to be with God in heaven. For Advaita, there are three paths to enlightenment (recognition of one's identity with Brahman): knowledge (philosophical reflection on scriptures, typically with a guru), works (good deeds and performance of rituals), and devotion (worship, and service). Doing the right things with detachment is important, since doing it any other way yields karmic debt. Escape from the cycle of rebirth (samsara) is the goal and correct knowledge the content, along with consciousness and bliss. For Shankara, the goal is to realize that all along you have been identical to qualityless Brahman. (It follows that if Chandra is identical to Bimal, and both are identical to qualityless Brahman, then Chandra is identical to Bimal, and of course conversely.) A conception of morality that has no application to the level of reality is so conceived as to provide opportunity to reach that level from the level of appearance. (We previously discussed the problems with interpretations of the levels.)

In each of our non-theistic cases, escape from samsara (the cycle of birth and rebirth under the law of karma) sets the framework in which life is lived.

Morality without Religion?

There remains the question as to whether you can have ethics without religion. The question is not whether a non-religious person can be ethical. That clearly is possible. Most people know people like that. The question is whether a person can consistently accept an ethical realist position—a position that believes that there are (human) mind-independent true moral principles, ways of acting that are objectively right or wrong, persons who are either good or bad independent of what anybody thinks—without believing that morality has a religious basis. The religion that usually comes into the discussion is monotheism: Can there be morality without God?

A more general question is whether there can be morality without metaphysics—whether a moral view of the world can be rationally justified unless some sort of metaphysical propositions are true. There is good reason to hope that the answer is affirmative. Metaphysics is a challenging area, chock full of interesting views and arguments. The same is true of ethics. It would be nice to be able to do one without the other. But one cannot, though it is possible to do ethics without noticing the metaphysical commitment one has made.

An example of a secular morality may be helpful at this point. Jeremy Bentham started classical utilitarianism. His version was Hedonistic. It should be stressed that there are non-Hedonistic versions of utilitarianism, but it was the view Bentham chose. Hedonism locates intrinsic goodness only in pleasure and intrinsic badness only in pain. On one philosophical view, persons have pleasures and pains, but are not composed of pleasures and pains. Conscious states are states, but not parts, of persons. Were Bentham to hold this view of persons, his view would entail that persons would have extrinsic worth, being conditions of there being items (certain conscious states) that possess (positive or negative) worth for their own sake. (Strictly, Bentham includes the conscious states of all sentient beings.) But on his view (shared for example with Hume) persons just are collections of conscious states, some of which possess positive, and some negative, intrinsic worth. Besides a doctrine of intrinsic worth, utilitarianism needs a principle of its distribution. It found this in the Utility Principle:

> UP. The right action for agent A at time T in circumstance C is the one that will bring about the greatest amount of pleasure over pain of any open to the agent, considering all sentient beings affected, in the long run.

(It may be that the best the agent can do is perform an action that brings about the least balance of pain over pleasure). Suppose there are ten thousand mice and one person in a room in which a fire starts. The person, or all the mice, can be rescued. It may well be that the mice, if they are rescued, will have sufficient pleasure so that their rescue brings about a greater balance of pleasure over pain than would rescuing the person. Then this is the best, and hence right, action.

(An agent's obligations may depend on what she knows; if so, assume the agent knows how the pleasure will be distributed.) Note that, on Benthamite grounds, one cannot object that this does not respect the rights of the person. For one thing, for Bentham a person just is a set of conscious states, the only ones of which have intrinsic (positive or negative) worth being ones that are pleasurable or painful. Second, to so appeal would be an appeal to rights. Rights would restrict the authority of the Utility Principle, which reigns supreme.

One can always develop the mice and men story more fully. Perhaps the story is broadcast worldwide and the result will be that a great many people are disturbed and saddened by the person not being rescued instead of the mice. Then the rescue of the person may be justified on utilitarian grounds. Of course the example can be broadened in a different way: the story never makes the paper, the person not rescued has no relatives, is a social outcast, is deeply depressed, and suffers severe migraine headaches. Then, on utilitarian grounds, perhaps rescuing the mice wins out. Bentham (in contrast to John Stuart Mill, his utilitarian disciple) does not distinguish between higher- and lower-level conscious states. The result is that only appeal to pleasure and pain serves to render decisions about actions, since they alone have intrinsic worth. As noted, there is no appeal possible to persons themselves (or mice themselves) as the subjects of those states, there being no such subject to which to appeal. Persons, as conceived in monotheistic, Jain, and Pudgala Buddhism (one school of Buddhism that was once numerous in India) views, are not reducible to bundles of conscious states, as they are in most of the Buddhist tradition. Given the deep non-violence of Jainism, plus the breadth of its view as to what is living, plus the karmic consequences of not rescuing the mice, there are more considerations relevant to the choice than is typical in at least the Semitic monotheisms. The point here is that metaphysical doctrines concerning the nature of persons are relevant to moral considerations. There is also the issue of determinism and libertarianism, since on the latter view there are no moral agents if the former view is true. Further, if nothing is either good or bad, there is nothing good to seek or bad to avoid. There being a right or wrong way to act, or an obligation to do or not do some sort of thing, presupposes there is some-thing good or bad. In a world where nothing has metaphysical value, nothing has moral worth. So in that important sense morality depends on metaphysics—on there being things possessing intrinsic worth. (It should be remembered here that by morality we mean objective values—values discovered rather than invented.) So issues concerning human nature (the good for anything depends on what that thing's nature is), freedom of choice, and mind-independent moral facts, are all relevant to morality and involve metaphysical considerations.

A morality presupposes a metaphysic. But need it be religious? For example—in order to be reasonably believed and followed—must morality have a monothe-istic basis? It is clear that it can have a monotheistic basis. The Semitic religions offer two commandments: Love the Lord your God, and love your neighbor as yourself. The commandments can be broken in three ways: by not loving God, not loving your neighbor, and not loving yourself. The parent who so loves her children that she is permanently lost when they grow up and leave home has failed to respect herself, and self-respect is part of legitimate love of self. Always plac-ing one's interest as one perceives them over the interests of others does not show them respect. Again, lack of respect is lack of healthy love. This is but the begin-ning of (one way of understanding) the basis of monotheistic morality.

Those who maintain that morality without God is logically inconsistent may have in mind various reasons. They may be assuming that morality requires moral laws, and moral laws require a law-giver. They may believe that if all we are is complex biological organisms produced by a process that has nothing in mind, so we are alone in the universe for so long as material conditions allow life to last for the race, and far less time for an individual, life has no purpose. All our plans amount to nothing in the end.

Depth, Breadth, and Length

The view that mores is as close as we get to ethics, stated in brief scope, goes like this. The appearance of human beings is recent, given how long the universe managed to get along without us. The evolutionary process with no foresight or purpose, developed biological things with sufficient complexity to support human life, and then the race moved from primitive to sophisticated culture, in the process developing means of destroying ourselves. Always survival ori-ented, enough of us came to see that warfare, plundering, and attempting to dominate was often not conducive to survival, and thus consider more peaceful alternatives. We came to have some limits on what we were willing to do to one another unless we felt really insecure. Since those who got together in groups and helped one another tended to live longer, we made up rules that were to hold societies together. After a while following these rules became something like second nature. The rules we somewhat internalized became accepted patterns for behavior, and we had mores—survival rules and rules to take off the sharp edges of life. Stories about a moral law are fiction. Morality has no place in a world in which this (and other things consistent with it) gives the whole story about felt obligations and duties. These are just feelings we have due to our history, to which no transcendent significance attaches. We can call this the Just Mores world.

There are secular moral realists—people who accept no religion but believe that there are items that are good and bad, right and wrong, independent of what anybody thinks. What might be added to the there-are-at-most-mores view to promote it to moral realism? Perhaps this. In the history of the development of humanity, there was a point at which non-living thing developed a new sort of property, that of being alive. If you have twenty pounds of rocks and add ten more, after the added weight, you can break glass meant to hold only twenty-five pounds. The causal properties of the heavier load are greater than that of the lighter. But the addition was just additive—more weight. If when the extra weight was added the result was a living thing, then the addition would be more than additive. An emergent property would have appeared—a property that invested its owner with being a new kind of thing. The same holds for going from living to conscious, and from conscious to self-aware. In each case, a new kind of thing has appeared. There is reason to claim that the new kind of thing is intrinsically "higher," of more metaphysical worth, than the old. This was in effect Aristotle's view, and much of the current environmental movement ascribes more worth to living things. Adding this perspective to the view described in the previous paragraph at least makes sense of contending for moral realism. We can call this a Moral Realist world.

Thus far the things to which intrinsic worth is ascribed—living things—are short-lived in cosmic terms. All things being equal, if it is good for Mary to live for seventy years, it is good for Mary to live seventy years and a day. Of course things may not be equal—they may be worse. But while some have thought that living for a thousand years, or forever, would of necessity be boring, many others have not agreed. There are additions to one's life one would turn down if offered—say, every added day filled with agony. But there are life extensions, even forever, that many would find attractive. Without trying to state criteria for life extensions being better for those who lived them, even forever, life after death has been something to be desired by most people. So greater longevity for Mary (and others) under good conditions would add to the moral desirability of a world in which it occurred. It would make the world a better world. Arguably, it would give more metaphysical worth to Mary. We can call this a Moral Realist Plus Afterlife world.

The idea of an afterlife in which the scales of justice are balanced is also attractive, so long as repentance and forgiveness are allowed as one way of balancing.

Further, the existence of a good God, as typically conceived by much of monotheism, would secure the continued life and the justice, and complete the picture. A monotheist will properly complain that we have pictured things in reverse—the actual sequence will be God, world, persons—but reversing the order is consistent with what has been said. We can call this a Moral Realist Plus Afterlife Plus Moral Providence world.

It seems clear that in the Moral Realist world described, morality does not cut deep into the world. Waiving the question of alien life far afield, the very much larger part of the cosmos is untouched by morality. Nothing deep in the universe favors it. Locally at least, its tenure is not long-lived. One can appeal to a moral realism that holds true moral principles to be necessarily true and grounded in abstract objects, namely propositions whose content is precisely those laws. Then the sense in which there will be morality without moral agents will be the sense that there are abstract truths about persons, all of the form *If there are persons, then . . .* But this sense will mean nothing to us.

In a monotheistic context Moral Realism has depth—it is, so to speak, sponsored by an Omnicompetent Creator. It has breadth in that it applies to all moral agents. It has length in that it applies to moral agents who live forever. It may be that the sense that morality requires monotheism is the recognition that the status of morality is most secure in a monotheistic universe.

There is also depth for morality in a universe governed by an impersonal law of karma that applies with rigid necessity and, being (like?) a natural law has no place for mercy. In Jainism, where personal identity is clearly said to be retained after enlightenment, and persons are held to be beginningless, it has breadth and length. For Advaita Vedanta, it seems to have similar depth, breadth, and length given the level of appearance, but that is trumped (sublated) by the distinctionless level of reality in which there is no morality at all. For those Buddhist traditions that accept a law of karma view, morality has depth, but the law operates on bundles that last barely long enough to exist at all and nirvana is often said to be either ineffable or a distinctionless state, neither of which allows continued personal identity. In sum: one of the most promising perspectives for being a metaphysically based morality comes from a view that ascribes intrinsic worth to persons. Aristotle's virtue ethics and Jainism are obvious examples. Neither view is theistic. A central contrast here is that persons are viewed as having great intrinsic worth without any appeal to God as having created them in God's image. In Aristotle there is resemblance to an Unmoved Mover who reflects on necessary truths and never changes. There is nothing analogous in Jainism even to the Unmoved Mover. On the other hand, in Jainism persons live forever and, if enlightened, do so in favorable circumstances, whereas in Aristotle there is little if any basis for belief in personal afterlife. (In Jainism, some persons are too defective to become enlightened.) In Jainism, persons are part of the fundamental, non-derivative features of the universe. In another jargon, they are ontologically primitive, not composed of or dependent on any other sort of thing. Aristotle's persons are not ontologically primitive, fundamental, non-derivative, or independent.

In both views, persons are rational, moral agents. At least arguably, a person being ontologically primitive grounds the value of persons more deeply in the nature of things than does its absence, but even if this is not granted, it does not follow that the worth of persons is annihilated.

There is the argument that since human persons simply are the product of blind forces with no foresight of their result, simply composed of material particles, a somewhat more complex animal than at least most other mammals, there is no value difference in kind between us and other animals—no metaphysical basis for granting humans any unique value. Whatever force this argument has, it goes against basing morality on the intrinsic worth of persons. Whatever force the argument has, with a little change in formulation, also goes against granting wider intrinsic worth to, say, mammals, fields of flowers, or landscapes.

As we noted, there are crucial leaps in evolutionary history to which emergentists draw attention, in particular from non-living to living, from living to conscious, and from conscious to self-awareness. This sort of hierarchy, a bit more detailed in Aristotle, led him to think in terms of a hierarchy of being and a corresponding hierarchy of value or worth. The two hierarchies corresponded to one another, the lowest rung on one corresponding to the lowest rung on the other, and the pattern following on through to the highest.

In monotheistic views, typically God is viewed as enjoying the highest possible metaphysical worth. Whether divine command theory is true, God is the cause and sustainer of moral agents in this life and the next, where justice and mercy are properly adjusted. On some views, morality does not apply to heaven, where there are no temptations to deal with. But this neglects the consideration that persons in heaven, even if their goodness is no longer tested, can be possessed of the properties that make for good moral persons.

If God is conceived as a moral agent, as is frequent but not universal among monotheists, then God's existence is the highest moral value and the core of morality relative to created persons is their being made in the image of God and their achieving their positive potential by imitation of God. A highly plausible view of morality takes moral principles to be, if true, then necessarily true. Monotheists who suppose God exists to be a logically necessary truth can take the necessary truth of true moral principles to be grounded in divine cognitive states; monotheists who view God exists as contingently true can ground necessarily true moral principles in abstract objects that possess logically necessary existence. On both views, if a moral principle is true, it is true whether God creates or not; a moral principle, being conditional—of the form possessed by *If X is a person then X ought to be respected*, for example—will be true under all possible conditions, including those in which God does not create. On both views, there will be persons[6] to whom moral principles apply only if God creates them.

It is sometimes argued that God cannot be said to be morally good in the same sense in which human beings—say, St. Paul—are said to be good. Two arguments often given for this view are:

Argument 1

1. *God is good* is a necessary truth.
2. *St. Paul is good*, even if true is a contingent truth.
3. If *X* in *Y is X* is used in a sentence expressing a necessary truth, and *X* in *Z is X* is used in a sentence expressing a contingent truth, then *X* as used in the one sentence bears a different meaning than does *X* as used in the other sentence.

Hence:

4. 'Good' as used in *God is good* has a different meaning than does 'good' in *St. Paul is good*.

The problem with this argument is that the principle expressed in premise 3 is false. Consider the sentences *Three is odd* and *The number of coins on the table is odd*. The proposition expressed by the first of these sentences is a necessary truth, and the proposition expressed by the second of these sentences is, if true at all, a contingent truth. But 'odd' means the same in both cases. Hence premise 3 is false.

The other line of reasoning is that if God is good, still God can do things, and allow things, without ceasing to be good that no human being could do, or allow,[7] without ceasing to be good. Jill, if she allows a person to suffer terribly when she could easily stop it, or causes someone to die even though her family needs her desperately, is not a good person. God, if God exists, at least allows such things all the time without ceasing to be called good. So 'good' must mean something else in heaven than on earth. This argument ignores the fact that ascriptions of goodness ultimately rest on motives, intentions, ends, and—in the end—character. Two persons, of equally good character, can act differently if their knowledge and powers differ, and greatly differently if their knowledge and powers differ greatly. A man on a train who is in sudden need of a delicate operation will rightly react differently to the idea of a skilled surgeon performing the operation immediately and a sincere lawyer with a knife and good intentions attempting to perform the same operation. Presumably the surgeon may, and perhaps ought, to operate; the lawyer ought to go get help. The claim that God is good is the claim that God's motives, ends, intentions, and character resemble those of a good human person, allowing for difference in knowledge and power. The range of things that God can allow and bring good out of thus vastly exceeds those available to any human being. Especially relevant in this regard is the monotheistic view that while a person's death ends our ability to affect them, for monotheism that makes no difference to God's power to affect them.

Thus in terms of depth, breadth, and length of morality, views of the world differ significantly as to the status they ascribe to morality. The differences find their source in competing metaphysical doctrines. To this point, we have considered the values treasured by our traditions and connections between metaphysical and moral worth. It is time to turn to responsibility.

Responsibility

Religious traditions are also concerned with responsibility—for example, to what degree can one act so as to become saved or enlightened? If one holds a reincarnation view, the matter is complex—for each lifetime one lives, there are previous ones that determine one's karmic condition. If this is complete determinism between lives, whether one ever becomes enlightened has always been determined, since one's lifetimes have never begun. If we have a monotheistic tradition with or without reincarnation, then God can determine what occurs down to the minutest detail. If so, can one be free in any sense in which one is morally responsible for one's actions? These questions raise a series of issues relevant to religion.

Deterministic Views

Fatalism: Determinism Based on Logical Necessity
   Fatalism is the view that these two things are true:

1.   Every truth is a necessary truth.
2.   Every falsehood is a necessary falsehood.

If one holds that God exists, and is a fatalist, one will think that God exists is a necessary truth and also that it, plus various necessary truths about God's nature, will explain other necessary truths about the existence and history of the world. In one sense, there can be no such thing as explaining why a particular necessary truth is true rather than false—its having been false is logically impossible and there is no need to eliminate a non-possibility. One can put the point here by contrasting a necessary truth like *Even an omnipotent being cannot fiat the actions of a libertarianly free person* and a contingent truth like *Boston's National Basketball franchise is named the Celtics*. The necessary truth concerning omnipotence and freedom can be explained by making its meaning clear; a detailed explanation of libertarian freedom is offered later in this chapter. But explaining the truth of a necessary truth amounts either to giving an account of its sense or offering an account of necessary truth generally—a theory of necessity such as *Necessary truths are grounded in abstract objects*. The contingent truth about the Celtics can be explained in terms of the history of the franchise; what makes it true is a series of events that might never have occurred, so this explanation is a matter of accounting for the fact that it is true rather than false. Consider a monotheistic version of fatalism. On this view, *Necessarily, God exists* is true, as are each of the following: *Necessarily, God has all those properties definitive of God's nature*; *Necessarily, God's choices are entirely determined by God's nature*; *Necessarily, whatever is true is true because God chose that it be true*. Then consider the consequences.
   One consequence is that God's existence and nature entirely determine God's choices, which in turn determine everything else. But it is, by hypothesis, logically impossible that God not exist or that God not have the nature that God

has. So it is logically impossible that any true proposition not be true or that any proposition that is not true have been true. The right way to think of the sort of scenario described is in terms of an axiomatic system in which all the theorems follow by rules of inference from the axioms; the axioms are necessary truths, the rules of inference truth preserving, and so the theorems are also necessary truths. A consequence would be that the actual world is also the only world possible.

Another consequence is that there would be at most one agent. Suppose that Tess and Tricia are related as follows. Tess has her own thought life, but Tricia thinks only when and what Tess deliberately, specifically causes her to think. Tess can act without Tricia, but Tricia acts only if Tess causes her to act. In fact, every feeling, mental image, dream, movement, attitude, pain, or pleasure Tricia experiences, Tess deliberately, specifically causes her to experience. Tess knows her power over Tricia, but Tricia is ignorant of it. Finally, this relationship between Tess and Tricia is one neither can break; its roots lie deep in the laws of nature. It is logically possible that Tess and Tricia not be so related, but only logically possible. Under these circumstances, however things seem to Tricia, she is not an agent; she does not act on her own, think on her own, feel on her own. But on the scenario with which we began, God is related to whatever persons there are as Tess is related to Tricia, only more so; here the roots of the relationship lie deep in the nature of a necessarily existing God and in the laws of logic. It is not even logically possible that God not be so related to any persons there may be. If persons must be moral agents, and moral agents must be libertarianly free, on the scenario being considered there is at most one person. In fact, God also lacks libertarian freedom. On this view, God is related to Tess in such a manner that her existence as well as her thoughts, feelings, and actions are entirely determined by God's existence and nature. It is no more logically possible that God exist and Tess not than it is logically possible that Tess exist and God not; that God exists, on the scenario in question, entails that Tess exists, and since the former is, by hypothesis, a necessary truth, so is the latter.[8] Thus that Tess exists also entails that God exists. Tess is not a person distinct from God; she is at most, as Spinoza would put it, a mode—a state—of God's.[9] It is not logically possible that "her" existence and "her" properties, thoughts, and actions exist without God's existing and having the nature that God possesses; the divine existence and nature determine "her" existence and properties in such a way that it is logically impossible that they be otherwise than as they are. In such a world, morality would be impossible. Even if we suppose that Tess is a person, it would be logically impossible that she or anyone act other than as they did, think other than as they did, feel other than as they did. Any suggestion to the effect that anyone might have acted, thought, or felt at some time other than as they did think, act, or feel at that time would be self-contradictory. If all truths were necessary truths, there would be no way things could be other than the way things were. The notions of responsibility and obligation, guilt and innocence, freedom and agency, all presuppose at least the logical possibility of alternatives. *Logical fatalism is true* and *There are moral agents* are logically incompatible propositions; while there is not much controversy concerning this point, there is considerable controversy regarding what sort of world it is within which agents can exist who are free in the sense required if they are to be morally responsible for their choices and actions.

This discussion of monotheistic fatalism raises some interesting questions regarding what is to come. If it is clear that the absence of logically possible alternatives entails the absence of freedom, is there any good reason to think the absence of all but counterfactual alternatives—alternatives available in other possible worlds but not in the real world, alternatives "available" only in a sense compatible with the actions actually performed being in fact inevitable—does not also entail the absence of freedom? If it is true that there is but one agent in a fatalistic monotheistic world, is there any good reason to think that there is more than one agent in a monotheistic deterministic world?

Determinism Not Based on Logical Necessity

Let a tensed universal description [TUD] be an accurate statement of everything that is contingently true in the world at a given time. Each such description should be viewed as tensed to some specific time that is specified in the description. Let LN be a correct account of all of the laws of nature, and LL a correct account of all of the laws of logic. Then determinism holds: for any TUD tensed earlier than time T, that TUD plus LN plus LL, entails any TUD tensed to time T or later. Thus, if determinism is true, the past determines a unique future. There are logical possibilities alternative to what happens at any given time; it is simply not compatible with the laws of logic, the laws of nature, and what has happened in the past that they be realized. So they will not happen, and there is no more that we can do about that than there is we can do about the truth of the laws of logic, the laws of nature, or what happened in the past.

Compatibilism and Incompatibilism

Compatibilism holds that it is logically possible that determinism be true and that persons have the sort of freedom that is required for them to be morally responsible for their choices and actions. The opposite position to compatibilism is incompatibilism, which holds that it is not logically possible (non-contradictory) that determinism be true and that persons have the sort of freedom that is required for them to be morally responsible for their choices and actions. Incompatibalism is part of Libertainism.[10]

Libertarianism holds that incompatibilism is true and determinism is false; in order for persons to have the sort of freedom that is required for them to be morally responsible for their choices and actions they must have genuine freedom, not compatibilist so-called freedom, regarding those choices and actions. Libertarians hold that persons do have this sort of freedom. Compatibilists are dubious that there is even possibly any sort of freedom beyond that which they affirm. The notion of libertarian freedom, often called categorical freedom, runs as follows.

> (CF) Jane is categorically (or libertarianly) free with respect to lying at T entails that Jane's lying is within her power at T and that Jane's refraining from lying is within her power at T.

In turn:

> (CFa) Jane's lying is within her power at T entails that Jane's lying at T does not require that Jane falsify some total universal description (TUD) tensed to a time earlier than T, make some law of nature false, or make some law of logic false.

and

> (CFb) Jane's refraining from lying is within her power at T entails that Jane's refraining from lying at T does not require that Jane falsify some TUD tensed to a time earlier than T, make some law of nature false, or make some law of logic false.
>
> (CF) is to be understood as containing the definitions provided by (CFa) and (CFb).

Relations between the Positions

It may be helpful in understanding these alternatives to see some of their relationship laid out.

1. One can consistently be a determinist and an incompatibilist.
2. One can consistently be a determinist and a compatibilist.
3. One cannot consistently be a determinist and a libertarian.
4. One cannot consistently be an incompatibilist and a compatibilist.
5. Being a libertarian entails being an incompatibilist.
6. Being an incompatibilist does not entail being a libertarian.
7. Being a compatibilist does not entail being a determinist.

Monotheistic Determinism and Monotheistic Libertarianism

A fundamental dispute within monotheism concerns whether possession of compatibilist freedom yields a world sufficiently different from (monotheistic) logical fatalism to allow for there to be human agents who are morally responsible for their thoughts and actions. Libertarian monotheists think that if the only sort of freedom human persons have is so-called compatibilist freedom then God is cause of whatever evils our thoughts and actions involve. Or they think that God is the only agent, and that human personhood is mere appearance. Compatibilist monotheists disagree. If compatibilism is false, then of course monotheists ought to reject it. There is an interesting and powerful argument against compatibilism.

An Argument against Compatibilism

Consider the TUD that is tensed to the time just before the last dinosaur died; let that be TUDdino. Then suppose that you will decide to have a cup of coffee at 3:00 this afternoon; let the TUD tensed to that time be TUDcup; TUDcup, of course, includes a statement to the effect that you decide to have a cup of coffee at 3:00. If determinism is true, then:

1. TUDdino and LL and LN entails TUDcup.
2. One is not responsible for anything that one has no control over.
3. One has no control over anything that is entailed by what one has no control over.
4. One is not responsible for anything that is entailed by what one has no control over. [from 2, 3]
5. You have no control over what is true in TUDdino.
6. You have no control over what the laws of logic are.
7. You have no control over what the laws of nature are.
8. You have no control over TUDdino and LL and LN. [from 5–7]
9. You have no control over what TUDdino and LL and LN entails. [from 4, 8]
10. You have no control over TUDcup. [from 1, 9]
11. TUDcup entails that you decide to have coffee at 3:00.
12. You have no control over whether you decide to have coffee at 3:00. [from 10, 11]

Note that you and your decision/action "stand in" here for everyone and every one of everyone's decisions/actions. So what follows is that if determinism is true then no one is ever responsible for any decision/action. Hence compatibilism, which claims otherwise, is false.[11] Central to controversy over the success of this argument is whether premise 3—*One has no control over anything that is entailed by what one has no control over*—is true. This claim is sometimes called the control principle. (One could challenge 9 as well, though it seems secure.)

Explanation and Determinism

If determinism is true, then for any TUD true at time T1 it is not merely the case that the TUD true at T1 plus the laws of logic plus the laws of nature entail the TUD true at any later time but that the TUD true at time T1 plus the laws of logic and the laws of nature also explain the truth of the TUD true at time T2, and so on. Even if it is a necessary element in explanation, entailment is not sufficient for explanation. The proposition *Either 1 and 3 are 7 or Oklahoma is a state, and 1 and 3 are not 7* entails the proposition *Oklahoma is a state*, but Oklahoma's statehood has not been explained.

The notion of an explanation is notoriously difficult, but this much can be said about it. Let us say that *If X obtains then Y obtains* is true and expresses a law, then there is an X/Y lawlike connection; let us also say that if there is a true non-lawlike proposition of the form *If X obtains then an agent with the power to do so typically will choose to bring about Y* then there is an X/Y teleological connection. In order that X obtains explain that Y obtains it must be the case that X does indeed obtain, and the case that there is a true proposition that expresses a lawlike or a teleological X/Y connection. Determinism assumes that for every state B that obtains, there is another state A such that A obtains and such that there is a lawlike A/B connection. In order for determinism to be true, the past must not only entail, but also explain, the future by virtue of there always being such lawlike connections.[12]

The Control Principle

What is most interestingly controversial about the argument, stated above, against compatibilism concerns the third premise, which states a version of the Control Principle:

> (CP) One has no control over anything that is entailed by what one has no control over.
> Is (CP), or some appropriate replacement, true? (CP) tells us this: one may properly infer from *Sam has no control over whether A obtains* and *That A obtains entails that B obtains* to *Sam has no control over whether B obtains*. There are two sorts of objection to (CP).

One is that there are analogous inferences that are not proper. For example, neither of these arguments is valid:

> Example One. Sue is obligated to do A; doing A entails doing B; hence Sue is obligated to do B. [Sue is obligated to wash her dog; washing her dog entails making a mammal wet; hence Sue is obligated to make a mammal wet. Making just any mammal wet is not among her obligations.]
> Example Two. Sue believes that P; that P is true entails that Q is true; hence Sue believes that Q. [Sue believes that figure F is a triangle; that F is a triangle entails that F's interior angles sum to 180 degrees; hence Sue believes that F's interior angles sum to 180 degrees. Sue can believe that F is a triangle but have learned no geometry sufficient for believing anything about what F's interior angles sum to.]

On the other hand, there are analogous inferences that are entirely proper.

> Example Three: Necessarily, P entails Q; necessarily P; hence necessarily Q.
> Example Four: P entails Q; P is true; hence Q is true.

Both example 3 and example 4 are valid inferences. Is it with these, or with the previous examples, that the Control Principle is properly compared? That is just the question all over again as to whether the Control Principle is true. No real progress is likely along these lines, either in favor or against the Control Principle. Each party to the dispute will simply put forward examples that exhibit their view of the matter, and claim—neither more nor less cogently than the other—that these are the genuinely parallel cases.

The other and better strategy involves looking very closely at what the Control Principle says. What it tells us is this. Hold LL and LN fixed. Let WT be the TUD true at time T. Let WT1 be the TUD true at T1. Then let WT entail WT1. What is the possibility of a person controlling whether WT is true if T has already past? The typical answer, quite plausibly, is *None at all*.

One thing that comes to mind is that one might travel back in time to T-minus-1 and do something that made T relevantly different. One problem is that we are not now in fact able to do this, even if it is theoretically possible. Suppose it is theoretically possible. Since we do not know how to do it, what difference does that make to anyone's responsibility? The usual sense of a compatibilist "could have done otherwise" is that doing otherwise was within the power of the agent in the sense that—to be brief—the agent was able in the actual situation not to do what she did given the abilities and knowledge she actually had, not some ability or knowledge she lacked.

But then knowing how to time travel is irrelevant, even if it is theoretically possible. One could claim that some at least of the fundamental natural laws yield only probabilities—are of the form *Given X, in circumstance C, y is N probable* where N is less than one. But then determinism has been abandoned and we have a new ball game.

The general idea of there being a problem with (CP) is that the laws of nature contain at least one contingent proposition that we could alter or time travel is possible so that one could tinker with the relevant TUD. Then one could alter things so that one controlled things determined by things over which it seems we have no control. The gist is that LN or a relevant TUD are really not beyond our control. But then the principle will be irrelevant, not false.

Further, we can replace (CP) by something along these lines:

> (CP*) Even if LL, LN, and TUDdino are not in principle beyond our control, they are in fact now beyond our control, and if LL, LN, and TUDT entail TUDT1, what happens at T1 is not under our control.
> (CP*) will do nicely as a replacement for (CP).

It is helpful, in approaching compatibilist accounts of freedom, to highlight three relevant concepts—logical inevitability, in fact inevitability, and causal impossibility:

> Logical inevitability: State of affairs A is logically inevitable if and only if that A obtains is a logically necessary truth.
> In fact inevitability: State of affairs A is in fact inevitable if and only if that A obtains is entailed by the truth about the past, the laws of nature, and the laws of logic.

These notions contrast to:

> Causal impossibility: State of affairs A is causally impossible if and only if A obtains only if some law of nature is false.

Compatibilists take it to be possible that a bit of behavior be in fact inevitable and one that one is morally responsible for performing. Compatibilists and incompatibilists typically agree that human beings never perform actions that are logically inevitable or causally impossible. Libertarians deny that human actions are typically in fact inevitable and add that were they, no one would ever be responsible for them.[13]

Compatibilism and Actions versus Nonactions

The compatibilist thinks that whether determinism is true or not, and hence even if it is true, we can have the sort of freedom required for moral responsibility. Hence it holds that this sort of freedom regarding some thought or action is compatible with that thought or action being in fact inevitable. One may be responsible for what one does, but also for what one does not do. A friend who could easily have stopped your progress and knew what would happen if he did not, but nonetheless allowed you to walk into the path of a moving vehicle, is not innocent merely because she did not push you into its path. For simplicity, however, focus here will be on responsibility for what one does. Regarding such responsibility, Karen is responsible for action A entails that Karen performed A.

Let Karen's states at time T refer to all of the physical states Karen's body is in at T and all of the mental states her mind is in at T. If determinism is true, each of those states is in fact inevitable, given the content of the past. Let us say that a causal chain passes through Karen at T if and only if at least one of its members is also one of Karen's states at T. If some action by Karen is a member of a causal chain—a chain whose earlier members result in Karen performing that action—let us call it an action chain relative to Karen; for short, an action chain. Any action chain relative to Karen must pass through Karen.

Consider the various sorts of mental states that one can be in that are relevant to how one acts—intentions, purposes, goals, preferences, likes, dislikes, desires, wants, choices, and so on. Let these be action-inclining states. Action-inclining states relative to chewing a stick of gum will include desiring to chew it, intending to chew it, having chewing it as a purpose or a goal, and the like. If a chain passes through Karen but contains no action-inclining state of Karen's, then even if it results in some motions of her body, it is dubious that it is an action chain regarding her. There is a difference between Karen's teeth gnashing and Karen gnashing her teeth, and if determinism being true is compatible with making that distinction between actual cases, presumably the difference will be one between a causal chain passing through that contains none of Karen's action-inclining states (Karen's teeth gnashing) and a causal chain passing through Karen that does contain some action-inclining state of her where the target of that state is her teeth being gnashed together (Karen gnashing her teeth). An action chain relative to Karen's performing action A must pass through Karen in such a way that it contains action-inclining states that are at least partial causes of A. This is one way, perhaps the most natural, for a determinist to endeavor to distinguish between what is, and what is not, an action: actions are the products of action-chains that pass through the person who acts in such a manner that the person's action-inclining states are at least among the action's causes.

Suppose Sam decides to commit murder. If determinism is true, this decision is in fact inevitable given things that occurred in the distant, pre-Sam past. The compatibilist will note that the causal chain that yields Sam's decision "runs through Sam," so to speak, whereas other causal chains do not do so. The earlier portion of the causal chain that yields the pre-Sam events whose occurrence, if determinism is true, render his choice in fact inevitable has not yet run through Sam. The compatibilist will add that there are logically possible worlds in which Sam's decision does not obtain; the events that render Sam's decision in fact inevitable would not obtain if one of those worlds was the actual world. This is the difference between Sam's decision being logically inevitable and its being in fact inevitable. Presumably, if determinism is true, it is not logically possible that the events that render his decision in fact inevitable occur without his decision also occurring—not unless one could have the same events but different causal laws. The core of the compatibilist's position will lie in the development of a notion of "is under the control of" where something is under one's control provided one could have done otherwise had things been different. Thus compatibilist freedom invites our attention.

Compatibilist Freedom

One suggestion regarding what this sort of freedom amount to is this: let D be a description of what has occurred up to time T,[14] LN a statement of the laws of nature, and LL a statement of the laws of logic. Let their conjunct be the whole past package. Jane wonders whether or not to lie to John. It turns out that *Jane lies to John* is compatible with the whole past package, and *Jane does not lie to John* is not compatible with the whole past package.[15] The idea is to leave room for Jane's being free even though what Jane will do must be compatible with the whole past package and only one of the logically possible alternatives is compatible with that package; on this view, whatever sort of freedom responsibility requires is constrained by this condition. Given the conditions described, Jane will lie to John, her lying to John is in fact inevitable, and *Jane is morally responsible for lying to John* is compatible with *Jane's not lying to John is incompatible with the whole past package*. Jane's lying, on this account, follows from what has happened prior to her lying, given the laws of logic and the laws of nature.[16]

The range of what can be said to give this alleged freedom content should be explored. If Jane's lying is an action on Jane's part, it must be related to Jane in certain ways—this, we might say, is the positive story regarding Jane's freely lying. The positive story is the story of the conditions regarding Jane's actually lying, the story of a causal chain that runs through Jane and presumably contains an action-inclining state. Further, if she is free in performing that action, her not performing it must have been available to her in certain ways—this, we might say, is the negative story regarding Jane's freely lying. The negative story is the story of the conditions regarding the availability to Jane of refraining from lying. The combination of the positive story and negative story, where both are told with compatibilist constraints, will be the whole compatibilist story regarding her freely lying. There is no universal agreement among compatibilists as to how this story goes, and we will give a very full account that captures a good many of the elements that compatibilists include in that story. What we say about the version of the story here can also be said about other compatibilist accounts.

Constraints

For an account of free action to be compatibilist, it must be the case that it can be a true account even if determinism is true. Hence that Jane's action is in fact inevitable, where 'in fact inevitable' is understood as we have defined it, and that Jane's action is free and she is morally responsible for so acting are logically compatible. Our formulation of the compatibilist account will endeavor to give as broad a definition as this constraint allows—to include as many elements as it allows.[17]

The Positive Story

Jane's lying to John at time T obviously entails that Jane lied to John at T. We have already noted that, on a compatibilist account, it entails that an action chain that includes Jane's lying to John at T passes through Jane.

A classic analysis of this sort of freedom goes like this:

> Jane is free in lying to John at time T if and only if (i) Jane lies to John at T, (ii) Jane wanted to lie to John at T, and (iii) Jane's lying is caused by her wanting. Let us say that if Jane and her lying are related as (i) through (iii) indicate, Jane's lying is congenial. This serves to emphasize that the relevant action chain contains states of Jane that are at least a partial cause of Jane's lying to John, where those states on the whole incline toward rather than against lying.

Here, then, is part of one compatibilist positive story regarding Jane's freely lying to John at time T:

> Jane's lying to John at time T is a free action entails that Jane lied to John at T, that an action chain that includes Jane's lying to John at T passes through Jane, and that Jane's lying to John at T is (in the sense defined) congenial to Jane. This is compatible with Jane's not liking to do it, but liking any other alternative still less. If Jim has hypnotized Jane to lie, puts a gun to her head to make her lie, or the like, John coerces Jane to lie. If Jane is related to her lying as a kleptomaniac to stealing, Jane is a compulsive liar. Suppose neither of these is the case; then Jane's lying is neither coerced nor compulsed. Thus far we have at least a fairly complete positive story—one that includes at least a great deal of what is available to such an account.

So we have:

> Jane's lying to John at T is a free action entails that Jane lied to John at T, an action chain that includes Jane's lying to John at T passes through Jane, Jane's lying to John at T is (in the sense defined) congenial to Jane, and at T, Jane is neither coerced nor compulsed to lie to John.

The Negative Story

If this is (one compatibilist version of) the positive story, there is also a compatibilist account of the availability to Jane of not lying to John at time T. If her not lying just plain is not available to her, then her lying isn't a free action. Jane's not lying is not logically impossible; it is, in that sense, logically available. It is not against the laws of nature; it is, in that sense, naturally available. It is within her capacity in the sense that she knows what a lie is and what she will say to John if she lies and she knows how to say those words; she is not dumb or paralyzed; she has whatever range of cognitive, psychological, and physical capacities are required by not lying. Thus Jane's not lying is, in that sense, competently available. Perhaps it is true that if she had chosen not to lie, she could have refrained from lying; then, in that sense, Jane's not lying is counterfactually available. Even if all this is so, either her choosing to lie or her not choosing to lie is incompatible with the whole past package.[18] Since she lies, her lying is in fact inevitable—it is in fact inevitable that she does not choose not to lie. So even if it is true that if she had not chosen to lie she would not have lied, it is also true that it was in fact inevitable that she not choose not to lie. Thus on one version, then, of the compatibilist account, Jane's lying to John at T is a free action entails Jane's not lying to John at T is logically, naturally, competently, and counterfactually available to Jane at T. Perhaps there is more. Perhaps this should be added. Suppose that Jane ordinarily has a set of only true beliefs about what one can expect from ordinary computers, but that one morning her colleagues discover her trying to fry eggs on her keyboard. Jane is, in this respect, irrational in the sense that, given beliefs anyone familiar with computers has, she should know that the result of her keyboard-and-egg behavior will not be breakfast.[19] A compatibilist may wish to add that actions that are irrational on Jane's part are not free actions. If so, we then get:

> Jane's lying to John at T is a free action entails Jane's not lying to John at T is logically, naturally, competently, and counterfactually available to Jane at T, and Jane's not lying to John at T would not be irrational.

It should be noted that being irrational here involves such things as having wildly implausible beliefs or reasoning in a chaotic fashion or the like; it is not a sense of irrational in which, for example, acting wrongly is inherently irrational.

Finally, perhaps lack of irrationality in the rough sense broadly characterized should also be added to Jane's act of lying. If we do this, and put the resultant positive and negative stories together, we get this result:

> Jane's lying to John at T is a free action entails that Jane lied to John at T, that an action chain that includes Jane's lying to John at T being congenial passes through Jane, Jane's lying to John at T is (in the sense defined) congenial to Jane. At T, Jane is neither coerced nor compulsed to lie to John, and Jane's lying to John at T is not irrational in the sense of resulting from her having wildly implausible beliefs or reasoning chaotically, and Jane's not lying to John at T is logically, naturally, competently, and counterfactually available to Jane at T, and Jane's not lying to John at T would not be irrational.

Perhaps there remains something that we must add in order to fairly express this sort of analysis of the freedom responsibility requires. But somewhere not too far along the road we have been traveling, presumably one gets to that point without having gotten to the point where both Jane's not lying and Jane's lying are compatible with the whole past package. We have come close at least to that point. For a compatibilist, to reach that point is to have gone too far.

The sort of freedom, if it is such, that we have been describing is a fairly complete rendering of compatibilist freedom. One could contest various elements included and perhaps contend for some additions. But it is a fair account of various elements that compatibilists have included in their accounts of compatibilist freedom, and that is all that we need. Is it true that compatibilist freedom is the sort of freedom a moral agent has if she is responsible for her actions?

The Control Principle Says:

> (CP) One has no control over anything that is entailed by what one has no control over.

The corresponding compatibilist claim is:

> (CC) One has control over what one has compatibilist freedom concerning.

The compatibilist will claim that in (CP) "having control of" is the sense of "has categorical or libertarian freedom regarding" and is thus a claim the compatibilist will reject in favor of (CC). Further, the compatibilist claims, being categorically or libertarianly free is not a necessary condition of being morally responsible. The libertarian response is that one can be neither free nor morally responsible regarding any action that is in fact inevitable. The compatibilist account of freedom may be fine as far as it goes, but it leaves out a crucial element—genuine alternatives that cannot coexist with in fact inevitable actions. The central principle in dispute here has been called the Principle of Alternative Possibilities.

The Principle of Alternative Possibilities

The libertarian typically embraces the Principle of Alternative Possibilities, which says that one is responsible for performing an action A on a given occasion only if on that occasion one has categorical freedom regarding performing A as well as categorical freedom regarding refraining from performing A. This principle has met with great resistance of late on grounds worth investigating.

Alleged Counter-examples to the Principle of Alternative Possibilities

Recent philosophy has seen a variety of alleged counter-examples to the claim that anyone lacking categorical freedom cannot properly be held morally responsible for anything. The basic idea of the objector is to present cases in which an agent who lacks categorical freedom is nonetheless morally responsible for what she does. Once one sees the relevant recipe, one can construct one alleged example after another; a couple of simple cases will convey the core idea. Suppose that in each case there is a morally right thing to do, and that 'responsible' means "morally responsible."

Case One. John sits in his room. He has a big chemistry exam tomorrow and can either study for it or go out to the Sherlock Holmes Movie Festival. He loves Holmes films and hates chemistry. Yet he decides to stay at his desk and study. Unknown to him, his parents in any case locked his door from the outside, so has could not have left anyway. Yet John is responsible for his choice to stay at his desk.

Case Two. Mary sits reflecting as to whether to send a bitter letter to her aunt, who has angered her greatly. But she also knows her aunt meant well and that it would be wrong to send the letter. Unknown to Mary, her sister Ann, a doctor, inserted a microchip into Mary's brain that allows Ann to monitor Mary's thoughts and control them if she wishes. Ann loves her aunt deeply and is monitoring Mary's thoughts; if Mary decides not to send the letter Ann will do nothing, but if Mary decides to send the letter Ann will make her reverse her decision. Mary decides on her own not to mail the letter, so Ann does nothing.

The argument then goes as follows: in Case One, John is responsible for having chosen to stay and study, even though he could not have left had he tried; in Case Two, Mary does not send the letter, even though she could not have sent it had she tried. Neither John nor Mary, in the cases described, possess categorical freedom, but both are praiseworthy for their actions. If they are praiseworthy, then they are responsible. So possessing categorical freedom is not a logically necessary condition of being responsible for what one does. Hence compatibilism is true.

Here is another way to put the argument. Since to make a choice is to act (an action need not be overt), reference to actions covers choices as well. Consider one version of the Principle of Alternative Possibilities:

> (PA) If person S is morally responsible for having performed action A at time T in context C, then S could have refrained from having performed action A at time T in context C.

According to (PA), if John is responsible for having stayed in his room, he could have left it; if Mary is responsible for not having sent the letter, she could have sent it. The point of the cases is that in them (PA) is false and John and Mary are responsible anyway. The alleged truth of (PA) is what justifies the claim that only possessors of categorical freedom are morally responsible for what they do. Since (PA) is false, that claim is not justified. But that claim is essential to incompatibilism. So incompatibilism is false. The core idea of this argument is this: if (PA) is false of a case in which an agent acts, it is also false of that agent in that case that he possesses categorical freedom, and there are cases in which an agent acts and is morally responsible for so acting even though (PA) is false of that agent.

Reply to the Objections

Regarding Case One, there are various moves open to an incompatibilist. Here are two:

> Move One. She can say that strictly what John is responsible for is not staying in the room (he could not have done otherwise) but choosing not to try to leave and deciding to study (he could have chosen to try to leave, or not to study). This is what he is responsible for, and (PA) is true of this.
>
> Move Two. While Move One is correct so far as it goes, there is an additional consideration. Suppose that a person is categorically free regarding whether she does something A at time T and in circumstance C, and she knows that, at T and in C, doing A is sufficient for the occurrence of B. Given this knowledge, she does A in order that B may occur. Then she is responsible for B occurring, even if B would have occurred had she not done A. John's deciding to stay in is sufficient for John's staying, and John has categorical freedom regarding trying to leave. He is also properly held responsible for what he knows his deciding to stay in is sufficient for, namely his studying. (He has firmly decided that if he stays, he studies.)

Move Two is neither problematic nor uncommon. Suppose a father knows that if he does not promise to pay for his daughter's tuition, her uncle will, but since she is his daughter and he loves her, he wants the tuition to be his gift to her, not anyone else's. What is in the father's power is whether he pays the tuition, but not whether it is paid. He is responsible for the tuition being paid, and his doing so is rightly taken, unless there is special reason to the contrary, as an action he could either have performed or refrained from performing. This fits the pattern described in Move Two. Move Two does suggest a clarification of (PA), which may now read:

> (PA*) If person S is morally responsible for having performed action A at time T in context C, then (i) S could have refrained from having performed action A at time T in context C, or (ii) there is some action B that S performed

such that S could have refrained from performing B, and S's performing B is, at T and in C, sufficient for S's performing A. The incompatibilist is in no danger from these cases.

Part of what has unfortunately made some philosophers think more of the alleged counter-examples than they should is their focusing only on the contrast between such things as freely choosing to send the letter versus freely choosing not to send the letter while ignoring such things as freely choosing to send the letter versus not freely choosing to send the letter. The alleged counter-examples are cases in which the subject does not know it, but must choose whether or not to be coerced regarding an action. This is a plausible candidate for describing a case in which an agent's freedom is minimal. The consequences regarding studying and the latter being sent will be the same whatever the agent does. But there will be an important difference regarding the agent who will either make the right choice freely or be coerced. The sort of person the agent becomes is a product of such choices—choices where he or she can do what is right uncoerced. Saying that Ann will cause Mary to choose not to send the letter if Mary does not choose not to send it on her own is misleading. Ann has access to a way of controlling Mary—if she must use it the proper way of describing things is that Ann decides that Mary does not send the letter. Mary is simply Ann's agent in carrying out Ann's wishes. Mary can escape coercion regarding sending the letter by choosing rightly on her own. Her character will be determined by what she does on this and similar occasions.

The difference between a libertarian and a compatibilist view of freedom is deep. The libertarian will distinguish between what we can call an aesthetic view of good character and a moral view of good character. If a painting is beautiful, it did not bring about its beauty; credit for that goes to the artist. If determinism is true, then if one has good character, the credit should go to the ultimate causes of the character. A person is unlike a painting in that she has mental states and those states are parts of a causal chain that leads to the way she thinks and acts, and her dispositions, which constitute her character. But the ultimate causes in the chain lie outside her mental, and for that matter her physical, states. They lie buried in the past before she was born.

Thus the person is like a living painting—one whose states play a causal role in determining her character. For monotheistic determinism, there is an artist to whom credit goes for her character.

(Theologically, the role of compatibilist freedom is to block the inference that God is responsible for what is bad in her character.) For atheistic determinism, there is no literal artist. Either way, the person is not the artist—not the determiner of her character. To say that she is the determined determiner of her character is a fancier way of saying that her character is to be viewed aesthetically—its ultimate causes lie elsewhere than with she herself. For the libertarian, her character—however similar in appearance to a good moral character it may be—is not the genuine article. The compatibilist will of course disagree. One way to focus the disagreement is to note that virtuous moral character is gained by voluntary actions known to be right and done because they are right, and the compatibilist glosses "voluntary" in one way and the libertarian in another.

Divine Knowledge and Human Freedom

Here is a standard argument to the conclusion that divine foreknowledge is incompatible with human freedom; it (and the analogous argument presented here) are concerned only with logically contingent statements. If successful, this argument would show that (i) libertarian monotheism is logically inconsistent, or (ii) that future tense statements are neither true nor false and so cannot be foreknown, or (iii) that for some other reason God does not know the future. Since (ii), as we will see, seems plainly false, we would be left with (i) and (iii).

1. If God knows today what Sally will do tomorrow, then Sally is not free regarding what Sally does tomorrow.
2. If God is omniscient, then God knows today what Sally will do tomorrow.
3. God is omniscient.

So:

4. God knows today what Sally will do tomorrow. [from 2, 3]

So:

5. Sally is not free regarding what Sally does tomorrow. [from 1, 4]

First, note that God knows that P entails that P is true, but God knows that P does not entail God makes P true. An omnipotent God can create a world in which things are true that God did not cause to be true. An omniscient God can know things to be true that God did not cause to be true.

Second, we should distinguish between direction of entailment and direction of truth determination. Entailment is defined this way: proposition P entails proposition Q if and only if *P is true but Q is false* is a contradiction. Truth determination is defined this way: A's obtaining determines B's truth if and only if the explanation that B is true is that A obtains. (To "obtain" is "to be the case" or "to be a fact".)

Third, suppose that Sally will be tempted to lie tomorrow, but will finally decide to tell the truth. Then it is true that (S) Sally will tell the truth tomorrow. Consider that claim, plus (G) God knows that Sally will tell the truth tomorrow. Note two things: (i) the direction of entailment goes from (G) to (S)—to get from (S) to (G) one would have to add that God is omniscient; (ii) the direction of truth determination goes from (S) to (G)—what makes (G) true is that (S) is true, not the other way round.

Fourth, given that the directions of truth determination goes as noted, it is perfectly compatible with (S) being true, and with (G) being true, that the explanation of Sally's telling the truth tomorrow is that tomorrow she freely chooses to tell the truth. Sally can be a libertarianly free moral agent whose decision to tell the truth explains the truth of (S). The explanation of (G)'s being true is just that God is omniscient and (S) is true. This is perfectly compatible with (S) being true because of a free choice by Sally. If this is so, then divine foreknowledge is compatible with human freedom. Hence divine foreknowledge is compatible with human freedom. The argument, then, fails to establish the intended incompatibility.

How Not to Understand God knows today what Sally will do tomorrow

1. As inferential knowledge. If X knows today that Sally will do B tomorrow, and X must infer Sally will do B tomorrow, then X must know something like this: X must know that A obtains now and that it is a law that if A obtains now then Sally does B tomorrow. Then something obtains now the obtaining of which is sufficient for Sally's doing B tomorrow. An omniscient being will have no need to make such inferences in order to know anything.

2. As a probability grid or its product. It is possible to think along these lines: if Sally does B freely tomorrow then her doing B is unpredictable other than probabilistically; if her doing B tomorrow is unpredictable other than probabilistically, then there is some chance that she not do B tomorrow; if X knows now that Sally will do B tomorrow, it follows that Sally will do B tomorrow; so if X knows now that Sally will do B tomorrow, then her doing B tomorrow is not to be understood probabilistically; so if X knows now that Sally will do B tomorrow, her doing B tomorrow is not free. But a monotheist who holds both that God has foreknowledge of human actions and that those actions are free is not thinking along these lines nor would or should she think in terms of a probability grid. That S does A freely does not entail that S does A is in principle unpredictable or S's doing A is only very probable or the like. Nor is an omnipotent being in the position of having to be content with probabilistic knowledge. Perhaps a being who learned what would happen in the future would suffer this limitation, but an omniscient being has no learning to do.[20]

Truth and the Future

Since it does not appeal to the idea that God causes whatever is true to be true, what force the above argument has for the incompatibility of divine foreknowledge and human freedom is also captured by this argument.[21]

1. Every true future tense statement is now true.
2. If every true future tense statement is now true, then determinism is true.

So:

3.   Determinism is true.

This argument could in principle be given at any time, regarding all future time. If it was always sound and valid, then determinism would be true.

An Argument Regarding Premise 1

The first premise assumes that (1*) future tense statements can be true. This claim can be defended as follows:

1a.   It is now true that (i) either (ii) the next president of the United States will be a former Celtic center or (iii) the next president of the United States will not be a former Celtic center.
1b.   (i) is of the form [(ii) or (iii)]
1c.   A proposition of the form [(ii) or (iii)] is true only if its components— i.e., (ii) and (iii)—are

either true or false.
   So (from 1a–1c):

   1d. (ii) and (iii) are either true or false.
   1e. (iii) = not(ii). [obvious]
   1f. If (ii) and (iii) are either true or false and (iii) = not(ii), then either (ii) is true or (iii) is true.

So (from 1d–1f):

   1g. Either (ii) is true or (iii) is true.
   1h. If (ii) is true, then some future tense statement is true.
   1i. If (iii) is true, then some future tense statement is true.

So (from 1g–1i):

   1j. Some future tense statement is true.
   1k. If some future tense statement is true, then future tense statements can be true.

So (from 1j and 1k):

   1*. Future tense statements can be true.

Further, if some future tense statements are now true, it seems arbitrary to deny that the true ones are now true. But does this entail determinism?
   That depends on what makes future tense statements true. Had Aristotle stopped lecturing one day and laconically commented that in the future a human being would stand on the surface of the moon, what he said would have been true.

What would have made it true was some human being standing on the surface of the moon at some time later than that at which Aristotle offered his comment. If instead Aristotle had said that sometime in the future someone would freely steal a pear, that would be made true by someone freely stealing a pear at some time later than that at which Aristotle's comment was made. There seems no more problem in this case than in the case of the human being standing on the surface of the moon. That a proposition is true at some time T does not entail that what makes it true obtains at T.[22]

Conclusion

After considerable searching, no genuine counter-example to the principle of alternative possibilities has surfaced. Suppose that Tricia is related to God as considered previously. If God creates a world in which the initial conditions come from God's hand and everything that comes afterward is in fact inevitable, it is hard to see why the fact that a causal chain passes through Tricia, or that in a world with different initial conditions different behavior by Tricia would have been causally inevitable, provides any reason to think that Tricia possesses any sort of freedom that makes her responsible for anything. What Tricia's possessing compatibilist freedom relative to an action comes down to is simply that a causal chain runs through Tricia's cognitive makeup and that in a world with different initial conditions different behavior by Tricia would have been causally inevitable. The libertarian seems right in thinking that this is not enough to make Tricia a free and responsible agent. If determinism and monotheism are both true, it is dubious that there can be more than one agent. If this is correct, consistent monotheists will be libertarians.

Compatibilism: An Authorial View

Suppose an agent S, who has ample time to reflect, performs a dangerous action A at great personal risk, and pulls it off. It is the structure of the situation that concerns us, so we can leave concrete details aside. That A has been done is known, and S remains anonymous. As the details become clear, however, S is identified as the agent and proudly owns the deed as his own—not only did he do it, he is proud of doing it; it fits his values, lifestyle, purposes, and goals. Further, he wrote down every argument he could think of for not doing it, and rejected them all. So he is surely responsible for doing A—what more could we want to establish that? Here the agent has, before and after, identified himself with A.

The libertarian will not be satisfied. The strength of the compatibilist case likely rests on our common sense assumption that S was libertarianly free at least at some point prior to doing A. The compatibilist proudly notes that all the conditions noted are compatible with determinism being true. This is precisely, for the libertarian, the problem. It is compatible with the whole story that the propositions that compose it are all entailed by L, N, and a set P of propositions true a million years ago.

Authorialism proposes three conditions sufficient for responsibility without denying that less might do:

1. S did A knowing what she was doing.
2. S owns up to doing A, happy to drape it with her approval as revelatory of what and who she is.
3. S would have done A had she considered every plausible argument against it.

The third element is important as making the action at least descriptively rational for S.

If S is rational, then (given 1–3) 5 is free.

The common sense assumption of libertarian freedom may well play a significant role in the apparent plausibility of the case as one of responsibility. Each of 1–3 is compatible with determinism being true. In none of 1–3 need there be more than counterfactual freedom. S could have done otherwise had things been different because S had all the resources for doing so, though given L, N, and P it followed that the proposition that she did otherwise could not be made true under prevailing conditions. There is plainly a causal sense in which S is responsible—she is a significant element in a causal series of iron necessity of sheer entailment from L, N, and P to *S does A*. The members of L are necessary truths, the members of N more difficult to settle but they are true, and the members of P largely if not entirely contingent truths about events. But the connection between [L, N, P] and *S does A* is entailment, as strong a relation as you can imagine. It is not one that S can break.

So the authorialist will put forth his view as the peak of compatibilist plausibility and the libertarian will find, not a position closer to her own than others of its kind, just across the border if not spanning it, but yet another view that raises for the libertarian an old question. Assume (LF) *For any proposition P, if P is true it is necessarily true and if P is false, then P is necessarily false.* Suppose S* wants chocolate and is told by a reliable authority that she can have it only if she makes a contradiction true. S* recognizes that she will not get her candy. If 1–3 are true of S* in a world of which (LF) is true, then the rest of the truths in that world will entail that S* remains chocolateless. But if things were different, S*could have chocolate. They just can't be different. Suppose S* is in our world in which, alas, [L, N, and P] entail that S* does not get chocolate. Things could be different but they are not. Consider whether S* is practically better off regarding chocolate than she would be in an (LF) world—ask if S* is freer regarding getting a chocolate in our world than in the (LF) world. Suppose the reliable authority tells S* she can have chocolate one if she makes one of [L, N, P] false. How much practical difference does not living in an (LF) world make to S* and her chocolate? Then generalize to every case in which [L, N, P] entail what happens at any time, given the appropriate tensing of P. The libertarian sees no practical difference. Either way, S* lacks chocolate. S*'s actual alternatives, in any given case, are limited to one—and that things could have been different changes nothing about responsibility in the case at hand. One's freedom is always conditional on what could be true elsewhere and elsewhen. That is, it never arrives.

Questions for Reflection

1. How can one tell whether moral values are fundamental within a particular religious tradition?
2. Does it make any difference to morality whether God exists or not? Why or why not?
3. Explain determinism, compatibilism, and libertarianism.
4. Suppose that God exists, determinism is true, and compatibilism is true. Does anything different follow regarding morality that would not follow if God didn't exist?
5. Suppose that God exists, determinism is true, and compatibilism is false. Does anything different follow regarding morality than would follow if compatibilism were true?
6. Sometimes religious believers claim that if there were no God, there would be no morality. Sometimes critics of religion claim that all religion perverts morality. Are either right?
7. Explain the notion of metaphysical value. Must the ultimate, fundamental value for a religious tradition be a moral value?
8. Explain and illustrate "The difference between compatibilist and incompatibilist notions of freedom relate to other basic concepts in an overall view."
9. Do moral claims need a metaphysical basis?
10. Does a person depending for existence on God prevent her from having libertarian freedom? (If you prefer: What exactly does it mean for a person to depend on God for her existence?)
11. What are the basic values embraced by our four traditions?

Notes

1. It is worth noting that something can have metaphysical worth in virtue of the sort of thing it is—of its nature—in a sense that makes it wrong to wantonly destroy it—without ascribing rights to it since it cannot take an interest in anything, nor can any member of its species do so.
2. There are various versions of divine command theory. One strong version holds that what is good is decided by God's nature and what is obligatory rests on God's commands, made in the light of what is good. We only touch the surface here in considering replies to the Euthyphro dilemma.
3. The Euthyphro dilemma thus is not properly stated in the form of *Either A or not-A*.
4. It is at this point that the conviction that moral law requires a lawgiver enters centrally into the theory.
5. This is not relativism in the sense that entails that there are no absolute obligations. It means only that where a person is not culpable in her ignorance of what is right, she is not blameworthy in not doing it.
6. Other than God.

7. Strictly, one needs to add here "without morally sufficient reason." It is left to the reader to consider the relevance to the argument of adding this needed qualification.

8. Indeed, any two necessary truths mutually entail one another. Further, since each truth about Tess's thoughts, by hypothesis, follows from a necessary truth, it is necessarily true, and so entails every truth about every thought that God has. So construed, God's existence, nature, and thought seems as much determined by Tess's as the reverse.

9. One need not put logical fatalism in somewhat monotheistic dress; it is the doctrine that all truths are necessary and all falsehoods contradictions, and *God exists*, for all logical fatalism cares, can be among the latter.

10. This is *metaphysical* libertarianism, to be distinguished from political views that use the same term.

11. For the argument's origin, see Peter Van Inwagen, *An Essay on Free Will*, referenced in the Suggested Readings at the end of this chapter.

12. Strictly, of course, sentences like *The past entails the future* are shorthand for sentences like *True propositions about the past entail the true propositions about the future.*

13. In fact, incompatibilists often hold that were determinism true, no one would, strictly speaking, *act* at all, since *Necessarily, if A is an action by Karen, then Karen is free relative to performing A.*

14. Thus D is an enormous set of TUDs.

15. There are problems with this sort of claim, to be noted later.

16. Strictly, given a set of propositions for which the laws are truth conditions.

17. Or at least to approximate this goal—sufficient ingenuity can fit a lot into this scope, and we may have left something interesting out. Fortunately, if the account is not quite as inclusive as it might be, it remains true that the account includes many important elements, and the inclusion of some other element of the same sort will not make any difference to our conclusion.

18. For convenience, let "choosing to do A" be a success term—that Jane can choose to lie only if, given that she so chooses, she lies.

19. Compatibilists sometimes suggest that actions out of character are unfree, though this would make most heroic action unfree. There are other possible fine-tunings, but by now the general compatibilist strategy should be clear.

20. The temptation to think so arises from noting that if S lives in a deterministic world, then what S does is both non-probabilistically predictable and unfree, so if what S does is free than it is probabilistically predictable. But the reasoning is fallacious. It is exactly parallel to this. Consider a world in which this is a law: *S eats chocolate at time T if and only if S eats peanut butter at time T.* Let this be a Reese's world (RW). If S lives in a Reese's world, and S eats peanut butter at T then S eats chocolate at T. Suppose that S moves from a Reese's world to a non-Reese's world (one where it is not a law that one eats peanut butter at a time if and only if one also eats chocolate at that time). Then S can eat chocolate without also eating peanut butter (and conversely). What temptation there was to deny this would go as follows. Let the law whose presence makes a world be a Reese's world be *LCPB*. Let *eating chocolate at T* be *CT* and *eating peanut butter at T* be *PBT*. Then the reasoning would be: since when *LCPB* holds, every *CT* is also a *PBT*, every *CT* is a *PBT* whether *LCPB* holds or not. But of course this is fallacious. Having moved, S can now eat her chocolate by itself.

21. One might argue that knowledge requires justified true belief so if God knows that something is true in the future, God must know something now from which this justification comes, and so the future is determined now. One can appeal to the highly controversial view that God is eternal here. Or one can simply say that divine omniscience

is an essential property of God and thus is, for a monotheistic view, a given in need of no further explanation.

22. This claim should be distinguished from the false claim that *A proposition that says that X will obtain at T can be true even if A does not obtain at T.*

Suggested Readings

Dundas, Paul (2002) *The Jains* (New York: Routledge). Discusses the history of Jainism in its doctrinal and social context.

Fischer, John Martin (2007) *My Way: Essays on Moral Responsibility* (Oxford: Oxford University Press). A sophisticated, nuanced version of compatibilism.

Frankfurt, H. G. (1988) *The Importance of What We Care About* (Cambridge: Cambridge University Press). A very influential contemporary defense of compatibilism.

Hare, John E. (2016) *God's Command* (Oxford: Oxford University Press). Argues that what is good is determined by God's nature and becomes obligatory by divine command, thereby uniting natural law theory with divine command theory.

Harvey, Peter (2000) *An Introduction to Buddhist Ethics: Foundations, Values, and Issues* (Cambridge: Cambridge University Press). Draws on traditional texts and contemporary practices to explore what Buddhist traditions have in common as well as where they differ.

Honderich, T. (1993) *How Free Are You?* (Oxford: Oxford University Press). Another defense of compatibilism.

Kane, Robert (2005) *A Contemporary Introduction to Free Will* (Oxford: Oxford University Press). A sophisticated, nuanced version of libertarianism.

Keown, Damien (2001) *The Nature of Buddhist Ethics* (Basingstoke: Palgrave Macmillan). An effort to see Buddhist ethics in terms not dominated by enlightenment.

Lemos, John (2013) *Freedom, Responsibility, and Determinism: A Philosophical Dialogue* (Indianapolis, IN: Hackett). An introduction to contemporary arguments and issues regarding its title topics, on their own and in relation to science and religion.

Molina, L. (1988) *On Divine Foreknowledge* (Ithaca, NY: Cornell University Press, trans. Alfred Fredoso). The standard presentation of the view that God knows what free persons, created or not, will or would do.

Perrett, Roy W. (1998) *Hindu Ethics: A Philosophical Study* (Honolulu: University of Hawaii' Press). Presents the structure of Hindu ethics.

Rowe, William L. (1991) *Thomas Reid on Freedom and Morality* (Ithaca, NY: Cornell University Press). An excellent discussion of Reid's libertarian views.

Van Inwagen, Peter (1983) *An Essay on Free Will* (Oxford: Clarendon Press). A powerful critique of compatibilism.

Watson, G., ed. (1982) *Free Will* (Oxford: Oxford University Press). An excellent collection of essays concerning libertarianism.

Zagzebski, Linda (1991) *The Dilemma of Freedom and Foreknowledge* (New York: Oxford University Press). A detailed discussion of divine foreknowledge.

15 Faith and Reason

Faith

To have faith involves belief; it cannot exist in a conceptual vacuum. Christianity talks about "the faith once delivered"—the central doctrines of the religion. All of our religions obviously have propositional content, things belief in which is essential to acceptance of their religion. The acceptance of these beliefs involves faith that what the texts say is true, and in particular true concerning diagnosis and cure. In turn this requires faith in those persons assigned central religious importance by those texts. (The role of oral tradition in the development and continuance of many religious traditions has been enormous; an oral tradition may develop into a textual one. This is a large topic and we can only mention it here. Oral tradition, in song or narrative, also has propositional content.) If there is no propositional content, there is no religion. Even religions that trade on paradox and contradiction, thinking that genuine religion can be found only after dismissing reason and rationality, preach doctrine of the need to do that in order to find what they believe is enlightenment or salvation. One needs propositional belief even to think there is any point to attempting to reject reason and to seek and follow a method for doing so. We have seen the significance of doctrine and belief in the religious traditions we have discussed.

In Shakespeare's phrase, "the unkindest cut of all" in critiques of religion is that religion's supposed beliefs are literally nonsense—that they are not true, nor do they even manage to be false.[1] The familiar tactic of critics of religion is to offer some theory of meaning, and then argue that the target of their criticism does not satisfy the theory's standard. Here, to be meaningful is to be either true or false. Thus "Buttercups created the world" and "Monkeys run congress"—taking both claims literally—are false, and hence meaningful, and their denials, being true, are also meaningful. As a sop thrown to religions being criticized it is sometimes suggested that their beliefs have emotive meaning, that is they may have the sort of sense that groans have. Religious phrases may elicit responses, so "God blesses us all" may elicit from a congregation "Amen" even though God-talk may be sheer nonsense. After all, the congregation could be trained to say "Amen" (roughly, "Let it be so") in response to "Wumba bunba," which the critic believes to be on a par with "God blesses us all" so far as being true or false goes.[2]

From the outside looking in, the proposal that for centuries millions of people have used monotheistic language to apparently say things they thought true, and all along were utterly misled—even the brightest and best who seemed to be brilliant thinkers—is surprising. The expectation given will be that the arguments in favor of this accusation must be incredibly powerful. Our tour of the arguments will endeavor to make clear the criticisms offered, and to see what can be said about the truth or falsehood of their conclusions. A theory of meaning will at least give what it takes to be a necessary condition of being true or false, and typically will suggest a sufficient condition. Only if these arguments fail with there be any possibility of religious faith.[3]

As good a place to start as any is the theories of meaning offered by David Hume, the immensely influential Scottish philosopher who wrote *A Treatise of Human Nature*.[4] He offered two theories of meaning, one for words and one for sentences. He called experiences with sensory content impressions of sensation and their copies in memory ideas of sensation. Experiences with introspective content he called impressions of reflection and their copies in memory ideas of reflection. He denied that we have any awareness of a self who has such experiences. Given that small background, here is his theory of meaning for words.

(W) A sound or mark is a word if and only if it is associated with (rarely he says "names") an impression or an idea.

A Humean will need to find a way of granting meaning to such terms as these: and, not, some, all, none, or, contradiction, consistent, entails, if-then, true, false. That task alone is unpromising—to what sensory or introspective contents do their terms correspond? Presumably, if a theory of meaning is offered, it should be meaningful on its own criterion. But to what sensory or introspective content does either "theory" or "meaning" correspond? For that matter, if *There is no self that is the subject of sensory or introspective experience* is true, it must be meaningful, and to what items of sensory or introspective experience does it correspond if there is no self of which to be aware? After all, on Hume's view, one must understand what the word 'self' means in order to tell that no such thing is experienced. His theory of meaning for sentences is:

(S) A string of words composes a sentence if and only if it, or its denial, is confirmable by reference to some sensory or introspective experience.

In addition there are sentences true or false by definition, a class supposed to contain all necessary truths and all necessary falsehoods, and to be trivial. A little reflection on (S) raises the obvious question as to what sensory or introspective experience confirms (S), and of course there is none. If it seems unlikely that these sorts of problems arise with an argument offered by an astute philosopher, perhaps the fact that it all happened again will be convincing. In the 1920s a group of philosophers, logicians, and scientists met informally in Vienna and came to be known as the Vienna Circle. They developed a view called Logical Positivism. The core of their program was a theory of meaning called the Verification Principle (VP). This theory dominated the Anglo-American philosophical scene for decades. In the exchange of arguments for and against the VP it underwent various subtle changes, but one example of its formulations will be sufficient to make our point.

VP. A string of words comprises a sentence if and only if

(1) it describes a sensory or introspective experience; or
(2) it is true or false by definition; and
(3) it can be confirmed or disconfirmed, in principle, by reference to some sensory or introspective experience; or
(4) it follows from sentences that fall under (1), (2), or (3).

The idea behind (3) is that if there is some possible sensory or introspective experience that would confirm or disconfirm what is expressed by a string of words, then that string of words is a sentence. It is not necessary that such an experience be available. For example, consider an area where dinosaurs are known to have roamed. Pick some place in that area, and offer the hypothesis that a dinosaur once slept there. Since we know what we would have to have seen in order to confirm the hypothesis, the sentence that expresses the hypothesis is meaningful. Hume's theory of sentence meaning is captured by the four conditions of (VP).

The first question to ask is where (VP) itself—a complex declarative sentence—fits into the four categories. It certainly is not a report of any sensory or introspective experience. On verificationist terms, any sentence falling under (2) is trivial. It does not fit under (3)—what sensory or introspective experience would confirm or disconfirm it? But (4) remains. Russell and Whitehead developed a system of logic published as *Principia Mathematica* (1907–1911), which contained the rule [If P, then (P or Q)]. The unpardonable sin for a rule of inference is that it sanction an inference from a truth to a falsehood. Consider an inference from P to (P or Q), with the 'or' being understood so that if either P or Q or both are true, then (P or Q) as a whole is true.

Suppose P is false. Then inferring (P or Q) from P will not involve inferring a falsehood from a truth—the premise is false. Suppose P is true. Then whatever one decides Q shall be, (P or Q) will be true since P is true. So we have the rule Addition: from P you may infer (P or Q). Then you replace (P) by something like *The sun is shining* and infer to *The sun is shining or the VP is true* and you have fitted VP into (4), so the VP does not rule itself out. Then imagine this dialogue:

Theist: Thank you! Now I see how to fit *God exists* under the VP fence; all I need to do is to infer *The sun is shining or God exists* from *The sun is shining*.

Critic: But that won't do. You have used Addition in your argument, and it only covers truths and falsehoods. *God exists* is neither.

Theist: Thank you again! You have assumed that the VP is true or false and that *God exists* is not true or false—you need the latter assumption to deny my inference. But you were supposed to argue from VP to the conclusion that *God exists* is not true or false, not to just assume it as part of your argument, as you have done here. So you have assumed that VP is true so that it comes under the rule called Addition, and assumed that *God exists* is neither true nor false. You have not shown either assumption to be true.

In any case, VP was just offered as a criterion of meaning, and then applied. There was no argument for it in the first place. It was crafted to include natural science, logic, and mathematics and rule out metaphysics, ethics, and religion. Toward the end of the dispute the suggestion was floated that the VP was really a piece of advice. Those who accepted claims in metaphysics, ethics, and religion declined to follow it.

There is no lack of other sources of conclusions that radical empiricists favor. One is the claim that God is ineffable.[5] One use of the term is for emphasis "Her beauty is ineffable." There are quite different uses that can be defined as follows:

A.   X is ineffableA if and only if, for any concept C, C does not apply to X.
B.   X is ineffableB if and only if, for any concept C, C does not fit X.

Concept C fits X if and only if C is true of X. Concept C applies to X if and only if C is true of X or C is false of X. Thus "is an elephant" fits an elephant but not a rose, but "is an elephant" applies to a rose since it is false of roses that they are elephants. So the claim that God is ineffable is either the claim that no concept fits God or the claim that no concept applies to God.

The claim that God is ineffableB—that claim that no concept fits God—is self-defeating, since "is ineffable" is a concept. A second problem concerns what reason there could be for saying that it is God who is said to be ineffableB. There is nothing that can be offered as a reason here—not that God is infinite, or not in space or time, or different in kind from anything else. Any of these reasons supposes that certain concepts—being infinite, not being in space or time, being different in kind—fit God, and that goes directly against the idea that God is ineffableB. The question as to why we should think it is God who is ineffable suggests another line of thought. To be God is to be omnipotent, omniscient, holy, sovereign, and the like, and an ineffable item can be none of these things. So how does God come into any of this? Further, presumably even an ineffable item must exist, and if anything exists, then the concept of existence fits it. Necessarily, to exist includes having properties and so the concept "has properties" fits an allegedly ineffable being. The notion of ineffabilityB, if one actually tries to draw out the idea as applying to God, turns out to be an acid that eats away the content of one's monotheism. The idea that God is ineffableB is incoherent. The claim that God is ineffableA entails the claim that God is ineffableB—if no concept even applies to God, then no concept fits God. What entails some incoherent claim is itself incoherent. Divine ineffability, as defined here, is not defensible.

That no proposition can be literally true of God but this does not empty theology of its content can be based on the view that all propositions that are true of God are to be understood analogically. The idea is that if two statements of the form *God is A* and *Socrates is A* are both true, then whatever the predicate term 'A' stands for means one thing when applied to Socrates and another thing when applied to God. Then the conclusion can be drawn that all predicates held to be true of God are used analogically. Actually, the conclusion does not follow.

Consider the propositions *God is omnipotent* and *Socrates is omnipotent*. They use 'omnipotent' in the same sense. More generally, the ideas are:

1. If statements of the form *God is A* and *Socrates is A* are both true, then 'A' is used analogically in the statement about God to that in which it is used in the statement about Socrates.
2. If statements of the form *God is A* and *Socrates is A* are such that one is true and the other false, then 'A' may be univocal (have the same sense) in both statements.

Thus in *Socrates is a citizen of Athens* and *God is not a citizen of Athens*, 'citizen of Athens' is used univocally. An easy extension allows *God does not weigh a hundred pounds* and *Socrates does not weigh a hundred pounds* to have univocal predicates, though both are true. This point deserves reinforcement.

There is still the idea that if two statements ascribe the same property to God and Socrates rather than both denying that property to God and Socrates, the predicates cannot be univocal and the properties ascribed cannot be the same. This too is dubious. Consider the properties *being able to raise ten pounds*, *knowing that Rhode Island is closer to New York than is California*, and *being self-aware*. The average citizen of Rhode Island and God have these properties, and there seems no reason to think that the properties are not the same in both cases.

One core of the doctrine that all predication of God must be merely analogous rather than literal is the idea that God belongs to no genus, and the meaning of a predicate differs as one applies it to things that differ in genus. Supposedly God belongs to no genus because there cannot be two Gods and every genus must be possibly shared by more than one thing. It is not clear why there cannot be a necessarily one-membered genus. There can be only one first person to climb Pike's Peak, but that is not a genus-defining feature. So just because there are properties necessarily had by only one thing if they are had by anything does not show that there cannot be a one-membered genus. God, however, is held to have an essence. Without getting into detail concerning how this essence should be stated, we will take one candidate for defining the divine essence as representative of others. We can put this briefly: being omnipotent, omniscient, and omnibenevolent. This defines a kind of being just as well as being H2O defines water as a kind.

Why then does it not define a genus? Relative to genus membership, the impossibility of multiple membership seems trumped by God having an essence. Even if it is not, the dictum that a term changes meaning when applied to members of different genuses does not follow. It is plainly false of number concepts, for example. It is false of many terms. You can have a dog that eats, drinks water, and sleeps in the same sense of these terms as they apply to you, and a rock can hold down a blanket in the same sense as you can. Your thumb can plug up a hole and then be replaced by a stick that plugs up the hole just as well and in the same sense, even though your thumb belongs to one genus and the stick to another. The *Meaning changes when used of a member of one genus and then of a member of another* is a dogma proclaimed without paying attention to the number and variety of cases where it is false.

The doctrine that all predicates ascribed to God, when the ascription is true, are used analogically dies hard. The point of analogical predication is to note a similarity. A typical pattern is *A is to B as C is to D*—for example, *Strength is to the body as intelligence is to the mind*. A simpler pattern involves the use of 'like.' *God is a rock* is not an intrusion of theology into geology. It means *God is like a rock*. Among the many properties that rocks have, God has at least one. The usual meaning of the comparison is that God is strong and reliable.

You are better off building your house on rock than on sand, and your life on God rather than riches. Whatever the pattern used, the analogy fails if one cannot identify the property on which resemblance is based. Part of what God being reliable means is that God will keep God's promises. Whatever one thinks of the theology, 'promise-keeping' is being ascribed to God and is meant literally. *As the author is to the novel so God is to the world* uses the more complex pattern. Two questions should be distinguished here. What resemblance has the speaker in mind?

When that is settled—when the resembling property is specified—can the ascription of that property to God be literal? A plausible candidate is *being a necessary condition for*. No author, no novel; no God, no world. *Being a necessary condition for the existence of* is a univocal term—the novelist bears the property it designates to the novel and God bears it to the world. *God is like oatmeal* apparently plays no role in monotheistic thought since it is opaque what the point of comparison might be. No doubt one could be supplied—as oatmeal is to physical health, so God is to spiritual health. That is lame at best. But even in cases that push the envelope, intelligibility of the analogy requires identification of the proposed resembling property. To claim that the property cannot be one that both God and humans have challenges the claim that anything can be said about God, and ignores numerous counter-examples.

Another related doctrine tells us that:

3.   For any property Q and substance S, if S's essence precludes S from having Q, the ascription of Q to S (that is, statements of the form *S has Q* or their equivalent) is meaningless (neither true nor false).

Thus *All cats are dogs* is meaningless, which is obviously false. *The number seven dances* is meaningless if 3 is true, since dancing is beyond the range of its natural skills. But precisely for that reason, a different tradition regards the statement as false. After all, the reason for regarding it as meaningless is that numbers are not the kind of thing that can dance. So it is true that (N) *Numbers are not the kind of thing that can dance*. This is logically incompatible with (D) *Numbers can dance*, since (N) entails not-(D). In giving the reason why (D) is meaningless, one relies on (N), which entails (D)'s denial. So if (N) has truth value, so does not-(D), and hence (D) does as well. The denial of a necessary truth is a necessary falsehood. So it turns out that the proposition that ascribes to something a property incompatible with its nature is false rather than meaningless. Not surprisingly, *God is a number* is false.

It is commonly said that God is infinite. The strict sense of infinite is this: a set S is infinite if and only if S contains subset S* such that each of the members of S* can be paired one-and-one with the members of S. Not being a set, God cannot be infinite in that sense. The looser sense those who ascribe *is infinite* to God is *unlimited*. But of course God is limited in all sorts of ways—God is not blue in color, round in shape, taller than six feet, younger than ten years, or the elected mayor of Cleveland. It can then be suggested that having properties limits whatever has them, since it then cannot have other properties that are incompatible with (contradictories or contraries to) the properties it already has. If having limitations is supposed to be negative, it is odd to think of having no properties as positive, since it entails not existing. Divine omnipotence is sometimes glossed as "infinite power," which is misleading, since it is so easily rendered as "can do anything" as if God could write your autobiography as autobiography (which would require that you be God). It is arguable that describing God as infinite is nothing like the best way of putting the various divine attributes or essential properties.

Monotheism is often accused of relying on anthropomorphism as essential to expressing its core content. Anthropomorphism, broadly construed, is describing God in terms of properties possessed by human beings. God is described as loving, just, and merciful. Anthropomorphic description is obviously a mistake if the properties ascribed to God are overtime parking, theft, or error on an exam. The properties in question are such properties as being self-aware, thinking, and acting—thinking of God as a person. The notion of a God who makes covenants with human beings created in God's image (an ascription often understood in terms of our volitional and rational capacities) is personal, and the idea that God cannot have personal properties is at best controversial. The objection to God being described in any terms at all of course is incompatible with any ascription of personal qualities to God. But we have argued that, at least when defended on the grounds discussed previously, this objection is not justified. The dictum that all language is non-literal long dominated departments of English in spite of its flagrant falsehood. The dictum itself is literal.

Those who complain about monotheistic anthropomorphism prefer terms like The Infinite, The Real, The One, Ground of Being, The Force, The Ultimate, and the like. Ground of Being suggests an independent existence on which all else depends, and thus has some use regarding God as conceived in the monotheistic traditions. The others suggest questions: The infinite what? The real what? The one what? The ultimate what? And which force? They are vaguer than 'God' in monotheistic traditions, though that need not be any advantage. A supposed advantage is that one can thereby describe various religious traditions using such terms. What that amounts to is that these terms serve as a blank into which various religious terms can be put. The project of reducing religions to their least common denominator is hardly obviously a good thing. It leaves out what each religion treasures most. The policy of doing so does not typically arise from concerns about the nature of religious language, though it is common in contemporary discussion of religious traditions and typical to treat religious claims non-literally.

The thesis that there can be no literal truths about God, even if monotheism is true, appears in much of monotheistic thought. It too seems mistaken. God is said to be omnipotent, omniscient, and morally perfect. It seems to follow that God can lift not only a mountain but also a feather, knows that twice two is four, and know that torturing for pleasure is wrong. We also can lift a feather, and know that twice two is four, and know that torture is wrong. In what respect is the meaning of *can lift a feather* not the same in God's case and the case of a human being? The way it is done may be different without the sense of the words being different. An immaterial omnipotent being will not have to touch a feather in order to move it upward from the ground. We will not have to touch it either—we can use tongs. But whatever means God uses to lift the feather and whatever means we use, we have both lifted the feather. If God knows that twice two is four, in what respect is the meaning of *knows twice two is four* not the same in God's case and in the case of a human being? It is true that an omniscient being will know all of mathematics and hence understand an enormous context of mathematical propositions in which the modest mathematical truth is included. One can then say that God knows it better than you do. But knowing better and knowing less well are still cases of knowing.

These are no doubt not profound religious truths, but if monotheism is true, they are truths. The importance of this small fact is evidence; in philosophy counterexamples are important. Further, if there can be literal trivial truths about God this raises the question as to why there cannot be significant literal truths as well. We have found no reason to think religious claims cannot be true or false. So far as these objections go at any rate, there can be religious faith. But what is that? And what is reason?

Reason and Rationality

Reasoning is an ability we have. In its full range, it is a very rich ability, including the capacity to believe, know, infer, imagine, remember, anticipate, plan, develop and test theories, offer explanations, develop and assess arguments, identify and reidentify thoughts and persons and things, and so on. Since attitudes and feelings can be irrational, there is not the grand divide between thought and feeling that is sometimes advertised. Without capacity to reason, irrationality is impossible. Parenthetically, there are circumstances in which one can be reasonable while nonetheless knowing one has contradictory beliefs. There is a paradox of authorship to this effect: Jeff writes a philosophy book in which he believes everything he said—he was honest in what he claimed. He is not arrogant, and so believes that the book contains some falsehood. If the book contains some falsehood, it follows that something he believes is false. If everything he believes is true, then at least one of his beliefs is false. But Jeff is not unreasonable in holding both of the incompatible beliefs. Notice he has (we will assume) good reason to think what he says in the book is true, and good reason to think that his book has not offered license for reasonable people to start believing contradictions, much less for pretending that contradictions are just paradoxes. The rule *If it is reasonable to believe that P is true and reasonable to believe that Q, then it is reasonable to believe that 'P and Q' is true* is false. Jeff, if he is reasonable, does not believe [There are no falsehoods in my book and there are falsehoods in my book]. He (let us suppose) has excellent reason to think that every argument in his book is sound and valid, so that every conclusion in his book is true. He has massive evidence that if not absolutely every, then very close to every, philosophy book contains some falsehood. (Perhaps a few short logic texts are exceptions.) He realizes they cannot be true together. But he also has what he rightly takes good reason in each case for belief. He does not try to imagine a world in which both are true. There are no such worlds. But he has not become irrational if he can shake neither belief so long as he knows that both claims cannot be true. The paradox of the author is not rarified. For each of us, it is almost certain that if we went into some impressive edifice where they put our heads in a comfortable hat connected to a sophisticated machine and thereby produced a list of every proposition we believe, it is hard to believe that there will be no incompatible beliefs on the list. But this is no rationale for ignoring inconsistencies that we discover.

Reasonable Belief

The focus in philosophy of religion now tends to be on whether religious belief can be reasonably held. This raises the question of what has to be true if someone is reasonable in holding a religious belief. The belief does not have to be true. It is possible to have superb evidence for a belief, and yet the belief is false. Evidence is truth-favoring but not truth-entailing.

W. K. Clifford became famous among philosophers for asserting that it was always wrong to believe on insufficient evidence.[6] This sounds like a high standard for belief, but before we worry about whether we sin if we go against this dictum, we should ask if it is true as a principle of proper belief. Of course what exactly the right criterion is for "sufficient evidence" is not clear, but suppose one is found. Then is the principle true? What evidence have we for:

(W) One ought never believe anything without sufficient evidence.

One problem concerns regress. If *You cannot believe P without sufficient evidence provided by Q, and cannot believe Q without sufficient evidence provided by R, and cannot . . .* then any belief you have will require support for another, which requires support for another, and you are like the man who will be let out of his cage so long as he always uses a key to unlock the door, which must always be unlocked by yet another key. The regress must end somewhere if one is to properly have a belief, but (W) suggests no stopping point. One way to escape this is to say that one accepts a foundationalism that notes that some beliefs are self-evident, belief-entailed, or evident to the senses. These classes are exemplified, respectively, by *No one can be taller than herself, I believe I exist, The computer screen is white*. Then the suggestion will be that there is sufficient evidence for these sorts of beliefs, as well as any belief that they entail or make probable. Only necessary truths are entailed by necessary truths, so no contingent truth can be derived from them. The set of contingent truths entailed or made probable by *I believe I exist* and its kin (*I believe I am conscious, I believe I have beliefs,* etc.) will not get us to other persons or external objects. *Propositions entailed or made probable by propositions that are evident to the senses* is a more tricky class than it appears. In perception am I simply having conscious states with sensory content, or am I having those states that are caused by external objects, or am I directly aware of those objects? Propositions from the first two classes will not help in deciding between these alternatives. The unclarity of "insufficient evidence" and the complexity of the epistemology of perception make the question as to how to deal with *is evident to the senses or is entailed or made probable by what is* a demanding one. A Cliffordian can hold this sort of foundationalism. Then the question concerns where (W) fits in the foundationalist scheme of things. It is not evident to the senses or belief entailed. A Cliffordian is likely to suggest self-evidence. (W) is not formally necessary—its denial lacks a contradictory structure and if it is not informally necessary it will lack the status claimed for it.

Religious doctrines are not likely to appear in a list of formally necessary truths—propositions that have self-contradictory denials, propositions whose logical structure is captured in such forms as *P and not-P, If Q then not-Q,* or the like. The most plausible relevant example of a proposition that is informally necessary is the familiar example already discussed, namely the claim that God is omnipotent, omniscient, and omnibenevolent in all possible worlds, which we discussed earlier, finding it to be controversial. Propositions that are belief-entailed are also unlikely to be a home to religious doctrines. The same seems to hold for propositions that are evident to the senses. But then where do religious doctrines fit? Considering this requires some examples. We can use our familiar examples.

G. God—an omnipotent, omniscient, omnibenevolent being—exists.
J. The essential nature of a person is that she is inherently everlasting and immaterial.
A. Ultimate reality is a qualityless being or state.
B. What we think of as persons are bundles of conscious states at a time and a series thereof over time.

Beginning with the conflicting J and B, we can note that the traditions that accept them agree that common sense sides with J. We seem to be enduring subjects of experience who are the same person at bedtime as we were upon waking, who once learned to read with focus on every word and later read sentences easily. Enlightenment experience confirms and supplements what common sense tells us regarding J. But we also commonsensically take our bodies to be essential to us if they are not simply us. We take our range of knowledge to be very limited. In enlightenment experience we recognize that we are distinct from and independent of our bodies, and enjoy a tremendous range of knowledge. For the tradition that embraces B, enlightenment experience corrects common sense. It reveals that we are not enduring beings but are subjectless causally connected states, each being related to other in one ephemeral bundle after another and every state being momentary. All of this is radically impermanent and causally dependent. So we have two radically different metaphysical views. Assuming all persons to belong to the same metaphysical kind with the same metaphysical structure, it is possible that experiences accepted as giving enlightenment be in error. The Jain can refer to common sense support, each will appeal to sacred texts, and each will refer to philosophical arguments. Neither view seems to fit nicely into the three-fold foundationalist division for basis propositions properly used in the foundations of knowledge and as premises from which conclusions can be produced by deductive, and perhaps inductive, arguments.

Turning to A, A obviously goes directly against common sense. Every perceptual and introspective experience in the history of humanity testifies against it. Shankara and other Advaitans know this. Their view is that sacred texts teach A. Other Vedantists interpret these texts differently, mainly theistically. Discussing the level of appearance, Shankara argues strongly for the reality of subjects of experience, the existence of mind-independent physical objects, and the general reality of the everyday world. He contrasts the level of reality—an undifferentiated being or states—on the basis (besides the texts) of enlightenment experience that is the goal of Advaita. Deriving A from foundationalist assumptions seems a hopeless enterprise.

The history of discussion of G includes efforts to base it on foundationally approved propositions. Central among these propositions is one or another version of a causal principle, such as:

1.   Whatever has a beginning has a cause.
2.   If X exists, might not have existed, and can be caused to exist, then X has a cause of existence.
3.   There cannot be an infinite series of caused and causing beings.

Relative to foundationalism, the proposal is that 1–3 are self-evident. None of them appear to have self-contradictory denials. If so, then if they are necessary truths, they are informally necessary. The basic idea behind these claims is that nothing can come from nothing. Alternatively, no item can just pop into existence. The claim that something exists fits into the "evident to the senses" basket if you think of perception and the "belief-entailed" basket if you think of introspection. Causal claims 1 and 3 are related in that both are relevant to whether the universe has a beginning. If 1 is to be used in a theistic argument, it must be supplemented. It is compatible with there being a beginningless series in which each item has a cause of existence. Thus it needs to be supplemented by something like 3. Claim 2, as noted when we discussed the cosmological argument, is neutral as to whether the universe has a beginning.

There is another theistic argument that, in one version, involves probability. It is the argument from design. It can be stated in these terms.

1. Artifacts behave in particular, repeated ways that we can anticipate. (Evident to the senses)
2. Nature (or natural objects) behave in particular, repeated ways that we can anticipate. (Evident to the senses)
3. Artifacts have that feature due to being designed by intelligent agents. (We know this by having seen them made, so evident to the senses.)

Probably:

4. Natural objects have that feature due to being designed by one or more intelligent agents.
5. Human intelligent agents did not design natural objects.

Probably:

6. One or more non-human intelligent agents designed natural objects.

The crucial issue regarding this argument concerns what justification there is for making the two probability inferences. One cannot claim to have observed any non-human agents design any natural objects, let alone universes. (The argument could be run by talking about an entire universe as well as by talking about natural objects.) There are lots of disanalogies between the two types of cases, and one who offers the argument will have to explain which are relevant and which are not, and then show that the relevant ones do hold between artifacts and natural objects. The conclusion is intended to concern only one designer, not many, and that must be justified (parsimony?). The list continues for some time, but ultimately the fundamental issue comes down to the degree to which mechanistic versus personal explanation has a right to claim ultimacy, not to claims about self-evidence.

We have explored some of the territory surrounding attempts to be foundationalists in thinking about attempting to assess religious belief. The motivation is to escape skepticism and have beliefs that are certainly true or highly probable—obviously of particular interest in the case of religious belief. Much of the history of attempts to do this, on both side of the fence, have followed this strategy. But the epistemic security of foundationalism itself is not great. It is not clear that it satisfies the very criterion it offers for proper belief. It is time to consider a different approach. We can do this by briefly considering two competing perspectives in the philosophy of science.

Confirmationism

The core of confirmation is the idea that the ability of a single proposition or a set of propositions S to explain some phenomena, the evidence for whose occurrence is strong, is a vote for S's truth. This favorable consideration can be countered by equal consideration against, for example, discovery of a defect in the explanation, the presentation of competitive theory at least as well supported that also explain the phenomena, and so on. The need for a framework in which to continue to work can keep a theory afloat even if there is good reason to doubt it, at least until a better is offered, so as to have a framework within which to work. There is an apparent glaring weakness to confirmationism as so far described. The logical structure of the argument seems to be:

Theory T predicts (entails or makes probable) that if X is in circumstance C, then Y will occur.
In C, Y occurs.
Therefore, T is true or probably true.

Unfortunately, this is also the logical form of:

If I have a million dollars, then I have at least one dollar.
I have at least one dollar.
Therefore I have a million dollars.

This is a fallacy with a long and unsavory history that has earned it the name "fallacy of affirming the consequent" (the proposition that follows 'then'). If that were part of a fair description of scientific reasoning, science would not be a rational enterprise. Of course things are more complex. There are lots of explanatory theories that are non-starters. The explanation of a building falling is not that someone frowned at it. A theory has to pass muster in terms of being consistent with present knowledge. (This does not rule out new scientific paradigms, but these typically come when a deep flaw in current theory is discovered.) This requirement is typically implicit and automatically applied. Second, having passed this test, the theory must be such that if it is true, the phenomena it is offered to explain are in fact explained. Explanation is more than entailment. That either three and seven are eleven or the water boils, and that three and seven are not eleven, entail that the water boils. It also offers no explanation whatever of the water boiling. Roughly, what connects the proposed explaining phenomenon PE and the phenomenon EP to be explained is a proposed law of the form *If PE then (at least probably) EP*. The law must fit into the nexus of laws already accepted. Broadly stated, the reasoning is: *We have two theories, one that entails that in condition C, X will occur or will probably occur. The other entails that in C, X won't or probably won't occur. Both theories would fit into our scientific picture of things. So we create condition C. If X occurs, the former theory is confirmed. If it does not, the latter theory is confirmed. Either way we have some reason to think that one of the theories is true.* With apologies for this very general and rough account, it should at least be enough to indicate how inadequate the affirming the consequent account is as a statement of confirmationism.

A contrasting perspective is offered by falsificationism. Falsificationism shares with confirmationism the respect due to Modus Tollens, the argument form *If P then Q, and not-Q; then not-P*. Finding a naturally black swan shows that the claim that all swans are white is false. Falsificationism is more cautious about the force of the positive feature made central by confirmationism. Being able to explain a phenomenon is by itself not much to brag about. That the powerful leprechaun Queen of the Irish wanting it to be so might do nicely as an explanation of there being many four-leaf clovers in Ireland, but it is unlikely to become a respected law in botany. Roughly, typically a plausible candidate for being a scientific theory must fit into what is already established in the field to which it is relevant and be subject to the testing techniques currently available. It must have explanatory power relative to phenomena in the field in which it is offered. It must explain some phenomenon that is currently puzzling. The practice of offering deductive arguments is not much pursued in assessing explanations, though the question of what an explanation entails or makes probable in specified circumstances is central. Scope matters—the more phenomena that fall within the class of what the explanation gives plausible account, the better the explanation. The falsificationalist is conservative in her claims. Suppose a theory has passed the primary elections, and there have been multiple attempts to falsify it, all of which have failed. So far, so good—other things being equal, we should include the theory in our tentative view of how the world is. Being strongly tested without falsification is the best we get in a theory so far as proof goes. The wider the range of phenomena a theory explains, and the more lower-level laws that fall under its laws, the more useful the theory is. But it is wisest to talk about one theory being better than another than to pronounce a confirmed theory true. Confirmation is essentially lack of disconfirmation.

The point here is not to go on to argue for confirmationism or falsificationism. It is rather to note the shift of procedure. The beginning is a description of something to be explained. The methods are similar if not identical. The conclusions are different—less or more conservative. The shift of focus to explanations is significant. The central question is not whether one or more propositions fit into one of four categories. Of course one could use only propositions that do so as providing confirmation or lack of disconfirmation, but there is no inherent limitation of this sort.

The falsifications method suggests something like the following. A good theory is one that has explanatory power regarding some phenomenon we have good reason to think exists, and has not been falsified after serious effort to do so. A theory has explanatory power relative to a phenomenon P only if, should the theory be true, it follows deductively that, or is probable that, P occurs. A theory with no explanatory power is not worth offering. Being confirmed is nothing more than having explanatory power and not having been falsified. If a theory has explanatory power, has not been falsified, and has no competitors with the same advantages, it is reasonable to believe that theory. Two theories are competitive if one entails or makes probable that under the same experimental conditions something will happen and the other theory entails or makes probable that something else (including nothing) will happen. Confirmationism differs only in its view of the significance of true predictions. One significant feature of both perspectives is that the focus is on theory assessment, which allows for assessment of sets of related propositions.

Religious traditions are not usually thought of as constituted by theories. If one's model for theories is scientific theories, this is altogether understandable. But they are partly and significantly constituted by explanation of what they regard as data desperately needing attention and response. They find us all in dire straits due to circumstances they describe in such a way as to make the distraught see their own condition, and describe a way out of those straits. All of this amounts to the core of a view of the world into which the relevant diagnosis and cure fit well, as they should as the worldview in part is developed from the content of the diagnosis and cure themselves. Thus religions centrally contain theories. Arguments for and against religious views often appeal to what are proposed as counter-examples to the core views of a tradition. Arguments for religious views often begin with phenomena that are viewed as well known and asserted to be well explained by the view. Monotheistic arguments from there being something rather than nothing, dependent things, moral values, natural order, and the like, are easily cast as arguments to best explanation. The varieties of arguments from evil are obviously falsifications in structure. Judgments regarding the reasonability of holding particular religious beliefs rest in part on the perceived results of such applications of confirmationism and falsificationism.

Consider the doctrine of the resurrection of Jesus Christ from the dead. There are at least five layers of claim here. One is that Jesus was an historical person who lived in the historical setting and time frame ascribed to him in the Gospels. The second is that he was crucified, dead, and buried. The third is that on the third day, his dead body returned to life. The fourth is that God caused this to happen. The fifth is that this event evidences the status of Jesus Christ as Jewish Messiah and Son of God. Each level is presupposed by the next highest. Each level that has a preceding level depends on it. Historical evidence is required, available, and disputed, for the first- and second-level claims. When we come to the third through fifth level we have a clear example of religious claims to which historical considerations are relevant. From a secular perspective, and from many religious perspectives, these claims have no plausibility. This would be expected from non-theistic views, secular and religious, since levels three through five are intimately connected in Christian theology. The doctrines are also rejected by Judaism and Islam. From a Christian perspective, while a resurrection claim about the Roman official Pilate would have a plausibility rating about that assigned to the resurrection of Jesus from secular and non-theistic viewpoints, it makes an enormous difference when the claim is made concerning Jesus, given the (contested) data we have concerning his life, teachings, and claims. There is thus a cluster of inter-related claims involved in the doctrine of the resurrection. There is the further claim that we are free moral agents, with disagreement as to whether we have compatibilist or libertarian freedom, and the further teaching that we are all sinners, morally wrong actions being violations of God's law. Thus we need to repent and ask for God's forgiveness, which is freely offered. Thus moral claims are added to historical claims as well as metaphysical claims starting with theism itself. The claims are interconnected and whether they are thought of as constituting an explanation, they are, if true, explanatory of much of the human condition and the prospects of its radically changing. The descriptions of the phenomena for which explanation is offered must be made carefully. Strictly, sin is falling short of divine requirements, so if sin occurs, then God exists. So the relevant phenomena must be described as morally wrong actions. That assumes that there is objective morality. Like other religious traditions, Christianity centers around a small number of claims that have wide metaphysical content and yet are focused on human salvation.

The Buddha is not related to Buddhism as Christ is to Christianity. Strictly, in the earlier parts of the complex tradition, the Buddha is a crucial figure because he found the path to enlightenment, fully followed it, and left the description with his followers. The texts recording this are viewed as authoritative because the Buddha was reporting his own experience and reciting a path that others could follow. Strictly, then, someone else following the prescribed path could have reached the same goal, and have recorded the prescription, and played a similar role had the Buddha not done so. But if one takes into account the history of Buddhism's developing doctrine regarding the Buddha, this scenario becomes less and less a possibility. In Theravada, we have a world in which everything is ephemeral save for nirvana, while in Mahayana Absolutism we have a view quite similar to Advaita. Whatever the sociological and psychological effects would be, at least were there good reasons to doubt that there was an historical figure, it would be logically possible that Theravada Buddhism be true. What the actual effect on the tradition would be is another matter beyond our argument. (No suggestion is being made that there was not an historical Buddha. The point I am making concerns the logic—in the strict sense—of early Buddhist thought.) There is the assertion that suffering—unsatisfactoriness in life—has its source in our attachments to this life and its contents. There is, as we have seen, a path described, the following of which will lead to release from attachments. These themes are woven into a metaphysic that includes reincarnation, karma, and a view of persons in which they are one time stage after another, each momentary stage filled by collections of physical and mental states, or just mental states. The fact that life is often, or at least seems to be, unsatisfactory is indisputable. The Buddhist view is that it is sufficiently so to make its end desirable. This is, as we have seen, a common theme in Indian philosophy, accompanied by the view that there is a state into which entry, of oneself or what there was of oneself, is far better.

Jainism is not a theistic religion and it does not ascribe to Mahavira properties similar to Catholic saints or God, save as he, like all enlightened Jains, is viewed as immortal and omniscient. Self-awareness is regarded as self-evidence so far as the existence of an enduring subject possessed of mental properties goes but it leaves out the part about immateriality, immortality, and omniscience. This further information is regarded as crucial features in escaping samsara, the cycle of rebirth.

While it is not obvious, it is true that that the central disagreement between Jainism and Buddhism concerns a philosophical dispute much discussed in contemporary metaphysics. The topic for our purposes concerns persons. Consider Geisha, who exists for 2 million seconds. For endurantism, all of Geisha is present at each of those seconds. For perdurantism, a time slice of Geisha is present—a temporally minimal bit that joins one million nine hundred thousand nine hundred ninety-nine more bits in a series. As is obvious, Jainism is endurantist and much of the Buddhist tradition is perdurantist. The arguments for and against these philosophical views are very relevant to the Jain and Buddhist doctrines. In addition, there are two views of time. One is the A-series perspective. The key temporal relations are past, present, and future. Time flows—an event that occurs now becomes past and what was present is replaced by the future. The other is a B-series view. The key temporal relations are before and after. One is to think of time as very much analogous to space. Think of a very long film strip stretched out full length, each frame representing one massive event (the state of things that obtain or exist at that slice of time). The frame goes on and on spatially, and as one observes the time slices, the ones that one viewed before remain in their place. Nothing goes out of existence. What happens is that as you observe, say, an Olympics race, the race is represented only in a limited number of frames so that as you move forward you move beyond the frame that represents the end of the race. Every thing that ever exists, every event that ever happens, also is there in its time frame, and the frames never go out of existence. Every time frame's contents are as real as every other's. Nero fiddles as Rome burns, Buzz Aldrin walks on the moon, cell phones are invented, Abraham Lincoln is elected president, and you take your first step—these contents of really existing time frames represent things that exist with tenure. Now end the story with two revisions. The time frames are really times, and there is no human observer. The view is neither theistic or non-theistic. Suppose that the B-series view of time is true. Then if Geisha exists for many lifetimes, Geisha still lingers in those unenlightened moments. Geisha still steals if he ever stole, and still saves a life if he ever saved a life. The Buddha still leaves wealth and comfort to seek enlightenment and still sits under the tree where he is believed to have been enlightened. So there is always a part of the Buddha that remains ever unenlightened. Mahavira still is enlightened as he still seeks enlightenment, though at different times, some before and some after each other. There is no past that falls away and no future that comes to pass. All of it, so to speak, is always there.

There are some interesting issues if either Jainism or Buddhism were to embrace the view that the B-series is right. In one respect, it is easier for much of the Buddhist tradition to do so, since on its view a person is a series of ephemeral bundles. A consequence of this Buddhist view, with or without a B-series view, is that nothing suffers or finds life unsatisfactory for more than a moment. Even the worst suffering accompanied by a memory of equally bad misery comes in very short bits. One can argue that on this view there is little motivation to care more about the bundles that occur some many thousands of bundles later in one's own series than one does about what happens thousands of bundles later in another series, and so leads to greater compassion. There is of course another way of viewing things. An equally possible result is the one not care about either. There is also the emphasis on lack of attachment. One is supposed to do one's charity without emotional investment in the outcome, and there is the short duration any one bundle exists to experience whatever degree of satisfactoriness or unsatisfactoriness occurs. The B-series fits very naturally with the bundle series in a manner that makes it quite dubious that it be acceptable to Jainism. There is a further consequence that is unfortunate from either a Jain or (much of) the Buddhist tradition. Consider a seeker for either Jain or Buddhist enlightenment to have lived many lifetimes. Suppose our seeker lives a thousand lives in the reincarnation-karma cycle. On a B-series view, every second of those lifetimes is written in stone in the tenured status of the pastless, presentless, futureless universe. Unless the Buddhist downplays the significance of the suffering of one bundle after another, the idea that reaching nirvana leaves all the bundles permanently in one unsatisfactory condition after another, unendingly. There is no remedy for them. Assuming that a B-series view requires a time slice view of persons—that a person-slice in time slice T1 cannot be numerically identical to a person-slice in time slice T2— then the consequence would be the same for Jainism after the core Jain doctrine regarding persons has been abandoned. But if the B-series view does require a time-slice view of persons, Jainism is logically incompatible with that view of time.

The point here has not been to argue for or against part of the Jain or part of the Buddhist tradition, but rather to point out some connections between doctrines of religious traditions and disputes in contemporary philosophy. These connections refute facile assumptions that religious traditions are immune to philosophical assessment, positive and negative.

Advaita is theistic in its view of what holds at the level of appearance and non-theistic concerning the level of reality. Shankara no more exists as a distinct individual who transcends appearance than anyone else. The same holds for gods, goddesses, and God. Even if one showed that the account of the world as the level of appearance was riddled with contradictions, there would remain what Shankara in his description of the level of appearance regards as an intractable fact—the existence of a subject who discovers and displays the contradictions. The Advaita view of the level of reality is reminiscent of the radical view that what there is "under" or "beyond" our conceptions of a world already filled with distinct items is an unindividuated "stuff" and that "our world" or "the external world"—made, not discovered, by us. The rough idea is that the ultimate stuff of the world can be "cut up or divided" into various ontologies—various objects in various relations, various worlds of perceptual content. Ultimate reality itself escapes us save for the knowledge given in enlightenment experience. There is plenty of discussion in the context of Indian philosophy, even within the Vedantic tradition. Another Vedantin, a following of Madhva who with Shankara and Ramanuja are central figures in monistic (Shankara) and theistic (Ramanuja and Madhva) Vedantic tradition, is also an impressive critic of Advaita. Vadiraja offers this argument, which is a more detailed version of a criticism offered earlier. Advaita's core doctrine is the identity of every Atman with Brahman, the latter being construed as undifferentiated blissful consciousness. There seems to be a world of objects and persons, and even God, but this is the way that Brahman appears rather than really is. According to Advaita, each Atman (the Atman is real) is associated with a jiva, a mind and body that seems to experience the world we all seem to experience. This experience gives us illusions. It is "within" this illusory world that suffering occurs and the reincarnation and karma cycle "occurs." This jiva, with its experiences, will cease forever upon enlightenment. The Atman then will no longer seem to be distinct from Brahman. One problem is that to seem to suffer is to suffer. (For Dvatin Vedantan Madhva there is no undifferentiated Brahman, but instead there is a personal God. There is no Atman in the Advaita sense, but instead there are real jivas, which are what gets enlightened.) The criticism is simple. The jiva is unreal and hence cannot have experiences. In the Advaitan view, there are only Atman and Brahman left, and they are identical. One can approach the issue in either of two ways. Going from Atman to Brahman, since Brahman cannot experience appearances, the Atman does the experiencing of appearances and hence is distinct from Brahman after all. Going from Brahman to Atman, Brahman cannot experience appearances, and since Atman is all that is left to have them, and hence must have them, Atman cannot be identical to Brahman or there cannot be a level of appearance. This is part of a long history of philosophical dialogue within Vedantin traditions that provides ample evidence that assessment of religious traditions is available in philosophy. The same holds for the rich philosophical traditions found in Buddhism. (There is also the fact that the philosophy/religion distinction is not traditionally Indian.)

Enlightenment traditions in effect treat what is, on their views, regarded as revealed by enlightenment experience as self-evident. Self-evidence does not merely mean, though it typically includes, being impossible for the subject not to believe. It includes the subject being entirely justified in accepting what is revealed in the experience (a revelation without a revealer in our non-theistic traditions). Each tradition, and each sub-tradition, has its own closely related cluster of doctrines, mutually related and aimed at a specifiable end. They define at least part of a worldview. They include claims as to what, if anything, exists independently of everything else (is existentially dependent on nothing),what the fundamental kinds of things in the world are, what (if anything) is the meaning of life, what future (if any) awaits persons, what (if any) fundamental religious problem we all face, and what (if any) solution there is to it. There are views as to what is and isn't without beginning and what does and does not have an ending; what is morally positive and what is morally negative. While obviously it is possible to consider their constitutive propositions, one can also view them as a whole. As assessment that does both is most informative concerning the object of assessment.

The fact, then, is that religious traditions are subject to philosophical assessment. We have tried to offer various examples of this, the bulk of which are taken from arguments actually given by proponents and critics of the religious traditions discussed. This completes our agenda—our argument that religious traditions are not safely walled off from rational assessment. Religious faith is not inherently unreasonable. The practice of accepting religious doctrines and living the lifestyle associated with them, accompanied by worship and trust of God in the monotheistic traditions, is reasonable to the degree that the doctrines are rational to accept. The process of trying to discover that regarding one or more traditions is complex. But there are religious truth-claims to assess and a long history of examples from which to learn.

Questions for Reflection

1. Distinguish between 'faith that' and 'faith in.'
2. What sort of faith is possible in a nonmonotheistic religious tradition?
3. Is it possible for a person to have faith in even if he has excellent reason for faith that?
4. What new possibilities does the notion of "argument to best explanation" introduce into the discussion in philosophy of religion?
5. Is the thesis that theories of meaning for which apparent claims central to religious traditions are neither true nor false, and hence not claims at all, at least insofar as they are discussed in this chapter, in fact failures to be true or false on their own terms?

Notes

1. This was the verdict of Logical Positivism, which was highly influential in its long heyday, roughly from the 1930s through the 1960s. Its classic expression came in A. J. Ayer (1952) *Language, Truth, and Logic* (New York: Dover). It was originally published in 1936.
2. Two sources of perspectives on the alleged problem of religious language are Ronald E. Santoni, ed. (1968) *Religious Language and the Problem of Religious Knowledge* (Indiana) and William P. Alston (1989) *Divine Nature and Human Language: Essays in Philosophical Theology* (Ithaca, NY: Cornell).
3. *God and Other Minds* (Ithaca, NY: Cornell, 1990—Sec. Ed.), Chapter Seven, provided a powerful 1967 response to Logical Positivism. No doubt it played a role in the almost universal demise of the view.
4. Available in many editions, it was published in parts from 1738–1740 and has become a classic empiricist text.
5. See Alston, William P. "Ineffability," *Philosophical Review*, Vol. 65, No. 4, 1956, pp. 506–522 for a good discussion of ineffability. Written in dialogue form, this essay probes various ways in which ineffabilist theses can be developed; each is found inadequate.
6. W. K. Clifford (1999) *The Ethics of Belief and Other Essays* (Amherst, NY: Prometheus). This book was originally published in 1947.

Suggested Readings

Audi, Robert (2011) *Rationality and Religious Commitment* (Oxford: Oxford University Press). An account of rationality followed by faith as an attitude including but not reducible to belief and conduct, with moral, political, social, and aesthetic dimensions of life; closes with a discussion of natural and moral evil and an account of the nature of persons.

Callahan, Laura Frances and O'Connor, Timothy, eds. (2014) *Religious Faith and Intellectual Virtue* (Oxford: Oxford University Press). Various questions are raised as to whether, and if so how, one's religious faith can be compatible with intellectual virtue in some defensible sense of the latter—e.g., can belief without evidence so count (cf. Reformed Epistemology)?

Evans, C. Stephen (1998) *Faith Beyond Reason: A Kierkegaardian Account* (Grand Rapids, MI: Eerdmans). A presentation of three kinds of "responsible fideism" favoring Kierkegaardian fideism, which is in part characterized by reason justifying a view of its own limitations.

Helm, Paul, ed. (1999) *Faith and Reason* (Oxford: Oxford University Press). A superbly wide-ranging selection from the classical period through the twentieth century—unlike any other in print.

Mavrodes, George, ed. (1970) *The Rationality of Belief in God* (Englewood Cliffs, NJ: Prentice-Hall). A good collection of essays on the reasonableness of monotheistic belief.

Mitchell, Basil (1981) *The Justification of Religious Belief* (Oxford: Oxford University Press). A clear presentation of the cumulative-case argument for monotheism.

Penelhum, Terence (1983) *God and Skepticism* (Dordrecht: D. Reidel). Clear discussion of monotheism and skepticism about monotheism.

Swinburne, Richard (1981) *Faith and Reason* (Oxford: Oxford University Press). A detailed account of faith and reason by a philosopher who thinks that one ought to have reasons for one's religious beliefs.

Wilkens, Steven, ed. (2014) *Faith and Reason: Three Views* (Downers Grove, IL: IVP Academic). Reason and faith in tension, cooperation, and subordination.

Yandell, Keith E. (1986) *Christianity and Philosophy* (Grand Rapids, MI: Eerdmans). A systematic exploration of issues relevant to monotheistic belief.

16 Some Further Vistas

Much of contemporary epistemology is divided into two camps regarding knowledge. One, called internalism, holds that for a person to know something she must be in possession of some consideration favoring its truth—that it is self-evident, evident to the senses, follows from propositions from one or both of these categories, is made highly probable by data known to be sound (in which case it is known to be highly probably true), is plain to introspection, or the like. The other, called externalism, holds that in order for a person to know some proposition to be true, his belief must have been caused in the proper way. The former position, allowing self-evidence to count as evidence, is properly thought of as evidentialist. The latter is not. Not surprisingly, both views are taken toward proposed religious knowledge. Neither requires that a known religious truth be a necessary truth, any more than a known truth about apples must be a necessary truth. The natural thing to think about when one turns to the idea of a religious internalist evidentialist is the theistic arguments, and we have considered that approach. A different approach from this is offered by Paul Moser, who offers a particularly clear appeal to moral experience as evidence for monotheistic belief. It is perhaps equally natural to expect a religious externalist non-evidentialist to favor fideism, the view that belief in God is to be held without, and perhaps without any consideration of, evidence. This is held to be true of the reformed epistemology of Alvin Plantinga. Moser and Plantinga are the most influential proponents of their particular views, and it is to those views we now turn. Each is sensitive to the issue of evidence contrary to Christian belief, which is their common interest. Moser holds that the explanation of the sort of experience that he makes central is that it is caused by God must be at least as reasonable as any competitive explanation, and Plantinga holds that the belief (religious or not) that is caused in the proper manner is knowledge only if it faces no undefeated defeater (no contrary evidence that is not successfully rebutted. These are not typical fideist views. That said, we turn to their positive presentations. While both philosophers are Christian, a non-Christian monotheist could accept at least much of their perspectives. Many moral realists are not Christians. The status of properly basic belief can be assigned and defended for other beliefs besides Christian ones. There are multiple religious doxastic practices.

Moser[1]

Moser notes that the arguments of natural theology such as we have considered earlier, whatever else their merits or defects, share the common feature that one can follow them and, even if one accepts them, respond with indifference. One can take the attitude that, at least for now, one has answered one of a great many philosophical questions, and turn to whatever is next on one's list. Basing his view on his reading of Biblical texts, he holds that God is little if any interested in one's ability to answer a true-false question *Does God exist?* on an examination. He proposes moral experience, particularly the sense of an obligation to act or not act in a certain manner, as the focal point of religious experience. In such experience, one has a sense, which Moser regards as veridical, of being encountered by a personal will other than one's own. While the subject of such an experience may not think of its apparent object in strictly monotheistic terms, feeling an obligation to act favorably to its content is, in Moser's view, the beginning of a reasonable faith. This requires a belief in objective morality—an acceptance of moral truths not simply based on conventions we have adopted. (Alternatively, it could be used as part of a case for moral objectivity.) Moral experiences Moser takes to provide evidence for and knowledge that God exists. His view raises issues discussed previously concerning monotheism and religious experience.

Plantinga[2]

A properly basic belief is one reasonably held without deriving it from some other belief. Examples are memory beliefs, introspective reports, and statements about one's physical environment. Such beliefs make use of clusters of concepts related to those used forming the beliefs—that there is a past, a self, an external world, for example. Plantinga's suggestion is that belief in God is a properly basic belief. This ties into his externalist account of knowledge. It comes along with its own bit of natural theology. Plantinga develops a cluster of concepts relevant to his non-evidentialist externalism as follows. We come to form beliefs, and thus we have a belief-forming mechanism. A belief-forming mechanism has the function of forming beliefs of a certain kind, description of which will vary from theory to theory. The term 'function' here is used neutrally as to whether having a function is built into what has it by a designer—atheists and theists can agree that it is the function of the heart to pump blood. According to evolutionary theory, Plantinga argues, it is the function of our belief-forming mechanism to deliver beliefs that promote survival, whether they are true or not. Plantinga's claim is that for your typical survival scenario—a tiger has you in mind for lunch—there are ever so many more false beliefs that will promote survival than there are true ones. For example, believing that tigers love to play games with humans but play too roughly, that the tiger is a human enemy in disguise, that the tiger's presence is a sign of enemy activity in the neighborhood, and so on. In Plantinga's view, if God created our belief-forming mechanism, it would be aimed at true belief. Hence, on theistic assumptions, we are the more reasonable in accepting our beliefs. The point here in adding this feature of Plantinga's view is not to argue for or against it. It has the dual purpose of noting a different sort of natural theology argument than the ontological and cosmological arguments, and correspondingly a new range of issues regarding its success, and of indicating more fully what his actual view is. If Plantinga is right, for example, the theist is more reasonable in believing pure evolutionary theory, simply as a theory in biology and without its frequently added metaphysical assumptions, than is the atheist. His account of knowledge goes as follows. If a person forms a belief due to her belief-forming mechanism, which is aimed at truth, functioning in an environment in which it functions well, the belief is true, and the belief faces no undefeated defeater, then the person has knowledge. Note that this is not offered as an independent test for knowledge—it cannot be since it requires that the relevant belief be true. Insofar as it favors Plantinga's own religious views, it does so to the degree that this is true: if the monotheist's belief is true, then if it is properly caused and faces no undefeated defeaters (no evidence that is unrebutted) it is knowledge.

Alston[3]

A third alternative is offered by William Alston. He makes the notion of a doxastic (belief-forming) practice central to his account in the sense that it is focus of assessment, not particular beliefs. The idea is that a community or culture will have belief-forming practices. An obvious example is sensory practice. We form beliefs about our observable physical environment, learning to do so from very early life. We learn what sorts of behavior are approved or disapproved, what sort of activity yields foodstuff, what sorts of economic doings are available, and so on, and thus acquire beliefs about these matters. There will also be religious belief-forming practices. A belief-forming practice will have at its core some set of fundamental beliefs assumed by those who follow it—for example, the belief in the mind-independent physical environment. Another example is belief in some sort of spiritual environment. Monotheists assume that God exists and come to have beliefs as to how God relates to the world. Since there are competing spiritual as well as other sorts of practices, the question arises as to how to compare them, if one can, in terms of their success. One question here concerns the consistency (lack of contradiction), coherence (mutual relevance), and empirical fit (accuracy to the content of relevant experience) of the comprising core beliefs. Another is the ability to change in response to new situations and accommodate new information and intrusions into the culture. Another is success at furthering survival and adequate living standard measured in some defensible manner. One result of this approach is to greatly broaden the considerations relevant to assessment of religious beliefs. It raises such questions as these, among many others: If one set of beliefs grounds a practice that serves a better life for its practitioners than does another, assuming some objective standard for being a better life, is this reason to think the former more likely true? Are there objective standards for being a better life? Is adaptability to new information a reliable guide to truth? Does adaptability mean more than simple logical consistency, and if so what more? These are only a few of the issues that Alston's suggestion raises.

Questions for Reflection

1. Is Moser's Internalist Evidentialism appeal to moral experience as evidence self-standing or in need of appeal to argument for an objective morality?
2. Is Plantinga right that at least typically there will be more false survival-promoting beliefs than true?
3. Is an internalist or an externalist account of moral knowledge more defensible?
4. Would the result of using Alston's sort of approach be a focus on justifiable belief in a sense relatively unrelated to true belief (contrary to its author's intent), and would it (equally against its author's intent) lead to an incoherent conceptual relativism?
5. Can Alston's suggestion be well integrated with either or both of the perspectives sketched just before it?

Notes

1. Moser, Paul K. (2009) *The Evidence for God: Religious Knowledge Reexamined* (Cambridge: Cambridge University Press). Presents the view that the evidence for God's existence comes in personal terms in moral experience rather than in third-person evidence that leaves the subject unchallenged to change her life and commitments.
2. Plantinga, Alvin (2000) *Warranted Christian Belief* (Oxford: Oxford University Press). The definitive statement of his externalist epistemology of Christian belief.
3. Alston, William P. (1993) *Perceiving God* (Ithaca, NY: Cornell). A thorough presentation and defense of Alston's religious epistemology for which it is possible to experience God, set in the context of a successful belief-forming practice. It still sets the standard.

Suggested Readings

Beilby, James (2002) *Naturalism Defeated?* (Ithaca, NY: Cornell). Plantinga's argument against the combination of naturalism and evolutionary theory is self-defeating is subjected to scrutiny by a large number of philosophers.

Moser, Paul K. (2013) *The Severity of God: Religion and Philosophy Reconceived* (Cambridge: Cambridge University Press). Argues that while God's gift of love is free, its reception involves stress and severity.

Plantinga, Alvin (2015) *Knowledge and Christian Belief* (Grand Rapids, MI: Eerdmans). A popular version of *Warranted Christian Belief*.

Schellenberg, J. L. (2015) *The Hiddenness Argument: Philosophy's New Challenge to Belief in God* (Oxford: Oxford University Press). Presents Schellenberg's anti-theistic argument in its most streamlined and persuasive terms.

Tooley, Michael and Plantinga, Alvin (2008) *Knowledge of God* (Oxford: Wiley-Blackwell). A high-level debate between an articulate non-believer and an articulate believer.

Glossary

This glossary defines some key philosophical and religious terms, giving them the sense they bear when used in this book. Not all of these terms, however, always have the same sense when they appear in other publications, and thus there is no claim that the definitions provided here are always inclusive.

Advaita (non-dual) Vedanta—the monistic religious tradition whose roots lie in the Vedas (Hindu Scriptures) and hold that all pluralism of objects, properties, and relations belong to how things appear rather than how they are

Alston's doxastic practice epistemology—the view that belief-forming practices are basic in the formation of religious belief and also in questions of the reasonability of such belief

appearance—the ways things seem

argument—a set of claims (premises) from which another claim (the conclusion) is supposed to follow in such a way that evidence has been provided for the conclusion's truth

argument to best explanation—reasoning in favor of the explanation of a phenomenon being the truth of some proposition or propositions offered

basic belief—a belief not based on propositional evidence

Brahman (with qualities)—God in Hindu philosophy and most forms of Hinduism

bundle—a collection of causally linked qualities or states

bundle reductionism—the view that a bundle is neither more nor less than its composing members

bundle theory—the view of persons on which a person at a time is a collection of momentary states and over time is a series of such collections

categorical system—an integrated set of claims composed of propositions formed by the use of categories

category—basic concept

causally necessary being—a being the existence of which cannot be caused

Christianity—a monotheistic religious tradition, the roots of which lie in Judaism and that affirms the deity, crucifixion, and resurrection of Jesus Christ

compatibilism—the view that even if determinism is true, we are responsible for our actions

compatibilist freedom—the sort of freedom one can have if determinism is true

cosmological argument—an argument to the effect that there being things that might never have existed and/or depend for existence on something else is best explained by reference to a being that cannot depend on anything else and has the power to create them; more briefly stated, an argument intended to prove that God is the sufficient cause of the world

counter-example—an example whose existence is incompatible with the truth of a proposal

creator—a being in virtue of whose activity there exists a world of things that might not have existed

criterion—a measure by which to determine distinct types by reference to a tradition's doctrines regarding diagnosis and cure

cure—the teaching of a religious tradition as to the means of curing the spiritual disease it posits

descriptive religious pluralism—the view that religious traditions differ by way of offering incompatible teachings

determinism—the view that the past determines a particular unique future

diagnosis—the teaching of a religious tradition as to the universal spiritual disease it is the religion's purpose to cure

doctrine—a teaching propounded by a religious tradition as part of its diagnosis or cure

doxastic practice—a procedure or method of belief-formation, in particular when it is embedded in a group

empiricist theory of meaning—the view that a non-definitional proposal is true or false only if it can in principle be confirmed or disconfirmed by sensory or introspective experience

enlightenment experience—an experience in which one cognitively and existentially recognizes the truth of the core doctrines of one's religious tradition and escapes reincarnation

enlightenment requirement—that if person A begins to seek enlightenment at T and finds it at time T, then the finder at T must be metaphysically identical to A

enlightenment-based argument—an argument based on an enlightenment experience

Euthyphro dilemma—either God decides what has value arbitrarily, or what has value has it independent of divine choice

evidential problem of evil—the claim that the existence of evil is evidence against the existence of God

evidentialism—the view that in order to know that a proposition is true one must believe it in the light of evidence for it (allowing for self-evidence to count)

externalism—the view that in order to know a proposition is true one's belief that the proposition is true must have been caused in right manner

faith—the acceptance of religious doctrine and the endeavor to live in accord with it; an essential element in faith is trust if the doctrine claims the existence of a cosmic person

faith in—personal trust

formal logical necessity—a proposition is formally necessary if and only if its denial is formally contradictory, as is any proposition of the form [P and not-P]

free will defense—the claim that at least much of the evil that exists is due to the free choices of agents, the value or whose existence as such counterbalances or outweighs the evil that they do

God—an omnipotent, omniscient, perfectly good being who creates the world

Greek monotheism—a set of ideas collected from Plato and Aristotle that view God as eternal, designer rather than creator, without providential rule over the world

Hindu monotheism—a variety of monotheism that holds that God everlasting creates the world, that reincarnation doctrine is true, and that salvation comes when one has an enlightenment experience

incompatibilism—the view that responsibility and determinism cannot coexist

indeterminism—the denial of determinism

ineffable—not describable, altogether beyond our concepts

informal logical necessity—a proposition is informally logically necessary if it is logically necessary (there are no possible conditions under which it would be false) but not formally logically necessary (it is not of the form *P and not-P* and it entails no proposition of this form); *If William draws a rectangle then William draws a figure* is informally logically necessary

inner-directed experience—an experience in which it at least seems to the subject that she is aware of something not distinct from and not independent of herself

Islam—a religious tradition that is monotheistic, holding that God gave a revelation to Mohammed in Arabic, the Koran, through which it interprets the Christian and Jewish Bibles

Jainism—an atheistic religious tradition that has its roots in the Jaina Sutras (Jain scriptures) and teaches that there are two kinds of substance, mental and physical, the mental ones being persons (jivas)

Judaism—a monotheistic religious tradition holding that God gave the law to Moses and called Abraham and made him the father of a chosen people; its sacred scriptures, the Hebrew Bible, includes the books of the Christian Old Testament.

karma—the doctrine of karma claims that one receives good consequences for good actions and bad consequences for bad actions, some of the consequences typically coming in a different lifetime than the deed from which they arise

kevala—Jain enlightenment experience in which one is said to recognize that one is distinct from and independent of one's body and unlimited in knowledge and escapes reincarnation

libertarian freedom—freedom to act in alternative ways, or to act or not act in a given way, on an actual condition of choice and not merely were things otherwise

libertarianism—the view that we have freedom of choice, and that compatibilism and determinism are false

logical problem of evil—the claim that the existence of God and the existence of evil are logically incompatible

logically necessary being—a being that exists under all possible conditions and so cannot not exist

memory requirement—that if person A remembers doing (seeing . . .) X then A must be metaphysically identical to the one who did (saw . . .) X

(metaphysical) personal identity—the non-conventional identity of a person at a time or over time

metaphysical value—the intrinsic worth a thing has due simply to its nature

moksha—Advaita enlightenment experience in which one is said to recognize one's identity with qualityless Brahman

monism—the view that the number of things there are is exactly between none and two

monotheism—the view that there exists one God, in contrast to atheism, which holds that there is no God, and polytheism, which holds that there are many gods but not one God

moral value—the dignity or worth inherent in being a self-conscious libertarianly free agent capable of making choices that are right or wrong

Moser's moral evidentialism—the view that moral experience of obligation is experience of God and that those who respond affirmatively to its challenge at least begin a positive relationship with God

(Nirguna) Brahman—the qualityless one thing there is

nirvana—Buddhist enlightenment experience in which one is said to recognize that one is merely a bundle of momentary states and achieves a condition that guarantees final nirvana at the end of one's current reincarnation

non-dualist view of experience—all experience that is of subject-consciousness-object or subject-consciousness structure is in error

normative religious pluralism—a view as to what to do about the fact that descriptive religious pluralism is true if one simply takes religious traditions as they stand—namely to understand the doctrines of the traditions non-literally

omnipotent—able to do anything that is not logically impossible

omniscient—knowing with regard to every proposition whether it is true or false

Ontological Argument—a line of reasoning intended to prove that God exists under all possible conditions

outer-directed experience—an experience in which it at least seems to the subject that she is aware of something distinct from and independent of herself

phenomenological description—a description of an experience based on the way things at least appear to the subject

Plantinga's reformed epistemology—the view that belief in God is properly basic and can be knowledge if it is caused in the right way and true

possible world—a total way a world might be

principle of experiential evidence—a criterion by which one can judge whether or not an experience is evidence for a claim

principle of sufficient reason—a proposition to the effect that whatever exists and can have a cause does have one

proposition—a proposition is anything that is either true or false; we use declarative sentences to express propositions, but the same proposition can be expressed by using different strings of words in one or more languages, so propositions are not sentences

providential—involving divine foresight or intervention especially in influencing the course of history

reality—the way things are

reincarnation—the series of birth after birth of every person that has no beginning and, without enlightenment, has no end

religious faith that—acceptance of a proposition due to acceptance of a religious authority

Semitic monotheism—a variety of monotheism including Judaism as source, Christianity, and Islam, that holds that God is creator and providential judge of humanity, right relationship to whom constitutes salvation

series of bundles—a temporal sequence of bundles, each causally related to its predecessor

series reductionism—a bundle series is neither more nor less than its composing bundles

subject-consciousness-object experience—an experience whose structure makes it outer-directed

subject-content experience—an experience whose structure makes it inner-directed

substance—a bearer of properties that is not a property or a bundle of properties and retains its identity in change of properties over time

teleological argument (argument from design)—an argument from the orderliness of nature to the existence of a non-human design

the Real—the proposed transcultural source of at least the major religious traditions

theistic inconsistency charge—the claim that theists are inconsistent when they judge God innocent in allowing preventable evils and judge humans guilty when they do the same

Theravada (tradition of the elders, the immediate followers of the Buddha) Buddhism—an Indian religious tradition that denies the existence of substances and teaches that what we think of as substances are really only causally connected properties

verification principle—an empiricist theory of meaning influential in twentieth century philosophy

virtue defense—the claim that there are virtues whose existence is worth the price of the evil that must exist in order for them to be achieved

Bibliography

Adams, R. M. (1999) *Finite and Infinite Goods* (Oxford: Oxford University Press)

Anthony, Louise (2011) The mental and the physical, in Le Poidevin, Robin, Peter Simons, *et al.*, eds. *The Routledge Companion to Metaphysics* (New York: Routledge) pp. 555–568

Athanassiadi, Polymnia and Michael Frede, eds. (1999) *Pagan Monotheism in Late Antiquity* (Oxford: Oxford University Press)

Audi, Robert (2010) *Epistemology: An Introduction to the Theory of Knowledge* (New York: Routledge)

Audi, Robert (2015) *Rational Belief: Structure, Grounds, and Intellectual Virtue* (Oxford: Oxford University Press)

Audi, Robert (2015) *Reasons, Rights, and Values* (Cambridge: Cambridge University Press)

Audi, Robert (2016) *Means, Ends, and Persons: The Meaning and Psychological Dimensions of Kant's Humanity Principle* (Oxford: Oxford University Press)

Baker, Lynn Rudder (2000) *Persons and Bodies: A Constitution View* (Cambridge: Cambridge University Press)

Bartley, Christopher J. (2002) *The Theology of Ramanuja* (London: Routledge-Curzon)

Bastow, David (1997) Rationality in Buddhist thought, in Deutsch, Eliot and Ron Bontekoe, eds. *A Companion to World Philosophies* (Cambridge, MA: Blackwell), pp. 410–419

Beebee, Helen (2010) Hume, in Benecker, Sven and Duncan Pritchard, eds. *The Routledge Companion to Epistemology* (New York: Routledge) pp. 730–739

Ben-Menaham, Yemina (2006) *Conventionalism* (Cambridge: Cambridge University Press)

Bergmann, Michael and Jeffrey Brower, eds. (2016) *Reason and Faith: Themes from Richard Swinburne* (Oxford: Oxford University Press)

Bernstein, Mark (2002) Fatalism, in Kane, Robert, ed. *The Oxford Handbook of Free Will* (Oxford: Oxford University Press) pp. 65–81

Berofsky, Bernard (2002) Ifs, cans, and free will: The issues, in Kane, Robert, ed. *The Oxford Handbook of Free Will* (Oxford: Oxford University Press) pp. 181–201

Berofsky, Bernard (2012) *Nature's Challenge to Free Will* (Oxford: Oxford University Press)

Bharadwaja, Vijay (1997) Logic and language in Indian philosophy, in Carr, Brian and Indira Mahalingam, eds. *Companion Encyclopedia of Asian Philosophy* (London: Routledge) pp. 230–250

Bigelow, John (2011) Truth-makers and truth-bearers, in Le Poidevin, Robin, Peter Simons, *et al.*, eds. *The Routledge Companion to Metaphysics* (New York: Routledge) pp. 389–400

BonJour, Laurence (2002) Internalism and externalism, in Moser, Paul K., ed. *The Oxford Handbook of Epistemology* (Oxford: Oxford University Press) pp. 234–263

BonJour, Laurence (2010) A priori knowledge, in Benecker, Sven and Duncan Pritchard, eds. *The Routledge Companion to Epistemology* (New York: Routledge) pp. 283–293

Boyer, Pascal (2001) *Religion Explained: The Evolutionary Origins of Religious Thought* (New York: Basic Books)

Brockington, John (1997) The origins of Indian philosophy, in Carr, Brian and Indira Mahalingam, eds. *Companion Encyclopedia of Asian Philosophy* (London: Routledge) pp. 97–113

Burton, David (2011) A Buddhist perspective, in Meister, Chad, ed. *The Oxford Handbook of Religious Diversity* (Oxford: Oxford University Press) pp. 321–336

Burton, David (2012) Buddhism, in Meister, Chad and Paul Copan, eds. *Routledge Companion to Philosophy of Religion* (New York: Routledge) pp. 7–27

Byrne, Peter (2011) A philosophical approach to religious diversity, in Meister, Chad, ed. *The Oxford Handbook of Religious Diversity* (Oxford: Oxford University Press) pp. 29–41

Byrne, Peter (2012) Theology and religious language, in Meister, Chad and Paul Copan, eds. *Routledge Companion to Philosophy of Religion* (New York: Routledge) pp. 581–592

Campbell, John (2011) The self, in Le Poidevin, Robin, Peter Simons, *et al.*, eds. *The Routledge Companion to Metaphysics* (New York: Routledge) pp. 569–577

Carr, Brian (1997) Śaṅkarācārya, in Carr, Brian and Indira Mahalingam, eds. *Companion Encyclopedia of Asian Philosophy* (London: Routledge) pp. 189–210

Carr, Brian (1999) Shankara, in Arrington, Robert L., ed. *A Companion to the Philosophers* (Oxford: Blackwell) pp. 613–620

Carr, Indira Mahalingham (1999) Ramanuja, in Arrington, Robert L., ed. *A Companion to the Philosophers* (Oxford: Blackwell) pp. 609–612

Carr, Indira Mahalingham and Brian Carr (1999) Madhva, in Arrington, Robert L., ed. *A Companion to the Philosophers* (Oxford: Blackwell) pp. 592–594

Carson, T. L. (2000) *Value and the Good Life* (Notre Dame: Notre Dame Press)

Casullo, Albert (2006) *A Priori Justification* (Oxford: Oxford University Press)

Casullo, Albert (2012) *Essays on A Priori Knowledge and Justification* (Oxford: Oxford University Press)

Casullo, Albert and Josh Thurow, eds. (2013) *The A Priori in Philosophy* (Oxford: Oxford University Press)

Chakrabarti, Arindam (1997) Rationality in Indian Philosophy, in Deutsch, Eliot and Ron Bontekoe, eds. *A Companion to World Philosophies* (Cambridge, MA: Blackwell), pp. 259–278

Chennakesavan, Sarasvati and K. Vasudeva Reddy (1997) Morals and society in Indian philosophy, in Carr, Brian and Indira Mahalingam, eds. *Companion Encyclopedia of Asian Philosophy* (London: Routledge) pp. 266–280

Clarke, Desmond M. and Catherine Wilson (2011) *The Oxford Handbook of Philosophy in Early Modern Europe* (Oxford: Oxford University Press)

Clarke, Randolph (2002) Libertarian views: Critical survey on noncausal and event-causal accounts of free agency, in Kane, Robert, ed. *The Oxford Handbook of Free Will* (Oxford: Oxford University Press) pp. 356–385

Clayton, J. (2006) *Religions, Reasons and Gods: Essays in Cross-Cultural Philosophy of Religion* (Cambridge: Cambridge University Press)

Collins, Robin (2012) The teleological argument, in Meister, Chad and Paul Copan, eds. *Routledge Companion to Philosophy of Religion* (New York: Routledge) pp. 411–421

Comans, Michael (1997) Later Vedānta, in Carr, Brian and Indira Mahalingam, eds. *Companion Encyclopedia of Asian Philosophy* (London: Routledge) pp. 211–229

Corcoran, Kevin (2001) *Body, Soul, and Survival* (Ithaca: Cornell University Press)

Crisp, Thomas M. (2003) Identity, in Loux, Michael J. and Dean W. Zimmerman, eds. *The Oxford Handbook of Metaphysics* (Oxford: Oxford University Press) pp. 211–245

Dasti, Matthew (2013) Asian philosophy, in Taliaferro, Charles, Victoria S. Harrison, and Steward Goetz, eds. *The Routledge Companion to Theism* (New York: Routledge) pp. 23–37

Davidson, Herbert A. (2005) *Moses Maimonides: The Man and His Work* (Oxford: Oxford University Press)

Davies, Brian (2006) *The Reality of God and the Problem of Evil* (London: Continuum)

Davies, Brian and Eleonore Stump (2014) *The Oxford Handbook of Aquinas* (Oxford: Oxford University Press)

D'Costa, Gavin (2012) Inter-religious dialogue, in Meister, Chad and Paul Copan, eds. *Routledge Companion to Philosophy of Religion* (New York: Routledge) pp. 261–270

Della Rocca, Michael (2002) Rene Descartes, in Nadler, Steven, ed. *A Companion to Early Modern Philosophy* (Oxford: Blackwell) pp. 60–79

Dicker, George (1999) Descartes, in Arrington, Robert L., ed. *A Companion to the Philosophers* (Oxford: Blackwell) pp. 209–216

Dickson, Owen Griffiths (2012) Religious experience, in Meister, Chad and Paul Copan, eds. *Routledge Companion to Philosophy of Religion* (New York: Routledge) pp. 765–744

Divers, John (2011) Possible worlds and *possibilia*, in Le Poidevin, Robin, Peter Simons, *et al.*, eds. *The Routledge Companion to Metaphysics* (New York: Routledge) pp. 335–345

Dombrowski, D. (2006) *Rethinking the Ontological Argument* (Cambridge: Cambridge University Press)

Dore, Clement (1997) Ontological arguments, in Quinn, Philip L. and Charles Taliaferro, eds. *A Companion to Philosophy of Religion* (Cambridge, MA: Blackwell) pp. 323–330

Dougherty, Trent and Justin P. McBrayer (2016) *Skeptical Theism: New Essays* (Oxford: Oxford University Press)

Dougherty, Trent and Jerry L. Walls (2013) Arguments from evil, in Taliaferro, Charles, Victoria S. Harrison, and Steward Goetz, eds. *The Routledge Companion to Theism* (New York: Routledge) pp. 369–382

Dreyfus, Hubert and Charles Taylor (2015) *Retrieving Realism* (Harvard: Belknap Press)

Evans, C. S. (2013) *God and Moral Obligation* (Oxford: Oxford University Press)

Everitt, Nicholas (2004) *The Non-Existence of God* (London: Routledge)

Fischer, John Martin (2002) Introduction: The contours of contemporary free will debates, in Kane, Robert, ed. *The Oxford Handbook of Free Will* (Oxford: Oxford University Press) pp. 281–308

Fischer, John Martin (2006) *My Way* (New York: Oxford University Press)

Fischer, John Martin, Robert Kane, Derk Pereboom, and Manuel Vargas (2007) *Four Views on Free Will* (Malden, MA: Blackwell Publishers)

Flew, Antony (2007) *There Is a God: How the World's Most Notorious Atheist Changed His Mind* (New York: HarperOne)

Flint, Thomas (1998) *Divine Providence* (Ithaca: Cornell University Press)

Foster, John (2004) *The Divine Lawmaker: Lectures on Induction, Laws of Nature, and the Existence of God* (Oxford: Oxford University Press)

Frasca-Spada, Marina (2002) David Hume, in Nadler, Steven, ed. *A Companion To Early Modern Philosophy* (Oxford: Blackwell) pp. 483–504

Gale, Richard (2008) *God and Metaphysics* (Amherst, NY: Prometheus Books)

Gale, Richard (2012) The problem of evil, in Meister, Chad and Paul Copan, eds. *Routledge Companion to Philosophy of Religion* (New York: Routledge) pp. 457–468

Gallagher, Shaun (2013) *The Oxford Handbook of the Self* (Oxford: Oxford University Press)

Gannsle, Greg and David Woodruff (2002) *God and Time: Essays on the Divine Nature* (Oxford: Oxford University Press)

Garcia, Laura L. (1997) Teleological and design arguments, in Quinn, Philip L. and Charles Taliaferro, eds. *A Companion to Philosophy of Religion* (Cambridge, MA: Blackwell) pp. 338–345

Gaukroger, Stephen (2010) Rene Descartes, in Benecker, Sven and Duncan Pritchard, eds. *The Routledge Companion to Epistemology* (New York: Routledge) pp. 678–687

Gendler, T. and J. Hawthorne, eds. (2002) *Conceivability and Possibility* (Oxford: Clarendon Press)

Gertler, Brie, ed. (2003) *Privileged Access: Philosophical Accounts of Self-Knowledge* (Aldershot: Ashgate Publishing)

Gertler, Brie (2011) *Self-Knowledge* (London: Routledge)

Ginet, Carl (2002) Reasons explanations of actions: Causalist versus noncausalist accounts, in Kane Robert, ed. *The Oxford Handbook of Free Will* (Oxford: Oxford University Press) pp. 386–405

Ginet, Carl (2003) Libertarianism, in Loux, Michael J. and Dean W. Zimmerman, eds. *The Oxford Handbook of Metaphysics* (Oxford: Oxford University Press) pp. 587–612

Goetz, Stewart and Charles Taliaferro (2008) *Naturalism* (Grand Rapids, MI: Eerdmans)

Gould, Paul, ed. (2014) *Beyond the Control of God? Six Views on the Problem of God and Abstract Objects* (New York: Bloomsbury)

Green, Adam and Eleonore Stump (2016) *Hidden Divinity and Religious Belief: New Perspectives* (Cambridge: Cambridge University Press)

Griffiths, Paul J. (1997) Buddhism, in Quinn, Philip L. and Charles Taliaferro, eds. *A Companion to Philosophy of Religion* (Cambridge, MA: Blackwell) pp. 15–24

Griffiths, Paul J. (1997) Comparative philosophy of religion, in Quinn, Philip L. and Charles Taliaferro, eds. *A Companion to Philosophy of Religion* (Cambridge, MA: Blackwell) pp. 615–620

Griffiths, Paul J. (2001) *Problems of Religious Diversity* (London: Wiley Blackwell)

Griffiths, Paul J. (2011) The religious alien, in Meister, Chad, ed. *The Oxford Handbook of Religious Diversity* (Oxford: Oxford University Press) pp. 115–126

Haji, Ishtiyaque (2002) Frankfurt-type examples and semi-compatibilism, in Kane, Robert, ed. *The Oxford Handbook of Free Will* (Oxford: Oxford University Press) pp. 202–228

Hampton. Jean (1998) *The Authority of Reason* (Cambridge: Cambridge University Press)

Hankey, Wayne J. (2012) Aquinas, in Meister, Chad and Paul Copan, eds. *Routledge Companion to Philosophy of Religion* (New York: Routledge) pp. 130–139

Hare, John (2006) *God and Morality: A Philosophical History* (Oxford: Blackwell)

Harris, H. and C.J. Insole, eds. (2005) *Faith and Philosophical Analysis: The Impact of Analytical Philosophy on the Philosophy of Religion* (Aldershot: Ashgate)

Harvey, Peter (1999) The Buddha, in Arrington, Robert L. ed. *A Companion to the Philoso-phers* (Oxford: Blackwell) pp. 568–573

Hasker, William (1999) *The Emergent Self* (Ithaca: Cornell University Press)

Hasker, William (2005) Analytic philosophy of religions, in Wainwright, William J., ed. *The Oxford Handbook of Philosophy of Religion* (Oxford: Oxford University Press) pp. 421–446

Hasker, William (2008) *The Triumph of God over Evil: Theodicy for a World of Suffering* (Downer's Grove: IVP Academic)

Hasker, William, David Basinger, and Ed Dekker, eds. (2000) *Middle Knowledge: Theory and Applications* (Frankfurt am Main: Peter Lang Publishers)

Haslinger, Sally (2003) Persistence through time, in Loux, Michael J. and Dean W. Zimmerman, eds. *The Oxford Handbook of Metaphysics* (Oxford: Oxford University Press) pp. 315–354

Hawthorne, John (2003) Identity, in Loux, Michael J. and Dean W. Zimmerman, eds. *The Oxford Handbook of Metaphysics* (Oxford: Oxford University Press) pp. 99–130

Hayes, Richard P. (2013) Philosophy of mind in Buddhism, in Emmanuel, Steven, ed. *A Companion to Buddhist Philosophy* (Oxford: Blackwell) pp. 395–405

Heim, Maria (2013) Mind in Theravada Buddhism, in Emmanuel, Steven, ed. *A Companion to Buddhist Philosophy* (Oxford: Blackwell) pp. 377–394

Helm, Paul (2000) *Faith and Reason* (Oxford: Oxford University Press)

Hick, John (1997) Religious pluralism, in Quinn, Philip L. and Charles Taliaferro, eds. *A Companion to Philosophy of Religion* (Cambridge, MA: Blackwell) pp. 607–614

Hick, John (2012) Religious pluralism, in Meister, Chad and Paul Copan, eds. *Routledge Companion to Philosophy of Religion* (New York: Routledge) pp. 240–249

Hill, D. (2005) *Divinity and Maximal Greatness* (London: Routledge)

Hochberg, Herbert (2011) Particulars, in Le Poidevin, Robin, Peter Simons, *et al.*, eds. *The Routledge Companion to Metaphysics* (New York: Routledge) pp. 286–295

Hoffman, Joshua and Gary S. Rosenkrantz (2002) *The Divine Attributes* (Oxford: Blackwell)

Honderich, Ted (2002) Determinism as true compatibilism and incompatibilism as false, and the real problem, in Kane, Robert, ed. *The Oxford Handbook of Free Will* (Oxford: Oxford University Press) pp. 461–476

Howard-Snyder, Daniel and Jeff Jordan, eds. (1996) *Faith, Freedom, and Rationality* (Lanham, MD: Rowman and Littlefield)

Hudson, Hud (2001) *A Materialist Metaphysics of the Human Person* (Ithaca: Cornell University Press)

Humber James M. (1999) Hume, in Arrington, Robert L., ed. *A Companion to the Philoso-phers* (Oxford: Blackwell) pp. 309–317

Idziac, Janine Marie (1997) Divine command ethics, in Quinn, Philip L. and Charles Taliaferro, eds. *A Companion to Philosophy of Religion* (Cambridge, MA: Blackwell) pp. 453–459

Inada, Kenneth K. (1997) Buddhist reality and divinity, in Deutsch, Eliot and Ron Bontekoe, eds. *A Companion to World Philosophies* (Cambridge, MA: Blackwell), pp. 392–399

Jackson, Frank and Michael Smith, eds. (2005) *The Oxford Handbook of Contemporary Philosophy* (New York: Oxford University Press)

Jackson, Frederick (2000) *From Metaphysics to Ethics: A Defense of Conceptual Analysis* (Oxford: Clarendon Press)

Jacobsen, Knut A. (1997) Humankind and nature in Buddhism, in Deutsch, Eliot and Ron Bontekoe, eds. *A Companion to World Philosophies* (Cambridge, MA: Blackwell), pp. 381–391

Kane, Robert (1996) *The Significance of Free Will* (Oxford: Oxford University Press)

Kane, Robert (2002) Introduction: The contours of contemporary free will debates, in Kane, Robert, ed. *The Oxford Handbook of Free Will* (Oxford: Oxford University Press) pp. 3–41

Kane, Robert (2002) Some neglected pathways in the free will labyrinth, in Kane, Robert, ed. *The Oxford Handbook of Free Will* (Oxford: Oxford University Press) pp. 406–437

Kapitan, Tomis (2002) A master argument for incompatibilism?, in Kane, Robert, ed. *The Oxford Handbook of Free Will* (Oxford: Oxford University Press) pp. 127–157

Kapstein, Matthew (1997) Buddhist perspectives on ontological truth, in Deutsch, Eliot and Ron Bontekoe, eds. *A Companion to World Philosophies* (Cambridge, MA: Blackwell), pp. 420–433

Kasulis, Thomas P. (1997) The Buddhist concept of self, in Deutsch, Eliot and Ron Bontekoe, eds. *A Companion to World Philosophies* (Cambridge, MA: Blackwell), pp. 400–409

Kerr, Gaven (2015) *Aquinas's Way to God: The Proof in* De Ente et Essentia (Oxford: Oxford University Press)

Kim, Jaegwon (2003) Supervenience, emergence, realization, reduction, in Loux, Michael J. and Dean W. Zimmerman, eds. *The Oxford Handbook of Metaphysics* (Oxford: Oxford University Press) pp. 556–584

Koller, John M. (1997) Humankind and nature in Indian philosophy, in Deutsch, Eliot and Ron Bontekoe, eds. *A Companion to World Philosophies* (Cambridge, MA: Blackwell), pp. 279–289

Koller, John M. (2012) Shankara, in Meister, Chad and Paul Copan, eds. *Routledge Companion to Philosophy of Religion* (New York: Routledge) pp. 99–108

Koons, Robert A. (2000) *Realism Regained: An Exact Theory of Causation, Teleology, and the Mind* (Oxford: Oxford University Press)

Koons, Robert A. and George Bealer, eds. (2010) *The Waning of Materialism* (Oxford: Oxford University Press)

Koons, Robert A. and Timothy Picavance (2015) *Metaphysics: The Fundamentals* (London: Wiley Blackwell)

Kretzmann, Norman (2002) *The Metaphysics of Creation: Aquinas's Natural Theology in Summa Cortra Gentiles I* (Oxford: Clarendon)

Kretzmann, Norman (2002) *The Metaphysics of Creation: Aquinas's Natural Theology in Summa Cortra Gentiles II* (Oxford: Clarendon)

Kvanvig, Johnathan L. (2010) Epistemic justification, in Benecker, Sven and Duncan Pritchard, eds. *The Routledge Companion to Epistemology* (New York: Routledge) pp. 25–36

Kwan, Kai-Man (2012) The argument from religious experience, in Craig, William Lane and J. P. Moreland, eds. *The Blackwell Companion to Natural Theology* (Oxford: Blackwell) pp. 498–552

Kwan, Kai-Man (2013) Religious experience, in Taliaferro, Charles, Victoria S. Harrison, and Steward Goetz, eds. *The Routledge Companion to Theism* (New York: Routledge) pp. 383–397

Larson, Gerald James (1997) Indian conceptions of reality and divinity, in Deutsch, Eliot and Ron Bontekoe, eds. *A Companion to World Philosophies* (Cambridge, MA: Blackwell), pp. 248–258

Laumakis, Stephen J. (2013) The philosophical context of Gotama's thought, in Emmanuel, Steven, ed. *A Companion to Buddhist Philosophy* (Oxford: Blackwell) pp. 13–25

Lawrence, David Peter (2013) Hindu theism, in Taliaferro, Charles, Victoria S. Harrison, and Steward Goetz, eds. *The Routledge Companion to Theism* (New York: Routledge) pp. 77–87

Leftow, Brian (2005) The ontological argument, in Wainwright, William J., ed. *The Oxford Handbook of Philosophy of Religion* (Oxford: Oxford University Press) pp. 80–115

LePoidevin, Robin, Peter Simons, *et al.*, eds. *The Routledge Companion to Metaphysics* (New York: Routledge) pp. 131–141

Libet, Benjamin (2002) Do we have free will?, in Kane, Robert, ed. *The Oxford Handbook of Free Will* (Oxford: Oxford University Press) pp. 551–564

Linville, Mark (2012) The moral argument, in Craig, William Lane and J.P. Moreland, eds. *The Blackwell Companion to Natural Theology* (Oxford: Blackwell) pp. 391–438

Lowe, E.J. (2001) *The Possibility of Metaphysics: Substance, Identity, Time* (Oxford: Oxford University Press)

Lowe, E.J. (2002) *A Survey of Metaphysics* (Oxford: Oxford University Press)

Lowe, E.J. (2003) Individuation, in Loux, Michael J. and Dean W. Zimmerman, eds. *The Oxford Handbook of Metaphysics* (Oxford: Oxford University Press) pp. 75–95

Lowe, E.J. (2007) *The Four-Category Ontology: A Metaphysical Foundation for Natural Science* (Oxford: Oxford University Press)

Lowe, E.J. (2009) *Truth and Truth-Making* (Montreal: McGill-Queens University Press)

Lowe, E.J. (2012) The ontological argument, in Meister, Chad and Paul Copan, eds. *Routledge Companion to Philosophy of Religion* (New York: Routledge) pp. 391–403

Lowe, E.J. (2013) *Forms of Thought: A Study in Philosophical Logic* (Cambridge: Cambridge University Press)

Lycan, William (2010) Epistemology and the role of intuition, in Benecker, Sven and Duncan Pritchard, eds. *The Routledge Companion to Epistemology* (New York: Routledge) pp. 313–322

MacDonald, Scott (1997) The Christian contribution to medieval philosophical theology, in Quinn, Philip L. and Charles Taliaferro, eds. *A Companion to Philosophy of Religion* (Cambridge, MA: Blackwell) pp. 80–87

Mann, William E. (1997) Necessity, in Quinn, Philip L. and Charles Taliaferro, eds. *A Companion to Philosophy of Religion* (Cambridge, MA: Blackwell) pp. 264–270

Mann, William E. (2005) Divine sovereignty and aseity, in Wainwright, William J., ed. *The Oxford Handbook of Philosophy of Religion* (Oxford: Oxford University Press) pp. 35–58

Markham, Ian S. (2012) Truth in religion, in Meister, Chad and Paul Copan, eds. *Routledge Companion to Philosophy of Religion* (New York: Routledge) pp. 212–227

Martin, Michael (1997) The verificationist challenge, in Quinn, Philip L. and Charles Taliaferro, eds. *A Companion to Philosophy of Religion* (Cambridge, MA: Blackwell) pp. 204–212

Martinich, A.P. and David Sosa, eds. (2001) *A Companion to Analytic Philosophy* (Oxford: Blackwell)

Matilal, Bimal Krishna (2015) *Ethics and Epics: The Collected Essays of Bimal Krishna Matilal Volume II* (Oxford: Oxford University Press)

Matilal, Bimal Krishna (2015) *Mind, Language and World: The Collected Essays of Bimal Krishna Matilal Volume I* (Oxford: Oxford University Press)

McInerny, Ralph (1997) Thomism, in Quinn, Philip L. and Charles Taliaferro, eds. *A Companion to Philosophy of Religion* (Cambridge, MA: Blackwell) pp. 158–165

McInerny, Ralph (1999) Aquinas, in Robert L. Arrington, ed. *A Companion to the Philosophers* (Oxford: Blackwell) pp. 124–129

McInerny, Ralph (2004) *Aquinas* (Cambridge: Polity Press)

McLaughlin, Brian, Ansgar Beckermann, and Sven Walter (2011) *The Oxford Handbook of Philosophy of Mind* (Oxford: Oxford University Press)

Meister, Chad V. (2010) *The Oxford Handbook of Religious Diversity* (Oxford: Oxford University Press)

Mele, Alfred R. (2006) *Free Will and Luck* (New York: Oxford University Press)

Mele, Alfred R. and Piers Rawling (2004) *The Oxford Handbook of Rationality* (Oxford: Oxford University Press)

Merenbon, John (2011) Medieval metaphysics II: Things, non-things, God and time, in Le Poidevin, Robin, Peter Simons, *et al.*, eds. *The Routledge Companion to Metaphysics* (New York: Routledge) pp. 58–67

Merricks, Trenton (2007) *Truth and Ontology* (Oxford: Oxford University Press)

Miller, Alexander (2011) Hume: Necessary connections and real existences, in Le Poidevin, Robin, Peter Simons, *et al.*, eds. *The Routledge Companion to Metaphysics* (New York: Routledge) pp. 131–141

Misak, Cheryl (2011) Anti-metaphysics II: Verificationism and kindred views, in Le Poidevin, Robin, Peter Simons, *et al.*, eds. *The Routledge Companion to Metaphysics* (New York: Routledge) pp. 201–208

Mittag, Daniel M. (2010) Evidentialism, in Benecker, Sven and Duncan Pritchard, eds. *The Routledge Companion to Epistemology* (New York: Routledge) pp. 167–175

Mohanty, J. N. (1997) A history of Indian philosophy, in Deutsch, Eliot and Ron Bontekoe, eds. *A Companion to World Philosophies* (Cambridge, MA: Blackwell), pp. 24–48

Mohanty, J. N. (1997) The idea of the good in Indian thought, in Deutsch, Eliot and Ron Bontekoe, eds. *A Companion to World Philosophies* (Cambridge, MA: Blackwell), pp. 304–323

Mohanty, J. N. (2000) *Classical Indian Philosophy* (Lanham, MD: Rowman and Littlefield)

Moreland, James Porter (2012) The argument from consciousness, in Craig, William Lane and J. P. Moreland, eds. *The Blackwell Companion to Natural Theology* (Oxford: Blackwell) pp. 282–343

Moreland, James Porter (2013) Arguments about human persons, in Taliaferro, Charles, Victoria S. Harrison, and Steward Goetz, eds. *The Routledge Companion to Theism* (New York: Routledge) pp. 398–411

Moreland, James Porter, Khaldoun A. Sweis, and Chad V. Meister (2013) *Debating Christian Theism* (Oxford: Oxford University Press)

Moser, Paul K. (2005) *The Oxford Handbook of Epistemology* (Oxford: Oxford University Press)

Moser, Paul K. (2011) Religious exclusivism, in Meister, Chad, ed. *The Oxford Handbook of Religious Diversity* (Oxford: Oxford University Press) pp. 77–88

Moser, Paul K. (2012) Christianity, in Meister, Chad and Paul Copan, eds. *Routledge Companion to Philosophy of Religion* (New York: Routledge) pp. 67–75

Murdoch, Dugold (2011) Descartes: The real distinction, in Le Poidevin, Robin, Peter Simons, *et al.*, eds. *The Routledge Companion to Metaphysics* (New York: Routledge) pp. 68–76

Murphy, Mark C. (2003) *An Essay on Divine Authority* (Ithaca: Cornell University Press)

Murphy, Mark C. (2012) *God and Moral Law: On the Theistic Explanation of Morality* (Oxford: Oxford University Press)

Murray, Michael J. and David E. Taylor (2012) Hiddenness, in Meister, Chad and Paul Copan, eds. *Routledge Companion to Philosophy of Religion* (New York: Routledge) pp. 368–377

Nerlich, Graham (2003) Space-time substantivalism, in Loux, Michael J. and Dean W. Zimmerman, eds. *The Oxford Handbook of Metaphysics* (Oxford: Oxford University Press) pp. 281–314

Netland, Harold A. (2012) Inclusivism and exclusivism, in Meister, Chad and Paul Copan, eds. *Routledge Companion to Philosophy of Religion* (New York: Routledge) pp. 250–260

Nielsen, Kai (1997) Naturalistic explanations of theistic belief, in Quinn, Philip L. and Charles Taliaferro, eds. *A Companion to Philosophy of Religion* (Cambridge, MA: Blackwell) pp. 402–409

O'Connor, Timothy (2000) *Persons and Causes: The Metaphysics of Free Will* (New York: Oxford University Press)

O'Connor, Timothy (2002) Libertarian views: Dualist and agent-causal theories, in Kane, Robert, ed. *The Oxford Handbook of Free Will* (Oxford: Oxford University Press) pp. 337–355

Oderberg, David S. (2007) *Real Essences* (New York: Routledge)

Oderberg, David S. (2012) The cosmological argument, in Meister, Chad and Paul Copan, eds. *Routledge Companion to Philosophy of Religion* (New York: Routledge) pp. 391–400

Oppy, Graham (2006) *Arguing About Gods* (Cambridge: Cambridge University Press)

Pande, G. C. (1997) Causality in Buddhist philosophy, in Deutsch, Eliot and Ron Bontekoe, eds. *A Companion to World Philosophies* (Cambridge, MA: Blackwell), pp. 370–380

Pandeya, R. C. and Manju (1997) Pūrva Mīmāṁsā and Vedānta, in Carr, Brian and Indira Mahalingam, eds. *Companion Encyclopedia of Asian Philosophy* (London: Routledge) pp. 172–188

Parsons, Keith M. (2012) Problems with theistic arguments, in Meister, Chad and Paul Copan, eds. *Routledge Companion to Philosophy of Religion* (New York: Routledge) pp. 460–469

Penelhum, Terence (1997) Fideism, in Quinn, Philip L. and Charles Taliaferro, eds. *A Companion to Philosophy of Religion* (Cambridge, MA: Blackwell) pp. 376–382

Penelhum, Terrence (2012) David Hume, in Meister, Chad and Paul Copan, eds. *Routledge Companion to Philosophy of Religion* (New York: Routledge) pp. 161–170

Pereboom, Derk (1997) Early modern philosophical theology, in Quinn, Philip L. and Charles Taliaferro, eds. *A Companion to Philosophy of Religion* (Cambridge, MA: Blackwell) pp. 103–110

Pereboom, Derk (2001) *Living Without Free Will* (Cambridge: Cambridge University Press)

Peterson, Michael L. (1997) The problem of evil, in Quinn, Philip L. and Charles Taliaferro, eds. *A Companion to Philosophy of Religion* (Cambridge, MA: Blackwell) pp. 393–401

Peterson, Michael L. (2011) Religious diversity, evil, and a variety of theodicies, in Meister, Chad, ed. *The Oxford Handbook of Religious Diversity* (Oxford: Oxford University Press) pp. 154–168

Peterson, Michael L. and Robert van Arragon, eds. (2004) *Contemporary Debates in Philosophy of Religion* (Oxford: Blackwell)

Pike, N. (2002) *God and Timelessness* (Eugene, OR: Wipf and Stock Publishers)

Plantinga, Alvin (1997) Reformed epistemology, in Quinn, Philip L. and Charles Taliaferro, eds. *A Companion to Philosophy of Religion* (Cambridge, MA: Blackwell) pp. 383–389

Plantinga, Alvin (2011) *Where the Conflict Really Lies: Science, Religion, and Naturalism* (Oxford: Oxford University Press)

Potter, Karl H. (1997) Knowledge and reality in Indian philosophy, in Carr, Brian and Indira Mahalingam, eds. *Companion Encyclopedia of Asian Philosophy* (London: Routledge) pp. 251–265

Premasiri, P. D. (1997) Ideas of the good in Buddhist philosophy, in Deutsch, Eliot and Ron Bontekoe, eds. *A Companion to World Philosophies* (Cambridge, MA: Blackwell), pp. 349–359

Pruss, Alexander R. (2006) *The Principle of Sufficient Reason* (Cambridge: Cambridge University Press)

Pruss, Alexander R. and Richard M. Gale (2005) Cosmological and design arguments, in Wainwright, William J., ed. *The Oxford Handbook of Philosophy of Religion* (Oxford: Oxford University Press) pp. 116–138

Quinn, Philip (2002) Epistemology in philosophy of religion, in Moser, Paul K., ed. *The Oxford Handbook of Epistemology* (Oxford: Oxford University Press) pp. 513–538

Ram-Prasad, Chakravarthi (2002) *Advaita Metaphysics and Epistemology* (London: Routledge Curzon)

Rea, Michael C. (2003) Four-dimensionalism, in Loux, Michael J. and Dean W. Zimmerman, eds. *The Oxford Handbook of Metaphysics* (Oxford: Oxford University Press) pp. 246–280

Rea, Michael C. (2009) *Oxford Readings in Philosophical Theology* (Oxford: Oxford University Press)

Reppert, Victor (2012) The argument from reason, in Craig, William Lane and J. P. Moreland, eds. *The Blackwell Companion to Natural Theology* (Oxford: Blackwell) pp. 344–390

Rist, John (2008) *What Is Truth?: From the Academy to the Vatican* (Cambridge: Cambridge University Press)

Robb, David (2011) Substance, in Le Poidevin, Robin, Peter Simons, *et al.*, eds. *The Routledge Companion to Metaphysics* (New York: Routledge) pp. 256–264

Robinson, Howard (2003) The ontology of the mental, in Loux, Michael J. and Dean W. Zimmerman, eds. *The Oxford Handbook of Metaphysics* (Oxford: Oxford University Press) pp. 527–555

Rowe, William L. (1997) Cosmological arguments, in Quinn, Philip L. and Charles Taliaferro, eds. *A Companion to Philosophy of Religion* (Cambridge, MA: Blackwell) pp. 331–337

Rowe, William L. (2004) *Can God Be Free?* (Oxford: Oxford University Press)

Roy, A. (1997) Contemporary Indian philosophy, in Carr, Brian and Indira Mahalingam, eds. *Companion Encyclopedia of Asian Philosophy* (London: Routledge) pp. 281–299

Rundle, Bede (2004) *Why There Is Something Rather Than Nothing* (Oxford: Clarendon Press)

Ruse, Michael (2012) The sociobiological account of religious belief, in Meister, Chad and Paul Copan, eds. *Routledge Companion to Philosophy of Religion* (New York: Routledge) pp. 511–522

Russell, Paul (2016) *The Oxford Handbook of Hume* (Oxford: Oxford University Press)

Scanlon, T. M. (1998) *What We Owe to Each Other* (Cambridge, MA: Harvard University Press)

Scanlon, T. M. (2008) *Moral Dimensions: Permissibility, Meaning, Blame* (Cambridge, MA: Belknap Harvard Press)

Schloss, J. and Murray, M., eds. (2009) *The Believing Primate: Scientific, Philosophical, and Theological Reflections on the Origins of Religion* (Oxford: Oxford University Press)

Sharma, Arvind (2011) A Hindu perspective, in Meister, Chad, ed. *The Oxford Handbook of Religious Diversity* (Oxford: Oxford University Press) pp. 309–320

Sharma, Arvind (2012) Hinduism, in Meister, Chad and Paul Copan, eds. *Routledge Companion to Philosophy of Religion* (New York: Routledge) pp. 7–17

Sider, Theodore (2001) *Four-Dimensionalism: An Ontology of Persistence and Time* (Oxford: Oxford University Press)

Sider, Theodore (2003) Reductive theories of modality, in Loux, Michael J. and Dean W. Zimmerman, eds. *The Oxford Handbook of Metaphysics* (Oxford: Oxford University Press) pp. 180–208

Skilton, Andrew (2013) Theravada, in Emmanuel, Steven, ed. *A Companion to Buddhist Philosophy* (Oxford: Blackwell) pp. 71–85

Smart, Ninian (1997) A survey of Buddhist thought, in Deutsch, Eliot and Ron Bontekoe, eds. *A Companion to World Philosophies* (Cambridge, MA: Blackwell), pp. 78–98

Smart, Ninian (1997) Hinduism, in Quinn, Philip L. and Charles Taliaferro, eds. *A Companion to Philosophy of Religion* (Cambridge, MA: Blackwell) pp. 7–14

Sobel, J. (2004) *Logic and Theism* (Cambridge: Cambridge University Press)

Strawson, Galen (2002) The bounds of freedom, in Kane, Robert, ed. *The Oxford Handbook of Free Will* (Oxford: Oxford University Press) pp. 441–460

Stroll, Avrum (2011) Metaphysics revivified, Le Poidevin, Robin, Peter Simons, *et al.*, eds. *The Routledge Companion to Metaphysics* (New York: Routledge) pp. 209–218

Stump, Eleonore (2003) *Aquinas* (London: Routledge)

Swinburne, Richard (2004, Sec. Ed.) *The Existence of God* (Oxford: Clarendon)

Swinburne, Richard (2013) *Mind, Brain, and Free Will* (Oxford: Oxford University Press)

Taliaferro, Charles (1997) Incorporeality, in Quinn, Philip L. and Charles Taliaferro, eds. *A Companion to Philosophy of Religion* (Cambridge, MA: Blackwell) pp. 271–278

Taliaferro, Charles (2005) *Evidence and Faith: Philosophy and Religion Since the Seventeenth Century* (Cambridge: Cambridge University Press)

Taliaferro, Charles (2011) A Christian perspective, in Meister, Chad, ed. *The Oxford Handbook of Religious Diversity* (Oxford: Oxford University Press) pp. 381–392

Taliaferro, C. and Meister, C. (2010) *The Cambridge Companion to Christian Philosophical Theology* (Cambridge: Cambridge University Press)

Taylor, Charles (2007) *A Secular Age* (Harvard: Belknap Press)

Timpe, Kevin and Daniel Speak (2016) *Free Will and Theism: Connections Contingencies and Concerns* (Oxford: Oxford University Press)

Trakakis, Nick and Daniel Cohen, eds. (2008) *Essays on Free Will and Moral Responsibility* (Newcastle upon Tyne, UK: Cambridge Scholars Publishing)

Tuske, Joerg (2013) The non-self theory and problems in philosophy of mind, in Emmanuel, Steven, ed. *A Companion to Buddhist Philosophy* (Oxford: Blackwell) pp. 419–428

Vahid, Hamid (2010) Externalism/Internalism, in Benecker, Sven and Duncan Pritchard, eds. *The Routledge Companion to Epistemology* (New York: Routledge) pp. 144–155 van Inwagen, Peter (2002) Free will remains a mystery, in Kane, Robert, ed. *The Oxford Handbook of Free Will* (Oxford: Oxford University Press) pp. 158–177

van Inwagen, Peter (2003) Existence, ontological commitment, and fictional Entities, in Loux, Michael J. and Dean W. Zimmerman, eds. *The Oxford Handbook of Metaphysics* (Oxford: Oxford University Press) pp. 131–157

van Inwagen, Peter (2008) *The Problem of Evil* (Oxford: Oxford University Press)

van Inwagen, Peter (2014) *Existence: Essays in Ontology* (Cambridge: Cambridge University Press)

Wainwright, William J. (1997) Christianity, in Quinn, Philip L. and Charles Taliaferro, eds. *A Companion to Philosophy of Religion* (Cambridge, MA: Blackwell) pp. 56–63

Wainwright, William J. (2005) *Religion and Morality* (Aldershot: Ashgate)

Wainwright, William J. (2013) Christianity, in Taliaferro, Charles, Victoria S. Harrison, and Steward Goetz, eds. *The Routledge Companion to Theism* (New York: Routledge) pp. 54–65

Walls, J.L., ed. (2007) *The Oxford Handbook of Eschatology* (Oxford: Oxford University Press)

Ward, Keith (2011) Religion and revelation, in Meister, Chad, ed. *The Oxford Handbook of Religious Diversity* (Oxford: Oxford University Press) pp. 169–184

Warfield, Ted (2003) Compatibilism and incompatibilism: Some arguments, in Loux, Michael J. and Dean W. Zimmerman, eds. *The Oxford Handbook of Metaphysics* (Oxford: Oxford University Press) pp. 613–630

Watson, Gary (2004) *Agency and Answerability* (New York: Oxford University Press)

Werner, Karel (1997) Non-orthodox Indian philosophies, in Carr, Brian and Indira Mahalingam, eds. *Companion Encyclopedia of Asian Philosophy* (London: Routledge) pp. 114–131

Westphal, Merold (1997) The emergence of modern philosophy of religion, in Quinn, Philip L. and Charles Taliaferro, eds. *A Companion to Philosophy of Religion* (Cambridge, MA: Blackwell) pp. 111–117

Widerker, David (2002) Responsibility and Frankfurt-type examples, in Kane, Robert, ed. *The Oxford Handbook of Free Will* (Oxford: Oxford University Press) pp. 323–334

Widerker, David and Michael McKenna, eds. (2003) *Moral Responsibility and Alternative Possibilities* (Aldershot, UK: Ashgate Press)

Wiggins, David (2001) *Sameness and Substance Renewed* (Cambridge: Cambridge University Press)

Wippel, John (2000) *The Metaphysical Thought of Thomas Aquinas* (Washington, DC: Catholic University of America Press)

Wolterstorff, Nicholas (1997) The reformed tradition, in Quinn, Philip L. and Charles Taliaferro, eds. *A Companion to Philosophy of Religion* (Cambridge, MA: Blackwell) pp. 165–170

Wolterstorff, Nicholas (2008) *Justice: Rights and Wrongs* (Princeton: Princeton University Press)

Wolterstorff, Nicholas (2014) Terrence Cuneo, ed. *Inquiring About God: Selected Essays, Series I* (Cambridge: Cambridge University Press)

Yandell, Keith E. (1997) Religious experience, in Quinn, Philip L. and Charles Taliaferro, eds. *A Companion to Philosophy of Religion* (Cambridge, MA: Blackwell) pp. 367–375

Yandell, Keith E. (2011) The diversity of religious experience, in Meister, Chad, ed. *The Oxford Handbook of Religious Diversity* (Oxford: Oxford University Press) pp. 89–101

Yandell, Keith E. (2012) Religious traditions and rational assessments, in Meister, Chad and Paul Copan, eds. *Routledge Companion to Philosophy of Religion* (New York: Routledge) pp. 228–239

Yandell, Keith E. (2013) Religious language, in Taliaferro, Charles, Victoria S. Harrison, and Steward Goetz, eds. *The Routledge Companion to Theism* (New York: Routledge) pp. 355–368

Zagzebski, Linda Trinkaus (2002) Recent work on divine foreknowledge and free will, in Kane, Robert, ed. *The Oxford Handbook of Free Will* (Oxford: Oxford University Press) pp. 45–64

Zagzebski, Linda Trinkaus (2004) *Divine Motivation Theory* (Cambridge: Cambridge University Press)

Zagzebski, Linda Trinkaus (2005) Morality and religion, in Wainwright, William J., ed. *The Oxford Handbook of Philosophy of Religion* (Oxford: Oxford University Press) pp. 344–365

Zimmerman, Dean W. (2003) Material people, in Loux, Michael J. and Dean W. Zimmerman, eds. *The Oxford Handbook of Metaphysics* (Oxford: Oxford University Press) pp. 491–526

Index

Absolutist Buddhism 55

action language 59–61

Advaita Vedanta 1, 16–17; appeal to enlightenment experience 217–18; arguments concerning 181–3; Atman theory 84; Brahman theory 84; causal theory of perception 84–5; compatibility 20–2; doctrines specific to 18; experience 181, 204; level of reality 19, 22, 27, 36, 83, 182, 213, 237, 239, 243, 279, 286; metaphysics 46; morality 46, 243; philosophers 80–3; reductionism and eliminativism 85–6; religious experience 27, 34, 36; religious neutrality 57; religious pluralism 55; religious traditions 49; self-authentication 207, 209–11, 214–15; two-theories account 83–4

Aldrin, Buzz 285

Alston, William 292–3, 293n3

anthropomorphism 54–5, 78n11, 275

Aquinas, Thomas 7; arguments by 130–54; change, potentiality, actuality 133–4; chronological vs. concurrent causes 132; cosmological argument (stage four) 145–8; cosmological argument (stage one) 141; cosmological argument (stage three) 143–4; cosmological argument (stage two) 141–2; domains, forwardness and backwardness 132–3; Fifth Way 148–52; First Way 134–5; Five Ways 130–1, 136, 140, 155–6n15; general structure of arguments 131–2; infinite series 136; Second Way 136–7; self-change 135; teleological argument 152–4; Third Way 137–45

Argument from Design 148–52

Aristotle 1, 7, 16, 119, 130, 133, 138, 194, 242–4, 263–4

atheism 48, 74–5, 114, 298

Atman: individual person 43, 60, 85–6, 94n12; real self 18–20, 34, 287; soul 182–3; theory 84

Augustine 128, 184

being, truth and goodness 13n3

belief-forming practice 161; Alston 292–3, 293n3; Plantinga 291–2

Berkeley, George (Bishop) 7, 86

Brahman 34, 151; Advaita Vedanta 181–3, 204–5, 217–18, 239, 287, 298; doctrine 39–40, 43, 46; enlightenment experience 207–9, 213, 217–18; experience 181–3; Hindu monotheism 71; nirguna 93, 182, 298; perception 85; qualityless 1, 16, 20–1, 27, 40, 46, 57, 60, 80–4, 93, 217–18, 239, 287, 298; reductionism and eliminativism 85–6; reincarnation 99; theory 84; ultimate reality 18, 19

Buddha: Buddhism 88–9, 92, 224, 284–5, 300

Buddhism: appeals to experience 223–5; Buddha 88–9, 92, 224, 284–5, 300; change 90, 94–5n31; Jainism vs. 87–93; memory 92–3; metaphysics 285–6; persons 88–9, 91–2, 183–4; reincarnation and karma 89–90, 190; self-authentication 207, 209–11, 215–16; simplicity 90–1; ultimate values 237–8

bundle theory: external critique of persons as bundles 188–9; fact of the matter